SharePoint 2013 WCM Advanced Cookbook

Over 110 recipes to engineer web content and master SharePoint 2013

John Chapman

[PACKT] enterprise 88

PUBLISHING   professional expertise distilled

BIRMINGHAM - MUMBAI

SharePoint 2013 WCM Advanced Cookbook

First published: January 2014

Production Reference: 1160114

Published by Packt Publishing Ltd.
Livery Place
35 Livery Street
Birmingham B3 2PB, UK.

ISBN 978-1-84968-658-7

www.packtpub.com

Cover Image by Abhishek Pandey (abhishek.pandey1210@gmail.com)

Credits

Author
John Chapman

Reviewers
Gary Arora

Zoltán Fiala

Moe Kahiel

Jiri Pik

Acquisition Editor
Sam Wood

Lead Technical Editor
Priya Singh

Technical Editors
Sharvari H. Baet

Mrunal Chavan

Pankaj Kadam

Copy Editors
Janbal Dharmaraj

Laxmi Subramanian

Project Coordinator
Joel Goveya

Proofreaders
Denise Dresner

Linda Morris

Indexer
Mariammal Chettiyar

Graphics
Yuvraj Mannari

Production Coordinator
Alwin Roy

Cover Work
Alwin Roy

About the Author

John Chapman is a software developer and designer, living in the Denver area, who specializes in SharePoint and .NET. Having worked in the higher education and telecommunications industries, he is now working as a software engineer for Sitrion, formerly NewsGator. He is working on the Social Sites product. Social Sites is the premier enterprise social software for Microsoft SharePoint.

John holds a B.S. and M.S. in Graphic Information Technology from Arizona State University. For more information about John Chapman, visit `http://www.sharepointjohn.com`.

I would like to thank my wife, Simone. Her support and patience have made everything I have accomplished in my life possible.

About the Reviewers

Gary Arora is a diehard technologist (read: Geek) and a seasoned consultant with over 10 years' experience. With a professional focus on SharePoint and the overall Microsoft stack, he has led and/or contributed to projects across industries in the United States and Europe.

Zoltán Fiala leads the Competence Center Microsoft of Adesso AG in Hamburg, Germany. He holds a PhD in web engineering from Dresden University of Technology and has worked as a SharePoint architect and project manager for several IT consultancy firms in the past. He has significant experience in the design and development of Web Content Management and portal solutions based on Microsoft technologies. For more information about Zoltán visit `http://www.z-fiala.net`.

Moe Kahiel is a senior SharePoint Enterprise architect with over 20 years of experience in a wide range of IT technologies. He has worked in the past with enterprise organizations such as EDS now HP and other Microsoft partners.

He is now an independent consultant focusing on Enterprise Content Management. He holds certifications of SharePoint (MCTS) and Microsoft (MCP), and is also a Certified Document Imaging Architect (CDIA).

I would like to thank the staff at Packt Publishing for giving me this opportunity and many thanks to my family for their help, support, and patience.

Jiri Pik is a finance and business intelligence consultant working with major investment banks, hedge funds, and other financial players. He has architected and delivered breakthrough trading, portfolio and risk management systems, and decision-support systems across industries.

His consulting firm WIXESYS provides their clients with certified expertise, judgment, and execution at the speed of light. WIXESYS's power tools include revolutionary Excel and Outlook add-ons available at `http://spearian.com`.

www.PacktPub.com

Support files, eBooks, discount offers and more

You might want to visit www.PacktPub.com for support files and downloads related to your book.

Did you know that Packt offers eBook versions of every book published, with PDF and ePub files available? You can upgrade to the eBook version at www.PacktPub.com and as a print book customer, you are entitled to a discount on the eBook copy. Get in touch with us at service@packtpub.com for more details.

At www.PacktPub.com, you can also read a collection of free technical articles, sign up for a range of free newsletters and receive exclusive discounts and offers on Packt books and eBooks.

http://PacktLib.PacktPub.com

Do you need instant solutions to your IT questions? PacktLib is Packt's online digital book library. Here, you can access, read and search across Packt's entire library of books.

Why Subscribe?

- ▶ Fully searchable across every book published by Packt
- ▶ Copy and paste, print and bookmark content
- ▶ On demand and accessible via web browser

Free Access for Packt account holders

If you have an account with Packt at www.PacktPub.com, you can use this to access PacktLib today and view nine entirely free books. Simply use your login credentials for immediate access.

Instant Updates on New Packt Books

Get notified! Find out when new books are published by following @PacktEnterprise on Twitter, or the *Packt Enterprise* Facebook page.

Table of Contents

Preface

Microsoft SharePoint Server 2013 is the latest release of the SharePoint Server product line that provides organizations with a full arsenal of tools to create a highly scalable and feature-rich **web content management** (**WCM**) system. This book is designed to provide a task-based approach for exploring the key WCM capabilities of SharePoint Server 2013. These include:

- ► Branding SharePoint
- ► Publishing content with SharePoint
- ► Managing content and navigation with taxonomy
- ► Customizing the SharePoint experience with code
- ► Translating content in SharePoint
- ► Staging SharePoint content

The recipes in this book cover each of the key areas for creating a full-fledged content management system that can be used for intranet, extranet, and Internet sites.

What this book covers

Chapter 1, Branding SharePoint with Composed Looks, covers how to brand SharePoint using composed looks, color palettes, and font schemes.

Chapter 2, Branding SharePoint with Device Channels and Design Packages, explains how to target SharePoint branding for specific devices and package branding customizations.

Chapter 3, Branding SharePoint with Custom Master Pages and Page Layouts, covers how to brand SharePoint with custom master pages and creating custom page layouts.

Chapter 4, Packaging Branding Elements in a SharePoint Solution with Visual Studio, explains how to create custom SharePoint solutions in Visual Studio to package and apply branding resources.

Chapter 5, Enhancing the Content Creation Process with the SharePoint Publishing Architecture, covers how to use the publishing features of SharePoint to manage web content.

Chapter 6, Centralizing and Structuring Content with Cross-site Publishing and Managed Metadata, explains how to use the cross-site publishing and managed metadata features of SharePoint to centrally structure and control content.

Chapter 7, Customizing the SharePoint Experience with Delegate Controls, covers how to create custom delegate user controls with Visual Studio.

Chapter 8, Enhancing User Input with InfoPath Forms, explains the basics of how to use InfoPath forms to customize the user input experience.

Chapter 9, Configuring Search, covers how to configure and manage search in SharePoint.

Chapter 10, Creating Multilingual Sites with SharePoint Variations, explains how to use SharePoint variations to create multilingual sites and manage content translation.

Chapter 11, Configuring Content Deployment, covers how to configure and perform deployment of SharePoint content from one site collection to another.

Chapter 12, Configuring Anonymous Access, explains how to make SharePoint sites available to end users without requiring them to login.

Who this book is for

This book is written for those who would like to expand their knowledge and abilities to configure, design, and develop for SharePoint web content management. They should be familiar with the SharePoint and web markup languages, such as HTML and CSS. In addition, knowledge of Windows PowerShell and programming .NET using C# is recommended, but not required.

What you need for this book

The recipes in this book utilize the Microsoft SharePoint Server 2013 web interface, Microsoft SharePoint Designer 2013, Microsoft InfoPath 2013, Windows PowerShell, and Microsoft C# .NET code. Most of the recipes that use the SharePoint web interface or SharePoint Designer can be used with SharePoint 2013 hosted on Office 365 as well as with a local SharePoint 2013 server. Recipes that use PowerShell or .NET code will require access to a local SharePoint 2013 server.

In order to make full use of all recipes in this book, it is highly recommended that you have a testing and development machine with the following software. These software applications can be obtained from the links provided or, in most cases, from MSDN with an active MSDN Subscription.

► Microsoft Windows Server 2012 available at `http://technet.microsoft.com/en-us/evalcenter/hh670538.aspx`

> The initial release of SharePoint Server 2013 does not support Windows Server 2012 R2. Service Pack 1 for SharePoint 2013 provides support for Windows Server 2012 R2.

► Microsoft SQL Server 2012 available at `http://www.microsoft.com/en-us/sqlserver/get-sql-server/try-it.aspx`

► Microsoft SharePoint Server 2013 Enterprise Edition available at `http://technet.microsoft.com/en-us/evalcenter/hh973397.aspx`

> Many of the publishing features we will explore in this book are only available in the enterprise edition of SharePoint Server 2013.

► Microsoft Visual Studio 2012 or 2013 (not the Express edition) available at `http://www.microsoft.com/visualstudio/eng/downloads`

► Microsoft Office Developer Tools for Visual Studio 2012 (not required for Visual Studio 2013) available at `http://msdn.microsoft.com/en-us/office/apps/fp123627.aspx`

► Microsoft InfoPath 2013 (part of Microsoft Office Professional Plus 2013) available at `http://technet.microsoft.com/en-us/evalcenter/jj192782.aspx`

> It is not recommended to install the InfoPath client software on the same computer as SharePoint Server. The assemblies from the InfoPath client software will conflict with the InfoPath server assemblies included with SharePoint Server.

► Microsoft SharePoint Designer 2013 available at `http://www.microsoft.com/en-ie/download/details.aspx?id=35491`

> This book does not cover the installation or configuration of these software applications. Most of the trial downloads, as well as TechNet (`http://technet.microsoft.com`) and MSDN (`http://msdn.microsoft.com`), provide documentation on installing and configuring these software products.

Conventions

In this book, you will find a number of styles of text that distinguish between different kinds of information. Here are some examples of these styles, and an explanation of their meaning.

Code words in text, database table names, folder names, filenames, file extensions, pathnames, dummy URLs, user input, and Twitter handles are shown as follows: "Composed looks are stored as list items in the _catalogs/design list of each SharePoint site."

A block of code is set as follows:

```
<s:latin typeface="Bodoni Book"
  eotsrc="/_layouts/15/fonts/BodoniBook.eot"
  woffsrc="/_layouts/15/fonts/BodoniBook.woff"
  ttfsrc="/_layouts/15/fonts/BodoniBook.ttf"
  svgsrc="/_layouts/15/fonts/BodoniBook.svg" />
```

Any command-line input or output is written as follows:

```
$web = Get-SPWeb http://sharepoint/site
```

New terms and important words are shown in bold. Words that you see on the screen, in menus or dialog boxes for example, appear in the text like this: "Select **Change the look** from the **Settings** menu."

> Warnings or important notes appear in a box like this.

> Tips and tricks appear like this.

Reader feedback

Feedback from our readers is always welcome. Let us know what you think about this book— what you liked or may have disliked. Reader feedback is important for us to develop titles that you really get the most out of.

To send us general feedback, simply send an e-mail to feedback@packtpub.com, and mention the book title via the subject of your message. If there is a topic that you have expertise in and you are interested in either writing or contributing to a book, see our author guide on www.packtpub.com/authors.

Customer support

Now that you are the proud owner of a Packt book, we have a number of things to help you to get the most from your purchase.

Downloading the example code

You can download the example code files for all Packt books you have purchased from your account at `http://www.packtpub.com`. If you purchased this book elsewhere, you can visit `http://www.packtpub.com/support` and register to have the files e-mailed directly to you.

Errata

Although we have taken every care to ensure the accuracy of our content, mistakes do happen. If you find a mistake in one of our books—maybe a mistake in the text or the code—we would be grateful if you would report this to us. By doing so, you can save other readers from frustration and help us improve subsequent versions of this book. If you find any errata, please report them by visiting `http://www.packtpub.com/submit-errata`, selecting your book, clicking on the **errata submission form** link, and entering the details of your errata. Once your errata are verified, your submission will be accepted and the errata will be uploaded on our website, or added to any list of existing errata, under the Errata section of that title. Any existing errata can be viewed by selecting your title from `http://www.packtpub.com/support`.

Piracy

Piracy of copyright material on the Internet is an ongoing problem across all media. At Packt, we take the protection of our copyright and licenses very seriously. If you come across any illegal copies of our works, in any form, on the Internet, please provide us with the location address or website name immediately so that we can pursue a remedy.

Please contact us at `copyright@packtpub.com` with a link to the suspected pirated material.

We appreciate your help in protecting our authors, and our ability to bring you valuable content.

Questions

You can contact us at `questions@packtpub.com` if you are having a problem with any aspect of the book, and we will do our best to address it.

1

Branding SharePoint with Composed Looks

In this chapter, we will cover the basics of branding SharePoint 2013 sites using **composed looks, color palettes**, and **font schemes**. We will discuss the following recipes:

- ▶ Applying a composed look
- ▶ Changing the site master pages
- ▶ Changing the site logo
- ▶ Uploading a custom color palette
- ▶ Uploading a custom font scheme
- ▶ Creating a custom composed look
- ▶ Using PowerShell to apply a composed look to all sites in a site collection
- ▶ Using PowerShell to apply master page and logo settings to all sites in a farm

Introduction

Microsoft SharePoint Server 2013 offers a variety of methods to apply styles and branding elements that range from simple configuration settings to custom code-based solutions. Before we explore the more advanced branding capabilities of SharePoint Server 2013, we will cover the basic branding offerings.

At the most basic level, branding and styling SharePoint includes applying one of the included **master pages**, setting the site logo, applying a color palette, and applying a font scheme. These elements, when combined, comprise a composed look.

Master pages are a feature of the ASP.NET web application framework that SharePoint leverages to provide a consistent look and feel for all pages within a SharePoint site.

Composed looks are stored as list items in the `_catalogs/design` list of each SharePoint site. Each composed look item contains the master page URL, color palette URL, font scheme URL, background image URL, and display order in relation to other composed looks.

SharePoint 2007 and 2010 each included theming capabilities. However, the theming capabilities in SharePoint 2013 are completely new in how they work and the level of customization they provide.

> Microsoft SharePoint has a number of online forums and communities that you can join and participate in. You can use the following communities to help you with all of your SharePoint endeavors:
>
> ▶ **Twitter #SharePoint**: `http://twitter.com/#sharepoint`
> ▶ **SharePoint StackExchange**: `http://sharepoint.stackexchange.com`
> ▶ **MSDN SharePoint forum**: `http://social.msdn.microsoft.com/Forums/en-US/category/sharepoint`
> ▶ **TechNet SharePoint forum**: `http://social.technet.microsoft.com/Forums/en-US/category/sharepoint`

Applying a composed look

When applying an existing composed look to an existing SharePoint site, it is important to note that the only method available for applying the composed look as it exists in the `_catalogs/design` list is with the SharePoint web interface. To apply the components of a composed look with PowerShell or .NET code, each property must be specified individually. In this recipe, we will use the SharePoint web interface to apply a composed look as well as use PowerShell and .NET code to apply the components of a composed look.

> From PowerShell or .NET code, the individual properties of the list item representing the composed look could be used when applying the individual components.

How to do it...

Follow these steps to apply the composed look:

1. Navigate to the site in your preferred web browser.

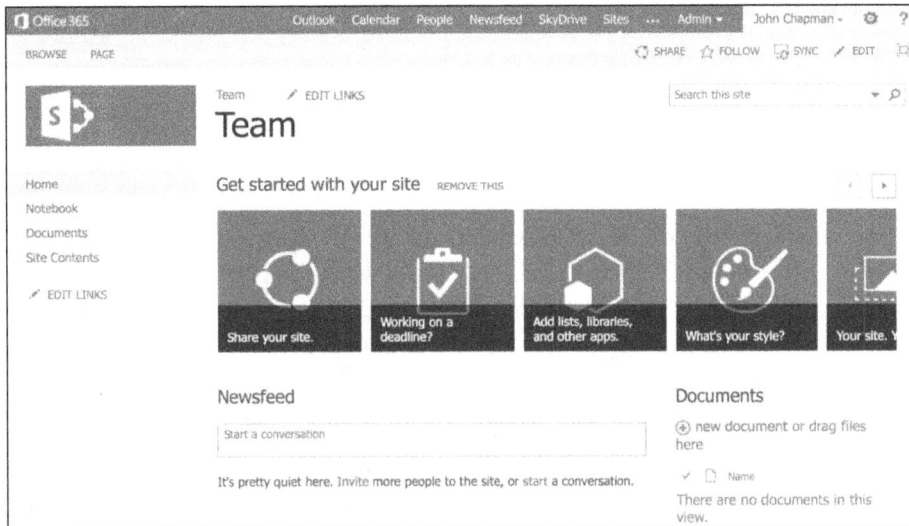

2. Navigate to the **Change the look** page. We can do this in two ways:

   ❑ Select **Change the look** from the **Settings** menu.

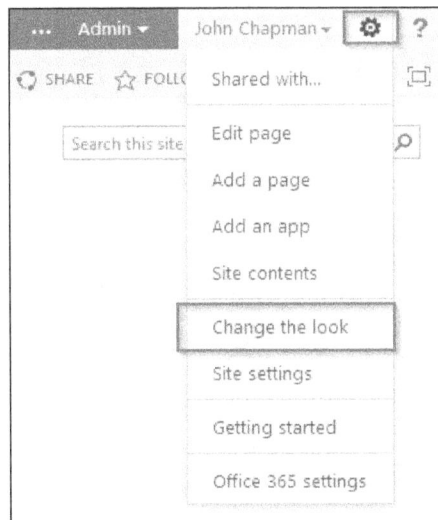

❑ Select **Site settings** from the **Settings** menu. Then select **Change the look** from the **Look and Feel** section.

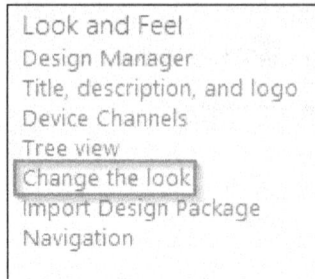

Look and Feel
Design Manager
Title, description, and logo
Device Channels
Tree view
Change the look
Import Design Package
Navigation

3. From the available composed looks, click on the preview image to select a composed look.

4. Before trying out the selected composed look, we can change the background image, color palette, site layout (master page), and font scheme.

Changing the various options will update the live preview automatically.

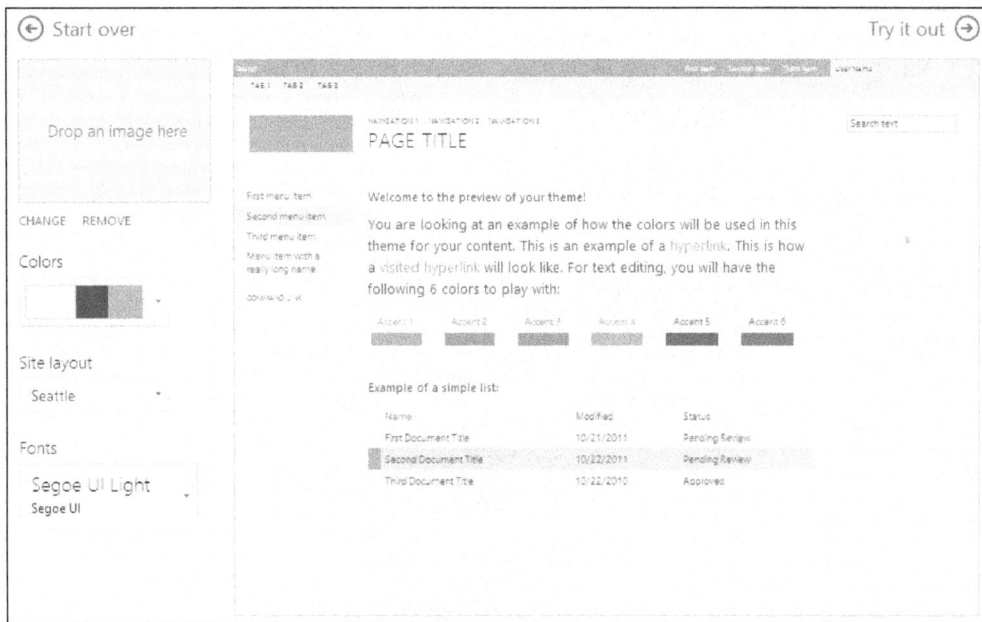

6. Select **Try it out** to preview the composed look and your configured options live on your SharePoint site.

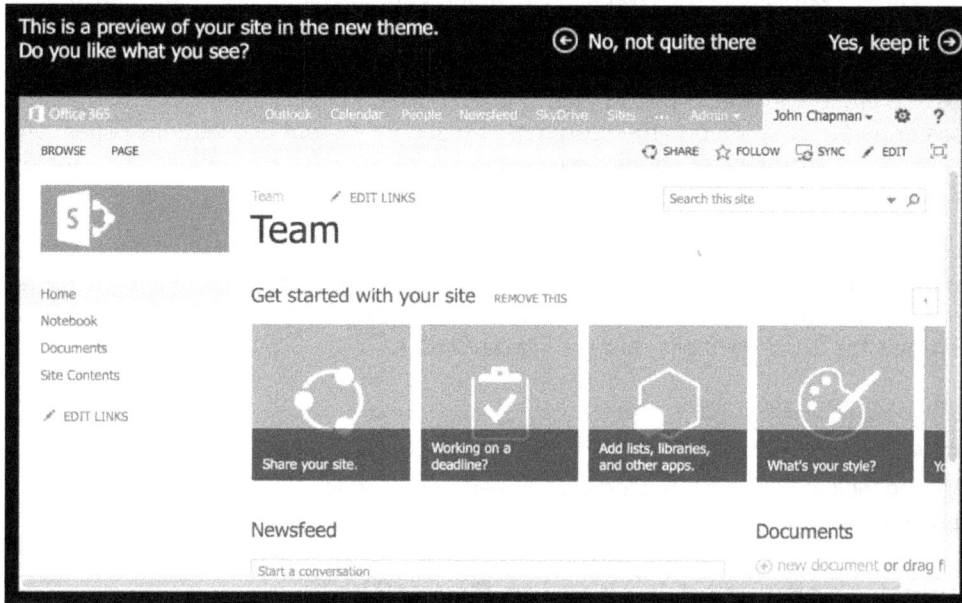

7. If you are satisfied with the design changes, select **Yes, keep it** to apply the styling. Otherwise, select **No, not quite there** to return to the previous screen.

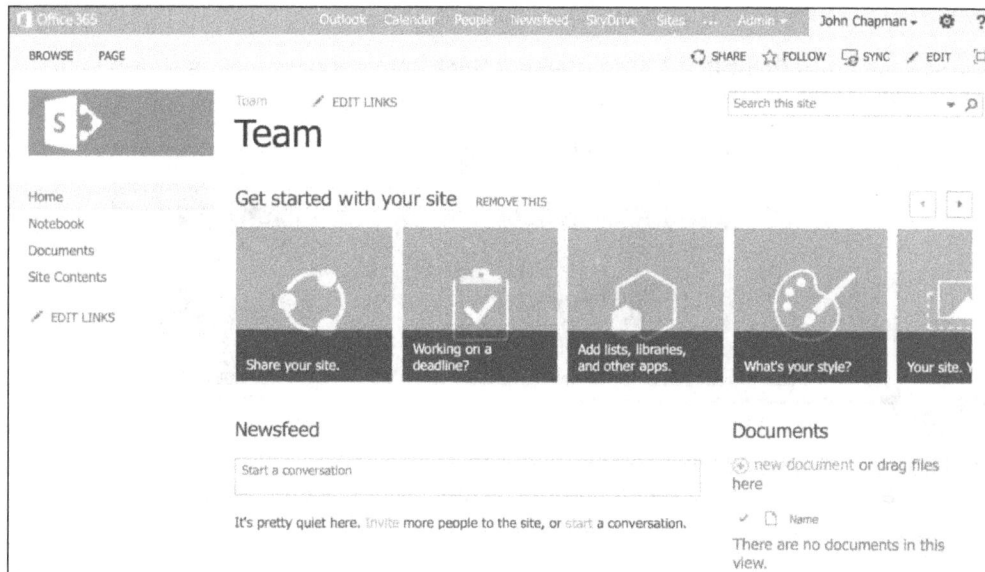

How it works...

An `SPWeb` object represents a SharePoint site in the SharePoint database and server-side object model. When we apply a composed look, the color palette, font scheme, and background image are used to create a new `SPTheme` object and it is assigned to the `ThemeInfo` property of the `SPWeb` object. The site layout, which is a reference to the URL of a master page, is assigned to the `MasterUrl` (used for system and settings pages) and `CustomMasterUrl` (used for content pages) properties of the `SPWeb` object. The `SPWeb` object is then saved to the SharePoint database.

When previewing the design changes live on your SharePoint site, SharePoint appends query strings to the home page of the site to instruct the site to use the provided theme information instead of what is currently configured. This is displayed within `IFRAME` on the page to allow us to preview the SharePoint site, but not interact with it.

There's more...

A composed look may also be applied with PowerShell or code using the server-side object model.

Applying a composed look using PowerShell

To launch PowerShell with the SharePoint snap-in loaded, you can select **SharePoint 2013 Management Shell** from the **Start** menu. You can also launch **Windows PowerShell** from the **Start** menu and manually load the SharePoint snap-in with the following command:

```
Add-PSSnapin Microsoft.SharePoint.PowerShell
```

You will see the **SharePoint 2013 Management Shell** command prompt as shown in the following screenshot:

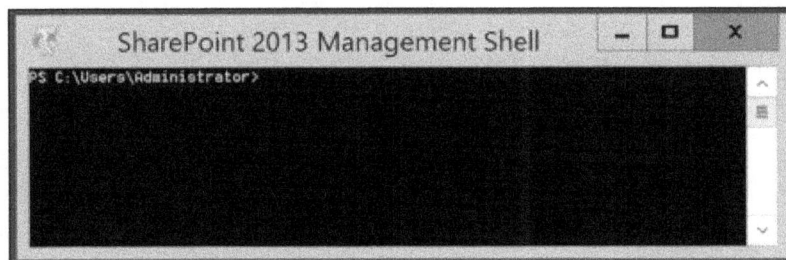

In addition, the **Windows PowerShell ISE** application provides the PowerShell command prompt with a user interface to simply create and execute PowerShell scripts.

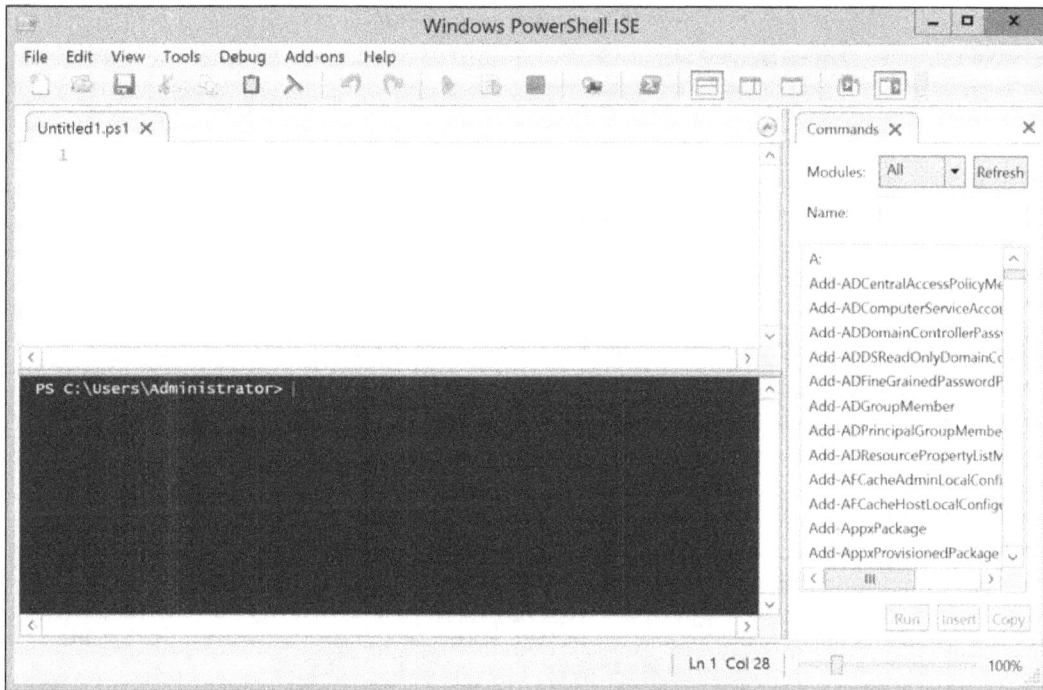

[
PowerShell scripts are plain text files with a `.ps1` file extension. You can create and edit them with Notepad, however applications such as PowerShell ISE provide additional editing capabilities that assist in writing PowerShell scripts.
]

Follow these steps to apply a composed look with PowerShell:

1. Use the `Get-SPWeb` Cmdlet to get the SharePoint site:

    ```
    $web = Get-SPWeb http://sharepoint/site
    ```

2. Use the `ApplyTheme` method to apply the color palette, font scheme, and background image by their URLs. Specify `false` for the last parameter to instruct SharePoint to place the files generated for this theme within the current site:

    ```
    $web.ApplyTheme("/_catalogs/theme/15/Palette015.spcolor",
      "/_catalogs/theme/15/fontscheme001.spfont",
      "/images/background.png", $false))
    ```

3. Use the `Update` method to apply the changes:

    ```
    $web.Update()
    ```

4. Use the `Dispose` method to discard the `SPWeb` object:

    ```
    $web.Dispose()
    ```

> You can download the example code files for all Packt books you have purchased from your account at http://www.packtpub.com. If you purchased this book elsewhere, you can visit http://www.packtpub.com/support and register to have the files e-mailed directly to you.

Applying a composed look with code using the server-side object model

Interacting with the server-side object model in C# requires a reference to the `Microsoft.SharePoint.dll` assembly found at `C:\Program Files\Common Files\Microsoft Shared\Web Server Extensions\15\ISAPI`. In addition, the code must be running in a `.NET` context on the SharePoint server. This includes, but is not limited to, Windows services, Windows applications, PowerShell Cmdlets, SharePoint timer jobs, SharePoint web parts, and SharePoint application pages.

Follow these steps to apply a composed look with code using the server-side object model:

1. Open the site collection containing the site in a `using` statement:

    ```
    using (var site = new SPSite("http://sharepoint/site"))
    ```

    If opening the `SPSite` or `SPWeb` objects from code without the `using` statement, dispose of the objects when you are done with them. This ensures that the objects are removed from memory and clears up connection resources for SharePoint.

2. Open the site in a `using` statement:

    ```
    using (var web = site.OpenWeb())
    ```

    In the SharePoint databases and server-side object model, the `SPSite` object represents a site collection and the `SPWeb` object represents a site.

3. Use the `ApplyTheme` method to apply the color palette, font scheme, and background image by their URLs. Specify `false` for the last parameter to instruct SharePoint to place the files generated for this theme within the current site:

    ```
    web.ApplyTheme("/_catalogs/theme/15/Palette015.spcolor",
      "/_catalogs/theme/15/fontscheme001.spfont",
      "/images/background.png", false);
    ```

4. Use the `Update` method to apply the changes:

    ```
    web.Update();
    ```

See also

See also

- The *Themes overview for SharePoint 2013* article on MSDN at `http://msdn.microsoft.com/en-us/library/jj927174.aspx`

- The *SPWeb class* topic on MSDN at `http://msdn.microsoft.com/en-us/library/Microsoft.SharePoint.SPWeb.aspx`

- The *SPSite class* topic on MSDN at `http://msdn.microsoft.com/en-us/library/microsoft.sharepoint.spsite.aspx`

- The *Get-SPWeb* topic on TechNet at `http://technet.microsoft.com/en-us/library/ff607807.aspx`

Changing the site master pages

Master pages are a feature of the ASP.NET web application framework that SharePoint leverages to provide a consistent look and feel for all pages within a SharePoint site. These can be used to provide various styling and branding configurations. SharePoint Server 2013 ships with two master pages that can be applied to SharePoint 2013 sites: **seattle** and **oslo**. The **seattle** master page is the default used when creating new SharePoint sites.

Each SharePoint site uses two configured master pages: the **site master page** and the **system master page**. The site master page is used when displaying content pages, libraries, lists, and so on, whereas the system master page is used when displaying settings and administrative pages.

SharePoint 2013 allows site collections to be configured to run in SharePoint 2010 or SharePoint 2013 compatibility modes. Master pages are only made available to the compatibility mode they are designed for. Thus, SharePoint 2010 master pages cannot be applied to a SharePoint 2013 site and vice versa.

Getting ready

In order to change the master page settings for a SharePoint site, the **SharePoint Server Publishing Infrastructure** site collection feature and **SharePoint Server Publishing** site feature must be activated.

Downloading the example code

You can download the example code files for all Packt books you have purchased from your account at `http://www.packtpub.com`. If you purchased this book elsewhere, you can visit `http://www.packtpub.com/support` and register to have the files e-mailed directly to you

How to do it...

Follow these steps to change the site master pages:

1. Navigate to the site in your preferred web browser. It should look like the following screenshot:

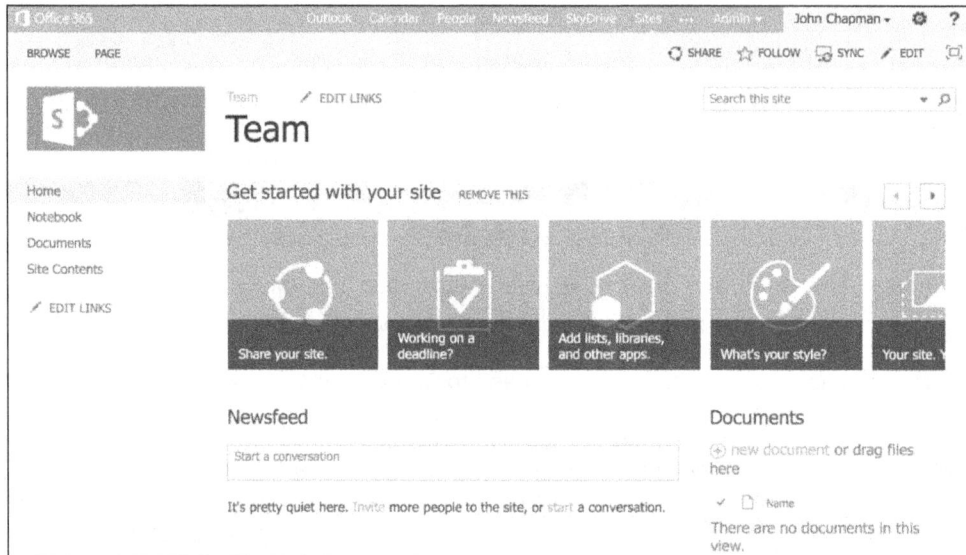

2. Select **Site settings** from the **Settings** menu.

3. Select **Master page** from the **Look and Feel** section, as shown in the following screenshot:

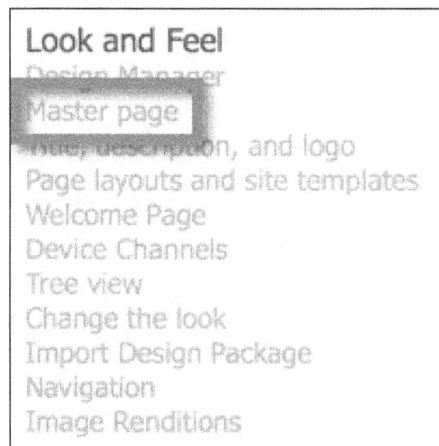

4. Select the site master page and the system master page to use. In this example, we will use the **oslo** master page:

Site Master Page

The site master page will be used by all publishing pages - the pages that visitors to your website will see. You can have a different master page for each Device Channel. If you don't see the master page you're looking for, go to the Master Page Gallery in Site Settings and make sure it has an approved version.

You may inherit these settings from the parent site or select unique settings for this site only.

○ Inherit site master page from parent of this site
◉ Specify a master page to be used by this site and all sites that inherit from it:

Default   oslo ▲▼

System Master Page

The system master page will be used by administrative pages, lists, and document library views on this site. If the desired master page does not appear, go to the Master Page Gallery in Site Settings and make sure the master page has an approved version.

You may inherit these settings from the parent site or select unique settings for this site only.

○ Inherit system master page from parent of this site
◉ Specify a system master page for this site and all sites that inherit from it:

All Channels   oslo ▲▼

5. Click on **OK** to save the changes. Now, the site will look like the following screenshot:

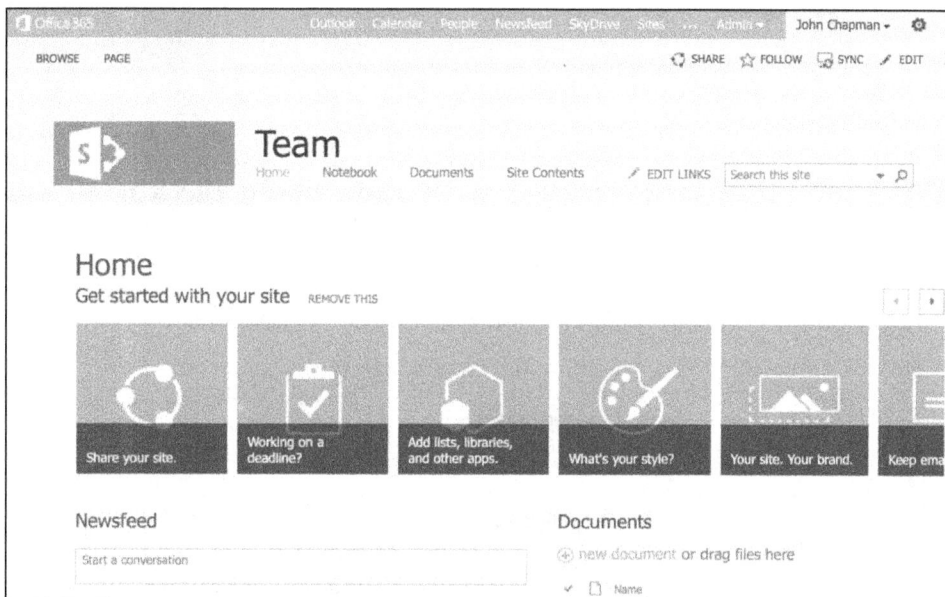

How it works...

The site relative URL for the selected site master page is assigned to the `MasterUrl` property of the `SPWeb` object representing the current site and the site relative URL for the system master page is set to the `CustomMasterUrl` property. The `SPWeb` object is then updated and saved to the SharePoint database.

There's more...

Site master pages may also be applied with PowerShell or code using the server-side object model.

Changing the site master pages using PowerShell

Follow these steps to change the site master pages using PowerShell:

1. Use the `Get-SPWeb` Cmdlet to get the SharePoint site:

   ```
   $web = Get-SPWeb http://sharepoint/site
   ```

2. Set the `MasterUrl` and `CustomMasterUrl` properties to configure the master pages by their URLs:

   ```
   $web.MasterUrl = "/_catalogs/masterpages/seattle.master"
   $web.CustomMasterUrl = "/_catalogs/masterpages/seattle.master"
   ```

3. Use the `Update` method to apply the changes:

   ```
   $web.Update()
   ```

4. Use the `Dispose` method to discard the `SPWeb` object:

   ```
   $web.Dispose()
   ```

Changing the site master pages with code using the server-side object model

Follow these steps to change the site master pages with code using the server-side object model:

1. Open the site collection containing the site in a `using` statement:

   ```
   using (var site = new SPSite("http://sharepoint/site"))
   ```

2. Open the site in a `using` statement:

   ```
   using (var web = site.OpenWeb())
   ```

3. Set the `MasterUrl` and `CustomMasterUrl` properties to configure the master pages by their URLs:

   ```
   web.MasterUrl = "/_catalogs/masterpages/seattle.master";
   ```

```
web.CustomMasterUrl =
  "/_catalogs/masterpages/seattle.master";
```

4. Use the `Update` method to apply the changes:

```
web.Update();
```

See also

▸ The *How to: Apply a master page to a site in SharePoint 2013* article on MSDN at `http://msdn.microsoft.com/en-us/library/jj862339.aspx`

▸ The *SPWeb class* topic on MSDN at `http://msdn.microsoft.com/en-us/library/Microsoft.SharePoint.SPWeb.aspx`

▸ The *SPSite class* topic on MSDN at `http://msdn.microsoft.com/en-us/library/microsoft.sharepoint.spsite.aspx`

▸ The *Get-SPWeb* topic on TechNet at `http://technet.microsoft.com/en-us/library/ff607807.aspx`

Changing the site logo

The logo is the image displayed, usually in the upper-left corner, on each page in a SharePoint site. Clicking on the logo returns the user to the root home page of the SharePoint site, as shown in the following screenshot:

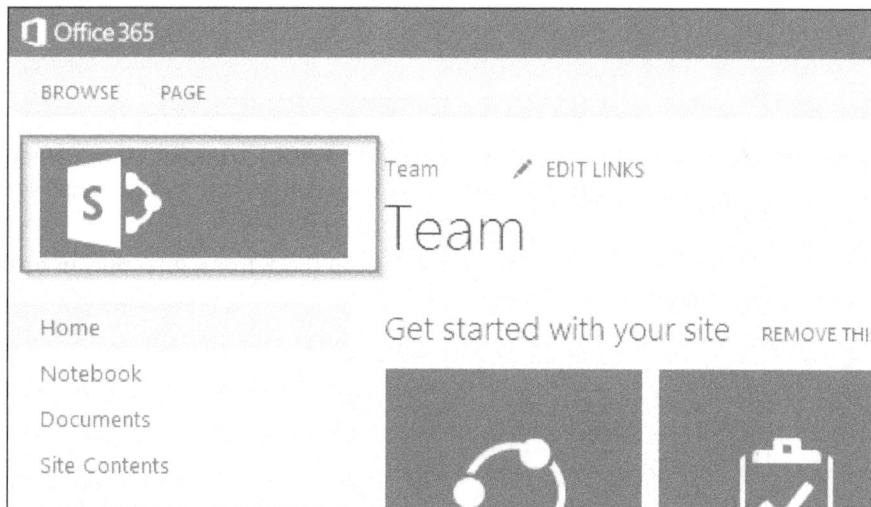

Getting ready

To complete this recipe you will need an image uploaded or available to upload to the SharePoint site.

How to do it...

Follow these steps to change the site logo:

1. Navigate to the site in your preferred web browser.
2. Select **Site settings** from the **Settings** menu.
3. Select **Title, description, and logo** from the **Look and Feel** section.

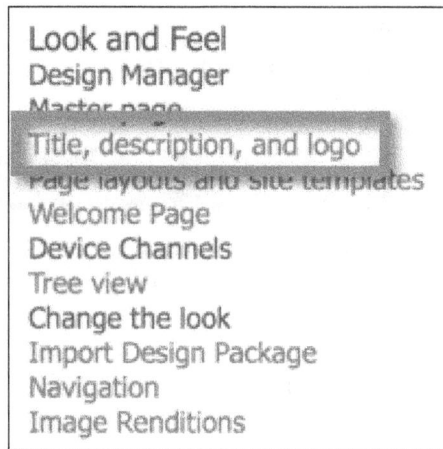

Look and Feel
Design Manager
Master page
Title, description, and logo
Page layouts and site templates
Welcome Page
Device Channels
Tree view
Change the look
Import Design Package
Navigation
Image Renditions

4. Under **Insert Logo**, select the logo by clicking on **FROM COMPUTER** to upload a new image or by clicking on **FROM SHAREPOINT** to use an image already existing in the SharePoint site.
5. Add a simple and short description for the logo in the **Enter a description** textbox as shown in the following screenshot:

Logo and Description

Associate a logo with this site. Add an optional
description for the image. Note: If the file location has a
local relative address, for example,
/_layouts/images/logo.gif, you must copy the graphics
file to that location on each front-end Web server.

Insert Logo:

FROM COMPUTER | FROM SHAREPOINT

/Team/SiteAssets/Office365.png

Office 365

Enter a description (used as alternative text for the picture):

Office 365 Team Site

6. Click on **OK** to save the changes. The logo should appear as shown in the following screenshot:

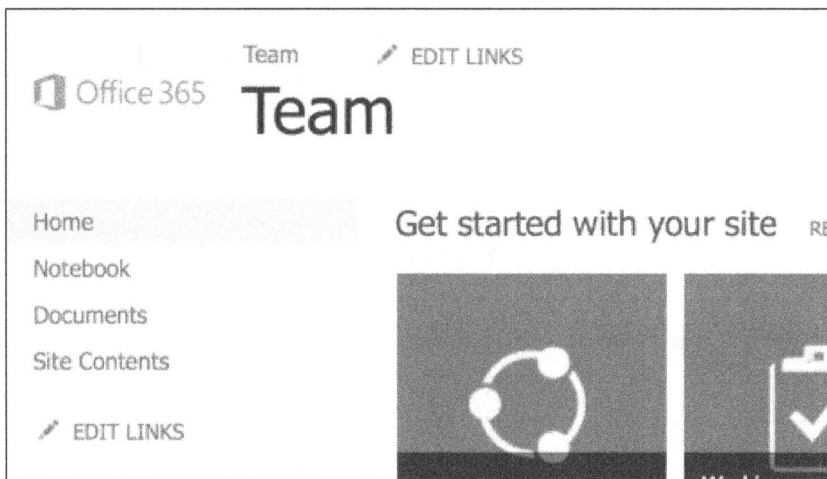

Office 365

Team   ✎ EDIT LINKS

Team

Home

Notebook

Documents

Site Contents

✎ EDIT LINKS

Get started with your site   RE

How it works...

The site relative URL for the logo image is assigned to the `SiteLogoUrl` property
of the `SPWeb` object representing the site, and the logo description is set to the
`SiteLogoDescription` property. The `SPWeb` object is then saved to the SharePoint
database. The logo description will be used as the alternative text for the logo that will be
displayed when hovering over the image with a mouse, as well as used by non-standard
browsers such as screen readers.

There's more...

The site logo and description may also be applied with PowerShell or code using the server-side object model.

Changing the site logo using PowerShell

Follow these steps to change the site logo using PowerShell:

1. Get the SharePoint site using the `Get-SPWeb` Cmdlet:

   ```
   $web = Get-SPWeb http://sharepoint/site
   ```

2. Set the `SiteLogoUrl` property to specify the URL of the image logo and the `SiteLogoDescription` property to specify the alternative text for the logo:

   ```
   $web.SiteLogoUrl = "/SiteAssets/logo.png"
   $web.SiteLogoDescription = "My PowerShell Site"
   ```

   > Setting the `SiteLogoUrl` property assumes that the referenced image has already been uploaded to the site.

3. Use the `Update` method to apply the changes:

   ```
   $web.Update()
   ```

4. Use the `Dispose` method to discard the `SPWeb` object:

   ```
   $web.Dispose()
   ```

Changing the site logo with code using the server-side object model

Follow these steps to change the site logo with code using the server-side object model:

1. Open the site collection containing the site in a `using` statement:

   ```
   using (var site = new SPSite("http://sharepoint/site"))
   ```

2. Open the site in a `using` statement:

   ```
   using (var web = site.OpenWeb())
   ```

3. Set the `SiteLogoUrl` property to specify the URL of the image logo and the `SiteLogoDescription` property to specify the alternative text for the logo:

   ```
   web.SiteLogoUrl = "/SiteAssets/logo.png";

   web.SiteLogoDescription = "My PowerShell Site";
   ```

4. Use the `Update` method to apply the changes:

   ```
   web.Update();
   ```

See also

▶ The *SPWeb class* topic on MSDN at `http://msdn.microsoft.com/en-us/library/Microsoft.SharePoint.SPWeb.aspx`

▶ The *SPSite class* topic on MSDN at `http://msdn.microsoft.com/en-us/library/microsoft.sharepoint.spsite.aspx`

▶ The *Get-SPWeb* topic on TechNet at `http://technet.microsoft.com/en-us/library/ff607807.aspx`

Uploading a custom color palette

SharePoint 2013 comes with 32 color palettes. If you are incorporating the branding of an organization you will likely need to customize the colors to match. Color palettes are simple XML files; however, they contain over 90 configured values. Identifying the appropriate values to update manually can be tedious. To simplify the process of creating new color palettes, Microsoft has made available the SharePoint Color Palette Tool for download. This tool can be downloaded from `http://www.microsoft.com/en-us/download/details.aspx?id=38182`.

The SharePoint Color Palette Tool provides:

▶ A live preview using the same layout as the live preview when configuring and applying a composed look, which we covered previously

▶ The configuration of each color element

▶ The configuration of which colors to use, when displaying in the color palette's drop-down list in the web interface

▶ The option to preview with a background image

▶ A preview utilizing various layouts in order to ensure the color palette applies well to the various page layouts and provides proper contrast between elements

We won't go into all of the details of using the tool to create color palettes. We will, however, cover how to upload the color palettes once created by the SharePoint Color Palette Tool.

Getting ready

To complete this recipe you will need a custom color palette created and ready to upload.

How to do it...

Follow these steps to upload a custom color palette:

1. Navigate to the site in your preferred web browser.
2. Select **Site settings** from the **Settings** menu.
3. Select **Themes** from the **Web Designer Galleries** section.

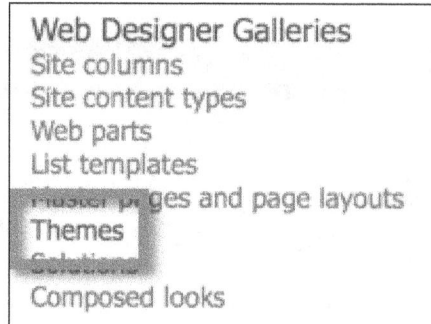

Web Designer Galleries
Site columns
Site content types
Web parts
List templates
~~Master p~~ges and page layouts
Themes
~~Solutions~~
Composed looks

4. Select the folder named 15.
5. Select **New Document** to upload and save the color palette file.

Alternatively, SharePoint 2013 also supports dragging-and-dropping files from Windows Explorer to the web interface in most browsers.

How it works...

The SharePoint color palettes are simply stored as files in a folder in a document library found at /_catalogs/theme/15. In this recipe, we uploaded our custom color palette to this document library and made it available for use when applying composed looks. The following screenshot shows our custom color palette in the folder named 15 which is inside the **Theme Gallery** library:

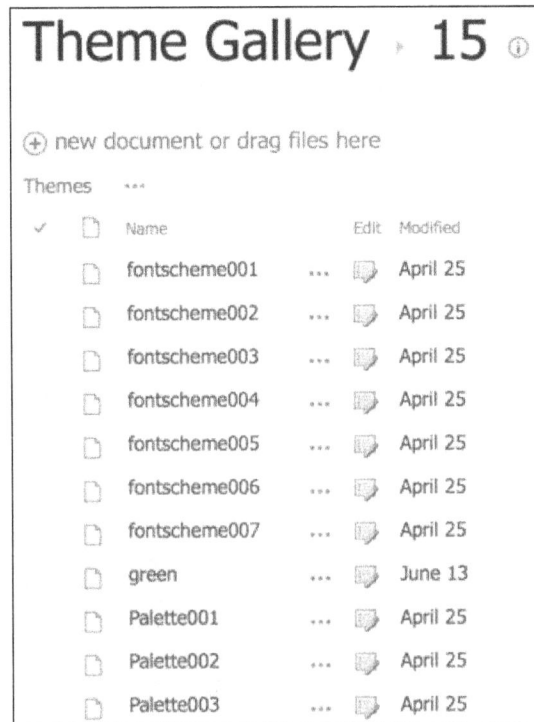

Theme Gallery · 15 ⓘ

⊕ new document or drag files here

Themes ···

✓	▢	Name		Edit	Modified
	▢	fontscheme001	...	▣	April 25
	▢	fontscheme002	...	▣	April 25
	▢	fontscheme003	...	▣	April 25
	▢	fontscheme004	...	▣	April 25
	▢	fontscheme005	...	▣	April 25
	▢	fontscheme006	...	▣	April 25
	▢	fontscheme007	...	▣	April 25
	▢	green	...	▣	June 13
	▢	Palette001	...	▣	April 25
	▢	Palette002	...	▣	April 25
	▢	Palette003	...	▣	April 25

There's more...

A color palette may also be uploaded with SharePoint Designer 2013, PowerShell, or code using the server-side object model.

Uploading a custom color palette using SharePoint Designer

SharePoint Designer 2013 can be used to browse and manage document libraries in SharePoint 2013. Follow these steps to upload a custom color palette using SharePoint Designer 2013:

1. Open the site in SharePoint Designer.

2. In the **Site Objects** pane on the left-hand side, select **All Files**.

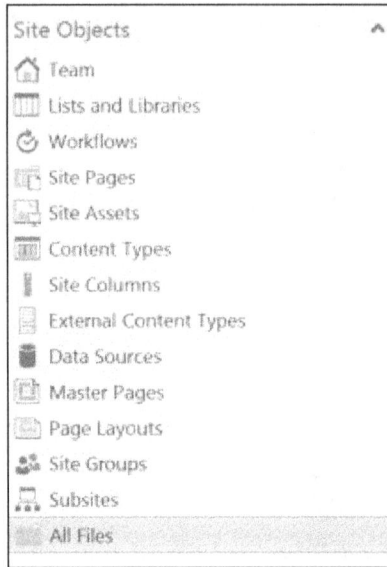

3. In the **All Files** list, navigate to **_catalogs | theme | 15**.

4. In the ribbon, click on **Import Files**.

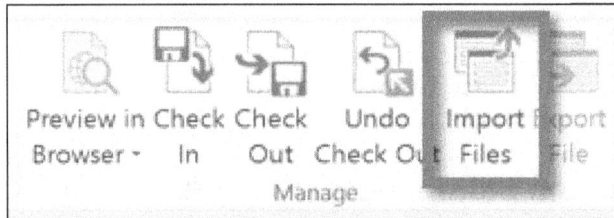

5. Select **Add File** to browse and select the color palette file.

6. Click on **OK** to import the color palette file.

Uploading a custom color palette using PowerShell

Follow these steps required to upload a custom color palette using PowerShell:

1. Get the site using the Get-SPWeb Cmdlet:

    ```
    $web = Get-SPWeb http://sharepoint/site
    ```

2. Assign the path of the color palette file to a variable:

    ```
    $filePath = "C:\mypalette.spcolor"
    ```

3. Get the /_catalogs/theme/15 folder from the SPWeb object:

```
$themeFolder =
$web.Folders["_catalogs"].Subfolders["theme"].Subfolders["15"]
```

4. Get the filename from the file path using the GetFileName method of the System.IO.Path class:

```
$fileName = [System.IO.Path]::GetFileName($filePath)
```

5. Get the contents of the file using the OpenRead method of the System.IO.File class:

```
$fileStream = [System.IO.File]::OpenRead($filePath)
```

6. Add the file to the Files collection of the folder using the name of the file and file contents. We are setting the third parameter to true to specify that this should override an existing file if it already exists by the same name:

```
$themeFolder.Files.Add($fileName, $fileStream, $true)
```

7. Call the Update method on the folder to update the Files collection:

```
$themeFolder.Update()
```

8. Use the Dispose method to discard the SPWeb object:

```
$web.Dispose()
```

Uploading a custom color palette with code using the server-side object model

Follow these steps to upload a custom color palette with code using the server-side object model:

1. Open the site collection containing the site in a using statement:

```
using (var site = new SPSite("http://sharepoint/site"))
```

2. Open the site in a using statement:

```
using (var web = site.OpenWeb())
```

3. Assign the path of the color palette file to a variable:

```
var filePath = "C:\mypalette.spcolor";
```

4. Get the /_catalogs/theme/15 folder from the SPWeb object:

```
var themeFolder =
  web.Folders["_catalogs"].SubFolders["theme"].SubFolders
  ["15"];
```

5. Get the filename using the GetFileName method of the System.IO.Path class:

```
var fileName = Path.GetFileName(filePath);
```

6. Get the contents of the file using the `OpenRead` method of the `System.IO.File` class:

```
var fileStream = File.OpenRead(filePath);
```

7. Add the file to the `Files` collection of the folder using the name of the file and file contents. We are setting the third parameter to `true` to specify that this should override an existing file if it already exists by the same name:

```
themeFolder.Files.Add(fileName, fileStream, true);
```

8. Call the `Update` method on the folder to update the `Files` collection:

```
themeFolder.Update();
```

See also

▸ The *Color palettes and fonts in SharePoint 2013* article on MSDN at `http://msdn.microsoft.com/en-us/library/jj945889.aspx`

▸ The *How to: Upload a file to a SharePoint Site from a Local Folder* article on MSDN at `http://msdn.microsoft.com/en-us/library/ms454491(v=office.14).aspx`

▸ The *SPWeb class* topic on MSDN at `http://msdn.microsoft.com/en-us/library/Microsoft.SharePoint.SPWeb.aspx`

▸ The *SPSite class* topic on MSDN at `http://msdn.microsoft.com/en-us/library/microsoft.sharepoint.spsite.aspx`

▸ The *Get-SPWeb* topic on TechNet at `http://technet.microsoft.com/en-us/library/ff607807.aspx`

Uploading a custom font scheme

Similar to color palettes, font schemes are XML files that define which fonts to use for displaying various texts in the web interface. Unlike color palettes, however, Microsoft has not released any tools to simplify the font scheme creation process. Font schemes are stored in the same location as that of color palettes in the `/_catalogs/theme/15` folder. SharePoint 2013 ships with eight font schemes with `SharePointPersonality.spfont` as the default.

When creating a new font scheme it is simplest to start with an existing one. If we download the `SharePointPersonality.spfont` font scheme file, we can use that as the basis for creating our own font scheme in any text editor.

There are three properties to define for our custom font scheme: `name`, `previewSlot1`, and `previewSlot2`. The preview slots use the fonts specified for those font slots when displaying the font scheme in the list of available font schemes to use in the web interface. There are seven font slots that can be configured:

- ▸ Title
- ▸ Navigation
- ▸ Large-heading
- ▸ Heading
- ▸ Small-heading
- ▸ Large-body
- ▸ Body

In the default font scheme, each font slot includes the following tags:

- ▸ Latin typeface (for example, `<s:latin typeface="Segoe UI Light" />`) that is used by languages that use Latin script
- ▸ East Asian typeface (for example, `<s:ea typeface="" />`) that is used by languages that use East Asian script
- ▸ Complex script typeface (for example, `<s:cs typeface="Segoe UI Light" />`) that is used by languages, which use complex scripts (languages whose characters require ligation or shaping)
- ▸ Fonts that target a specific script with a typeface (for example, `<s:font script="Arab" typeface="Segoe UI Light" />`, `<s:font script="Deva" typeface="Nirmala UI" />`, and so on)

In order to be compatible with SharePoint, each font slot requires the Latin typeface, East Asian typeface, and complex script typeface tags. The additional fonts included for specific scripts are optional and may be removed if you do not require support for those scripts.

In addition to system fonts that will be broadly available, we can use fonts that will be downloaded by the browser if they do not exist on the local system. Using the example from `fontscheme001.spfont`, we can specify the source locations for the various font formats:

```
<s:latin typeface="Bodoni Book"
  eotsrc="/_layouts/15/fonts/BodoniBook.eot"
  woffsrc="/_layouts/15/fonts/BodoniBook.woff"
  ttfsrc="/_layouts/15/fonts/BodoniBook.ttf"
  svgsrc="/_layouts/15/fonts/BodoniBook.svg" />
```

When using custom fonts, it is important to include all four formats for maximum compatibility with web browsers. In addition, it is important to ensure that you have rights to use a font before distributing it via your SharePoint site. There are a number of Internet sites that can convert a font into these four formats for you. One such site is `http://www.web-font-generator.com/`.

Getting ready

To complete this recipe you will need a custom font scheme created and ready to upload.

How to do it...

Follow these steps to upload a custom font scheme:

1. Navigate to the site in your preferred web browser.
2. Select **Site settings** from the **Settings** menu.
3. Select **Themes** in the **Web Designer Galleries** section.
4. Select the folder named 15.
5. Select **New Document** to upload and save the font scheme file.

How it works...

SharePoint font schemes are simply stored as files in a folder in a document library found at /_catalogs/theme/15. In this recipe, we uploaded our custom font scheme to this document library and made it available for use when applying composed looks.

There's more...

A font scheme may also be uploaded with SharePoint Designer 2013, PowerShell, or code using the server-side object model. We covered how to do this in the previous recipe, *Uploading a custom color palette*.

See also

▶ The *Color palettes and fonts in SharePoint 2013* article on MSDN at http://msdn.microsoft.com/en-us/library/jj945889.aspx

▶ The *How to: Upload a File to a SharePoint Site from a Local Folder* article on MSDN at http://msdn.microsoft.com/en-us/library/ms454491(v=office.14).aspx

▶ The *SPWeb class* topic on MSDN at http://msdn.microsoft.com/en-us/library/Microsoft.SharePoint.SPWeb.aspx

▶ The *SPSite class* topic on MSDN at http://msdn.microsoft.com/en-us/library/microsoft.sharepoint.spsite.aspx

▶ The *Get-SPWeb* topic on TechNet at http://technet.microsoft.com/en-us/library/ff607807.aspx

Creating a custom composed look

Composed looks are stored as items in the _catalogs/design list within each SharePoint site. They can specify the master page, color palette, font scheme, background image, and display order in relation to other composed looks.

How to do it...

Follow these steps to create a custom composed look:

1. Navigate to the site in your preferred web browser.
2. Select **Site settings** from the **Settings** menu.
3. Select **Composed looks** in the **Web Designer Galleries** section.

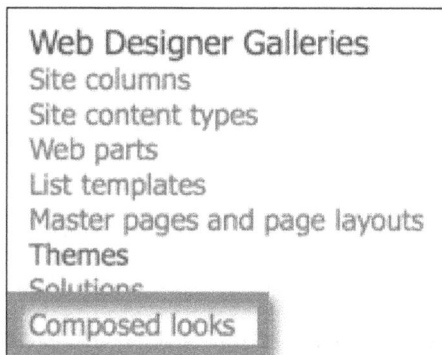

Web Designer Galleries
Site columns
Site content types
Web parts
List templates
Master pages and page layouts
Themes
Solutions
Composed looks

4. Click on **New Item** to create a new composed look item in the list.
5. Enter the name for the composed look in both the **Title** and **Name** fields.
6. Enter the URLs to the master page, color palette, background image, and font scheme files in both the **Web Address** and **Description** fields for each section.
7. Enter the **Display Order**.
8. Click on **Save**.

How it works...

Composed looks are simply stored as items in the _catalogs/design list. When a composed look is applied to a site the items specified in the composed look are used to create a SPTheme object that then gets applied to the SPWeb object representing the site. If no background image is specified, none will be applied when using this composed look. If no font scheme is specified, the default SharePointPersonality.spfont font scheme will be applied when using this composed look.

Lastly, the **Display Order** option is used to sort the available composed looks when choosing which composed look to apply to a site. Have a look at the following screenshot:

Composed Looks ⓘ

⊕ new item or edit this list

All Items   ⋯

✓	Name	Master Page URL	Theme URL	Image URL
	Current			
	Orange	/_catalogs/masterpage/seattle.master	/_catalogs/theme/15/palette015.spcolor	
	Sea Monster	/_catalogs/masterpage/oslo.master	/_catalogs/theme/15/palette005.spcolor	/_layouts/15/images/im
	Green	/_catalogs/masterpage/seattle.master	/_catalogs/theme/15/palette013.spcolor	
	Lime	/_catalogs/masterpage/seattle.master	/_catalogs/theme/15/palette026.spcolor	
	Nature	/_catalogs/masterpage/seattle.master	/_catalogs/theme/15/palette006.spcolor	/_layouts/15/images/im
	Blossom	/_catalogs/masterpage/seattle.master	/_catalogs/theme/15/palette002.spcolor	/_layouts/15/images/im
	Sketch	/_catalogs/masterpage/oslo.master	/_catalogs/theme/15/palette008.spcolor	/_layouts/15/images/im
	City	/_catalogs/masterpage/seattle.master	/_catalogs/theme/15/palette004.spcolor	/_layouts/15/images/im
	Orbit	/_catalogs/masterpage/seattle.master	/_catalogs/theme/15/palette009.spcolor	/_layouts/15/images/im

There's more...

A composed look can be created with PowerShell or code using the server-side object model.

Creating a custom composed look using PowerShell

Follow these steps to create a custom composed look using PowerShell:

1. Get the site using the `Get-SPWeb` Cmdlet:

   ```
   $web = Get-SPWeb http://sharepoint/site
   ```

2. Get the `SPList` object representing the `_catalogs/design` list from the `SPWeb` object:

   ```
   $list = $web.Lists["Composed Looks"]
   ```

3. Add a new `SPListItem` to the `Items` collection of the `SPList` object:

   ```
   $item = $list.Items.Add()
   ```

4. Assign the values to each of the properties of the `SPListItem` object:

   ```
   $item["Title"] = "PowerShell"

   $item["Name"] = "PowerShell"

   $item["Master Page URL"] =
   ```

```
"/_catalogs/masterpages/seattle.master"

$item["Theme URL"] = "/_catalogs/theme/15/palette005.spcolor"

$item["Image URL"] = "/_layouts/15/images/image_bg005.jpg"

$item["Font Scheme URL"] =
"/_catalogs/theme/15/fontscheme003.spfont"
$item["Display Order"] = "200"
```

5. Use the `Update` method on `SPList` to update the `Items` collection:

   ```
   $item.Update()
   ```

6. Use the `Dispose` method to discard the `SPWeb` object:

   ```
   $web.Dispose()
   ```

Creating a custom composed look with code using the server-side object model

Follow these steps to create a custom composed look with code using the server-side object model:

1. Open the site collection containing the site in a `using` statement:

   ```
   using (var site = new SPSite("http://sharepoint/site"))
   ```

2. Open the site in a `using` statement:

   ```
   using (var web = site.OpenWeb())
   ```

3. Get the `SPList` object representing the `_catalogs/design` list from the `SPWeb` object:

   ```
   var list = web.Lists["Composed Looks"];
   ```

4. Add a new `SPListItem` to the `Items` collection of the `SPList` object:

   ```
   var item = list.Items.Add();
   ```

5. Assign the values to each of the properties of the `SPListItem` object:

   ```
   item["Title"] = "PowerShell";

   item["Name"] = "PowerShell";

   item["Master Page URL"] =
     "/_catalogs/masterpages/seattle.master";

   item["Theme URL"] =
     "/_catalogs/theme/15/palette005.spcolor";

   item["Image URL"] = "/_layouts/15/images/image_bg005.jpg";
   ```

```
item["Font Scheme URL"] =
  "/_catalogs/theme/15/fontscheme003.spfont";

item["Display Order"] = "200";
```

6. Use the `Update` method on the `SPList` object to update the `Items` collection:

```
item.Update();
```

See also

▶ The *Themes overview for SharePoint 2013* article on MSDN at `http://msdn.microsoft.com/en-us/library/jj927174.aspx`

▶ The *How to: Add or Delete List Items* article on MSDN at `http://msdn.microsoft.com/en-us/library/ms467435(v=office.14).aspx`

▶ The *SPWeb class* topic on MSDN at `http://msdn.microsoft.com/en-us/library/Microsoft.SharePoint.SPWeb.aspx`

▶ The *SPSite class* topic on MSDN at `http://msdn.microsoft.com/en-us/library/microsoft.sharepoint.spsite.aspx`

▶ The *Get-SPWeb* topic on TechNet at `http://technet.microsoft.com/en-us/library/ff607807.aspx`

Using PowerShell to apply a composed look to all sites in a site collection

Windows PowerShell provides administrators with the ability to create complex scripts that utilize Cmdlets and .NET code. The Microsoft SharePoint PowerShell snap-in exposes many of the common administrative functions of SharePoint as Cmdlets. For the rest, we can use the server-side object model.

Since composed looks are applied at the site level, it can be cumbersome to apply them to a large number of sites. In this recipe, we are going to use PowerShell to iterate through all of the SharePoint sites in a site collection to apply a composed look.

> When using complex PowerShell, it is ideal to write the commands in a text file with a `.ps1` extension and then execute the script from the PowerShell session. This allows us to easily use the `foreach` loops and other techniques that are common to programming.

How to do it...

Follow these steps to apply a composed look to all sites in a site collection using PowerShell:

1. Open your preferred text editor to create the `.ps1` script file.

2. Get the site collection with the `Get-SPSite` Cmdlet:

    ```
    $site = Get-SPSite http://sharepoint/site
    ```

3. Use a `foreach` loop to iterate through each `SPWeb` in the `AllWebs` property of the `SPSite` object:

    ```
    foreach ($web in $site.AllWebs)
    ```

4. Check if `SPWeb` exists:

    ```
    if ($web.Exists)
    ```

5. Apply the composed look using the `ApplyTheme` method:

    ```
    $web.ApplyTheme("/_catalogs/theme/15/Palette015.spcolor",
    "/_catalogs/theme/15/SharePointPersonality.spfont",
    "/_layouts/15/images/image_bg011.jpg", $false)
    ```

6. Use the `Dispose` method to discard the `SPWeb` object:

    ```
    $web.Dispose()
    ```

7. Use the `Dispose` method to discard the `SPSite` object:

    ```
    $site.Dispose()
    ```

8. Save the file as a PS1 file, for example, `applycomposedlook.ps1`.

9. Execute the script in the PowerShell session:

    ```
    ./applycomposedlook.ps1
    ```

How it works...

Using PowerShell we can easily create scripts to perform tasks that would normally require a tedious amount of manual work. In this recipe, we iterated through each site in the `AllWebs` property of the site collection that we obtained using the `Get-SPSite` Cmdlet. For each SharePoint site, we used the `ApplyTheme` method to apply our composed look.

There's more...

The steps performed in PowerShell may also be completed with code using the server-side object model. Follow these steps to apply a composed look to all sites in a site collection with code using the server-side object model:

1. Open the site collection in a `using` statement:

   ```
   using (var site = new SPSite("http://sharepoint/site")
   ```

2. Use a `foreach` loop to iterate through each `SPWeb` in the `AllWebs` property of the `SPSite` object:

   ```
   foreach (var web in site.AllWebs)
   ```

3. Check if the `SPWeb` exists:

   ```
   if (web.Exists)
   ```

4. Apply the composed look using the `ApplyTheme` method:

   ```
   web.ApplyTheme("/_catalogs/theme/15/Palette015.spcolor",
     "/_catalogs/theme/15/SharePointPersonality.spfont",
     "/_layouts/15/images/image_bg011.jpg", false);
   ```

5. Use the `Dispose` method to discard the `SPWeb` object:

   ```
   web.Dispose();
   ```

See also

▸ The *Themes overview for SharePoint 2013* article on MSDN at `http://msdn.microsoft.com/en-us/library/jj927174.aspx`

▸ The *SPWeb class* topic on MSDN at `http://msdn.microsoft.com/en-us/library/Microsoft.SharePoint.SPWeb.aspx`

▸ The *SPSite class* topic on MSDN at `http://msdn.microsoft.com/en-us/library/microsoft.sharepoint.spsite.aspx`

▸ The *Get-SPSite* topic on TechNet at `http://technet.microsoft.com/en-us/library/ff607950.aspx`

Using PowerShell to apply master page and logo settings to all sites in a farm

For this recipe, we are using a PowerShell script to apply master page and logo settings to each SharePoint site in every site collection of each web application on the local SharePoint farm.

How to do it...

Follow these steps to apply master page and logo settings to all sites in the local SharePoint farm using PowerShell:

1. Open your preferred text editor to create the `.ps1` script file.

2. Use a `foreach` loop to iterate through each content of `SPWebApplication` on the local SharePoint farm using the `Get-SPWebApplication` Cmdlet:

    ```
    foreach($webApp in (Get-SPWebApplication))
    ```

3. Use a `foreach` loop to iterate through each `SPSite` in the `Sites` property of the `SPWebApplication` object:

    ```
    foreach($site in $webApp.Sites)
    ```

4. Verify the `CompatibilityLevel` property of `SPSite` to ensure it is in SharePoint 2013 (Version 15) mode and not in SharePoint 2010 (Version 14) mode.

    ```
    if ($site.CompatibilityLevel -eq 15)
    ```

5. Use a `foreach` loop to iterate through each `SPWeb` in the `AllWebs` property of the `SPSite` object:

    ```
    foreach ($web in $site.AllWebs)
    ```

6. Check if the `SPWeb` object exists:

    ```
    if ($web.Exists)
    ```

7. Set the master page and logo properties for the `SPWeb` object:

    ```
    $web.SiteLogoUrl = "/SiteAssets/logo.png"

    $web.SiteLogoDescription = "My PowerShell Site"

    $web.MasterUrl = "/_catalogs/masterpages/seattle.master"

    $web.CustomMasterUrl = "/_catalogs/masterpages/seattle.master"
    ```

8. Use the `Update` method on the `SPWeb` object to save the changes:

    ```
    $web.Update()
    ```

9. Use the `Dispose` method to discard the `SPWeb` object:

    ```
    $web.Dispose()
    ```

10. Use the `Dispose` method to discard the `SPSite` object:

    ```
    $site.Dispose()
    ```

11. Save the file as a `PS1` file, for example, `applymasterpageandlogo.ps1`.

12. Execute the script in the PowerShell session:

```
./applymasterpageandlogo.ps1
```

How it works...

In this recipe, we retrieved all of the content web applications using the Get-SPWebApplication Cmdlet. We then iterated through each site collection in the Sites property of each web application and then iterated through each site in the AllWebs property of each site collection. For each site, we updated the properties for the logo and master pages.

There's more...

The steps performed in PowerShell may also be completed in code using the server-side object model. Follow these steps to apply master page and logo settings to all sites on the local SharePoint farm with code using the server-side object model:

1. Use a foreach loop to iterate through each content SPWebApplication on the local SharePoint farm:

```
foreach (var webApp in
  SPWebService.ContentService.WebApplications)
```

2. Use a foreach loop to iterate through each SPSite in the Sites property of the SPWebApplication object:

```
foreach (var site in webApp.Sites)
```

3. Verify the CompatibilityLevel property of SPSite to ensure it is in SharePoint 2013 (Version 15) mode and not in SharePoint 2010 (Version 14) mode:

```
if (site.CompatibilityLevel == 15)
```

4. Use a foreach loop for iterating through each SPWeb in the AllWebs property of the SPSite object:

```
foreach (var web in site.AllWebs)
```

5. Check if the SPWeb exists:

```
if (web.Exists)
```

6. Set the master page and logo properties on the SPWeb object:

```
web.SiteLogoUrl = "/SiteAssets/logo.png";

web.SiteLogoDescription = "My Code Site";

web.MasterUrl = "/_catalogs/masterpages/seattle.master";
```

```
web.CustomMasterUrl =
  "/_catalogs/masterpages/seattle.master";
```

7. Use the `Update` method on the `SPWeb` object to save the changes:

   ```
   web.Update();
   ```

8. Use the `Dispose` method to discard the `SPSite` and `SPWeb` objects:

   ```
   web.Dispose();
   site.Dispose();
   ```

See also

▸ The *SPWebApplication class* topic on MSDN at `http://msdn.microsoft.com/en-us/library/microsoft.sharepoint.administration.spwebapplication.aspx`

▸ The *SPWeb class* topic on MSDN at `http://msdn.microsoft.com/en-us/library/Microsoft.SharePoint.SPWeb.aspx`

▸ The *SPSite class* topic on MSDN at `http://msdn.microsoft.com/en-us/library/microsoft.sharepoint.spsite.aspx`

▸ The *Get-SPWebApplication* topic on TechNet at `http://technet.microsoft.com/en-us/library/ff607562.aspx`

2
Branding SharePoint with Device Channels and Design Packages

In this chapter, we will cover packaging out-of-the-box branding elements and targeting the branding for specific devices. We will cover the following recipes:

- ▶ Creating a device channel for mobile devices
- ▶ Applying a master page to a device channel
- ▶ Creating and exporting a design package
- ▶ Importing and applying a design package
- ▶ Importing a design package to all site collections with PowerShell
- ▶ Listing the device channel master pages

Introduction

With the 2013 release of SharePoint, Microsoft has added two new capabilities that assist with full-scale branding of SharePoint sites: **device channels** and **design packages**. A device channel uses the user agent of the web browser sending the incoming web request to determine which master page to render the content pages with. A common use of the device channels is to detect tablets and smartphones to use a more touch-friendly interface design. For instance, a device channel can be configured to look for an iPad in the following user agent to identify the iPad devices:

```
Mozilla/5.0 (iPad; CPU OS 7_0_4 like Mac OS X)
  AppleWebKit/537.51.1 (KHTML, like Gecko) Version/7.0
    Mobile/11B554a Safari/9537.53
```

> Any portion of the user agent can be used for a device channel. It is important to be specific, but not too specific. Using iPad would apply to all the devices that specify iPad in their user agent, whereas iPad; U; CPU OS 7_0 would only apply to iPads running on iOS Version 7.0.

A design package is a SharePoint solution, packaged as a WSP file containing branding customizations, such as master pages and cascading style sheets. This provides a simple method of exporting a site design from one site and applying it to another. A design package will only contain items that are not default to SharePoint. Default items, such as the included master pages, will be referenced, but are not included as part of the package.

Prior to SharePoint 2013, packaged design solutions could only be created manually or with Visual Studio. Design packages allow any site collection administrator to create and apply packaged designs. This allows the site collection administrators to obtain packaged designs (from third parties, and so on) and apply them, without having to manually upload and configure each piece of the design.

Creating a device channel for mobile devices

One of the most common scenarios for using device channels is to identify the tablet and smartphone browsers. Applying a mobile-specific master page, when appropriate, can provide the users with a design that is more touch friendly and is laid out in a specific manner for smaller screens. In this recipe, we are going to create a device channel that will identify Android, iOS, BlackBerry, WebOS, and Windows mobile devices. There are hundreds of mobile-specific browsers that we can detect with the user agent. However, for this recipe we are going to keep it simple.

Getting ready

In order to view and modify the device channels for a SharePoint site, the **SharePoint Server Publishing Infrastructure** site collection feature and **SharePoint Server** Publishing site feature must be activated.

How to do it...

Follow these steps to create a device channel for mobile devices:

1. Navigate to the site in your preferred web browser.
2. Select **Site settings** from the **Settings** menu.
3. Select **Device Channels** from the **Look and Feel** section.

```
Look and Feel
Design Manager
Master page
Title, description, and logo
Page layouts and site templates
Welcome Page
Device Channels
Tree view
Change the look
Import Design Package
Navigation
Image Renditions
```

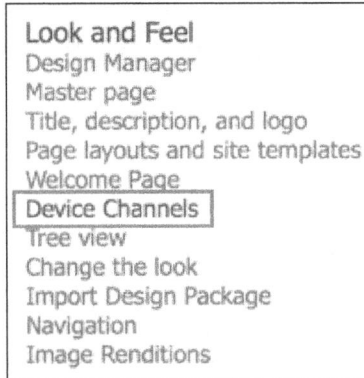

You can also navigate to the **Device Channels** page from the **Design Manager** page.

4. Select **New Item**.

5. Provide a **Name**, **Description**, and **Alias** for the device channel.

> The **Alias** field specified will be used when specifying which master page to use with the device channel in the device channel mappings file. We will learn about this in the next recipe, *Applying a master page to a device channel*.

6. Specify the **Device Inclusion Rules** to be included in the device channel.

```
Android
iPad
iPod
iPhone
BlackBerry
IEMobile
WebOS
```

7. When using multiple device inclusion rules, place each string on a new line to match the user agent. **Device Inclusion Rules** are simply strings that are looked for in the user agent of incoming web requests.

Name *	Mobile
	The name used by authors and others to identify this channel
Alias *	Mobile
	Pick a word to identify this channel in code, Device Channel panels, previews and other contexts. Warning: If you later change the channel alias, you will have to manually update Master Page mappings, Device Channel panels, and any custom code or markup.
Description	Device channel for mobile devices.
	A quick description of the Device Channel
Device Inclusion Rules *	Android iPad iPod iPhone BlackBerry IEMobile
	Specify one or more user agent substrings (for example: Windows Phone OS), placing each substring on its own line. When the user agent string of a visiting device contains any of the specified substrings, the channel will force site pages to display using that channel's optimizations, like a different Master Page or Device Channel Panel. You can also trigger this special rendering by using query strings, cookies or custom code, in which case the substrings don't matter.

8. Mark the **Active** checkbox and click on **Save**.

How it works...

Device channels are created and stored in the /DeviceChannels SharePoint list in the root site of a site collection. When an incoming browser request is received, SharePoint checks whether the incoming user agent matches any of the **Device Inclusion Rules** before selecting the master page to use.

Device Channels ⓘ

⊕ new item or edit this list

All Items   All Device Channels: Simple Listing   ...

✓	Active	Name	Alias	Description
	Yes	Mobile	Mobile	Targets mobile devices
	Yes	Default	Default	This channel is the default for your site. A device will see the look and feel specified by this channel when no other channels are active or when the device's user-agent string does not match the device inclusion rules for any active channels.

Many web browsers have developer tools that allow changing the user agent reported by the browser. Switching the user agent is one way in which we can test to ensure our device channels are working correctly. Internet Explorer 11, for instance, includes this option in the **Emulation** section of the **F12 Developer Tools**.

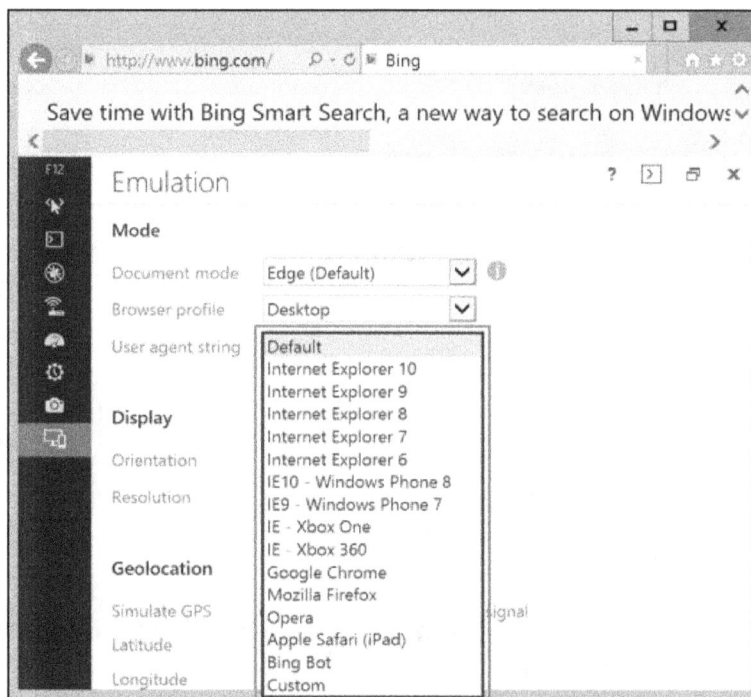

There's more...

A device channel may also be created with PowerShell or with code using the server-side object model.

Creating a device channel for mobile devices using PowerShell

Follow these steps to create a device channel for mobile devices using PowerShell:

1. Get the site using the `Get-SPWeb` Cmdlet.

   ```
   $web = Get-SPWeb http://sharepoint/site
   ```

2. Get the `DeviceChannels` list.

   ```
   $list = $web.Lists["Device Channels"]
   ```

3. Add a new `SPListItem` item to the `Items` collection of the list.

   ```
   $item = $list.Items.Add()
   ```

4. Assign the values to each of the properties on the `SPListItem` item.

   ```
   $item["Name"] = "PowerShell"

   $item["Alias"] = "PowerShell"

   $item["Description"] = "PowerShell Channel"

   $item["Device Inclusion Rules"] =
       "Android`niPad`niPod`niPhone`nBlackBerry`nIEMobile`nWebOS"

   $item["Active"] = $true
   ```

> When a line break is required within a string, in PowerShell, an escape character can be used. Escape characters in PowerShell use the tilde character. For example, a new line is represented by `n.

5. Call the `Update` method on the list to update the `Items` collection.

   ```
   $item.Update()
   ```

6. Use the `Dispose` method to discard the `SPWeb` object.

   ```
   $web.Dispose()
   ```

Creating a device channel for mobile devices with code using the server-side object model

Follow these steps to create a device channel for mobile devices with code using the server-side object model:

1. Open the site collection containing the site in a `using` statement.

   ```
   using (var site = new SPSite("http://sharepoint/site"))
   ```

2. Open the site in a `using` statement.

```
using (var web = site.OpenWeb())
```

3. Get the `DeviceChannels` list.

```
var list = web.Lists["Device Channels"];
```

4. Add a new `SPListItem` item to the `Items` collection of the list.

```
var item = list.Items.Add();
```

5. Assign the values to each of the properties on the `SPListItem` item.

```
item["Name"] = "Code";

item["Alias"] = "Code ";

item["Description"] = "Code Channel";

item["Device Inclusion Rules"] =
   "Android\niPad\niPod\niPhone\nBlackBerry\nIEMobile\nWebOS";

item["Active"] = true;
```

> When a line break is required within a string in C#, an escape character can be used. Escape characters in C# use the backslash character. For example, a new line is represented by \n.

6. Call the `Update` method on the list to update the `Items` collection.

```
item.Update();
```

See also

▸ The *SharePoint 2013 Design Manager device channels* article on MSDN at `http://msdn.microsoft.com/en-us/library/jj862343.aspx`

▸ The *How to: Add or Delete List Items* topic on MSDN at `http://msdn.microsoft.com/en-us/library/ms467435(v=office.14).aspx`

▸ The *SPWeb class* topic on MSDN at `http://msdn.microsoft.com/en-us/library/Microsoft.SharePoint.SPWeb.aspx`

▸ The *SPSite class* topic on MSDN at `http://msdn.microsoft.com/en-us/library/microsoft.sharepoint.spsite.aspx`

▸ The *Get-SPWeb* article on TechNet at `http://technet.microsoft.com/en-us/library/ff607807.aspx`

Applying a master page to a device channel

Once a device channel has been created, it can be configured to use as a different site master page rather than the default site master page. For instance, browsers targeted by a mobile device channel could display the content using the **oslo** master page whereas all other browsers could display the same content using the **seattle** master page.

The **System Master Page** is configured for all device channels and cannot be configured for individual device channels.

How to do it...

Follow these steps to apply a master page to a device channel:

1. Navigate to the site in your preferred web browser.
2. Select **Site settings** from the **Settings** menu.
3. Select **Master page** from the **Look and Feel** section.
4. Specify which **Site Master Page** to use for each device channel.

Site Master Page

The site master page will be used by all publishing pages - the pages that visitors to your website will see. You can have a different master page for each Device Channel. If you don't see the master page you're looking for, go to the Master Page Gallery in Site Settings and make sure it has an approved version.

You may inherit these settings from the parent site or select unique settings for this site only.

○ Inherit site master page from parent of this site

◉ Specify a master page to be used by this site and all sites that inherit from it:

Mobile	oslo	⬍
Default	seattle	⬍

☐ Reset all subsites to inherit this site master page setting

---

5. Click on **Save**.

How it works...

The master page to device channel mappings are stored in the `_catalogs/masterpages/__DeviceChannelMappings.aspx` file as XML within the root site of a site collection. For each incoming browser web request, this file is used by SharePoint to determine which master page to use with the content returned to the browser.

```
<%@ Reference VirtualPath="~CustomMasterUrlForMapping0" %><%@ Reference VirtualPath="~CustomMasterUrlForMapping1" %><%@ Page Lan
<head>
<meta name="WebPartPageExpansion" content="full" />
<!--[if gte mso 9]>
<SharePoint:CTFieldRefs runat=server Prefix="mso:" FieldList="FileLeafRef"><xml>

<mso:CustomDocumentProperties>
<mso:ContentTypeId msdt:dt="string">0x010100FDA260FD09A244B183A666F2AE2475A6</mso:ContentTypeId>
</mso:CustomDocumentProperties>
</xml></SharePoint:CTFieldRefs><![endif]-->
</head><body><mappings>
  <mapping>
    <channelAlias>Mobile</channelAlias>
    <masterUrl href="/_catalogs/masterpage/oslo.master" token="~sitecollection/_catalogs/masterpage/oslo.master" />
  </mapping>
  <defaultChannelMapping>
    <siteMasterUrl token="~sitecollection/_catalogs/masterpage/seattle.master" href="/_catalogs/masterpage/seattle.master" />
    <systemMasterUrl token="~sitecollection/_catalogs/masterpage/seattle.master" href="/_catalogs/masterpage/seattle.master" />
    <alternateCssUrl token="" href="" />
    <themedCssFolderUrl token="" href="" isthemeshared="false" />
  </defaultChannelMapping>
</mappings></body></html>
```

There's more...

A device channel mapping may also be configured with PowerShell or with code using the server-side object model. In this recipe, these two methods are similar. However, the .NET reflection methods used are slightly different. When an object is instantiated with reflection in PowerShell, its public properties and methods become available to the command line. However, when an object is instantiated with reflection in the .NET code, each property and method needs to be searched for before being able to access them.

> The methods that provide the functionality to configure the device channel mappings are not publicly exposed in the SharePoint assemblies. As a result, we will use the .NET reflection to instantiate the objects required. It is important to note that non-public classes in the SharePoint assemblies can change between SharePoint versions and updates without notice. Using reflection tools, such as .NET Reflector (http://www.red-gate.com/products/dotnet-development/reflector/) and dotPeek (http://www.jetbrains.com/decompiler/), we can browse the assemblies to adjust the references accordingly.

Applying a master page to a device channel using PowerShell

Follow these steps to apply a master page to a device channel using PowerShell:

1. Load the `Microsoft.SharePoint.dll` and `Microsoft.SharePoint.Publishing.dll` assemblies into the PowerShell session.

   ```
   [Reflection.Assembly]::LoadFrom("C:\Program Files\Common
   Files\microsoft shared\Web Server
   Extensions\15\ISAPI\Microsoft.SharePoint.Publishing.dll")
   ```

   ```
   [Reflection.Assembly]::LoadFrom("C:\Program Files\Common
   Files\microsoft shared\Web Server
   Extensions\15\ISAPI\Microsoft.SharePoint.dll")
   ```

2. Get the object types for the parameters that will be used when getting the class constructor for the `MasterPageMappingsFile` object and later instantiating the object.

```
$typeWeb = [Microsoft.SharePoint.SPWeb]

$typeBool = [System.Boolean]

$typeMappingFile =
[System.Type]::GetType("Microsoft.SharePoint.Publishing.Mobile.
MasterPageMappingsFile, Microsoft.SharePoint.Publishing,
Version=15.0.0.0, Culture=neutral, PublicKeyToken=71e9bce111e942
9c")
```

3. Create an array of the object types.

```
$consMappingFileParams = ($typeWeb, $typeBool, $typeWeb)
```

4. Get the class constructor for the `MasterPageMappingsFile` object.

```
$consMappingFile =
$typeMappingFile.GetConstructor($consMappingFileParams)
```

5. Create an array of the parameters required to instantiate the `MasterPageMappingsFile` object.

```
$mappingFileParams =
[System.Array]::CreateInstance([System.Object], 3)

$mappingFileParams[0] = (Get-SPSite
http://sharepoint/sitecollection).RootWeb

$mappingFileParams[1] = $false

$mappingFileParams[2] = $null
```

When invoking a constructor to create an instance of a .NET object in PowerShell, we have to create a `System.Object` array rather than using a PowerShell array. Even though the base class for a PowerShell array is `System.Object[]`, when calling the `Invoke` method on the class constructor, it will see it as a `PSObject` object instead. The same goes for the `SPWeb` object we are passing as the first parameter. .NET will see the object as a `PSObject` object instead of a `SPWeb` object if we use `Get-SPWeb`. However, if we get the `SPWeb` object from the `SPSite` object, it will not get treated as a `PSObject` object.

6. Invoke the class constructor to create an instance of the `MasterPageMappingsFile` object.

   ```
   $mappingFile = $consMappingFile.Invoke($mappingFileParams)
   ```

7. Set the `MasterPageUrl` property for the device channel on the `MasterPageMappingsFile` object.

   ```
   $mappingFile["PowerShell"].MasterPageUrl =
   "/_catalogs/masterpage/oslo.master"
   ```

8. Save the changes using the `UpdateSingleChannel` method.

   ```
   $mappingFile.UpdateSingleChannel("PowerShell")
   ```

Applying a master page to a device channel with code using the server-side object model

Follow these steps to apply a master page to a device channel with code using the server-side object model:

> A reference to the `Microsoft.SharePoint.Publishing.dll` assembly is required for this recipe.

1. Get the site collection in a `using` statement.

   ```
   using (var site = new SPSite("http://sharepoint/sitecollection"))
   ```

2. Get the root site of the site collection in a `using` statement.

   ```
   using (var web = site.RootWeb)
   ```

3. Get the object type that will be used when getting the class constructor for the `MasterPageMappingsFile` object and later instantiating the object.

   ```
   var typeMappingFile =
     Type.GetType("Microsoft.SharePoint.Publishing.Mobile.
   MasterPageMappingsFile, Microsoft.SharePoint.Publishing,
   Version=15.0.0.0, Culture=neutral, PublicKeyToken=71e9bce111e942
   9c");
   ```

4. Get the class constructor for the `MasterPageMappingsFile` object.

   ```
   var consMappingFile =
     typeMappingFile.GetConstructor(new Type[] { typeof(SPWeb),
       typeof(bool), typeof(SPWeb) });
   ```

5. Invoke the constructor to create an instance of the `MasterPageMappingsFile` object.

```
var mappingFile = consMappingFile.Invoke(new object[]
  { web, false, null });
```

6. Get the `mappings` field of the `MasterPageMappingsFile` object, and cast the field as an `IDictionary`.

```
var mappings = (IDictionary)typeMappingFile.GetField("mappings",
  BindingFlags.Instance | BindingFlags.NonPublic).
GetValue(mappingFile);
```

7. Set the `MasterPageUrl` property for the device channel on the `mappings` field.

```
mappings["PowerShell"].GetType().GetProperty("MasterPageUrl",
  BindingFlags.Instance |
    BindingFlags.Public).SetValue(mappings["PowerShell"],
      "/_catalogs/masterpage/seattle.master", null);
```

8. Set the `mappings` field of the `MasterPageMappingsFile` object.

```
typeMappingFile.GetField("mappings", BindingFlags.Instance |
  BindingFlags.NonPublic).SetValue(mappingFile, mappings);
```

9. Get the `UpdateSingleChannel` method from the type of the `MasterPageMappingsFile` object.

```
var updateMethod = typeMappingFile.GetMethod("UpdateSingleChann
el",
  BindingFlags.Instance | BindingFlags.Public, null, new Type[]
    { typeof(string) }, null);
```

10. Save the changes by invoking the `UpdateSingleChannel` method.

```
updateMethod.Invoke(mappingFile, new object[] { "Code" });
```

See also

▶ The *SharePoint 2013 Design Manager device channels* article on MSDN at `http://msdn.microsoft.com/en-us/library/jj862343.aspx`

▶ The *Reflection in the .NET Framework* article on MSDN at `http://msdn.microsoft.com/en-us/library/f7ykdhsy.aspx`

▶ The *SPWeb class* topic on MSDN at `http://msdn.microsoft.com/en-us/library/Microsoft.SharePoint.SPWeb.aspx`

▶ The *SPSite class* topic on MSDN at `http://msdn.microsoft.com/en-us/library/microsoft.sharepoint.spsite.aspx`

▶ The *Get-SPSite* topic on TechNet at `http://technet.microsoft.com/en-us/library/ff607950.aspx`

Creating and exporting a design package

Design packages in SharePoint 2013 allow us to package our customized branding from one SharePoint site and apply it to another. Design packages can include:

- ▸ Device channels
- ▸ Design files stored in `_catalogs/masterpage/`
- ▸ Master pages
- ▸ Display templates
- ▸ Page layouts

When a design package is created, it will only include the preceding elements that were customized or added. It will not include the items that come by default with SharePoint. In this recipe, we will cover how to create a design package from a site that is already customized.

How to do it...

Follow these steps to create and export a design package:

1. Navigate to the site in your preferred web browser.
2. Select **Site settings** from the **Settings** menu.
3. Select **Design Manager** from the **Look and Feel** section.

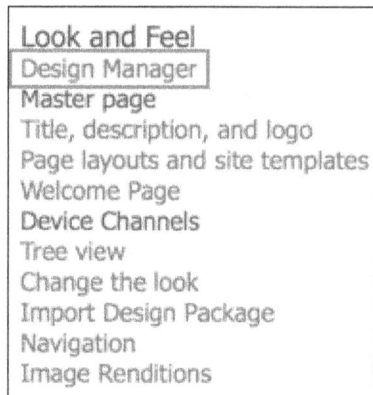

Look and Feel
Design Manager
Master page
Title, description, and logo
Page layouts and site templates
Welcome Page
Device Channels
Tree view
Change the look
Import Design Package
Navigation
Image Renditions

4. There are eight steps present on the left-hand side of the page to manage every aspect of the SharePoint site design customizations that will be included in the design package. Perform each step to verify that the elements are being included in the site design package.

1. Welcome
2. Manage Device Channels
3. Upload Design Files
4. Edit Master Pages
5. Edit Display Templates
6. Edit Page Layouts
7. Publish and Apply Design
8. Create Design Package

5. Select the final step **8. Create Design Package** as shown in the previous screenshot.
6. Provide a **Design Name**.
7. Select **Create**. Creating the design package may take some time depending on the amount of customizations being included and the server resources.
8. Once complete, click on the link to download the design package.

How it works...

When creating a design package, each site design customization is reviewed in the wizard steps. These design customizations include master pages, page layouts, device channels, and design files (cascading style sheets, images, JavaScript, and so on). The design customizations are then packaged in a SharePoint solution file (WSP). These SharePoint solutions are sandboxed solutions that allow the site collection administrators to upload and deploy them rather than requiring a farm administrator.

There's more...

A design package may also be exported with PowerShell or with code using the server-side object model.

Creating and exporting a design package using PowerShell

Follow these steps to create and export a design package using PowerShell:

1. Load the `Microsoft.SharePoint.dll` and `Microsoft.SharePoint.Publishing.dll` assemblies into the PowerShell session.

    ```
    [Reflection.Assembly]::LoadFrom("C:\Program Files\Common
    Files\microsoft shared\Web Server
    ```

```
Extensions\15\ISAPI\Microsoft.SharePoint.Publishing.dll")

[Reflection.Assembly]::LoadFrom("C:\Program Files\Common
Files\microsoft shared\Web Server
Extensions\15\ISAPI\Microsoft.SharePoint.dll")
```

2. Get the site collection using the `Get-SPSite` Cmdlet.

```
$site = Get-SPSite http://sharepoint/sitecollection
```

3. Create the design package using the `Export` method of `Microsoft.SharePoint.Publishing.DesignPackage`.

```
$package =
[Microsoft.SharePoint.Publishing.DesignPackage]::Export($site,
"My PowerShell Design", $false)
```

4. Get the filename using the specified format and design the package details.

```
$fileName = "{0}-{1}.{2}.wsp" -f ($package.PackageName,
$package.MajorVersion, $package.MinorVersion)
```

5. Get the `SPFile` object representing the design package WSP file from the `RootWeb` property of the `SPSite` object.

```
fileBinary = $site.RootWeb.GetFile("/_catalogs/solutions/" +
$fileName).OpenBinary()
```

6. Use `System.IO.FileStream` to save the contents of the `SPFile` object to the local filesystem.

```
$fileStream = New-Object System.IO.FileStream("C:\" +
$fileName, [System.IO.FileMode]::OpenOrCreate,
[System.IO.FileAccess]::Write)

$fileStream.Write($fileBinary, 0, $fileBinary.Length)

$fileStream.Close()
```

7. Use the `Dispose` method to discard the `SPSite` object.

```
$site.Dispose()
```

Creating and exporting a design package with code using the server-side object model

Follow these steps to create and export a design package with code using the server-side object model:

> A reference to the `Microsoft.SharePoint.Publishing.dll` assembly is required for this recipe.

1. Get the site collection in a `using` statement.

    ```
    using (var site = new SPSite("http://sharepoint/sitecollection"))
    ```

2. Get the root site of the site collection in a `using` statement.

    ```
    using (var web = site.RootWeb)
    ```

3. Create the design package using the `Export` method of `Microsoft.SharePoint.Publishing.DesignPackage`.

    ```
    var package = DesignPackage.Export(site, "My Code Design", false);
    ```

4. Get the filename using the specified format and design the package details.

    ```
    var fileName = string.Format(CultureInfo.InvariantCulture,
      "{0}-{1}.{2}.wsp", package.PackageName, package.MajorVersion,
      package.MinorVersion);
    ```

5. Get the `SPFile` object representing the design package WSP file from the `RootWeb` property of the `SPSite` object.

    ```
    var fileBinary = web.GetFile("/_catalogs/solutions" +
      filename).OpenBinary();
    ```

6. Use `System.IO.FileStream` to save the contents of the `SPFile` object to the local filesystem.

    ```
    var fileStream = new FileStream("C:\\" + fileName,
      FileMode.OpenOrCreate, FileAccess.Write);

    fileStream.Write(fileBinary, 0, fileBinary.Length);

    fileStream.Close();
    ```

See also

▶ The *SharePoint 2013 Design Manager design packages* article on MSDN at `http://msdn.microsoft.com/en-us/library/jj862342.aspx`

▶ The *SPWeb class* topic on MSDN at `http://msdn.microsoft.com/en-us/library/Microsoft.SharePoint.SPWeb.aspx`

▶ The *SPSite class* topic on MSDN at `http://msdn.microsoft.com/en-us/library/microsoft.sharepoint.spsite.aspx`

▶ The *Get-SPSite* topic on TechNet at `http://technet.microsoft.com/en-us/library/ff607950.aspx`

Importing and applying a design package

With SharePoint 2013, a user only needs to be a site collection administrator to apply a packaged design rather than be a farm administrator. This offloads the burden of applying site collection level designs from farm administrators and makes it simpler for site collection administrators to obtain packaged designs from third parties and apply them.

How to do it...

Follow these steps to import and apply a design package:

1. Navigate to the site in your preferred web browser.
2. Select **Site settings** from the **Settings** menu.
3. Select **Import Design Package** from the **Look and Feel** section.

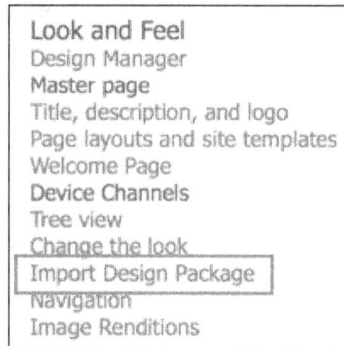

> Look and Feel
> Design Manager
> Master page
> Title, description, and logo
> Page layouts and site templates
> Welcome Page
> Device Channels
> Tree view
> Change the look
> Import Design Package
> Navigation
> Image Renditions

4. Select the design package to import.
5. Select **Import**.

How it works...

Importing a design package adds the SharePoint solution file (WSP) to the **Solutions Gallery** of the site collection and applies the customizations it contains. These SharePoint solutions are sandboxed solutions that allow the site collection administrators to upload and deploy them rather than requiring a farm administrator.

There's more...

A design package may also be imported and applied with PowerShell or with code using the server-side object model.

Importing and applying a design package using PowerShell

Follow these steps to import and apply a design package using PowerShell:

1. Load the `Microsoft.SharePoint.dll` and `Microsoft.SharePoint.Publishing.dll` assemblies into the PowerShell session.

   ```
   [Reflection.Assembly]::LoadFrom("C:\Program Files\Common
   Files\microsoft shared\Web Server
   Extensions\15\ISAPI\Microsoft.SharePoint.Publishing.dll")

   [Reflection.Assembly]::LoadFrom("C:\Program Files\Common
   Files\microsoft shared\Web Server Extensions\15\ISAPI\Microsoft.
   SharePoint.dll")
   ```

2. Get the site collection using the `Get-SPSite` Cmdlet.

   ```
   $site = Get-SPSite http://sharepoint/sitecollection
   ```

3. Specify the path to the design package WSP file and get the file name from the path.

   ```
   $filePath = "C:\My PowerShell Design-1.0.wsp"

   $fileName = [System.IO.Path]::GetFileName($filePath)
   ```

4. Create a `DesignPackageInfo` object to represent the design package we are about to upload. In the constructor, specify the major and minor version of the design package.

   ```
   $package = New-Object
   Microsoft.SharePoint.Publishing.DesignPackageInfo($fileName,
   [Guid]::Empty, 1, 0)
   ```

5. Create a temporary folder in the `RootWeb` site to upload the design package to:

   ```
   $tempFolderName = "temp_designupload_" +
   ([Guid]::NewGuid).ToString()

   $tempFolder =
   $site.RootWeb.RootFolder.SubFolders.Add($tempFolderName)
   ```

6. Use the `OpenRead` method of `System.IO.File` to read the contents of the design package WSP file and add the file to the `Files` collection of the temporary folder.

   ```
   $fileBinary = [System.IO.File]::OpenRead($filePath)

   $file = $tempFolder.Files.Add($fileName, $fileBinary, $true)

   $fileBinary.Close()
   ```

7. Use the `Install` method of `Microsoft.SharePoint.Publishing.DesignPackage` to add the design package to the **Solutions Gallery** and apply the customizations in the design package to the site collection.

   ```
   [Microsoft.SharePoint.Publishing.DesignPackage]::Install($site,
   $package, $file.Url)
   ```

8. Delete the temporary folder.

   ```
   $tempFolder.Delete()
   ```

9. Use the `Dispose` method to discard the `SPSite` object.

   ```
   $site.Dispose()
   ```

Importing and applying a design package with code using the server-side object model

Follow these steps to import and apply a design package with code using the server-side object model:

> A reference to the `Microsoft.SharePoint.Publishing.dll` assembly is required for this recipe.

1. Get the site collection in a `using` statement.

   ```
   using (var site = new SPSite("http://sharepoint/sitecollection"))
   ```

2. Get the root site of the site collection in a `using` statement.

   ```
   using (var web = site.RootWeb)
   ```

3. Specify the path to the design package WSP file and get the file name from the path.

   ```
   var filePath = "C:\My Code Design-1.0.wsp";
   var fileName = Path.GetFileName(filePath);
   ```

4. Create a `DesignPackageInfo` object to represent the design package we are about to upload. In the constructor, specify the major and minor versions of the design package.

   ```
   var package = new DesignPackageInfo(fileName, Guid.Empty, 1, 0);
   ```

5. Create a temporary folder in the `RootWeb` site to upload the design package to.

   ```
   var tempFolderName = "temp_designupload_" +
     Guid.NewGuid().ToString();
   var tempFolder = web.RootFolder.SubFolders.Add(tempFolderName);
   ```

6. Use the `OpenRead` method of `System.IO.File` to read the contents of the design package WSP file and add the file to the `Files` collection of the temporary folder.

```
var fileBinary = File.OpenRead(filePath);

var file = tempFolder.Files.Add(fileName, fileBinary, true);

var fileBinary.Close();
```

7. Use the `Install` method of `Microsoft.SharePoint.Publishing.DesignPackage` to add the design package to the **Solutions Gallery** and apply the customizations in the design package to the site collection.

```
DesignPackage.Install(site, package, file.Url);
```

8. Delete the temporary folder.

```
tempFolder.Delete();
```

See also

- ▶ The *SharePoint 2013 Design Manager design packages* article on MSDN at `http://msdn.microsoft.com/en-us/library/jj862342.aspx`

- ▶ The *How to: Upload a File to a SharePoint Site from a Local Folder* article on MSDN at `http://msdn.microsoft.com/en-us/library/ms454491(v=office.14).aspx`

- ▶ The *SPWeb class* topic on MSDN at `http://msdn.microsoft.com/en-us/library/Microsoft.SharePoint.SPWeb.aspx`

- ▶ The *SPSite class* topic on MSDN at `http://msdn.microsoft.com/en-us/library/microsoft.sharepoint.spsite.aspx`

- ▶ The *Get-SPSite* topic on TechNet at `http://technet.microsoft.com/en-us/library/ff607950.aspx`

Importing a design package to all site collections with PowerShell

Applying a design package to a large number of site collections can be a tedious task. To expedite the process, we can use PowerShell. In this recipe, we are going to use a PowerShell script (PS1) to upload and apply a design package to each content site collection in each web application on the local SharePoint farm.

How to do it...

Follow these steps to import a design package to all site collections with PowerShell:

1. Open your preferred text editor to create the PS1 script file.

2. Load the `Microsoft.SharePoint.dll` and `Microsoft.SharePoint.Publishing.dll` assemblies into the PowerShell session.

   ```
   [Reflection.Assembly]::LoadFrom("C:\Program Files\Common
   Files\microsoft shared\Web Server
   Extensions\15\ISAPI\Microsoft.SharePoint.Publishing.dll")
   ```

   ```
   [Reflection.Assembly]::LoadFrom("C:\Program Files\Common
   Files\microsoft shared\Web Server
   Extensions\15\ISAPI\Microsoft.SharePoint.dll")
   ```

3. Specify the path to the design package WSP file and get the filename from the path.

   ```
   $filePath = "C:\My PowerShell Design-1.0.wsp"
   ```

   ```
   $fileName = [System.IO.Path]::GetFileName($filePath)
   ```

4. Create a `DesignPackageInfo` object to represent the design package we are about to upload. In the constructor, specify the major and minor versions of the design package.

   ```
   $package = New-Object
   Microsoft.SharePoint.Publishing.DesignPackageInfo($fileName,
   [Guid]::Empty, 1, 0)
   ```

5. Create a temporary folder name to upload the design package in each site collection.

   ```
   $tempFolderName = "temp_designupload_" +
   ([Guid]::NewGuid).ToString()
   ```

6. Use the `OpenRead` method of `System.IO.File` to read the contents of the design package WSP file and add the file to the `Files` collection of the temporary folder.

   ```
   $fileBinary = [System.IO.File]::OpenRead($filePath)
   ```

7. Use a `foreach` loop to iterate through each content `SPWebApplication` on the local SharePoint farm using the `Get-SPWebApplication` Cmdlet.

   ```
   foreach($webApp in (Get-SPWebApplication))
   ```

8. Use a `foreach` loop to iterate through each `SPSite` Cmdlet in the `Sites` property of the `SPWebApplication` object.

   ```
   foreach($site in $webApp.Sites)
   ```

9. Verify the `CompatibilityLevel` property of the `SPSite` object to ensure it is in SharePoint 2013 (Version 15) mode and not in SharePoint 2010 (Version 14) mode.

   ```
   if ($site.CompatibilityLevel -eq 15)
   ```

10. Using the following command, create a temporary folder in the `RootWeb` site to upload the design package:

    ```
    $tempFolder =
    $site.RootWeb.RootFolder.SubFolders.Add($tempFolderName)
    ```

11. Add the file to the `Files` collection of the temporary folder.

    ```
    $file = $tempFolder.Files.Add($fileName, $fileBinary, $true)
    ```

12. Use the `Install` method of `Microsoft.SharePoint.Publishing.DesignPackage` to add the design package to the **Solutions Gallery** and apply the customizations in the design package to the site collection.

    ```
    [Microsoft.SharePoint.Publishing.DesignPackage]::Install($site,
    $package, $file.Url)
    ```

13. Delete the temporary folder.

    ```
    $tempFolder.Delete()
    ```

14. After the `foreach` loops are completed, close the design package WSP file.

    ```
    $fileBinary.Close()
    ```

15. Use the `Dispose` method to discard the `SPSite` object.

    ```
    $site.Dispose()
    ```

16. Save the file as a PS1 file, for example, `importdesignpackage.ps1`.

17. Execute the script in the PowerShell session.

    ```
    ./importdesignpackage.ps1
    ```

How it works...

PowerShell provides a scripting environment that can simplify repetitive administrative tasks. Using PowerShell, we are able to use a combination of the Cmdlets provided and the .NET code to iterate through each site collection in each web application to import and apply our design package.

In this recipe, we used the `Get-SPWebApplication` Cmdlet to retrieve all of the content web applications on the local SharePoint farm. We then iterated through each site collection in the `Sites` property of each web application. For each site collection, we uploaded the design package to a temporary folder. Lastly, we installed the design package to each site collection from the temporary folder.

There's more...

This recipe may also be accomplished with code using the server-side object model.

> A reference to the `Microsoft.SharePoint.Publishing.dll` assembly is required for this recipe.

Follow these steps to import and apply a design package to all site collections using the server-side object model:

1. Specify the path to the design package **WSP** file and get the filename from the path.

   ```
   var filePath = "C:\My Code Design-1.0.wsp";
   var fileName = Path.GetFileName(filePath);
   ```

2. Create a `DesignPackageInfo` object to represent the design package we are about to upload. In the constructor, specify the major and minor versions of the design package.

   ```
   var package = new DesignPackageInfo(fileName, Guid.Empty, 1, 0);
   ```

3. Create a temporary folder name to upload the design package in each site collection.

   ```
   var tempFolderName = "temp_designupload_" +
     Guid.NewGuid().ToString();
   ```

4. Use the `OpenRead` method of `System.IO.File` to read the contents of the design package WSP file and add the file to the `Files` collection of the temporary folder.

   ```
   var fileBinary = File.OpenRead(filePath);
   ```

5. Use a `foreach` loop to iterate through each content `SPWebApplication` on the local SharePoint farm.

   ```
   foreach(var webApp in SPWebService.ContentService.WebApplications)
   ```

6. Use a `foreach` loop to iterate through each `SPSite` in the `Sites` property of the `SPWebApplication` object.

   ```
   foreach(SPSite site in webApp.Sites)
   ```

7. Verify the `CompatibilityLevel` property of the `SPSite` object to ensure it is in SharePoint 2013 (Version 15) mode and not in SharePoint 2010 (Version 14) mode.

   ```
   if (site.CompatibilityLevel == 15)
   ```

8. Create a temporary folder in the `RootWeb` site to upload the design package to.

   ```
   var tempFolder =
     site.RootWeb.RootFolder.SubFolders.Add(tempFolderName);
   ```

9. Add the file to the `Files` collection of the temporary folder.

```
var file = tempFolder.Files.Add(fileName, fileBinary, true);
```

10. Use the `Install` method of `DesignPackage` to add the design package to the **Solutions Gallery** and apply the customizations in the design package to the site collection.

```
DesignPackage.Install(site, package, file.Url);
```

11. Delete the temporary folder.

```
tempFolder.Delete();
```

12. Discard the `SPSite` object using the `Dispose` method.

```
site.Dispose();
```

13. After the `foreach` loops are completed, close the design package WSP file.

```
fileBinary.Close();
```

See also

▶ The *SharePoint 2013 Design Manager design packages* article on MSDN at `http://msdn.microsoft.com/en-us/library/jj862342.aspx`

▶ The *How to: Upload a File to a SharePoint Site from a Local Folder* article on MSDN at `http://msdn.microsoft.com/en-us/library/ms454491(v=office.14).aspx`

▶ The *SPWeb class* topic on MSDN at `http://msdn.microsoft.com/en-us/library/Microsoft.SharePoint.SPWeb.aspx`

▶ The *SPSite class* topic on MSDN at `http://msdn.microsoft.com/en-us/library/microsoft.sharepoint.spsite.aspx`

▶ The *Get-SPWebApplication* topic on TechNet at `http://technet.microsoft.com/en-us/library/ff607562.aspx`

Listing the device channel master pages

Identifying the master pages used by each device channel for each site in a SharePoint farm can be cumbersome. Using PowerShell, the administrators are able to quickly iterate through each site to accomplish this. In this recipe, we are going to use a PowerShell script (PS1) to output the device channels and master pages configured for each site in a site collection.

How to do it...

Follow these steps to list the device channel master page configurations for each site in a site collection with PowerShell:

1. Open your preferred text editor to create the PS1 script file.

2. Load the `Microsoft.SharePoint.dll` and `Microsoft.SharePoint.Publishing.dll` assemblies into the PowerShell session.

    ```
    [Reflection.Assembly]::LoadFrom("C:\Program Files\Common
    Files\microsoft shared\Web Server
    Extensions\15\ISAPI\Microsoft.SharePoint.Publishing.dll")

    [Reflection.Assembly]::LoadFrom("C:\Program Files\Common
    Files\microsoft shared\Web Server
    Extensions\15\ISAPI\Microsoft.SharePoint.dll")
    ```

3. Get the site collection using the `Get-SPSite` Cmdlet.

    ```
    $site = Get-SPSite http://sharepoint/sitecollection
    ```

4. Get the object types for the parameters that will be used when getting the class constructor for the `MasterPageMappingsFile` object and later instantiating the object.

    ```
    $typeWeb = [Microsoft.SharePoint.SPWeb]

    $typeBool = [System.Boolean]

    $typeMappingFile =
    [System.Type]::GetType("Microsoft.SharePoint.Publishing.Mobile.
    MasterPageMappingsFile,
    Microsoft.SharePoint.Publishing, Version=15.0.0.0,
    Culture=neutral,
    PublicKeyToken=71e9bce111e9429c")
    ```

5. Create an array of the object types.

    ```
    $consMappingFileParams = ($typeWeb, $typeBool, $typeWeb)
    ```

6. Get the class constructor for the `MasterPageMappingsFile` object.

    ```
    $consMappingFile =
    $typeMappingFile.GetConstructor($consMappingFileParams)
    ```

7. Create an array of the default parameters required to instantiate the `MasterPageMappingsFile` object.

    ```
    $mappingFileParams =
    [System.Array]::CreateInstance([System.Object], 3)

    $mappingFileParams[1] = $false

    $mappingFileParams[2] = $null
    ```

8. Use a `foreach` loop to iterate through each `SPWeb` in the `AllWebs` property of the `SPSite` object.

   ```
   foreach ($web in $site.AllWebs)
   ```

9. Add the `SPWeb` object to the parameters array and invoke the constructor to create an instance of the `MasterPageMappingsFile` object.

   ```
   $mappingFileParams[0] = [Microsoft.SharePoint.SPWeb] $web

   $mappingFile = $consMappingFile.Invoke($mappingFileParams)
   ```

10. Output the master page settings for the default channel.

    ```
    Write-Host ""

    Write-Host "Site: " $web.Url

    Write-Host "Device Channel: Default"

    Write-Host "Master Page: " $web.CustomMasterUrl
    ```

11. Use a `foreach` loop for each device channel key in the `Keys` collection of the mapping file.

    ```
    foreach ($key in $mappingFile.Keys)
    ```

12. Output the master page settings for the device channel.

    ```
    Write-Host ""

    Write-Host "Site: " $web.Url

    Write-Host "Device Channel: " $key

    Write-Host "Master Page: " $mappingFile[$key].MasterPageUrl
    ```

13. Use the `Dispose` method to discard the `SPWeb` object.

    ```
    $web.Dispose()
    ```

14. Use the `Dispose` method to discard the `SPSite` object.

    ```
    $site.Dispose()
    ```

15. Save the file as a `PS1` file, for example, `getdevicechannels.ps1`.

16. Execute the script in the PowerShell session.

    ```
    ./getdevicechannels.ps1
    ```

```
Administrator: SharePoint 2013 Management Shell          -  □  X

PS H:\> .\GetDeviceChannelMappings.ps1

GAC     Version          Location
---     -------          --------
True    v4.0.30319       C:\Windows\Microsoft.Net\assembly\GAC_MSIL\Microsoft.S...
True    v4.0.30319       C:\Windows\Microsoft.Net\assembly\GAC_MSIL\Microsoft.S...

Site:   http://volantis
Device Channel: Default
Master Page:   /_catalogs/masterpage/seattle.master

Site:   http://volantis
Device Channel:  PowerShell
Master Page:   /_catalogs/masterpage/seattle.master

Site:   http://volantis
Device Channel:  iPhone
Master Page:   /_catalogs/masterpage/Seattle_Responsive.master

Site:   http://volantis/blog
Device Channel: Default
Master Page:   /blog/_catalogs/masterpage/seattle.master

Site:   http://volantis/chinese
Device Channel: Default
```

How it works...

Using .NET reflection we are able to interact with the private methods and classes in the SharePoint assemblies that provide the mapping information of the device channel. In this recipe, we used .NET reflection to instantiate the MasterPageMappingsFile object for each site in the AllWebs property of the site collection we obtained with the Get-SPSite Cmdlet. From the MasterPageMappingsFile object, we were able to output the master page configured for each device channel. In addition, we output the default master page configured for each site.

There's more...

This recipe may also be accomplished with code using the server-side object model.

> A reference to the Microsoft.SharePoint.Publishing.dll assembly is required for this recipe.

Follow these steps to list the device channel master page configurations for each site in a site collection using the server-side object model:

1. Get the site collection with a using statement.

```
using (var site = new SPSite("http://sharepoint/sitecollection"))
```

2. Get the object type that will be used when getting the class constructor for the `MasterPageMappingsFile` object and later instantiating the object.

```
var typeMappingFile =
  Type.GetType("Microsoft.SharePoint.Publishing.Mobile.
MasterPageMappingsFile,
    Microsoft.SharePoint.Publishing, Version=15.0.0.0,
      Culture=neutral, PublicKeyToken=71e9bce111e9429c");
```

3. Get the class constructor for the `MasterPageMappingsFile` object.

```
var consMappingFile = typeMappingFile.GetConstructor(new Type[]
  {typeof(SPWeb), typeof(bool), typeof(SPWeb)});
```

4. Use a `foreach` loop to iterate through each site in the `AllWebs` property of the site collection.

```
foreach (var web in site.AllWebs)
```

5. Ensure that the site exists.

```
if (web.Exists)
```

6. Invoke the constructor to create an instance of the `MasterPageMappingsFile` object.

```
var mappingFile = consMappingFile.Invoke(new object[]
  { web, false, null });
```

7. Output the master page settings for the default channel.

```
Console.WriteLine("");

Console.WriteLine("Site: " + web.Url);

Console.WriteLine("Device Channel: Default");

Console.WriteLine("Master Page: " + web.CustomMasterUrl);
```

8. Get the `mappings` field from the mapping file and cast the object as an `IDictionary`.

```
var mappings =
  (IDictionary)typeMappingFile.GetField("mappings",
    BindingFlags.Instance |
      BindingFlags.NonPublic).GetValue(mappingFile);
```

9. Use a `foreach` loop for each device channel key in the `Keys` collection of the mappings dictionary.

```
foreach (var key in mappings.Keys)
```

10. Get the master page URL from the mappings dictionary.

```
var mappingObject = mappings[key];
```

```
var masterUrl =
  (string)mappingObject.GetType().GetProperty("MasterPageUrl",
    BindingFlags.Instance |
      BindingFlags.Public).GetValue(mappingObject, null);
```

11. Output the master page settings for the device channel.

```
Console.WriteLine("");

Console.WriteLine("Site: " + web.Url);

Console.WriteLine("Device Channel: " + key);

Console.WriteLine("Master Page: " + masterUrl);
```

12. Use the `Dispose` method to discard the `SPWeb` object.

```
web.Dispose();
```

See also

▸ The *SharePoint 2013 Design Manager device channels* article on MSDN at `http://msdn.microsoft.com/en-us/library/jj862343.aspx`

▸ The *Reflection in the .NET Framework* article on MSDN at `http://msdn.microsoft.com/en-us/library/f7ykdhsy.aspx`

▸ The *SPWeb class* topic on MSDN at `http://msdn.microsoft.com/en-us/library/Microsoft.SharePoint.SPWeb.aspx`

▸ The *SPSite class* topic on MSDN at `http://msdn.microsoft.com/en-us/library/microsoft.sharepoint.spsite.aspx`

▸ The *Get-SPSite* topic on TechNet at `http://technet.microsoft.com/en-us/library/ff607950.aspx`

3
Branding SharePoint with Custom Master Pages and Page Layouts

In this chapter, we will use SharePoint Designer 2013 to create and customize master pages and page layouts. We will cover the following recipes:

- ▸ Editing a master page in SharePoint Designer
- ▸ Changing the site master pages in SharePoint Designer
- ▸ Hiding unwanted master page controls
- ▸ Restoring the Navigate Up button using a master page
- ▸ Adding JavaScript and cascading stylesheet references to a master page
- ▸ Creating a fixed width master page
- ▸ Creating an expanding width master page with content padding
- ▸ Creating a minimalistic master page
- ▸ Creating a responsive mobile master page
- ▸ Customizing the Windows 8 Start menu tile for pinning sites using a master page
- ▸ Customizing the shortcut icon (favicon) using a master page
- ▸ Creating a page layout with three columns of web part zones
- ▸ Creating a page layout with web parts added to the page

- ▶ Creating a page layout with a picture-library-based image carousel using JavaScript
- ▶ Displaying specific content only to authenticated users
- ▶ Displaying specific content only to anonymous users
- ▶ Displaying specific content only to site administrators
- ▶ Creating a master page with editing controls only available to editors

Introduction

With the 2.0 release of ASP.NET (.NET Framework 2.0), Microsoft added the concept of master pages. Master pages are used by ASP.NET web applications to provide a template, which the content pages use when rendering content. These master pages can also be nested, allowing for a main template with subtemplates used in different contexts. In addition, there is no limit to the number of master pages an ASP.NET web application can use. Being built on ASP.NET, SharePoint utilizes master pages for nearly every page rendered.

In addition to master pages, SharePoint uses page layouts to provide templates for creating content pages. Page layouts provide the content layout for a SharePoint page within the confines of the master page. The following diagram shows the SharePoint content page structure:

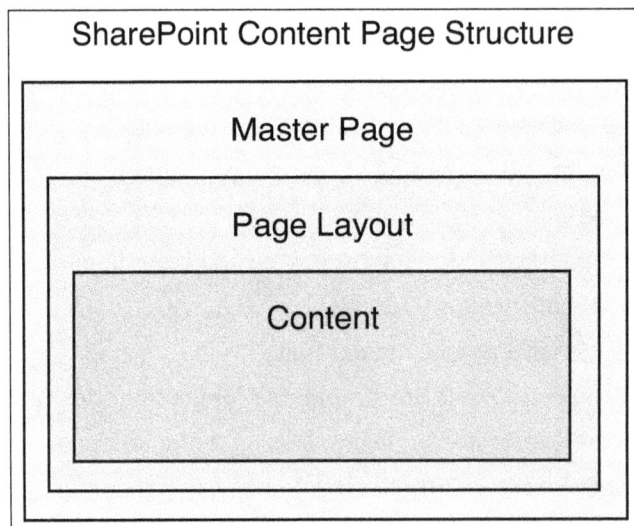

```
┌─────────────────────────────────────────────┐
│        SharePoint Content Page Structure      │
│  ┌─────────────────────────────────────────┐ │
│  │              Master Page                 │ │
│  │  ┌───────────────────────────────────┐  │ │
│  │  │           Page Layout             │  │ │
│  │  │  ┌─────────────────────────────┐  │  │ │
│  │  │  │          Content            │  │  │ │
│  │  │  │                             │  │  │ │
│  │  │  └─────────────────────────────┘  │  │ │
│  │  └───────────────────────────────────┘  │ │
│  └─────────────────────────────────────────┘ │
└─────────────────────────────────────────────┘
```

Editing a master page in SharePoint Designer

Since SharePoint 2007, Microsoft has released a companion application called SharePoint Designer with each version of SharePoint. Originally the successor to Microsoft FrontPage, SharePoint Designer provides users the ability to customize SharePoint sites based on their permissions. This includes master pages, page layouts, workflows, lists, libraries, and so on.

> The design view for editing master pages that was available in the previous versions has been removed from the 2013 version of SharePoint Designer.

SharePoint Designer uses the SharePoint web service APIs and **remote procedure calls (RPC)** to interact with the SharePoint server. This allows connecting to SharePoint from remote computers rather than requiring the software be run on the SharePoint server itself. This also allows SharePoint Designer to be used with hosted SharePoint implementations, such as the SharePoint Online service of Microsoft Office 365. In addition, any user with access to a SharePoint site can connect with SharePoint Designer (when not disabled by a site collection or farm administrator). Users will only be able to see and interact with the SharePoint site based on the permissions they have.

How to do it...

Follow these steps to edit a master page in SharePoint Designer:

1. Open SharePoint Designer.
2. Select **Open Site**. Enter the complete URL to the SharePoint site and select **Open**.

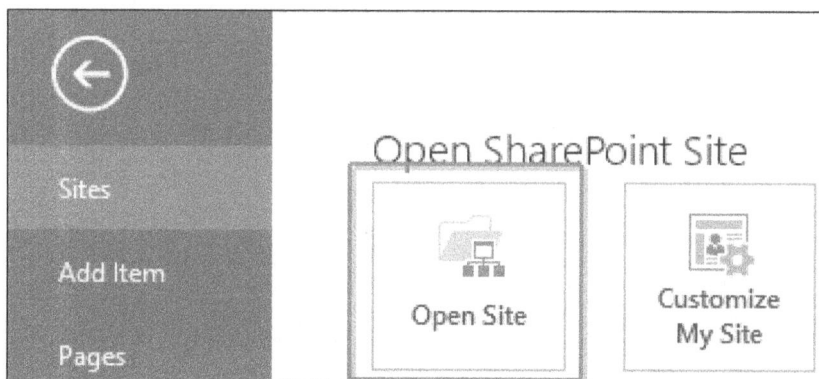

3. From the **Navigation** pane, select **Master Pages** as shown in the following screenshot:

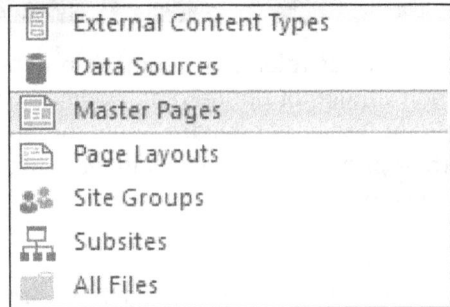

External Content Types	
Data Sources	
Master Pages	
Page Layouts	
Site Groups	
Subsites	
All Files	

4. From the list of files in the **Master Pages** library, select `seattle.master`.

5. From the ribbon, select **Check Out**.

Preview in Browser ▾ | Check In | Check Out | Undo Check Out

Manage

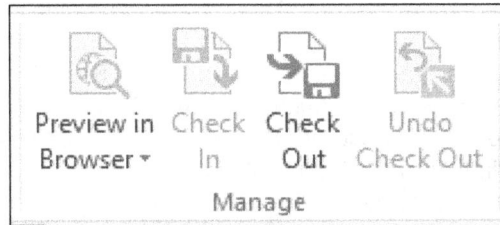

6. Under **Customization**, select **Edit file** as shown in the following screenshot:

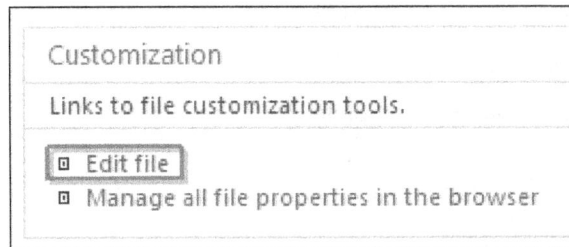

Customization

Links to file customization tools.

☐ Edit file
☐ Manage all file properties in the browser

7. Once the file has been edited and saved, select the back icon to return to the **Properties** page for `seattle.master`:

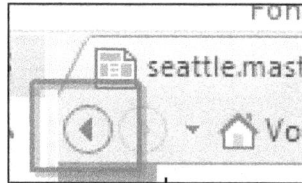

8. Select the back icon again to return to the **Master Pages** library.
9. Right-click on the `seattle.master` file.
10. Select **Check In** as shown in the following screenshot:

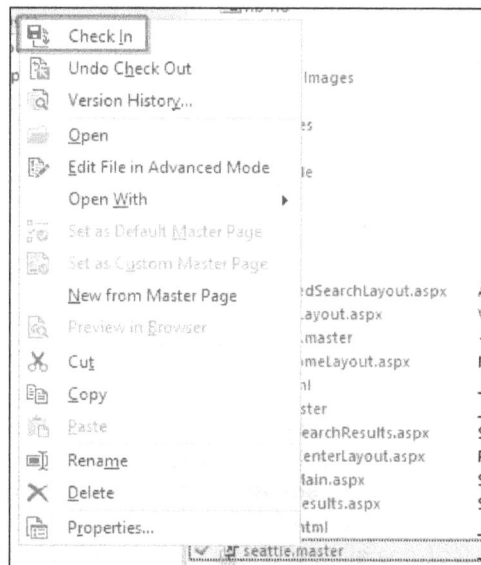

Using the **Check In** option from the ribbon where we used the **Check Out** option will allow you to check in the file using the **Check In** option. However, it does not allow you to **Check In** and **Publish** the file at the same time. Right-clicking on the file and selecting the **Check In** option will allow you to do both at the same time.

11. Select **Publish a major version** as shown in the following screenshot:

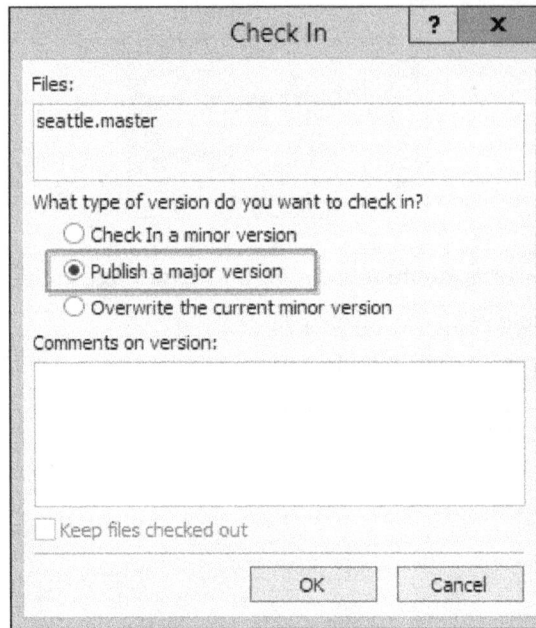

12. Click on **OK**.

How it works...

Using the SharePoint web services API and remote procedure calls, SharePoint Designer allows us to modify files in a SharePoint site. Using the versioning and publishing features of SharePoint, we can **Check Out** and **Check In** content to ensure only one person is editing the content at a time. In addition, this allows for that content to have **published** versions that noneditors can view. These features allow multiple content editors to work with content and only have published versions visible to everyone else.

SharePoint Designer 2013 allows us to edit the code of the master pages, but does not provide a WYSIWYG (design view) editor.

See also

 ▸ The *SharePoint Designer for Developers* article on MSDN at http://msdn.
    microsoft.com/en-us/sharepoint/hh850380.aspx

Changing the site master pages in SharePoint Designer

In addition to creating and editing master pages, SharePoint Designer allows us to configure the master pages used by the SharePoint site. Each site has two assigned master pages, the **Site Master Page** and the **System Master Page**. The **Site Master Page** is used when displaying content pages, such as publishing pages, whereas the **System Master Page** is used when displaying administrative pages, such as the **Site settings** page.

This is the only method available to set the master page settings if the SharePoint publishing features are not activated on the SharePoint site or access to PowerShell on the SharePoint servers is not available.

How to do it...

Follow these steps to change the site master pages in SharePoint Designer:

1. Open SharePoint Designer and select **Open Site**. Enter the complete URL to the SharePoint site and select **Open**.
2. From the **Navigation** pane, select **Master Pages**.
3. In the list of files in the **Master Pages** library, right-click on the master page you wish to set.

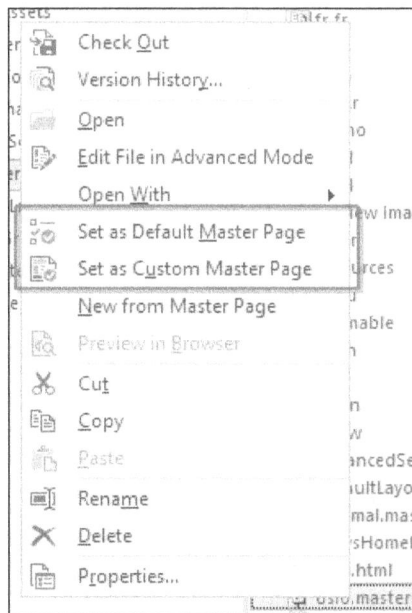

4. Select **Set as Default Master Page** to set the **System Master Page**.

5. Select **Set as Custom Master Page** to set the **Site Master Page**.

How it works...

Using the SharePoint web services API and remote procedure calls, SharePoint Designer allows us to set the master page settings for a SharePoint site. The master pages configured will only apply to the default device channel. Any additional device channels would need to be configured through the web interface, PowerShell, or code using the server-side object model.

See also

▶ The *SharePoint Designer for Developers* article on MSDN at `http://msdn.microsoft.com/en-us/sharepoint/hh850380.aspx`

Hiding unwanted master page controls

By default, SharePoint has a large number of SharePoint-specific controls and content zones added to each master page. SharePoint requires most of these controls in order to work correctly. When removing an undesirable control from the master page, we generally hide the control rather than removing it completely. This ensures SharePoint has access to the control, but does not render it to the end user.

Many of the controls included on the SharePoint master pages are required for the page to render correctly. When removing a control we can test whether it can be removed completely. If the page generates errors about the missing control, we know we need to hide it instead of removing it completely.

In this recipe, we will hide the suite bar branding (**SharePoint** or **Office 365**) and suite bar links (**Newsfeed**, **SkyDrive**, and **Sites**) using our customized master page.

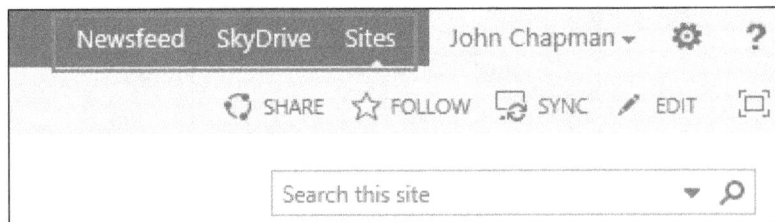

How to do it...

Follow these steps to hide unwanted master page controls:

1. Open SharePoint Designer.

2. Select **Open Site**. Enter the complete URL to the SharePoint site and select **Open**.

3. From the **Navigation** pane, select **Master Pages**.

4. In the list of files in the **Master Pages** library, make a copy of `seattle.master` (in our example, we have renamed it `Seattle_HideControls.master`).

   When modifying master pages included with SharePoint, do not modify the included master page. Make a copy of the master page and make your changes to the copy and then check out the new `Seattle_HideControls.master` master page.

5. Open the `Seattle_HideControls.master` master page.

6. Locate the `</SharePoint:SharePointForm>` closing tag for the `SharePointForm` element as shown in the following screenshot:

```
711 <SharePoint:AjaxDelta id="DeltaPageInstrumentation" runat="server">
712     <SharePoint:FlightedContent runat="server" ExpFeature="UserActivityLogging" RenderIfInFlight="true">
713         <SharePoint:PageInstrumentationControl runat="server" Id="PageInstrumentationControl" />
714     </SharePoint:FlightedContent>
715 </SharePoint:AjaxDelta>
716         </div>
717 </SharePoint:SharePointForm>
718 <SharePoint:AjaxDelta id="DeltaPlaceHolderUtilityContent" runat="server">
719     <asp:ContentPlaceHolder id="PlaceHolderUtilityContent" runat="server"/>
720 </SharePoint:AjaxDelta><SharePoint:ScriptBlock runat="server">
721     var g_Workspace = &quot;s4-workspace&quot;;
722 </SharePoint:ScriptBlock>
723
724 </body>
725 </SharePoint:SPHtmlTag>
```

> The `<SharePoint:SharePointForm>` tag results in the `<form>` tag when rendered in the browser. It is important to ensure our SharePoint controls remain inside the `<SharePoint:SharePointForm>` tag to prevent errors on the page.

7. Add a `<div>` container to hide our controls before the `</SharePoint:SharePointForm>` element as shown in the following code:

```
<div style="display: none;">
</div>
```

   The following screenshot shows these elements:

```
716 </SharePoint:AjaxDelta>
717         </div>
718 <div style="display: none;">
719
720 </div>
721 </SharePoint:SharePointForm>
722 <SharePoint:AjaxDelta id="DeltaPlaceHolderUtilityContent" runat="server">
723         <asp:ContentPlaceHolder id="PlaceHolderUtilityContent" runat="server"/>
```

8. Locate the `<div id="suiteBarLeft">` element.

```
<SharePoint:FlightedContent runat="server" ExpFeature="ShellNavBar" FarmPropertyRequiredForFeature="SpoTAConfigPath" RenderIfInFlight="false">
  <div id="suiteBar" class="ms-fullWidth">
    <div id="suiteBarLeft">
      <div class="ms-table ms-fullWidth">
        <div class="ms-tableRow">
          <div class="ms-tableCell ms-verticalAlignMiddle">
            <SharePoint:DelegateControl id="ID_SuiteBarBrandingDelegate" ControlId="SuiteBarBrandingDelegate" runat="server" />
          </div>
          <div class="ms-core-deltaSuiteLinks">
            <div id="suiteLinksBox">
              <SharePoint:DelegateControl id="ID_SuiteLinksDelegate" ControlId="SuiteLinksDelegate" runat="server" />
            </div>
          </div>
        </div>
      </div>
    </div>
  </div>
  <div id="suiteBarRight">
```

9. Cut the contents of the `<div id="suiteBarLeft">` element to remove them from this location and allow us to paste them later. The following screenshot shows this `<div>` element:

```
<div id="suiteBarLeft">

</div>
```

10. Paste the following contents into the `<div>` tag that we created earlier to hide the elements:

```
<div style="display: none;">
<SharePoint:DelegateControl id="ID_SuiteBarBrandingDelegate" Contr
olId="SuiteBarBrandingDelegate" runat="server"/>

<SharePoint:AjaxDelta runat="server" id="DeltaSuiteLinks"
BlockElement="true" CssClass="ms-core-deltaSuiteLinks">
    <div id="suiteLinksBox">
        <SharePoint:DelegateControl
          id="ID_SuiteLinksDelegate"
          ControlId="SuiteLinksDelegate" runat="server" />
    </div>
</SharePoint:AjaxDelta>
</div>
```

We can remove the `<div>` elements we pasted, which surround the SharePoint controls. All we need to ensure is that the controls are on the page.

```
<div style="display: none;">
    <SharePoint:DelegateControl id="ID_SuiteBarBrandingDelegate" ControlId="SuiteBarBrandingDelegate" runat="server"/>

    <SharePoint:AjaxDelta runat="server" id="DeltaSuiteLinks" BlockElement="true" CssClass="ms-core-deltaSuiteLinks">
            <div id="suiteLinksBox">
                <SharePoint:DelegateControl id="ID_SuiteLinksDelegate" ControlId="SuiteLinksDelegate" runat="server" />
            </div>
    </SharePoint:AjaxDelta>
</div>
```

11. Save the master page.

12. Check in and publish the master page using the **Check In** and **Publish** options.

13. Set the master page as the **Site Master Page**.

14. Navigate to the site in your preferred web browser to observe the results. You will see a screen similar to the following screenshot:

How it works...

In order for SharePoint pages to render correctly, most of the server controls included on the default master pages are required. Using CSS to hide server controls allows for SharePoint to render the control while the browser hides it for the end user. Rendering the control, even though hidden, still requires server and browser resources. It will still impact the page load performance.

See also

▶ The *CSS Display and Visibility* article on W3 Schools at `http://www.w3schools.com/css/css_display_visibility.asp`

▶ The *Overview of the SharePoint 2013 Page Model* topic on MSDN at `http://msdn.microsoft.com/en-us/library/jj191506.aspx`

Restoring the Navigate Up button using a master page

In the default SharePoint 2010 interface, there was a button to navigate up the breadcrumb structure, which looked like a Windows Explorer folder (see the following screenshot for reference). In SharePoint 2013, this control still exists, but has been hidden. In this recipe, we will restore it using our customized master page.

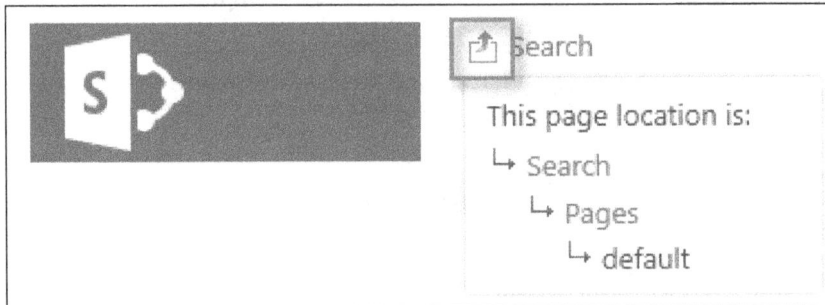

How to do it...

Follow these steps to restore the Navigate Up breadcrumb control using a master page:

1. Open SharePoint Designer.

2. Select **Open Site**. Enter the complete URL to the SharePoint site and select **Open**.

3. From the **Navigation** pane, select **Master Pages**.

4. In the list of files in the **Master Pages** library, make a copy of `seattle.master` (for our example, we have renamed it as `Seattle_RestoreNavigateUp.master`).

5. Check out the new `Seattle_RestoreNavigateUp.master` master page.

6. Open the `Seattle_RestoreNavigateUp.master` master page.

7. Locate the `<div class="ms-breadcrumb-dropdownBox"` element. The following code shows the content inside this element:

```
<div class="ms-breadcrumb-dropdownBox" style="display:none;">
<SharePoint:AjaxDelta id="DeltaBreadcrumbDropdown" runat="server">
  <SharePoint:PopoutMenu
    Visible="false"
    runat="server"
    ID="GlobalBreadCrumbNavPopout"
    IconUrl="/_layouts/15/images/spcommon.png?rev=23"
    IconAlt="<%$Resources:wss,master_breadcrumbIconAlt%>"
            ThemeKey="v15breadcrumb"
```

```
                        IconOffsetX="215"
                        IconOffsetY="120"
                        IconWidth="16"
                        IconHeight="16"
                        AnchorCss="ms-breadcrumb-anchor"
                        AnchorOpenCss="ms-breadcrumb-anchor-open"
                        MenuCss="ms-breadcrumb-menu ms-noList">
```

8. Remove `style="display:none;"` from the `<div>` element.

9. Set the `Visible` attribute to `true`.

10. Set the `ThemeKey` attribute to `spcommon`.

11. Set the `IconUrl` attribute to `/_layouts/15/images/spcommon.png`.

```
<div class="ms-breadcrumb-dropdownBox">
<SharePoint:AjaxDelta id="DeltaBreadcrumbDropdown" runat="server">
  <SharePoint:PopoutMenu
    Visible="true"
    runat="server"
    ID="GlobalBreadCrumbNavPopout"
    IconUrl="/_layouts/15/images/spcommon.png"
    IconAlt="<%$Resources:wss,master_breadcrumbIconAlt%>"
                ThemeKey="spcommon"
                IconOffsetX="215"
                IconOffsetY="120"
                IconWidth="16"
                IconHeight="16"
                AnchorCss="ms-breadcrumb-anchor"
                AnchorOpenCss="ms-breadcrumb-anchor-open"
                MenuCss="ms-breadcrumb-menu ms-noList">
```

12. Save the master page.

13. Check in and publish the master page using the **Check In** and **Publish** options.

14. Set the master page as the **Site Master Page**.

15. Navigate to the site in your preferred web browser to observe the results.

How it works...

The default SharePoint 2013 master pages already include the server control to create and render the breadcrumb navigation. By default, however, it is hidden. By modifying the properties of the control on the master page, we are instructing SharePoint to display the control.

See also

▶ The *PopoutMenu class* topic on MSDN at `http://msdn.microsoft.com/en-us/library/microsoft.sharepoint.webcontrols.popoutmenu.aspx`

Adding JavaScript and cascading stylesheet references to a master page

Most of our customizations to the master pages require some CSS or **JavaScript (JS)** references. CSS and JS files should be located in one of the following places:

▶ In the SharePoint site inside the `_catalogs/masterpage` folder. This allows for the files to be included when exporting a design package.

▶ In the `_layouts` folder on the filesystems of the SharePoint servers. This is primarily accomplished with custom SharePoint solutions created with Visual Studio.

▶ On an external content source, such as a content delivery network.

> If you are using an external content source, ensure that all users accessing the SharePoint site have access to the external content source. The external content source may not be available to some users if their network configuration does not permit it.

When referencing files in the SharePoint site or in the `_layouts` folder, relative URLs should be used to allow alternate access maps to work. When referencing files on an external site, the exact, complete URL should be used.

> Alternate access mapping in SharePoint allows access to SharePoint web applications using multiple URLs. For instance, `http://sharepoint/` and `http://sharepoint.local/` could be the same SharePoint web application. A relative URL does not specify the protocol or domain in the URL. For instance, `/_layouts/mystyles.css` is a relative URL, while `http://sharepoint/_layouts/mystyles.css` is an absolute URL.

How to do it...

Follow these steps to add JavaScript and CSS references to a master page:

1. Open SharePoint Designer.

2. Select **Open Site**. Enter the complete URL to the SharePoint site and select **Open**.

3. From the **Navigation** pane, select **Master Pages**.

4. In the list of files in the **Master Pages** library, make a copy of seattle.master (for our example, we have renamed it Seattle_AddJavaScriptAndCSS.master).

5. Check out the new Seattle_AddJavaScriptAndCSS.master master page using the **Check Out** feature.

6. Open the Seattle_AddJavaScriptAndCSS.master master page.

7. Locate the <head> element. The following screenshot shows the <head> element highlighted in the code:

```
<%@Master language="C#"%>
<%@ Register Tagprefix="SharePoint" Namespace="Microsoft.SharePoint.WebControls" Assembly="Microsoft.SharePoint,
<%@ Import Namespace="Microsoft.SharePoint.ApplicationPages" %>
<%@ Register Tagprefix="WebPartPages" Namespace="Microsoft.SharePoint.WebPartPages" Assembly="Microsoft.SharePoi
<%@ Register TagPrefix="wssuc" TagName="Welcome" src="~/_controltemplates/15/Welcome.ascx" %>
<!DOCTYPE html PUBLIC "-//W3C//DTD XHTML 1.0 Strict//EN"
    "http://www.w3.org/TR/xhtml1/DTD/xhtml1-strict.dtd">
<SharePoint:SPHtmlTag dir="<%$Resources:wss,multipages_direction_dir_value%>" ID="SPHtmlTag" runat="server" >
<head runat="server">
```

8. Add the following JavaScript reference:

```
<SharePoint:ScriptLink ID="customJavaScript" Name="<%
$SPUrl:~Site/_catalogs/masterpage/resources/SampleJavaScript.js
%>" runat="server"></SharePoint:ScriptLink>
```

> In our JavaScript reference, we are using the ~Site variable to get the URL of the file relative to the SharePoint site. The ~SiteCollection variable can be used if the URL is relative to the SharePoint site collection instead.

9. Add the following CSS reference:

```
<SharePoint:CssRegistration ID="customCssRegistration" Name="<%
$SPUrl:~Site/_catalogs/masterpage/resources/SampleStyleSheet.css
%>" runat="server"></SharePoint:CssRegistration>
```

10. Save the master page.

11. Check in and publish the master page using the **Check In** and **Publish** options.

12. Set the master page as the **Site Master Page**.

How it works...

For traditional websites, the `<link>` and `<script>` tags are used to reference CSS and JavaScript files on a web page. While we can still use those in our SharePoint master pages, SharePoint provides server controls to reference CSS and JavaScript files. Using the `ScriptLink` and `CssRegistration` server controls will ultimately result in the `<link>` and `<script>` tags being added to the page when rendered. However, these server controls provide additional management by SharePoint to prevent duplication and allow for scripts to be loaded on demand rather than on every page load. In addition, these server controls allow variables, such as the site or site collection URLs, to be used in the path to the resource.

See also

▸ The *ScriptLink class* topic on MSDN at `http://msdn.microsoft.com/en-us/library/microsoft.sharepoint.webcontrols.scriptlink.aspx`

▸ The *CssRegistration class* topic on MSDN at `http://msdn.microsoft.com/en-us/library/microsoft.sharepoint.webcontrols.cssregistration.aspx`

Creating a fixed width master page

The default SharePoint 2013 master page, `seattle.master`, expands to fill the browser window. In this recipe, we will modify the `seattle.master` master page to have a fixed width using CSS.

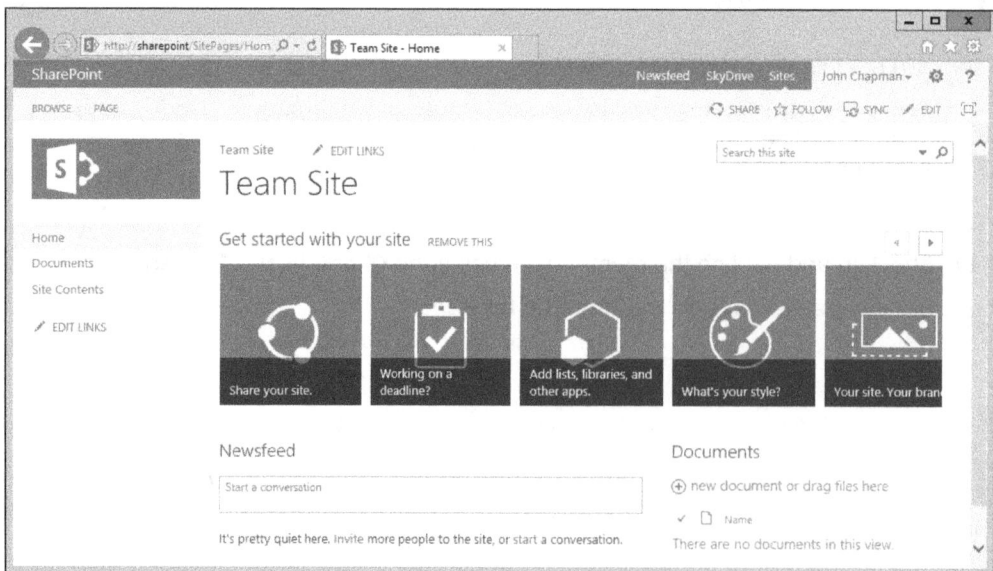

How to do it...

Follow these steps to create a fixed width master page:

1. Open SharePoint Designer.
2. Select **Open Site**. Enter the complete URL to the SharePoint site and select **Open**.
3. From the **Navigation** pane, select **Master Pages**.
4. In the list of files in the **Master Pages** library, make a copy of `seattle.master` (for our example, we have renamed it `Seattle_FixedWidth.master`).
5. Check out the new `Seattle_FixedWidth.master` master page.
6. Open the `Seattle_FixedWidth.master` master page.
7. Locate the `<head>` element.
8. Add the CSS reference to the `FixedWidth.css` file we will create.

    ```
    <SharePoint:CssRegistration ID="customCssRegistration" Name="<%
    $SPUrl:~Site/_catalogs/masterpage/resources/FixedWidth.css %>"
    runat="server"></SharePoint:CssRegistration>
    ```

9. Save the master page.
10. Check in and publish the master page using the **Check In** and **Publish** options.
11. Set the master page as **Site Master Page**.
12. From the **Navigation** pane, select **All Files**.
13. In the **All Files** content pane, navigate to **_catalogs | masterpage | resources**.

> If the `resources` folder in `_catalogs/masterpage` has not been created yet, select **Folder** from the **New** section on the ribbon.

14. From the **New** section on the ribbon, navigate to **File | CSS** as shown in the following screenshot:

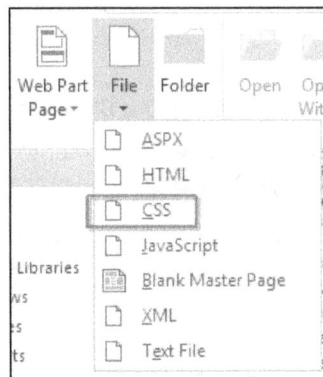

15. Name the new CSS file as `FixedWidth.css`.

16. Check out the new `FixedWidth.css` file using the **Check Out** option.

17. Open the `FixedWidth.css` file.

18. Specify a background color for the `#s4-workspace` element using the following lines of code:

```
#s4-workspace {

    background: #999999;

}
```

19. Give the `#s4-titlerow` and `#contentRow` elements a white background, a fixed width of `1024px`, and set the left-hand side and right-hand side margins to automatically center align the elements.

```
#s4-titlerow, #contentRow {

    background: #FFFFFF;

    width: 1024px;

    margin-left: auto;

    margin-right: auto;

}
```

20. Add a top margin to the `#s4-titlerow` element to separate it from the header controls on the page:

```
#s4-titlerow {

    margin-top: 50px;

}
```

21. Save the CSS file.

22. Check in and publish the CSS file using the **Check In** and **Publish** options.

23. Navigate to the site in your preferred web browser to observe the results. The result will be similar to the following screenshot:

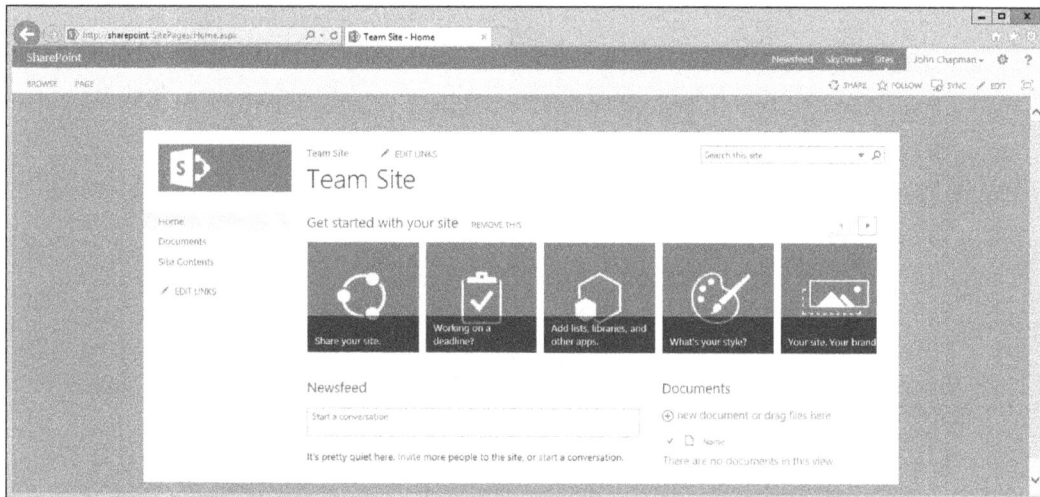

How it works...

The page content for SharePoint pages is rendered within the `s4-workspace` DIV element. In our recipe, we used CSS to provide a grey background color for `s4-workspace`. We then used CSS to center align the content of the `s4-workspace` element in a white box with a fixed width. An HTML element that has its left and right margins set to `auto` will be centered in the element that contains it.

The `#s4-workspace` DIV element is used by SharePoint to contain the majority of the page content. The `#s4-titlerow` DIV element is used to contain the site logo, navigation, and search box in default configurations. The `#contentRow` DIV element is used to contain the quick launch navigation and page content.

See also

▶ The *CssRegistration class* topic on MSDN at `http://msdn.microsoft.com/en-us/library/microsoft.sharepoint.webcontrols.cssregistration.aspx`

Creating an expanding width master page with content padding

In this recipe, we will modify the `seattle.master` master page to have padding added around the expanding width content for a contained look that still expands with the browser window using CSS.

How to do it...

Follow these steps to create an expanding width master page with content padding:

1. Open SharePoint Designer.

2. Select **Open Site**. Enter the complete URL to the SharePoint site and select **Open**.

3. From the **Navigation** pane, select **Master Pages**.

4. In the list of files in the **Master Pages** library, make a copy of `seattle.master` (for our example, we have renamed it `Seattle_ExpandingWidthWithPadding.master`).

5. Check out the new `Seattle_ExpandingWidthWithPadding.master` master page using the **Check Out** feature.

6. Open the `Seattle_ExpandingWidthWithPadding.master` master page.

7. Locate the `<head>` element.

8. Add the following CSS reference to the `ExpandingWidthWithPadding.css` file we created:

```
<SharePoint:CssRegistration ID="customCssRegistration"
Name="<% $SPUrl:~Site/_catalogs/masterpage/resources/
ExpandingWidthWithPadding.css %>" runat="server"></
SharePoint:CssRegistration>
```

9. Save the master page.

10. Check in and publish the master page using the **Check In** and **Publish** options.

11. Set the master page as **Site Master Page**.

12. From the **Navigation** pane, select **All Files**.

13. In the **All Files** content pane, navigate to **_catalogs | masterpage | resources**.

14. From the **New** section on the ribbon, navigate to **File | CSS**.

15. Name the new CSS file `ExpandingWidthWithPadding.css`.

16. Check out the new `ExpandingWidthWithPadding.css` file.

17. Open the `ExpandingWidthWithPadding.css` file.

18. Specify a background color for the `#s4-workspace` element.

```
#s4-workspace {

    background: #999999;

}
```

19. Give the `#s4-titlerow` and `#contentRow` elements a white background and set the left-hand side and right-hand side margins to `100px`.

```
#s4-titlerow, #contentRow {

    background: #FFFFFF;

    margin-left: 100px;

    margin-right: 100px;

}
```

20. Add a top margin to the `#s4-titlerow` element to separate it from the header controls on the page as shown in the following code:

```
#s4-titlerow {

    margin-top: 50px;

}
```

21. Save the CSS file.

22. Check in and publish the CSS file using the **Check In** and **Publish** options.

23. Navigate to the site in your preferred web browser. Resize the browser window to observe the results. Compare the behavior to the results of the previous recipe, *Creating a fixed width master page*.

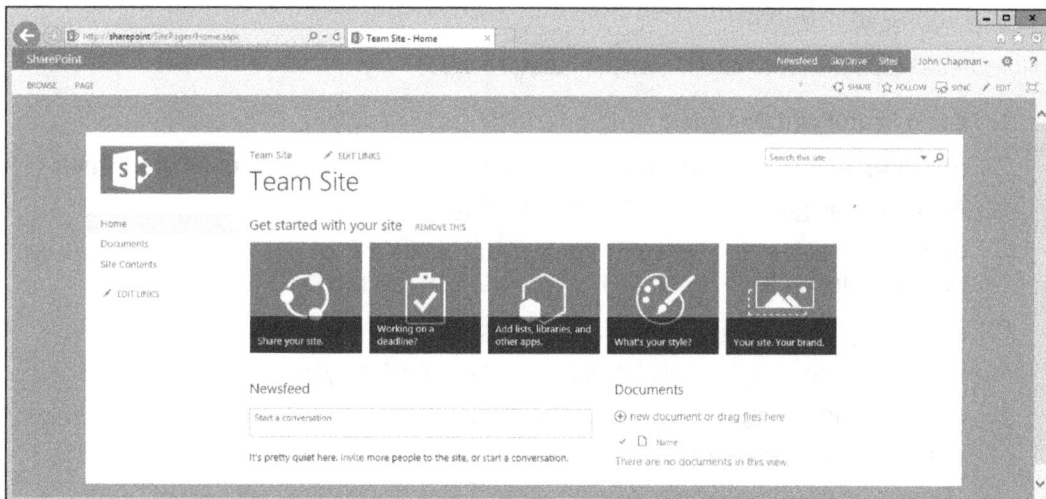

How it works...

The page content for SharePoint pages is rendered within the `s4-workspace DIV` element. In our recipe, we used CSS to provide a grey background color for the `s4-workspace` element. We then used CSS to center the content of the `s4-workspace` element in a white box that expands with the size of the browser window. An HTML element that has its left and right margins set to the same size will be centered in the element that contains it and will expand in size as the element containing it expands in size.

See also

▶ The *CssRegistration class* topic on MSDN at `http://msdn.microsoft.com/en-us/library/microsoft.sharepoint.webcontrols.cssregistration.aspx`

Creating a minimalistic master page

SharePoint 2013 comes with an out of the box fairly minimalistic design. In this recipe, we will modify the `seattle.master` master page to hide many of the SharePoint controls to create an even more minimalistic look. A minimalistic-design approach usually provides more emphasis on the page content and less emphasis on gratuitous design elements.

How to do it...

Follow these steps to create a minimalistic master page:

1. Open SharePoint Designer.
2. Select **Open Site**. Enter the complete URL to the SharePoint site and select **Open**.
3. From the **Navigation** pane, select **Master Pages**.
4. In the list of files in the **Master Pages** library, make a copy of `seattle.master` (in our example, we have renamed it `Seattle_Minimalistic.master`).
5. Check out the new `Seattle_Minimalistic.master` master page.
6. Open the `Seattle_Minimalistic.master` master page.
7. Locate the following closing tag for the `SharePointForm` element:

   ```
   </SharePoint:SharePointForm>
   ```

8. Add the following `<div>` container to hide our controls before the `</SharePoint:SharePointForm>` element:

   ```
   <div style="display: none;">
   </div>
   ```

9. Locate the `<div id="suiteBarLeft">` element.

10. Cut the contents of the `<div id="suiteBarLeft">` element (not the opening and closing `DIV` tags of the element) and paste them into our hidden `<div>` tag.

11. Locate the `<SharePoint:SPRibbonPeripheralContent>` element with the ID `RibbonTabRowRight`.

12. Cut the `<SharePoint:SPRibbonPeripheralContent>` element with its contents and paste it into our hidden `<div>` tag.

13. Locate the `<div id="s4-titlerow">` element.

14. Cut the `<div id="s4-titlerow">` element with its contents and paste it into our hidden `<div>` tag.

15. Locate the `<div id="sideNavBox">` element.

16. Cut the `<div id="sideNavBox">` element with its contents and paste it into our hidden `<div>` tag.

17. Locate the `<div id="contentBox">` element.

18. Add the following style attribute to the `<div id="contentBox">` element to override its left margin to `20px`:

    ```
    <div id="contentBox" style="margin-left: 20px;"
    ```

19. Save the master page.

20. Check in and publish the master page using the **Check In** and **Publish** options.

21. Set the master page as the **Site Master Page**.

22. Navigate to the site in your preferred web browser to observe the results. The result will be similar to the following screenshot:

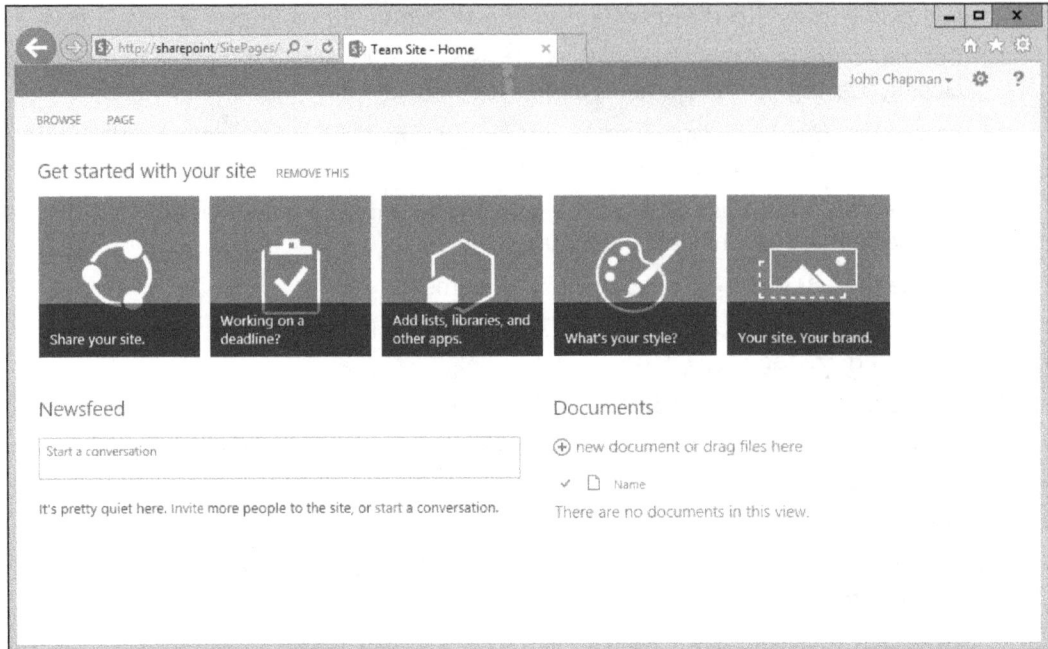

How it works...

In order for SharePoint pages to render correctly, most of the server controls included in the default master pages are required. Using CSS to hide server controls allows SharePoint to render the control while the browser hides it for the end user. In our recipe, we have hidden controls to provide the default SharePoint master page with a more minimalistic look.

See also

▸ The CSS *Display and Visibility* article on W3 Schools at `http://www.w3schools.com/css/css_display_visibility.asp`

Creating a responsive mobile master page

In this recipe, we will modify the `seattle.master` master page to hide the header controls and float all of the page elements to make them appear vertically stacked. This will allow users to view the site on mobile devices and only require the user to scroll vertically rather than both vertically and horizontally.

This recipe will only cover the basic aspects of making a responsive design master page friendlier to mobile devices. Additional styling and design would be required to provide a more complete mobile user experience.

Responsive designs are usually flexible, allowing pages to render well in various web browsers and are not limited to mobile browsers. Creating responsive designs is a good practice for all web browsers. In this recipe, however, we will focus on a responsive design geared at mobile browsers.

Getting ready

For this recipe, we should have a device channel created to target our mobile browsers.

How to do it...

Follow these steps to create a responsive mobile master page:

1. Open SharePoint Designer.

2. Select **Open Site**. Enter the complete URL to the SharePoint site and select **Open**.

3. From the **Navigation** pane, select **Master Pages**.

4. In the list of files in the **Master Pages** library, make a copy of `seattle.master` (for our example, we have renamed it `Seattle_Responsive.master`).

5. Check out the new `Seattle_Responsive.master` master page.

6. Open the `Seattle_Responsive.master` master page.

7. Locate the `<head>` element.

8. Add the following CSS reference to the `Responsive.css` file that we created:

   ```
   <SharePoint:CssRegistration ID="customCssRegistration" Name="<%
   $SPUrl:~Site/_catalogs/masterpage/resources/Responsive.css %>"
   runat="server"></SharePoint:CssRegistration>
   ```

9. Save the master page.

10. Check in and publish the master page using the **Check In** and **Publish** options.

11. Set the master page as the **Site Master Page** or assign the master page to the device channel that targets your mobile device.

12. From the **Navigation** pane, select **All Files**.

13. In the **All Files** content pane, navigate to **_catalogs | masterpage | resources**.

14. From the **New** section on the ribbon, navigate to **File | CSS**.

15. Name the new CSS file `Responsive.css`.

16. Check out the new `Responsive.css` file.

17. Open the `Responsive.css` file.

18. Hide the header controls using the following code:

```
#suiteBar, #s4-ribbonrow {

    display: none;

}
```

19. Set the title area to have an automatic width using the following code:

```
#titleAreaRow, #s4-titlerow {

    height: auto;

    width: auto;

}
```

20. Set the content of the title and content areas to float using the following code:

```
#titleAreaRow > div, #contentRow > div, #layoutsTable td {

    float: left;

    display: inline-block;

}
```

21. Set the page content to have a minimum width and set its left-hand side margin to override the default margin using the following code:

```
#contentBox {

    min-width: 100px;

    margin-left: 20px;

}
```

22. Set the workspace container to have a forced automatic width using the following code:

```
#s4-workspace {

    width: auto !important;

}
```

23. Save the CSS file.

24. Check in and publish the CSS file using the **Check In** and **Publish** options.

25. Navigate to the site in your preferred web browser or your mobile device to observe the results. The results will be similar to the following screenshot:

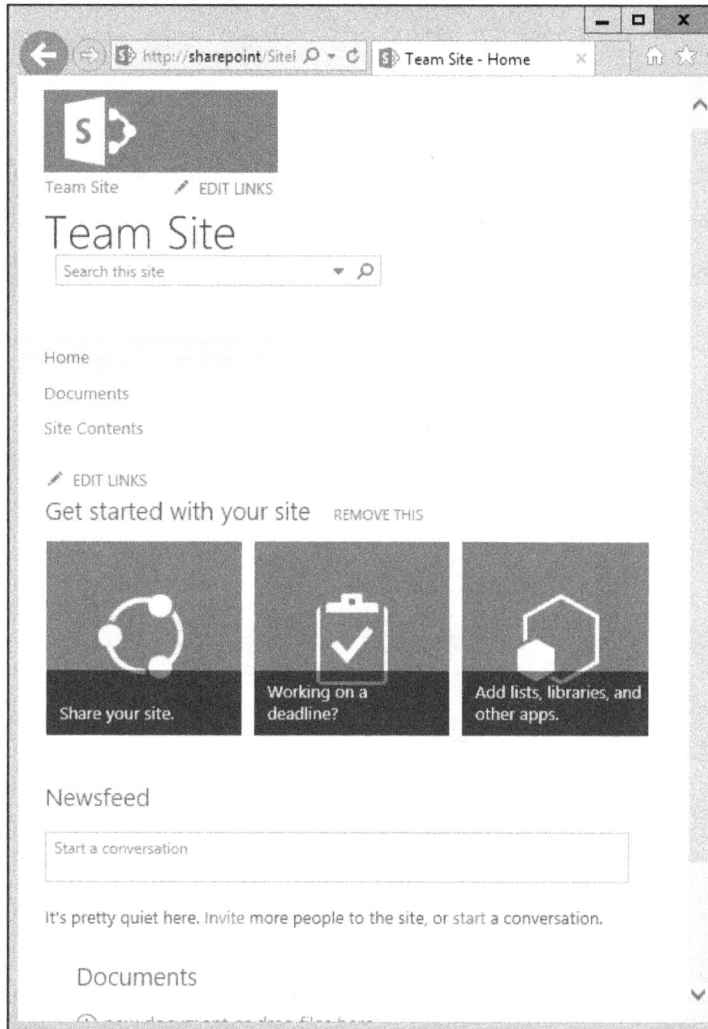

How it works...

In this recipe, we have used CSS to hide controls and to make the remaining controls float and use automatic widths. By making these controls float and use automatic widths, we are making them appear stacked vertically to provide smaller screens with better visibility of the content. The content on the screen will be adjusted based on the width of the screen and so on.

See also

► The *CssRegistration class* topic on MSDN at `http://msdn.microsoft.com/en-us/library/microsoft.sharepoint.webcontrols.cssregistration.aspx`

Customizing the Windows 8 Start menu tile for pinning sites using a master page

The Windows 8 **Start** menu allows users to pin sites from Internet Explorer as tiles. SharePoint 2013 provides a simple control to manage how the tile looks and what icon to use. In this recipe, we will customize the tile settings with our customized master page.

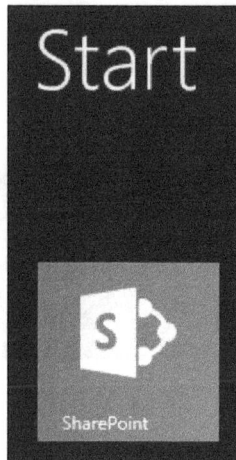

How to do it...

Follow these steps to customize the Windows 8 **Start** menu tile for pinning sites using a master page:

1. Open SharePoint Designer.
2. Select **Open Site**. Enter the full URL to the SharePoint site and select **Open**.
3. From the **Navigation** pane, select **Master Pages**.
4. In the list of files in the **Master Pages** library, make a copy of `seattle.master` (for our example, we have renamed it `Seattle_Windows8Tile.master`).
5. Check out the new `Seattle_Windows8Tile.master` master page.

6. Open the `Seattle_Windows8Tile.master` master page.

7. Locate the `<SharePoint:SPPinnedSiteTile>` element.

8. Provide a custom image URL and hex color using the following code:

```
<SharePoint:SPPinnedSiteTile runat="server" TileUrl="/_catalogs/
masterpage/resources/SimpleSmiley.png" TileColor="#d17601" />
```

> Images used for the pin style should be a 144 px by 144 px transparent PNG file.

9. Save the master page.

10. Check in and publish the master page using the **Check In** and **Publish** option.

11. Set the master page as the **Site Master Page**.

12. Navigate to the site in Internet Explorer on Windows 8.

13. Pin the site to the Windows 8 **Start** menu to observe the results. The following screenshot shows the option that allows us to pin the page to the **Start** menu:

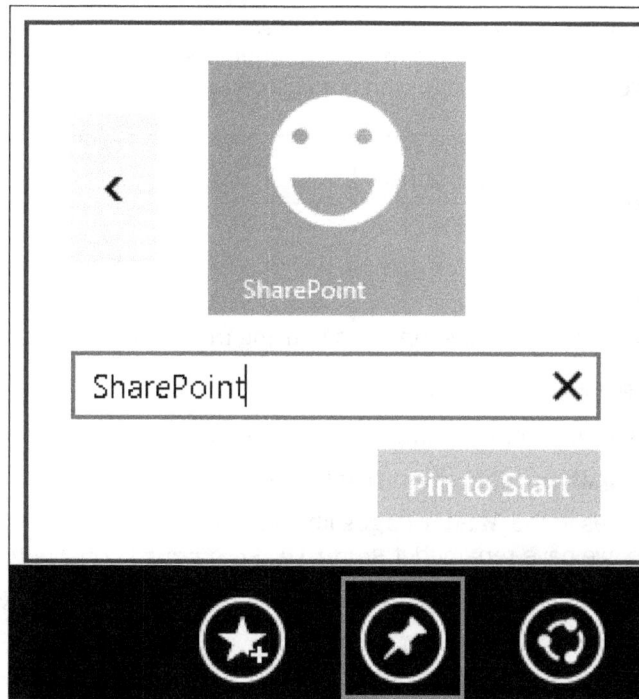

How it works...

The `SPPinnedSiteTile` server control outputs `<meta>` tags to the `<head>` element of the SharePoint page when rendered. When Internet Explorer on Windows 8 pins a site, it will look for these `<meta>` tags when creating the pin. In this recipe, we provided a custom image and color to be used when adding these tags. This replaces the default SharePoint logo and the blue color.

See also

▶ The *SPPinnedSiteTile class* topic on MSDN at `http://msdn.microsoft.com/en-us/library/microsoft.sharepoint.webcontrols.sppinnedsitetile.aspx`

Customizing the shortcut icon (favicon) using a master page

The shortcut icon, or favicon, is a 16 px by 16 px image that most browsers will display as part of the title bar when viewing a web page as well as when bookmarking the web part. In this recipe, we will change the shortcut icon with our customized master page.

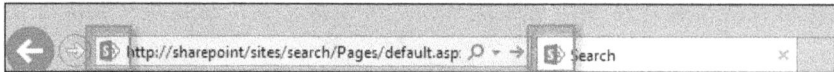

How to do it...

Follow these steps to customize the shortcut icon using the master page:

1. Open SharePoint Designer.
2. Select **Open Site**. Enter the complete URL to the SharePoint site and select **Open**.
3. From the **Navigation** pane, select **Master Pages**.
4. In the list of files in the **Master Pages** library, make a copy of `seattle.master` (for our example, we have renamed it `Seattle_ShortcutIcon.master`).
5. Check out the new `Seattle_ShortcutIcon.master` master page.
6. Open the `Seattle_ShortcutIcon.master` master page.
7. Locate the `<SharePoint:SPShortcutIcon>` element.

8. Provide a custom image URL using the following code:

```
<SharePoint:SPShortcutIcon runat="server" IconUrl="/_catalogs/
masterpage/resources/favicon.png" />v
```

> Images used for the shortcut icon should be a 16 px by 16 px transparent `.png` or `.ico` file.

9. Save the master page.

10. Check in and publish the master page using the **Check In** and **Publish** options.

11. Set the master page as the **Site Master Page**.

12. Navigate to the site in your preferred web browser to observe the results. The result will be similar to the following screenshot:

How it works...

The `SPShortCutIcon` server control outputs a `<link>` tag for the shortcut icon (or favicon) to the `<head>` element of the SharePoint page when rendered. When most web browsers render the page, they will use this image in the title bar or bookmark for the page. In this recipe, we provided a custom image that replaces the default SharePoint logo when adding the tag.

There's more...

Apple devices, such as iPhones and iPads, look for specific images when determining what to display as the icon for a site when pinning it to the home screen. We can add `<link>` tags to instruct these devices to use images we have provided. For instance, let's look at the following link tags:

```
<!-- Standard iPhone -->
<link rel="apple-touch-icon" sizes="57x57" href="apple-touch-icon-57.
png" />
<!-- Retina iPhone -->
<link rel="apple-touch-icon" sizes="114x114" href="t apple-touch-
icon-114.png" />
<!-- Standard iPad -->
<link rel="apple-touch-icon" sizes="72x72" href=" apple-touch-icon-72.
png" />
<!-- Retina iPad -->
<link rel="apple-touch-icon" sizes="144x144" href=" apple-touch-
icon-144.png" />
```

See also

▶ The *Configuring Web Applications* article in the *Safari Web Content Guide* at `https://developer.apple.com/library/ios/documentation/ AppleApplications/Reference/SafariWebContent/ ConfiguringWebApplications/ConfiguringWebApplications.html`

▶ The *SPShortCutIcon class* topic on MSDN at `http://msdn.microsoft.com/en- us/library/microsoft.sharepoint.webcontrols.spshortcuticon.aspx`

Creating a page layout with three columns of web part zones

A page layout is a template used when creating new content pages in SharePoint. There are a number of page layouts included with SharePoint out of the box. When one of those doesn't suffice, we can easily create our own. In this recipe, we will modify the `BlankWebPartPage. aspx` page layout to have three columns, each with a web part zone. A **web part zone** is an area of the page where users can add web parts. A **web part** is an ASP.NET user control under the covers.

How to do it...

Follow these steps to create a page layout with three columns of web part zones:

1. Open SharePoint Designer.

2. Select **Open Site**. Enter the complete URL to the SharePoint site and select **Open**.

3. From the **Navigation** pane, select **Page Layouts**.

4. In the list of files in the **Page Layouts** library, make a copy of `BlankWebPartPage. aspx` (for our example, we have renamed it `PageLayout_ThreeColumn.aspx`).

> The **Page Layouts** view is a view of the `_catalogs/masterpage` library that is limited to show **Page Layouts** only.

5. Check out the new `PageLayout_ThreeColumn.aspx` page layout.

6. Open the `PageLayout_ThreeColumn.aspx` page layout.

7. Locate the first `<div class="ms-table ms-fullWidth">` element.

8. Remove the following `<div>` elements it contains:

```
<div class="ms-table ms-fullWidth">

<SharePointWebControls:ScriptBlock runat="server">
```

```
if(typeof(MSOLayout_MakeInvisibleIfEmpty) == &quot;function&quot;)
{MSOLayout_MakeInvisibleIfEmpty();}</SharePointWebControls:ScriptB
lock>
</div>
```

9. Using the SharePoint table layout styles, add three `<div>` column containers as shown in the following code:

```
<div class="ms-table ms-fullWidth">
<div class="ms-table ms-fullWidth">
<div class="cell-margin tableCol-33">
</div>
<div class="cell-margin tableCol-33">
</div>
<div class="cell-margin tableCol-33">
</div>
</div>
<SharePointWebControls:ScriptBlock runat="server">
if(typeof(MSOLayout_MakeInvisibleIfEmpty) == &quot;function&quot;)
{MSOLayout_MakeInvisibleIfEmpty();}</SharePointWebControls:ScriptB
lock>
</div>
```

10. In each `<div>` column container, add a `WebPartZone` element as shown in the following code:

```
<div class="cell-margin tableCol-33">
<WebPartPages:WebPartZone runat="server" Title="<%$Resources:cms
,WebPartZoneTitle_Left%>" ID="CenterLeftColumn"><ZoneTemplate></
ZoneTemplate></WebPartPages:WebPartZone>
</div>
<div class="cell-margin tableCol-33">
<WebPartPages:WebPartZone runat="server" Title="<%$Resources:cm
s,WebPartZoneTitle_Center%>" ID="CenterColumn"><ZoneTemplate></
ZoneTemplate></WebPartPages:WebPartZone>
</div>
<div class="cell-margin tableCol-33">
<WebPartPages:WebPartZone runat="server" Title="<%$Resources:cms,
WebPartZoneTitle_Right%>" ID="CenterRightColumn"><ZoneTemplate></
ZoneTemplate></WebPartPages:WebPartZone>
</div>
```

11. Save the page layout.

12. Navigate back to the **Properties** page for the page layout.

13. Select **Manage all file properties in the browser** from the **Customization** section as shown in the following screenshot:

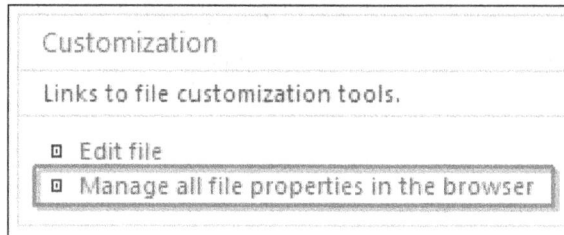

14. From the ribbon, select **Edit Item** as shown in the following screenshot:

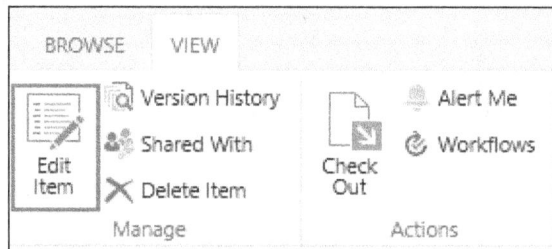

15. Ensure the **Content Type** option is set to **Page Layout** as shown in the following screenshot:

16. Provide a new title in the **Title** field for the page layout (for example, `Three Column`).

17. In the **Associated Content Type** field, set **Content Type Group** to **Page Layout Content Types** and **Content Type Name** to **Article Page**, as shown in the following screenshot:

Associated Content Type	
	Content Type Group
	Page Layout Content Types ⌄
	Content Type Name
	Article Page ⌄

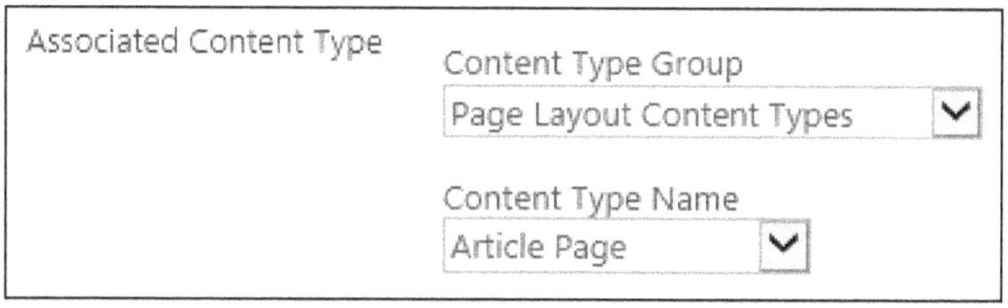

18. Save the item.

19. Check in and publish the page layout using the **Check In** and **Publish** options.

20. Navigate to the **Pages** library of the SharePoint site using your preferred web browser.

> If the **Pages** library is not on the quick launch, it can be accessed from the **Settings** menu under **Site Content**.

21. Select **New Document** from the **FILES** tab on the ribbon.

22. Provide a title and URL for the new page in the **Title** and **URL** fields.

23. Select the newly created page layout as shown in the following screenshot:

Page Layout

Select a page layout to control how the page will be displayed.

(Article Page) Body only
(Article Page) Image on left
(Article Page) Image on right
(Article Page) Summary links
(Article Page) Three Column
(Catalog-Item Reuse) Blank Catalog Item
(Catalog-Item Reuse) Catalog Item Image on Left
(Enterprise Wiki Page) Basic Page
(Error Page) Error
(Project Page) Basic Project Page

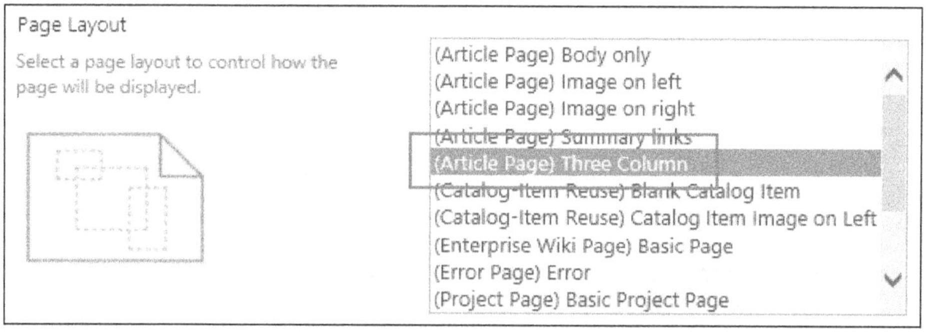

24. Click on **Create**.

25. Edit the new page to observe our new layout and web part zones. The following screenshot shows the editing window of the page:

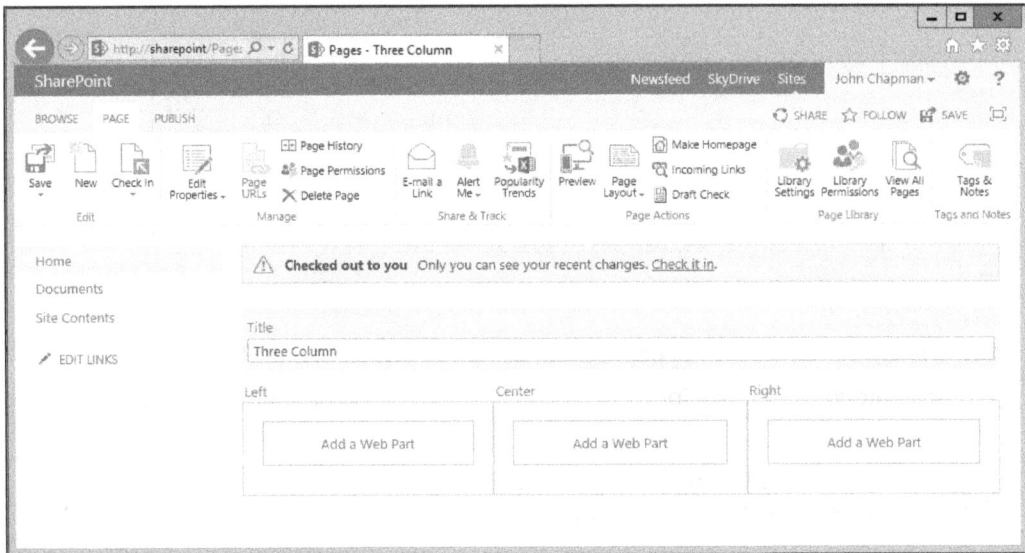

How it works...

For content pages, SharePoint uses the master page and the page layout to provide the content structure of the pages. This allows the master page to provide the overall design of the SharePoint site and the page layout to provide the structure within the master page for specific pages. When a content page is rendered, the page content is rendered in the areas provided by the page layout. Then the content and page layout are rendered in the content area of the master page.

See also

▶ The *WebPartZone class* topic on MSDN at http://msdn.microsoft.com/en-us/library/system.web.ui.webcontrols.webparts.webpartzone.aspx

Creating a page layout with web parts added to the page

In our custom page layouts, we can add web parts to the templates in two ways. First, we can add them to a web part zone template. This adds the web part to the web part zone when a page is created with the page layout and they can be modified or removed after the page has been created.

Secondly, we can reference the web part directly on the page outside of web part zones. This will insert the web part onto the page, but it cannot be modified or removed from the page when editing the page in the SharePoint web interface.

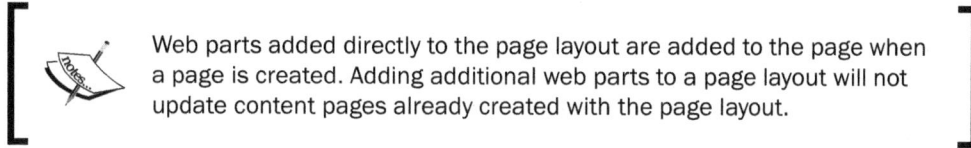

> Web parts added directly to the page layout are added to the page when a page is created. Adding additional web parts to a page layout will not update content pages already created with the page layout.

In this recipe, we will add two web parts to our page layout (one inside a web part zone template and one outside a web part zone). We will use the page layout we created previously with the three web part zone columns as a starting point.

How to do it...

Follow these steps to create a page layout with web parts added to the page:

1. Open SharePoint Designer.
2. Select **Open Site**. Enter the complete URL to the SharePoint site and select **Open**.
3. From the **Navigation** pane, select **Page Layouts**.
4. In the list of files in the **Page Layouts** library, make a copy of `PageLayout_ThreeColumn.aspx` (for our example, we have renamed it `PageLayout_WebPartsAdded.aspx`).
5. Check out the new `PageLayout_WebPartsAdded.aspx` page layout.
6. Open the `PageLayout_WebPartsAdded.aspx` page layout.
7. Locate the first `<div class="ms-table ms-fullWidth">` element.
8. Before the `<div>` elements, add a `TableOfContentsWebPart` element.

   ```
   <PublishingWebControls:TableOfContentsWebPart
   ID="TableOfContentsWebPart" Title="Table of Contents"
   runat="server" />
   ```

> Web parts added outside of a `WebPartZone ZoneTemplate` are added to the page, but are not editable from the SharePoint web interface.

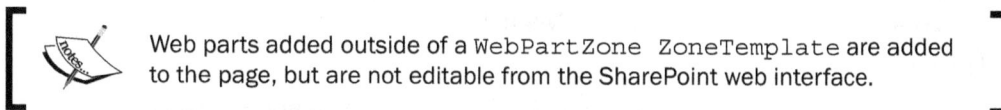

9. Using the SharePoint table layout styles, add three `<div>` column containers as shown in the following code:

   ```
   <div class="ms-table ms-fullWidth">
   <div class="ms-table ms-fullWidth">
   <div class="cell-margin tableCol-33">
   </div>
   ```

```
<div class="cell-margin tableCol-33">
</div>
<div class="cell-margin tableCol-33">
</div>
</div>
<SharePointWebControls:ScriptBlock runat="server">
if(typeof(MSOLayout_MakeInvisibleIfEmpty) == &quot;function&quot;)
{MSOLayout_MakeInvisibleIfEmpty();}</SharePointWebControls:ScriptB
lock>
</div>
```

10. In `ZoneTemplate` of one of the `WebPartZone` elements, add a `MediaWebPart` as shown in the following code:

```
<WebPartPages:WebPartZone runat="server" Title="<%$Resources:cms,W
ebPartZoneTitle_Center%>" ID="CenterColumn">
<ZoneTemplate>
<PublishingWebControls:MediaWebPart ID="MediaWebPart" Title="Media
Web Part" runat="server" />
</ZoneTemplate>
</WebPartPages:WebPartZone>
```

> Web parts added in a `WebPartZone` `ZoneTemplate` are added to the page when created and are editable from the SharePoint web interface.

11. Save the page layout.

12. Navigate back to the **Properties** page for the page layout.

13. Under **Customization**, select **Manage all file properties in the browser**.

14. Select **Edit Item** from the ribbon.

15. Ensure that the **Content Type** option is set to **Page Layout**.

16. Provide a new title for the page layout (for example, `Web Parts Added`).

17. In the **Associated Content Type** option, set **Content Type Group** to **Page Layout Content Types** and **Content Type Name** to **Article Page**.

18. Save the item.

19. Check in and publish the page layout using the **Check In** and **Publish** options.

20. Navigate to the **Pages** library of the site using your preferred web browser.

21. Select **New Document** from the **FILES** tab on the ribbon.

22. Provide a title and URL for the new page in the **Title** and **URL** fields.

23. Select the newly created page layout.

24. Select **Create**.

25. Edit the new page to observe our new layout and web parts. The following screenshot shows the page where we can edit our web parts:

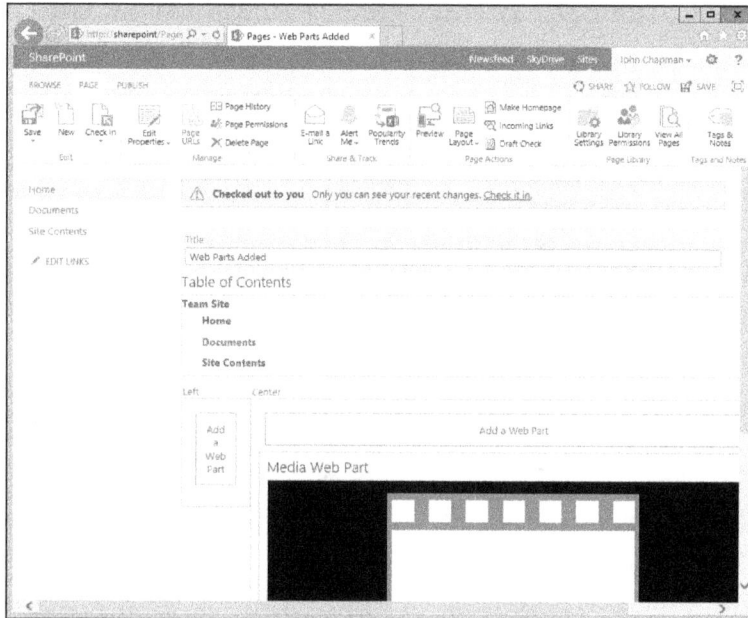

How it works...

Web parts are ultimately ASP.NET server controls at their core. As such, they can be added directly to a page layout like any other server control. Doing so puts them on the page, but does not let users edit them in the web interface.

Web part zones are server controls that provide a section of the page that users can add web parts to in the web interface. They also have a template that allows a page layout to include web parts in the zone by default when the content page is created. These web parts can be edited in the web interface after the content page is created.

See also

▸ The *WebPartZone class* topic on MSDN at http://msdn.microsoft.com/en-us/library/system.web.ui.webcontrols.webparts.webpartzone.aspx

Creating a page layout with a picture-library-based image carousel using JavaScript

Page layouts provide easy-to-use templates for content creators to use when creating SharePoint site content. In scenarios where a certain page design is used repetitively, a page layout is ideal. One example of this is an image carousel used by landing pages. In this recipe, we will create a JavaScript-based image carousel that displays images from a picture library in the SharePoint site.

To simplify the process of creating the JavaScript image carousel, we will use the jQuery framework (`http://www.jquery.com`) and jQuery bxSlider plugin (`http://www.bxslider.com`).

> This recipe will look for images in the **Images** picture library in the SharePoint site. Upload a few 750 px wide images (each with a constant height) for the image carousel to use.

Getting ready

For this recipe, we will use the page layout we previously created in the *Creating a page layout with three columns of web part zones* recipe.

How to do it...

Follow these steps to create a page layout with an image carousel:

1. Open SharePoint Designer.

2. Select **Open Site**. Enter the complete URL to the SharePoint site and select **Open**.

3. From the **Navigation** pane, select **Page Layouts**.

4. In the list of files in the **Page Layouts** library, make a copy of `PageLayout_ThreeColumn.aspx` (for our example, we have renamed it `PageLayout_ImageCarousel.aspx`).

5. Check out the new `PageLayout_ImageCarousel.aspx` page layout.

6. Open the `PageLayout_ImageCarousel.aspx` page layout.

7. Add an `ImageCarousel.css stylesheet` file and an `ImageCarousel.js` JavaScript file to the `resources` folder located at `_catalogs/masterpage/resources`.

8. Add references to our custom stylesheet, the jQuery bxSlider stylesheet, the jQuery JavaScript, and the jQuery bxSlider plugin JavaScript to the page. In addition, reference the SharePoint JavaScript files to ensure they are loaded on the page.

```
<SharePointWebControls:CssRegistration ID="customCss" name="<%
$SPUrl:~Site/_catalogs/masterpage/resources/imagecarousel.css %>"
runat="server"/>
<SharePointWebControls:CssRegistration ID="bxSliderCss" name="<%
$SPUrl:~Site/_catalogs/masterpage/resources/jquery.bxslider.css
%>" runat="server"/>

<SharePointWebControls:ScriptLink ID="jQuery" Name="~site/_
catalogs/masterpage/resources/jquery-2.0.2.min.js"
runat="server"></SharePointWebControls:ScriptLink>
<SharePointWebControls:ScriptLink ID="bxSliderJs"
Name="~site/_catalogs/masterpage/resources/jquery.bxslider.js"
runat="server"></SharePointWebControls:ScriptLink>
<SharePointWebControls:ScriptLink ID="customJavaScript"
Name="~site/_catalogs/masterpage/resources/imagecarousel.js"
runat="server"></SharePointWebControls:ScriptLink>

<SharePointWebControls:ScriptLink Name="sp.js" runat="server"
Localizable="false" LoadAfterUI="true" />
<SharePointWebControls:ScriptLink Name="sp.runtime.js"
runat="server" Localizable="false" LoadAfterUI="true" />
<SharePointWebControls:ScriptLink Name="sp.core.js" runat="server"
Localizable="false" LoadAfterUI="true" />
```

9. Locate the first `<div class="ms-table ms-fullWidth">` element.

10. Before the `<div>` elements it contains, add the following `<div>` tag to contain the image carousel:

    ```
    <div class="ImageCarousel"></div>
    ```

11. In our `ImageCarousel.css` stylesheet, provide a default height, width, and display for the image carousel as follows:

    ```
    .ImageCarousel {

        height: 400px;

        width: 800px;

        display: block;
    }
    ```

12. In our `ImageCarousel.js` JavaScript file, create a function to initialize the carousel and use the `ExecuteOrDelayUntilScriptLoaded` function to execute the function after the SharePoint JavaScript files load as shown in the following code:

    ```
    function InitializeImageCarousel() {
    }
    ExecuteOrDelayUntilScriptLoaded(InitializeImageCarousel, "sp.js");
    ```

> The ExecuteOrDelayUntilScriptLoaded function is provided by SharePoint to allow us to instruct SharePoint to load the required core JavaScript and then execute our function.

13. In our initialization function, get the current SharePoint context:

```
var context = new SP.ClientContext.get_current();
```

14. From the context, get the current SharePoint site:

```
var web = context.get_web();
```

15. Get the Images picture library from the SharePoint site as follows:

```
var list = web.get_lists().getByTitle('Images');
```

16. Use a CAML query to limit the number of returned items to five:

```
var camlQuery = new SP.CamlQuery();
camlQuery.set_viewXml('<View><RowLimit>5</RowLimit></View>');
```

> CAML is an XML-based query schema used by SharePoint to query SharePoint lists.

17. Get the items from the list with the CAML query as follows:

```
var items = list.getItems(camlQuery);
```

18. Instruct the context to load the items with the Id, Title, and FileRef properties as follows:

```
context.load(items, 'Include(Id, Title, FileRef)');
```

19. Call the executeQueryAsync method on the context to execute the query and provide delegate functions to execute on success or failure of the request, as shown in the following code:

```
context.executeQueryAsync(
Function.createDelegate(this, function (sender, args) {
   // Success
}),
Function.createDelegate(this, function (sender, args) {
    // Failed
}));
```

20. In the failure delegate function (the second function), use the SharePoint debug trace function to write the error to the browser console as follows:

```
Sys.Debug.trace('Request failed. ' + args.get_message() + '\n' +
args.get_stackTrace());
```

21. In the success delegate function (this first function), create the `<ul>` container object for the image carousel using the following line of code:

    ```
    var slider = $('<ul class="bxslider"></ul>');
    ```

22. Iterate through each item and add the `<li>` element representing the image using the following code:

    ```
    var listItemEnumerator = items.getEnumerator();
    while (listItemEnumerator.moveNext()) {
    var oListItem = listItemEnumerator.get_current();

    var itemHtml = $('<li><img title="' + oListItem.get_item("Title")
    + '" src="' + oListItem.get_item("FileRef") + '" /></li>');
    itemHtml.appendTo(slider);
    }
    ```

23. Add the `<ul>` image carousel container to the following image carousel `<div>` we have on the page:

    ```
    var imageCarousel = $('.ImageCarousel');
    slider.appendTo(imageCarousel);
    ```

24. Initialize the jQuery bxSlider plugin using the following line of code:

    ```
    $('.bxslider').bxSlider({ captions: true, slideWidth: 750 });
    ```

25. Set the height of the image carousel `<div>` to match the `bxSlider` height to ensure there is no overlapping content:

    ```
    $('.ImageCarousel').height($('.bx-wrapper', $('.ImageCarousel')).
    height());
    ```

26. Save the page layout.

27. Navigate back to the **Properties** page for the page layout.

28. Select **Manage all file properties in the browser** from the **Customization** section.

29. Select **Edit Item** from the ribbon and ensure that the **Content Type** is set to **Page Layout**.

30. Provide a new title for the page layout (for example, Image Carousel).

31. For the **Associated Content Type** option, set **Content Type Group** to **Page Layout Content Types** and **Content Type Name** to **Article Page**.

32. Save the item.

33. Check in and publish the page layout using the **Check In** and **Publish** options.

34. Navigate to the **Pages** library of the SharePoint site using your preferred web browser.

35. Select **New Document** from the **Files** tab on the ribbon.

36. Provide a title and URL for the new page in the **Title** and **URL** fields.

37. Select the newly created page layout.

38. Click on **Create**.

39. View the page to observe our image carousel. The following screenshot shows the **Image Carousel** window:

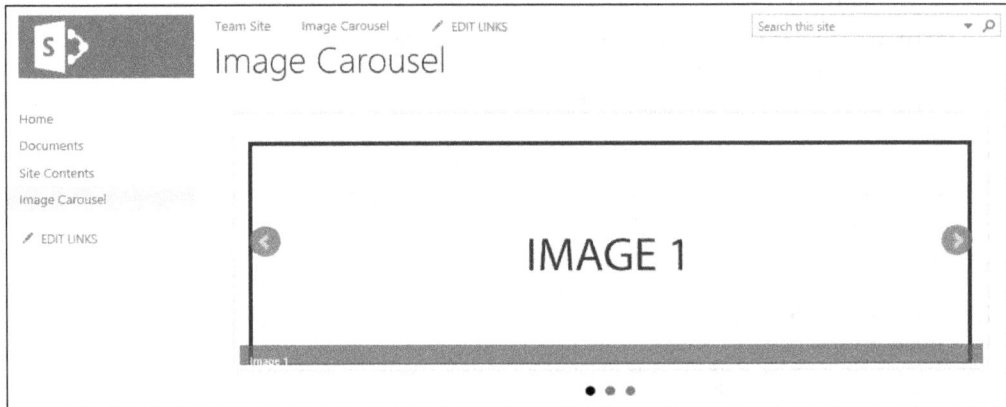

How it works...

In addition to the server-side object model, SharePoint provides additional object models to interact with SharePoint content. In this recipe, we used the **JavaScript object model** (**JSOM**). Using JSOM, we retrieved the current site from the current SharePoint context. We used a CAML query to retrieve the **Images** picture library in the current site. We then created an unordered list with the images and used our JavaScript libraries and plugins (jQuery and bxSlider) to create our image carousel. Once we had our page layout created, we created a page with it to observe our image carousel.

See also

▶ The *JavaScript API Reference for SharePoint 2013* topic on MSDN at `http://msdn.microsoft.com/en-us/library/jj193034.aspx`

▶ The *ScriptLink class* topic on MSDN at `http://msdn.microsoft.com/en-us/library/microsoft.sharepoint.webcontrols.scriptlink.aspx`

▶ The *CssRegistration class* topic on MSDN at `http://msdn.microsoft.com/en-us/library/microsoft.sharepoint.webcontrols.cssregistration.aspx`

▶ The *Overview of the SharePoint 2013 Page Model* article on MSDN at `http://msdn.microsoft.com/en-us/library/jj191506.aspx`

▶ The *SharePoint Designer for Developers* article on MSDN at `http://msdn.microsoft.com/en-us/sharepoint/hh850380.aspx`

Displaying specific content only to authenticated users

When working with public-facing SharePoint sites, it is common to display content only to users who have logged in. In this recipe, we will add some content to our customized master page that only authenticated users can see.

To see the results of this recipe, you will need to be able to access the SharePoint site both anonymously and logged in.

How to do it...

Follow these steps to display specific content only to authenticated users:

1. Open SharePoint Designer.
2. Select **Open Site**. Enter the complete URL to the SharePoint site and select **Open**.
3. From the **Navigation** pane, select **Master Pages**.
4. In the list of files in the **Master Pages** library, make a copy of `seattle.master` (for our example, we have renamed it `Seattle_DisplayAuthenticatedContent.master`).
5. Check out the new `Seattle_DisplayAuthenticatedContent.master` master page.
6. Open the `Seattle_DisplayAuthenticatedContent.master` master page.
7. Locate the element with the `ID_SuiteBarBrandingDelegate` ID.
8. After the delegate control, add the following `<asp:LoginView>` control with content in the `LoggedInTemplate`:

   ```
   <asp:LoginView ID="customLoginView" runat="server">
   <LoggedInTemplate>
   <span style="color: #FFFFFF; float: right;">Only Authenticated
   Users Can See This</span>
   </LoggedInTemplate>
   </asp:LoginView>
   ```

9. Save the master page.
10. Check in and publish the master page using the **Check In** and **Publish** options.
11. Set the master page as the **Site Master Page**.

12. Navigate to the site in your preferred web browser as an anonymous user to observe the results.

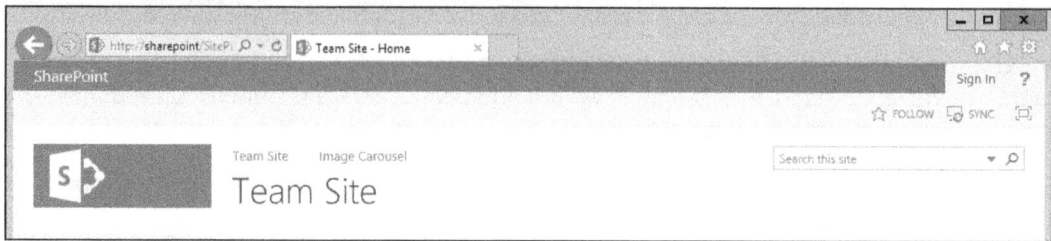

13. Navigate to the site in your preferred web browser as an authenticated user to observe the results.

How it works...

The ASP.NET `LoginView` control is a simple server control that can have a template for logged in users and a template for anonymous users. The `LoggedInTemplate` content only renders when a user is logged in. In this recipe, we added some text to the `LoggedInTemplate` that only authenticated users should see.

See also

▸ Chapter 12, *Configuring Anonymous Access*

▸ The *LoginView class* topic on MSDN at `http://msdn.microsoft.com/en-us/library/system.web.ui.webcontrols.loginview.aspx`

Displaying specific content only to anonymous users

Similar to the previous recipe, it is common to display certain content on a page only to users who have not logged in. In this recipe, we will add some content to our customized master page that only anonymous users can see.

To see the results of this recipe, you will need to be able to access the SharePoint site both anonymously and logged in.

How to do it...

To display specific content only to anonymous users, we will use the following steps:

1. Open SharePoint Designer.

2. Select **Open Site**. Enter the full URL to the SharePoint site and select **Open**.

3. From the **Navigation** pane, select **Master Pages**.

4. In the list of files in the **Master Pages** library, make a copy of `seattle.master` (for our example, we have renamed it `Seattle_DisplayAnonymousContent.master`).

5. Check out the new `Seattle_DisplayAnonymousContent.master` master page.

6. Open the `Seattle_DisplayAnonymousContent.master` master page.

7. Locate the element with the `ID_SuiteBarBrandingDelegate` ID.

8. After the delegate control, add an `<asp:LoginView>` control with content in the `AnonymousTemplate`.

   ```
   <asp:LoginView ID="customLoginView" runat="server">
   <AnonymousTemplate>
   <span style="color: #FFFFFF; float: right;">Only Anonymous Users
   Can See This</span>
   </AnonymousTemplate>
   </asp:LoginView>
   ```

9. Save the master page.

10. Check in and publish the master page using the **Check In** and **Publish** options.

11. Set the master page as the **Site Master Page**.

12. Navigate to the site in your preferred web browser as an anonymous user and as an authenticated user to observe the results.

How it works...

The ASP.NET `LoginView` control is a simple server control that can have a template for logged in users and a template for anonymous users. The `AnonymousTemplate` content only renders when a user is not logged in. In this recipe, we added text to the `AnonymousTemplate` that only users who are not logged in should see.

See also

▶ *Chapter 12, Configuring Anonymous Access*

▶ The *LoginView class* topic on MSDN at `http://msdn.microsoft.com/en-us/library/system.web.ui.webcontrols.loginview.aspx`

Displaying specific content only to site administrators

When working with intranet or extranet sites, as well as public-facing sites that allow users to log in, it is common to only allow administrators of the SharePoint site to see certain content. In this recipe, we will use our customized master page to hide content from users who are not site administrators.

How to do it...

Follow these steps to display specific content only to site:

1. Open SharePoint Designer.

2. Select **Open Site**. Enter the complete URL to the SharePoint site and select **Open**.

3. From the **Navigation** pane, select **Master Pages**.

4. In the list of files in the **Master Pages** library, make a copy of `seattle.master` (for our example, we have renamed it as `Seattle_DisplayAdministratorContent.master`).

5. Check out the new `Seattle_DisplayAdministratorContent.master` master page.

6. Open the `Seattle_DisplayAdministratorContent.master` master page.

7. Locate the element with the `ID_SuiteBarBrandingDelegate` ID.

8. After the delegate control, add a `<SharePoint:SPSecurityTrimmedControl>` control with the following content:

```
<SharePoint:SPSecurityTrimmedControl ID="customSecurityTrimmedCont
rol" PermissionContext="CurrentSite" PermissionsString="ManageWeb"
runat="server">
<span style="color: #FFFFFF; float: right;">Only Admins Can See
This</span>
</SharePoint:SPSecurityTrimmedControl>
```

9. Save the master page.

10. Check in and publish the master page using the **Check In** and **Publish** options.

11. Set the master page as the **Site Master Page**.

12. Navigate to the site in your preferred web browser as an administrator user and as a nonadministrator user to observe the results.

How it works...

The `SPSecurityTrimmedControl` is a simple server control that displays its content based on the permission levels of the current user. When this control renders, it simply looks to the current SharePoint context to determine if the current user has the permission level required.

See also

▸ The *SPSecurityTrimmedControl class* topic on MSDN `http://msdn.microsoft.com/en-us/library/microsoft.sharepoint.webcontrols.spsecuritytrimmedcontrol.aspx`

Creating a master page with editing controls only available to editors

In this recipe, we will create a custom master page that is branded for a public-facing SharePoint site. In addition, this master page will only show the page editing controls to those with contribute access to the SharePoint site.

To see the results of this recipe, you will need to be able to access the SharePoint site both anonymously and logged in.

How to do it...

Follow these steps to create a master page with editing controls only available to editors:

1. Open SharePoint Designer.

2. Select **Open Site**. Enter the complete URL to the SharePoint site and select **Open**.

3. Add a `PublicMasterPage.css` stylesheet file to the `resources` folder located at `_catalogs/masterpage/resources`.

4. From the **Navigation** pane, select **Master Pages**.

5. In the list of files in the **Master Pages** library, make a copy of `seattle.master` (for our example, we have renamed it `Seattle_PublicWebsite.master`).

6. Check out the new `Seattle_PublicWebsite.master` master page.

7. Open the `Seattle_PublicWebsite.master` master page.

8. Add a reference to our `PublicMasterPage.css` stylesheet file.

```
<SharePoint:CssRegistration ID="customCssRegistration" Name="<%
$SPUrl:~Site/_catalogs/masterpage/resources/PublicMasterPage.css
%>" runat="server"></SharePoint:CssRegistration>
```

9. In our stylesheet file, add the following content padding to the workspace and a background color for the body:

```
#s4-workspace {

    background: #FFFFFF;

    margin: 50px 100px 50px 100px;
}
body {

    background: #999999;
}
#s4-ribbonrow, #suiteBar {

    background: #FFFFFF;
}
```

10. In our custom master page, locate the element with the `suiteBar` ID as follows:

11. Before the `suiteBar` element, add the beginning tag for a `<SharePoint:SPSec urityTrimmedControl>` control with the permissions set to `EditListItems` as shown in the following line of code:

```
<SharePoint:SPSecurityTrimmedControl ID="customSecurityTrimmedCont
rol" PermissionContext="CurrentSite" PermissionsString="EditListIt
ems" runat="server">
```

> The `EditListItems` permission level will require the user to have contribute access to the site in order to see the items in the control.

12. In our custom master page, locate the element with the `s4-workspace` ID.

13. Before the `s4-workspace` element, add the following end tag for the `<SharePoint :SPSecurityTrimmedControl>` control:

```
</SharePoint:SPSecurityTrimmedControl>
```

14. Save the master page.

15. Check in and publish the master page using the **Check In** and **Publish** options.

16. Set the master page as the **Site Master Page**.

17. Navigate to the site in your preferred web browser anonymously and log in to observe the results.

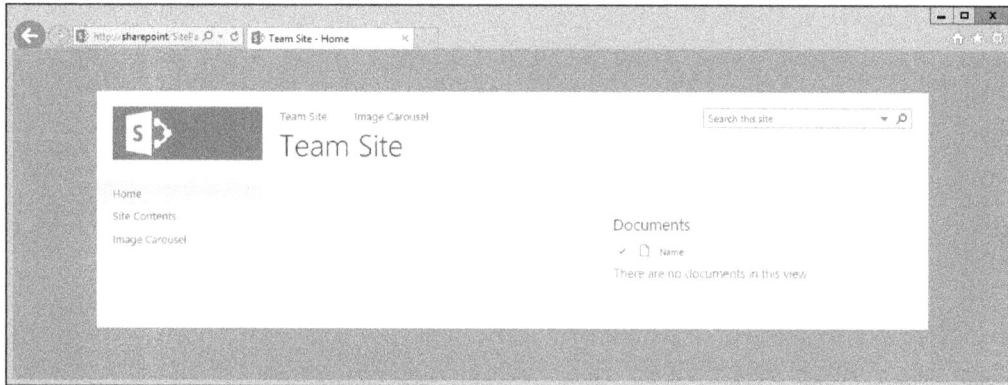

How it works...

In this recipe, we used CSS to provide padding around the content of the page and used an `SPSecurityTrimmedControl` control to hide the page editing controls to users who do not have access to edit the pages.

See also

- ▸ *Chapter 12, Configuring Anonymous Access*
- ▸ The *SPSecurityTrimmedControl class* topic on MSDN at `http://msdn.microsoft.com/en-us/library/microsoft.sharepoint.webcontrols.spsecuritytrimmedcontrol.aspx`
- ▸ The *ScriptLink class* topic on MSDN at `http://msdn.microsoft.com/en-us/library/microsoft.sharepoint.webcontrols.scriptlink.aspx`
- ▸ The *CssRegistration class* topic on MSDN at `http://msdn.microsoft.com/en-us/library/microsoft.sharepoint.webcontrols.cssregistration.aspx`

4
Packaging Branding Elements in a SharePoint Solution with Visual Studio

In this chapter, we will use Visual Studio to create a custom SharePoint solution project that will package our branding elements. We will cover the following recipes:

- ▶ Creating a Visual Studio SharePoint solution
- ▶ Including image, cascading stylesheets, and JavaScript resources in a SharePoint solution
- ▶ Including master pages in a SharePoint solution
- ▶ Including page layouts in a SharePoint solution
- ▶ Adding localization to a SharePoint solution
- ▶ Creating site feature to apply branding
- ▶ Creating the site collection feature to apply the feature to new and existing sites
- ▶ Creating a timer job to ensure the site branding feature is activated
- ▶ Packaging and deploying the SharePoint solution
- ▶ Activating the site collection feature on all site collections with PowerShell

Introduction

To package, distribute, and deploy custom solutions in SharePoint, Microsoft has provided the SharePoint solution concept. A SharePoint solution is a compressed Microsoft Cabinet file with the `.wsp` file extension. This file contains an XML manifest defining the solution with all the files and assemblies required for the solution.

In this chapter, we will create a SharePoint solution with Visual Studio to package our branding elements.

Creating a Visual Studio SharePoint solution

In this recipe, we will be creating a SharePoint 2013 farm solution. Farm solutions allow us to deploy content to the filesystem of the SharePoint servers and interact with SharePoint farm elements outside of a site collection, such as the web application.

How to do it...

Follow these steps to create a SharePoint solution:

1. Open Visual Studio and select **New Project** from the **FILE** menu as shown in the following screenshot:

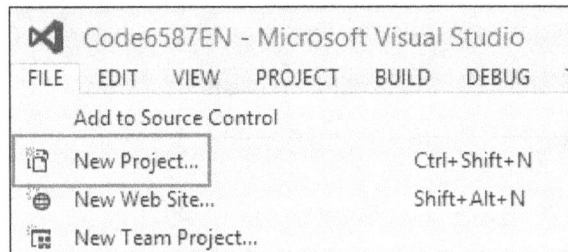

2. Navigate to **Visual C#** | **Office/SharePoint** | **SharePoint Solution** and select **SharePoint 2013 - Empty Project** as shown in the following screenshot:

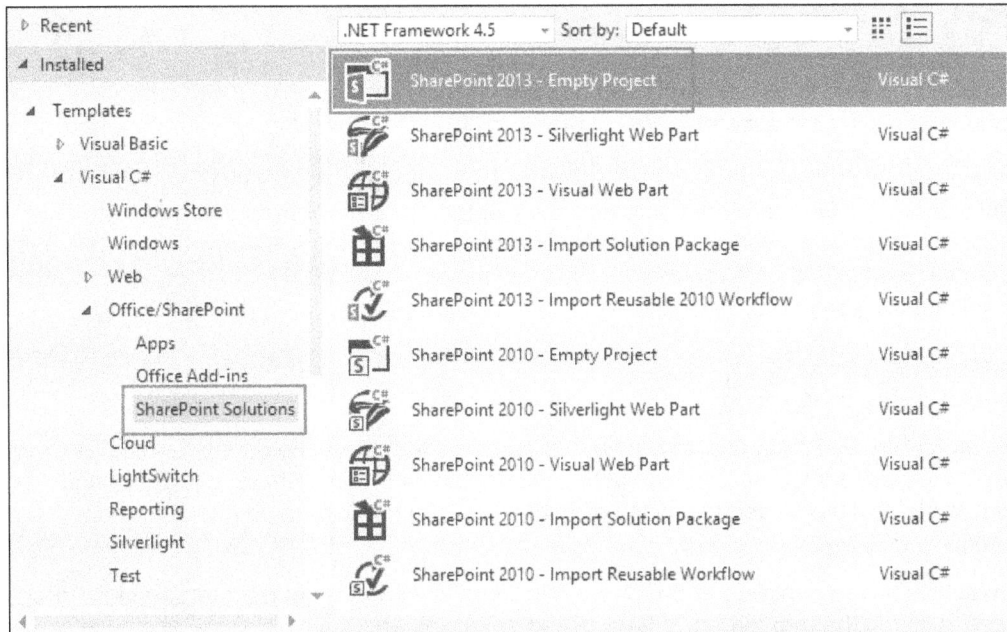

3. Provide a name and location for the project.

Name:	Code6587EN07
Location:	c:\users\administrator\documents\visual studio 2013\Projects
Solution name:	Code6587EN07

4. Click on **OK**.

5. Provide the URL to the local SharePoint site.

6. Select the **Deploy as a farm solution** option.

What site do you want to use for debugging?

http://sharepoint/ | ∨ | Validate

What is the trust level for this SharePoint solution?

○ Deploy as a sandboxed solution

> Clicking this option causes the solution to be deployed as a Sandboxed solution. Sandboxed solutions can be deployed by the site collection owner and are run in a secure, monitored process that has limited resource access.

◉ Deploy as a farm solution

> Clicking this option means that users must have SharePoint administrator privileges to run or deploy the solution.

7. Click on **OK**.

How it works...

A Visual Studio SharePoint project builds a **class library** (an assembly) when compiled. In addition to building the assembly, Visual Studio provides a publishing function that packages the assembly, the manifest, and all the included files into a SharePoint solution (.wsp) file.

When creating a new SharePoint solution, it will default to a sandboxed solution. With any programming, it is a good idea to only have access to what is required for your solution. If your SharePoint project does not require access to elements not allowed in a sandboxed solution, use a sandboxed solution.

There's more...

With SharePoint 2010 and Visual Studio 2010, Microsoft introduced project templates to create, package, deploy, and debug custom SharePoint solutions. SharePoint 2010 and Visual Studio 2010 provided two types of SharePoint solutions: farm solutions and sandboxed solutions.

Farm solutions are deployed at the SharePoint farm level and require a farm administrator access to install them to the farm. **Sandboxed solutions** are deployed at the site collection level and only require a site collection administrator access to install them to the site collection. Farm solutions are provided full access to the SharePoint farm, whereas sandboxed solutions are only provided access to elements within the site collection.

Farm solutions can only be added with PowerShell Cmdlets or the stsadm.exe command. They cannot be added or updated with the web interface. They can, however, be deployed and retracted with the web interface.

Sandboxed solutions can be added, deployed, updated, and retracted with the web interface or PowerShell Cmdlets. They cannot be managed with the stsadm.exe command.

The primary differences between farm and sandboxed solutions are illustrated in the following table (note that this is not a comprehensive list):

Type	Farm solution	Sandboxed solution
Deploys to	Farm solutions store	Site collection solutions gallery
Installation methods	PowerShell Cmdlets and the stsadm.exe command	PowerShell Cmdlets and web interface
Farm features	Yes	No
Web application features	Yes	No
Site collection features	Yes	Yes
Site features	Yes	Yes
Application pages (/_layouts)	Yes	No

Type	Farm solution	Sandboxed solution
Custom action groups	Yes	No
Code-based workflows	Yes	No
Content types and fields	Yes	Yes
Custom actions	Yes	Yes
Declarative workflows	Yes	Yes
Event receivers	Yes	Yes
List definitions and instances	Yes	Yes
Modules	Yes	Yes
Web parts	Yes	Yes
Timer jobs	Yes	No

The IIS worker processes (`w3wp.exe`) executes the farm solution code, whereas the user code solution worker processes (`spucworkerprocess.exe`) executes the sandboxed solution code.

With SharePoint 2013 and Visual Studio 2012, Microsoft has added a third type of SharePoint solution, the SharePoint app. A SharePoint app solution runs isolated from the SharePoint stack, only allows for the client-side and JavaScript object models to be used to interact with SharePoint, and provides a framework to publish apps to and install apps from the SharePoint app store.

Using the SharePoint version as reference, the tools and solutions available in SharePoint are illustrated in the following table:

SharePoint version	2007	2010	2013
Tools available	<ul><li>The assemblies are created with Visual Studio</li><li>The solutions are packaged manually or with third-party tools</li><li>Deployment and debugging during development is done manually</li></ul>	<ul><li>The assemblies and solutions are created in Visual Studio</li><li>One-click deployment and debugging is available in Visual Studio</li></ul>	<ul><li>The assemblies and solutions are created in Visual Studio</li><li>One-click deployment and debugging is available in Visual Studio</li></ul>

SharePoint version	2007	2010	2013
Farm solutions	Yes	Yes	Yes
Sandboxed solutions	No	Yes	Yes
Apps	No	No	Yes

Packaging branding elements, such as master pages and page layouts, can be accomplished with a sandboxed solution. However, since we will be interacting with the web application and a custom timer job in this chapter, we will work with a farm solution throughout this chapter.

See also

▸ The *Solution Schema* topic on MSDN at `http://msdn.microsoft.com/en-us/library/office/ms442108.aspx`

▸ The *Apps for SharePoint Overview* article on MSDN at `http://msdn.microsoft.com/en-us/library/office/fp179930.aspx`

▸ The *Sandboxed Solution Considerations* article on MSDN at `http://msdn.microsoft.com/en-us/library/ee231562.aspx`

▸ The *SharePoint for Developers* article on MSDN at `http://msdn.microsoft.com/en-us/office/dn448478`

Including images, cascading stylesheets, and JavaScript resources in a SharePoint solution

Within a Visual Studio SharePoint solution, we can map project folders to folders on the SharePoint server filesystem. For static content resources, such as images and style sheets, it is ideal to store them on the filesystem of the SharePoint server rather than in the content database of the SharePoint web applications. This allows **Internet Information Services** (**IIS**) to serve up content directly from the filesystem rather than having to request the file from the SQL database before serving it to the client.

There are a number of folders that we can map to, however, the most commonly mapped folders are the `Layouts` and `Images` folders. Files in our project mapped to the `Layouts` folder will be served to the client from the `_layouts/15` URL and files mapped to the `Images` folder will be served from the `_layouts/15/images` URL.

SharePoint 2013 allows SharePoint 2010 solutions to be installed. To accommodate the possibility of two compatibility levels for solutions to be installed, 2013 solution files are served from the _layouts/15 URL, whereas files from the 2010 solution are served from the _layouts URL. This applies to the Layouts and Images folder mappings. Most other folder mapping options do not have two version-specific locations.

In this recipe, we will map the Layouts and Images folders. We will then add content to both.

How to do it...

Follow these steps to map folders and include static resources:

1. From the **Solution Explorer** pane in Visual Studio, right-click on the project name.

2. Select **Add** and then select **SharePoint "Images" Mapped Folder**, as shown in the following screenshot:

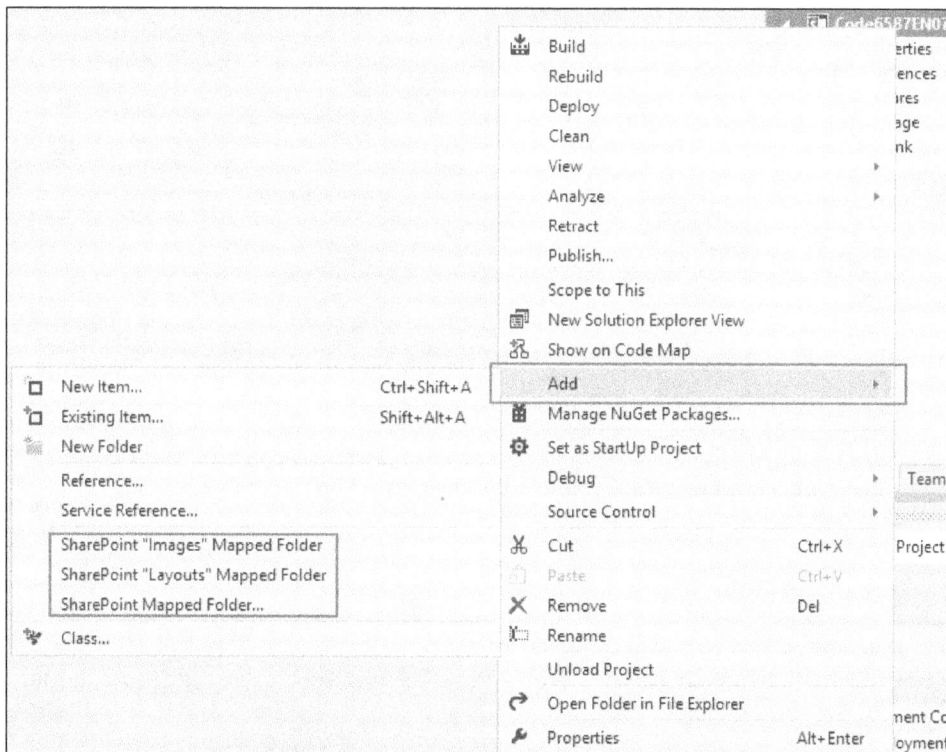

3. From the **Solution Explorer** pane, right-click on the project name.

4. Select **Add** and then select **SharePoint "Layouts" Mapped Folder**.

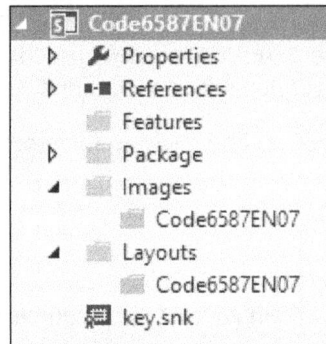

5. Right-click on the folder created under `Images`.

6. Select **Add** and then select **Existing Item**.

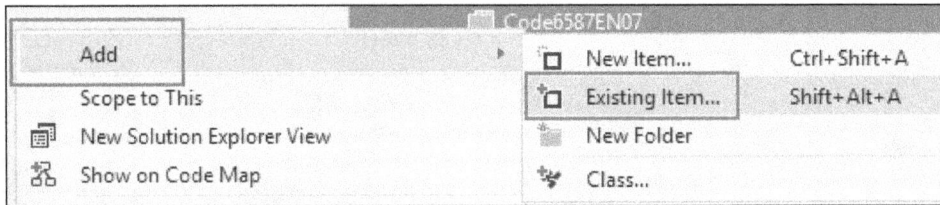

7. Select an image from your filesystem to be included in the folder.

8. Right-click on the folder created under `Layouts`.

9. Select **Add** and then select **New Item**.

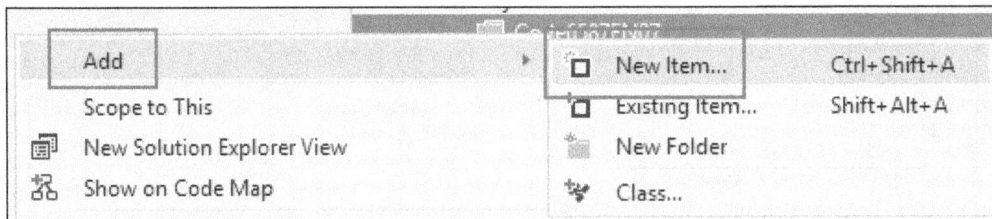

10. Navigate to **Visual C# Items | Web** and select **JavaScript File**, as shown in the following screenshot:

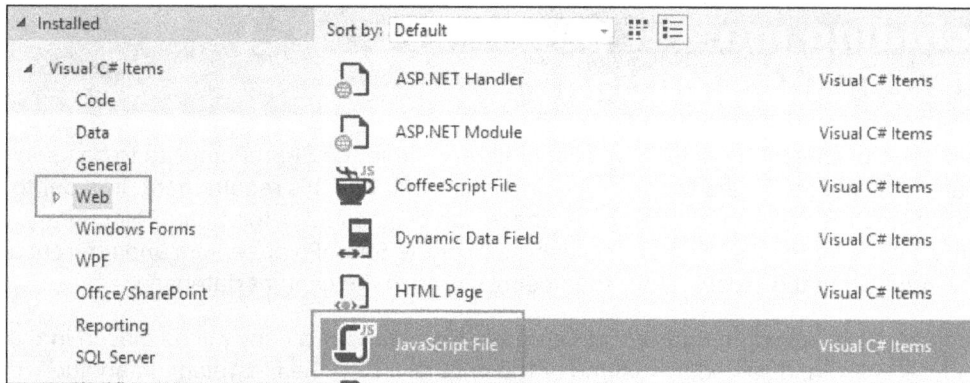

11. Give the new file a name (for example, `Custom.js`).

12. Click on **Add**.

13. Right-click on the folder created under `Layouts`.

14. Click on **Add** and then select **New Item**.

15. Navigate to **Visual C# Items | Web** and select **Style Sheet**.

16. Give the new file a name (for example, `Custom.css`).

17. Click on **Add**.

How it works...

Contents of a mapped folder in a SharePoint solution are added directly to the filesystem of each SharePoint server in the farm when the solution is deployed. The `Layouts` mapped folder, which serves content from the `_layouts/15` URL, is mapped to `C:\Program Files\Common Files\Microsoft Shared\Web Server Extensions\15\Template\Layouts` on the filesystem of the SharePoint servers. The `Images` mapped folder, which serves content from the `_layouts/15/images` URL, is mapped to `C:\Program Files\Common Files\Microsoft Shared\Web Server Extensions\15\Template\Layouts\Images` on the filesystem of the SharePoint servers.

When adding most mapped folders to a SharePoint project, Visual Studio will create subfolders matching the name of the project within the mapped folders. It is important to ensure the files and folders we add to a mapped folder do not conflict with the files and folders included with SharePoint.

See also

► The *How to: Add and Remove Mapped Folders* article on MSDN at `http://msdn.microsoft.com/en-us/library/ee231521.aspx`

Including master pages in a SharePoint solution

Certain types of content must exist in a list or library within the SharePoint site to be usable by SharePoint. Master pages are one type of content that has this requirement. In order to reduce calls to the SQL content database, these can be ghosted in the SharePoint library. Ghosting allows for the file to be on the filesystem of the SharePoint servers and referenced by a placeholder in the library rather than being stored in the content database.

If a ghosted file is edited (in SharePoint Designer, for instance), a copy will be placed in the content database and served up instead of the original file on the filesystem. In addition, the file can be reverted back to being served up by the filesystem.

In this recipe, we will include a copy of the `Seattle.master` master page that we have renamed `Tacoma.master`. You can download a copy of `Seattle.master` from the web interface or with SharePoint Designer.

How to do it...

Follow these steps to include a master page in the solution:

1. From the **Solution Explorer** pane in Visual Studio, right-click on the project name.
2. Click on **Add** and select **New Item**.
3. Navigate to **Visual C# Items | Office/SharePoint** and select **Module**, as shown in the following screenshot:

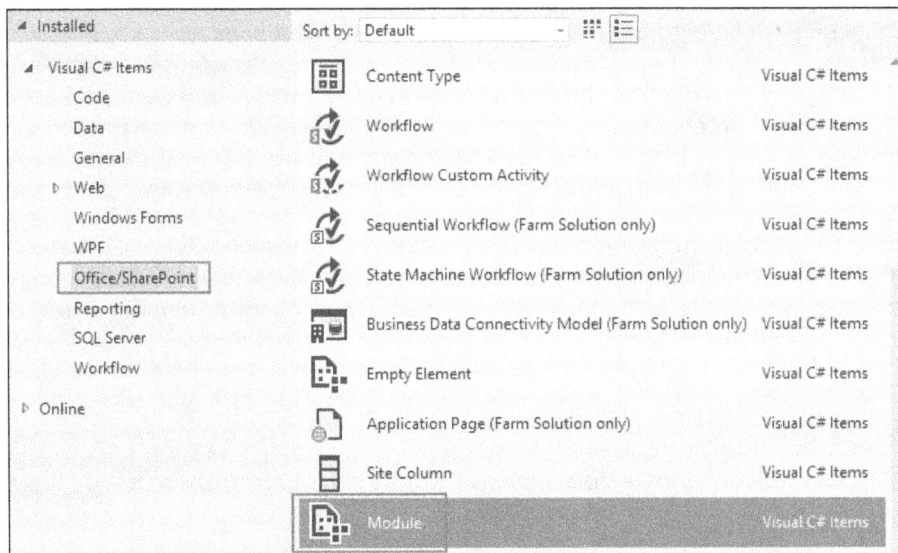

4. Give the module a name (for example, `MasterPages`).

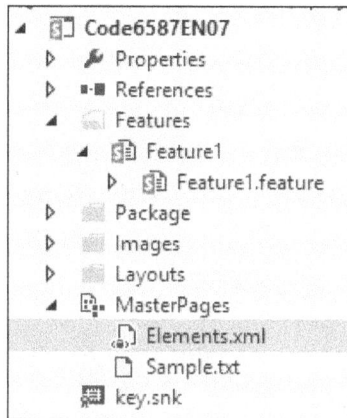

5. Click on **Add**.

```
▲ 🔲 Code6587EN07
   ▷ 🔧 Properties
   ▷ ■·■ References
   ▲ 📄 Features
      ▲ 📄 Feature1
         ▷ 📄 Feature1.feature
   ▷ 📦 Package
   ▷ 🖼 Images
   ▷ 📁 Layouts
   ▲ 📄 MasterPages
      📄 Elements.xml
      📄 Sample.txt
   🔑 key.snk
```

> When adding a new module, Visual Studio will add a `Sample.txt` example file. In addition, if a feature already exists in the project, it will add the module to it. Otherwise, it will add a new feature to the project.

6. Delete the `Sample.txt` file in the `MasterPages` module.

7. Right-click on the `MasterPages` module.

8. Click on **Add** and select **Existing Item**.

9. Select the `Tacoma.master` master page from your filesystem.

10. In the `MasterPages` module, open the `Elements.xml` file.

11. On the `<Module>` element, set the `Url` property to `_catalogs/masterpage`, the `Path` property to null, and the `RootWebOnly` property to `FALSE`, as shown in the following line of code:

```
<Module Name="MasterPages" Url="_catalogs/masterpage" Path=""
RootWebOnly="FALSE">
```

12. On the `<File>` element, set the `Type` property to `GhostableInLibrary`, the `IgnoreIfAlreadyExists` property to `TRUE` and the `Url` property to `Tacoma.master`, as shown in the following line of code:

```
<File Path="MasterPages\Tacoma.master" Type="GhostableInLibrary"
IgnoreIfAlreadyExists="TRUE" Url="Tacoma.master" />
```

The following screenshot shows the `<Module>` and `<File>` elements:

```
Elements.xml
1  <?xml version="1.0" encoding="utf-8"?>
2  <Elements xmlns="http://schemas.microsoft.com/sharepoint/">
3    <Module Name="MasterPages" Url="_catalogs/masterpage" Path="" RootWebOnly="FALSE">
4      <File Path="MasterPages\Tacoma.master" Type="GhostableInLibrary" IgnoreIfAlreadyExists="TRUE" Url="Tacoma.master" />
5    </Module>
6  </Elements>
```

13. Save the `Elements.xml` file.
14. Right-click on the `Feature1` folder in the `Features` folder.
15. Select `Rename`.
16. Rename `Feature1` to `SiteBranding`.
17. Open the **SiteBranding** feature.
18. Set the **Scope** to **Web**.
19. Set the **Title** to `$Resources:Code6587ENCh04,Feature_SiteBranding_Title`; and the **Description** to `$Resources:Code6587ENCh04,Feature_SiteBranding_Description;`.
20. Save the **SiteBranding** feature.

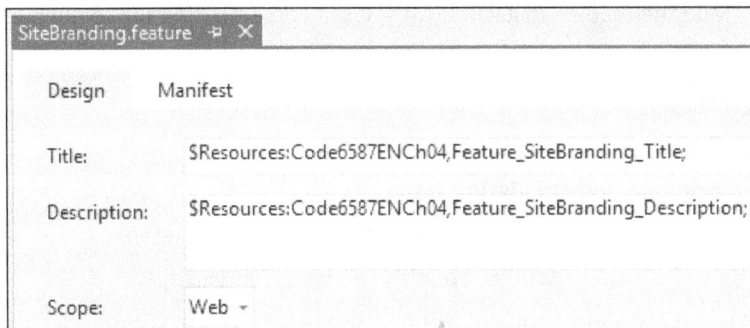

SiteBranding.feature	
Design	Manifest
Title:	$Resources:Code6587ENCh04,Feature_SiteBranding_Title;
Description:	$Resources:Code6587ENCh04,Feature_SiteBranding_Description;
Scope:	Web

How it works...

Adding features to a SharePoint solution creates a feature definition that is deployed to the filesystem of the SharePoint servers. They can be scoped to web (site), site (site collection), web application, or farm. The values entered for the **Title** and **Description** fields are references to string resources that we will create later in the *Adding localization to a SharePoint solution* recipe.

The content that SharePoint needs to refer to in libraries rather than from the `Layouts` folder, such as master pages and page layouts, can be ghosted. Ghosting a file places it in the folder of the feature definition on the filesystem of the SharePoint servers. A placeholder is added to the library to allow access to the file from the library as if it were in the library.

Ghosted files are added to the SharePoint project in a SharePoint module. A SharePoint module can be used to add files to a site. The `Elements.xml` file in a module defines what files are included in the module and the options for adding each file to the site. The `Url` property provides the location of the files in the module that will be added to in the site. With the `Type` property set to `GhostableInLibrary`, the file will be ghosted from the filesystem into the library.

See also

▸   The *Using Modules to Include Files in the Solution* article on MSDN at `http://msdn.microsoft.com/en-us/library/ee231567.aspx`

▸   The *File Element (Module)* topic on MSDN `http://msdn.microsoft.com/en-us/library/ms459213.aspx`

Including page layouts in a SharePoint solution

Page layouts included in a SharePoint solution require additional data to be added to their library properties to associate them with the page layout content type. In this recipe, we will include a copy of the `BlankWebPartPage.aspx` page layout that we have renamed `Tacoma_BlankWebPartPage.aspx` with the appropriate properties. You can download a copy of `BlankWebPartPage.aspx` from the web interface or with SharePoint Designer.

How to do it...

Follow these steps to include a page layout in the solution:

1.   From the **Solution Explorer** pane in Visual Studio, right-click on the project name.

2.   Click on **Add** and then select **New Item**.

3.   Navigate to **Visual C# Items | Office/SharePoint** and select **Module**.

4.   Give a name to the **Module** (for example, `PageLayouts`).

5.   Click on **Add**.

> Since both master pages and page layouts are added to the same SharePoint library, they could both exist in the same module.

6. Delete the `Sample.txt` file in the `PageLayouts` module.

7. Right-click on the `PageLayouts` module.

8. Select **Add** and then select **Existing Item**.

9. Select the `Tacoma_BlankWebPartPage.aspx` page layout from your filesystem.

10. In the `PageLayouts` module, open the `Elements.xml` file.

11. On the `<Module>` element, set the `Url` property to `_catalogs/masterpage`, the `Path` property to null, and the `RootWebOnly` property to FALSE.

    ```
    <Module Name="PageLayouts" Url="_catalogs/masterpage" Path=""
    RootWebOnly="FALSE">
    ```

12. On the `<File>` element, set the `Type` property to `GhostableInLibrary`, the `IgnoreIfAlreadyExists` property to TRUE, and the `Url` property to `Tacoma_BlankWebPartPage.aspx`.

13. In the `<File>` element, add the properties that will be assigned to the file in the SharePoint library.

    ```
    <File Path="PageLayouts\Tacoma_BlankWebPartPage.aspx"
    Type="GhostableInLibrary" IgnoreIfAlreadyExists="TRUE"
    Url="Tacoma_BlankWebPartPage.aspx">

    <Property Name="Title" Value="$Resources:Code6587ENCh04,Tacoma_
    PageLayout_Name;" />

    <Property Name="Description" Value="$Resources:Code6587ENCh04,Taco
    ma_PageLayout_Description;" />

    <Property Name="ContentType" Value="$Resources:cmscore,contentty
    pe_pagelayout_name;" />

    <Property Name="PublishingAssociatedContentType" Value=";#$Resourc
    es:cmscore,contenttype_articlepage_name;;#0x010100C568DB52D9D0A14D
    9B2FDCC96666E9F2007948130EC3DB064584E219954237AF3900242457EFB8B242
    47815D688C526CD44D;#"/>

    </File>
    ```

14. Save the `Elements.xml` file. The following screenshot shows the contents of the `Elements.xml` file:

```
Elements.xml  X
  1    <?xml version="1.0" encoding="utf-8"?>
  2  ⊟<Elements xmlns="http://schemas.microsoft.com/sharepoint/">
  3  ⊟  <Module Name="PageLayouts" Url="_catalogs/masterpage" Path="" RootWebOnly="FALSE">
  4  ⊟    <File Path="PageLayouts\Tacoma_BlankWebPartPage.aspx" Type="GhostableInLibrary" IgnoreIfAlreadyExists="TRUE" Url="Tacoma_BlankWebPartPage.aspx">
  5        <Property Name="Title" Value="$Resources:Code6587ENCh04,Tacoma_PageLayout_Name;" />
  6        <Property Name="Description" Value="$Resources:Code6587ENCh04,Tacoma_PageLayout_Description;" />
  7        <Property Name="ContentType" Value="$Resources:cmscore,contenttype_pagelayout_name;" />
  8        <Property Name="PublishingAssociatedContentType" Value=";#
             $Resources:cmscore,contenttype_articlepage_name;;#0x010100C5880852D9D0A14D9B2FDCC9668669F200794813DEC3D8064584E219954237AF3900242457EF88B24247815D888C525CD44D;#"/>
  9      </File>
 10    </Module>
 11  </Elements>
```

How it works...

In addition to adding files to a SharePoint library, a module can also set the properties of the file in the library. In this recipe, we added a custom page layout to a module and set the properties of the file to provide it with a page layout title and associate it with the page layout content type.

The values of the `Title` and `Description` properties are resource strings that we will create in the *Adding localization to a SharePoint solution* recipe. The `ContentType` property uses a resource string from SharePoint and the `PublishingAssociatedContentType` property instructs SharePoint to make this file a page layout.

The `/_catalog/masterpage` library, where master pages and page layouts are stored, contains multiple content types. If a page layout file is not associated with the page layout content type, it will not be available in the web interface when creating a new content page.

See also

- ▸ The *Using Modules to Include Files in the Solution* article on MSDN at `http://msdn.microsoft.com/en-us/library/ee231567.aspx`

- ▸ The *File Element (Module)* topic on MSDN at `http://msdn.microsoft.com/en-us/library/ms459213.aspx`

Adding localization to a SharePoint solution

To localize the names and descriptions of user interface elements, such as features and web parts, externalized resource files need to be added to the `Resources` mapped folder. In this recipe, we will create English and French language resource files that include resource strings for the names and descriptions of the features we will create in the subsequent recipes.

How to do it...

Follow these steps to add localization resources to the solution:

1. Right-click on the project name in the **Solution Explorer** pane.

2. Click on **Add** and then select **SharePoint Mapped Folder**. The **SharePoint Mapped Folder** dialog will display all of the available folders to map in a tree view as shown in the following screenshot:

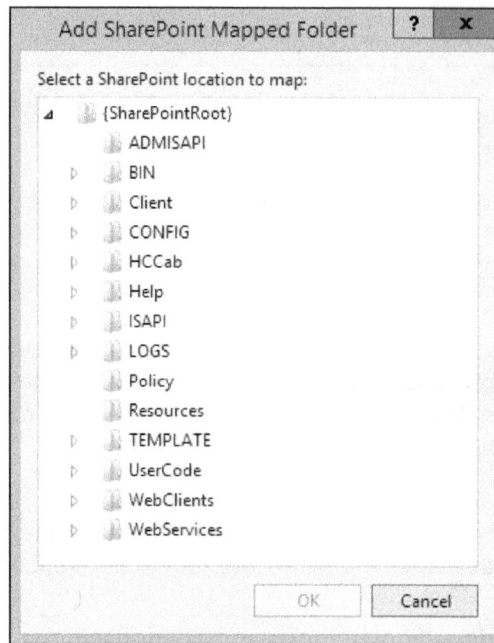

3. Select Resources and click on **OK**.

4. Right-click on the Resources folder.

5. Click on **Add** and then select **New Item**.

6. Navigate to **Visual C# Items | General** and select **Resource File**, as shown in the following screenshot:

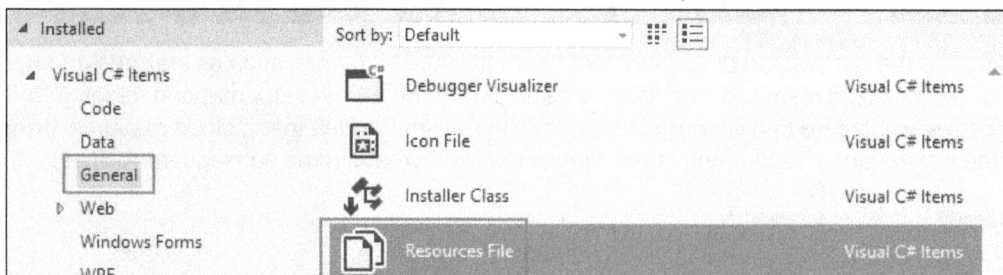

7. Provide a name for the resource file (for example, Code6587ENCh04.resx).

8. Click on **Add**.

9. Repeat steps 5 through 9 to create two additional resource files with the language codes appended to the filename (for example, `Code6587ENCh04.en-US.resx` and `Code6587ENCh04.fr-FR.resx`).

   For resource files, SharePoint requires a default file without the language code added and a resource file for each language code supported. In our example, both the `Code6587ENCh04.resx` and `Code6587ENCh04.en-US.resx` resource files will contain our strings in U.S. English and `Code6587ENCh04.fr-FR.resx` will contain our strings in French.

   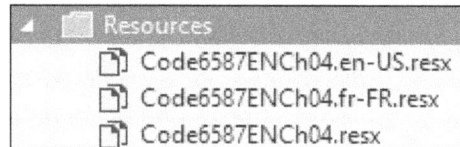

10. Open each resource file and set **Access Modifier** to **No Code Generation**. Since we are not referencing the resource strings in our C# code, we do not need any code generated for the resource files.

    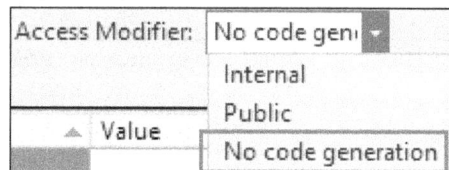

11. In both the default and en-US resource files, add the following English resource strings:

Name	Value
Feature_SiteBranding_Description	Apply our custom branding solution to this SharePoint site
Feature_SiteBranding_Title	Custom branding: Apply to SharePoint site
Feature_SiteCollectionBranding_Description	Apply our custom branding site feature to all sites in this site collection
Feature_SiteCollectionBranding_Title	Custom branding: Apply to all sites in site collection
Tacoma_PageLayout_Description	Demo blank web part page for our custom branding solution
Tacoma_PageLayout_Name	Tacoma blank web part page

The following screenshot shows the English resource strings added to the `Code6587ENCh04.resx` file:

Name	Value	Comment
Feature_SiteBranding_Description	Apply our custom branding solution to this SharePoint Site.	
Feature_SiteBranding_Title	Custom Branding: Apply to SharePoint Site	
Feature_SiteCollectionBranding_Description	Apply our custom branding Site feature to all Sites in this Site Collection.	
Feature_SiteCollectionBranding_Title	Custom Branding: Apply to All Sites in Site Collection	
Tacoma_PageLayout_Description	Demo blank web part page for our custom branding solution.	
Tacoma_PageLayout_Name	Tacoma Blank Web Part Page	

12. In the fr-FR resource file, add the following French resource strings:

Name	Value
Feature_SiteBranding_Description	Appliquer notre solution de personnalisation de SharePoint site
Feature_SiteBranding_Title	Branding personnalisé: Appliquer au site SharePoint
Feature_SiteCollectionBranding_Description	Appliquer notre image de marque fonctionnalités de site personnalisé à tous les sites dans cette collection de sites
Feature_SiteCollectionBranding_Title	Branding personnalisé: S'applique à tous les sites dans la collection de sites
Tacoma_PageLayout_Description	Démo vide page WebPart pour notre solution de personnalisation
Tacoma_PageLayout_Name	Tacoma page web part vierge

The following screenshot shows the French resource strings added to the `Code6587ENCh04.fr-FR.resx` file:

Name	Value	Comment
Code6587ENCh04.fr-FR.resx		
Strings ▾ Add Resource ▾ Remove Resource ▾ Access Modifier: No code gen ▾		
Feature_SiteBranding_Description	Appliquer notre solution de personnalisation de SharePoint Site.	
Feature_SiteBranding_Title	Branding personnalisé : Appliquer au Site SharePoint	
Feature_SiteCollectionBranding_Description	Appliquer notre image de marque fonctionnalités de Site personnalisé à tous les Sites dans cette Collection de sites.	
Feature_SiteCollectionBranding_Title	Branding personnalisé : S'applique à tous les Sites dans la Collection de sites	
Tacoma_PageLayout_Description	Démo vide page WebPart pour notre solution de personnalisation.	
Tacoma_PageLayout_Name	Tacoma Page WebPart vierge	

13. Save the resource files.

How it works...

Localization strings for feature names, web part titles, and other interface elements are stored as resource files (`.resx`) in the Resources folder of the 15 HIVE (`C:\Program Files\ Common Files\Microsoft Shared\Web Server Extensions\15\Resources`). These are standard .NET resource files with no code generation and are stored in XML format.

When IIS is started or restarted, all of the resources in this folder are loaded into memory. If a resource was recently added, but is not being displayed, restarting IIS will force the resources to load.

The French language resource strings were translated from English using the Bing Translator for demonstration purposes. When translating resource strings, a human translator will provide a more accurate translation. Displaying sites in other languages requires the installation of language packs.

See also

▸ *Chapter 10, Creating Multilingual Sites with SharePoint Variations*

▸ The *Resources in .Resx File Format* article on MSDN at `http://msdn.microsoft. com/en-us/library/ekyft91f(v=vs.90).aspx`

▸ The *Localizing SharePoint Solutions* article on MSDN at `http://msdn. microsoft.com/en-us/library/vstudio/ee696750.aspx`

Creating a site feature to apply branding

SharePoint features provide a mechanism to add our custom branding elements to the SharePoint farm at four different scopes. Features can be scoped to the farm level, web application level, site collection level, or site (web) level. In addition to adding content, they can run custom code when activated, upgraded, deactivated, and so on in feature event receivers.

In this recipe, we will create a site (web) scoped feature that adds and configures our branding elements on the site.

How to do it...

Follow these steps to create a feature event receiver:

1. Open the **SiteBranding** feature that was created when creating for our `MasterPages` and `PageLayouts` modules.

2. Verify that both the modules are listed in the **Items in the feature** section.

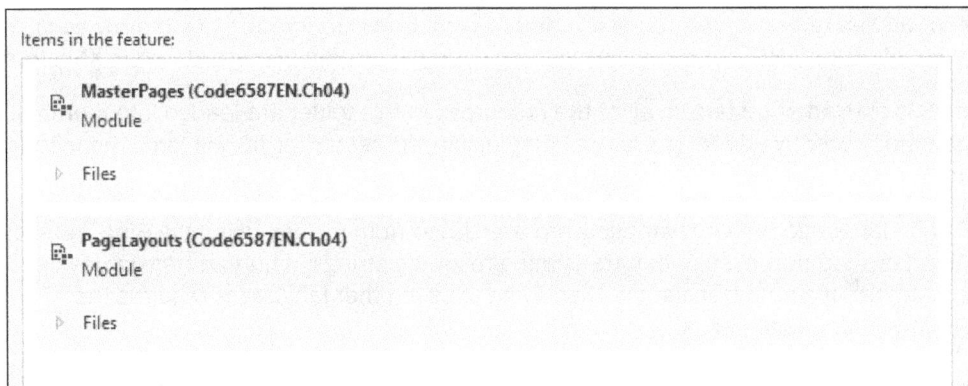

3. Right-click on **SiteBranding.feature** in the `Features` folder.

4. Select **Add Event Receiver** as shown in the following screenshot:

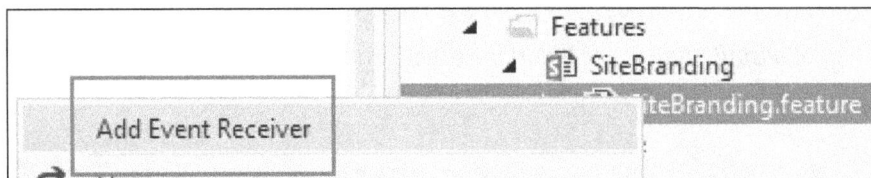

5. In our new `SiteBrandingEventReceiver` class, add the following constant strings that we will use for property names and master page URLs:

```
public class SiteBrandingEventReceiver : SPFeatureReceiver
{

private const string PropertyOldMasterUrl =
"CustomProp::OldMasterUrl";

private const string PropertyOldCustomMasterUrl = "CustomProp::Old
CustomMasterUrl";

private const string TacomaMasterUrl = "_catalogs/masterpage/
Tacoma.master";

private const string SeattleMasterUrl = "_catalogs/masterpage/
Seattle.master";
```

6. Uncomment the `FeatureActivated` and `FeatureDeactivating` methods as shown in the following code:

```
public override void FeatureActivated(SPFeatureReceiverProperties
properties)
{
}

public override void FeatureDeactivating(SPFeatureReceiverProperti
es properties)
{
}
```

7. In the `FeatureActivated` method, get the site in a `using` statement as follows:

```
using (var web = properties.Feature.Parent as SPWeb)
```

8. Ensure the site is not null using the following line of code:

```
if (web != null)
```

9. Get the current value for the `AllowUnsafeUpdates` property on the site and set the value to `true` as follows:

```
var allowUnsafeUpdates = web.AllowUnsafeUpdates;

web.AllowUnsafeUpdates = true;

web.Update();
```

10. Using the following code, remove our custom master page properties if they already exist on the site:

```
if (web.AllProperties.ContainsKey(PropertyOldMasterUrl))
web.AllProperties.Remove(PropertyOldMasterUrl);

if (web.AllProperties.ContainsKey(PropertyOldCustomMasterUrl))
web.AllProperties.Remove(PropertyOldCustomMasterUrl);
```

11. Get the current master page settings for the site using the following code:

```
var masterUrl = web.MasterUrl;

var customMasterUrl = web.CustomMasterUrl;
```

12. Set the current master page settings as the values to our custom master page properties.

```
web.AllProperties.Add(PropertyOldMasterUrl, masterUrl);

web.AllProperties.Add(PropertyOldCustomMasterUrl,
customMasterUrl);
```

13. Set the `Tacoma.master` master page as the master page for the site and system master pages using the following code:

```
web.MasterUrl = TacomaMasterUrl;

web.CustomMasterUrl = TacomaMasterUrl;

web.Update();
```

14. Set the `AllowUnsafeUpdates` property of the site back to its original value.

```
web.AllowUnsafeUpdates = allowUnsafeUpdates;

web.Update();
```

15. In the `FeatureDeactivating` method, get the site in a `using` statement.

```
using (var web = properties.Feature.Parent as SPWeb)
```

16. Ensure the site is not `null`, using the following code:

```
if (web != null)
```

17. Get the current value for the `AllowUnsafeUpdates` property on the site and set the value to `true`.

```
var allowUnsafeUpdates = web.AllowUnsafeUpdates;
web.AllowUnsafeUpdates = true;
web.Update();
```

18. Get the default `Seattle.master` master page URL using the following code:

```
var masterUrl = SeattleMasterUrl;

var customMasterUrl = SeattleMasterUrl;
```

19. Using the following code, check the site properties for the original master page settings we added in the `FeatureActivating` method:

```
if (web.AllProperties.ContainsKey(PropertyOldMasterUrl))
{

    var propertyValue = web.AllProperties[PropertyOldMasterUrl] as
    string;

    if (!string.IsNullOrEmpty(propertyValue))
    masterUrl = propertyValue;

    web.AllProperties.Remove(PropertyOldMasterUrl);

}

if (web.AllProperties.ContainsKey(PropertyOldCustomMasterUrl))
{

    var propertyValue = web.AllProperties[PropertyOldCustomMasterUrl]
    as string;

    if (!string.IsNullOrEmpty(propertyValue))
    customMasterUrl = propertyValue;

    web.AllProperties.Remove(PropertyOldCustomMasterUrl);

}
```

20. Set the original master page as the master page for the site and system master pages.

```
web.MasterUrl = masterUrl;

web.CustomMasterUrl = customMasterUrl;

web.Update();
```

21. Set the `AllowUnsafeUpdates` property of the site back to its original value, using the following code:

```
web.AllowUnsafeUpdates = allowUnsafeUpdates;

web.Update();
```

How it works...

SharePoint features may include event receivers that execute at different points in the life cycle of the feature. In our example, we created `FeatureActivated` and `FeatureDeactivating` event receivers to configure the master page settings when activated or deactivated. In addition, we stored the old master page settings as properties on the site to allow us to restore the settings when the feature is deactivated.

See also

▶ The *Creating SharePoint Features* article on MSDN at `http://msdn.microsoft.com/en-us/library/vstudio/ee231541(v=vs.110).aspx`

▶ The *How to: Create an Event Receiver* article on MSDN at `http://msdn.microsoft.com/en-us/library/vstudio/ee231563.aspx`

▶ The *SPFeatureReceiver.FeatureActivated method* topic on MSDN at `http://msdn.microsoft.com/en-us/library/microsoft.sharepoint.spfeaturereceiver.featureactivated.aspx`

▶ The *SPFeatureReceiver.FeatureDeactivating method* topic on MSDN at `http://msdn.microsoft.com/en-us/library/microsoft.sharepoint.spfeaturereceiver.featuredeactivating.aspx`

▶ The *Walkthough: Add Feature Event Receivers* article on MSDN at `http://msdn.microsoft.com/en-us/library/vstudio/ee231604.aspx`

Creating the site collection feature to apply the feature to new and existing sites

In this recipe, we will create a site collection scoped feature that will activate the site scoped branding feature to all sites in the site collection. In addition, we will add an event receiver to activate the site branding feature on all newly created sites.

How to do it...

Follow these steps to create a site collection feature and the event receivers:

1. Right-click on the `Features` folder.

2. Click on **Add Feature** as shown in the following screenshot:

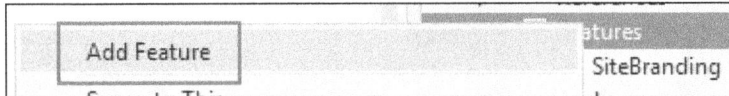

3. Rename the new feature `SiteCollectionBranding`.

4. Open the new **SiteCollectionBranding** feature.

5. Set **Scope** to **Site**.

6. Set **Title** to `$Resources:Code6587ENCh04,Feature_`
   `SiteCollectionBranding_Title;` and **Description** to `$Resources:Code6587`
   `ENCh04,Feature_SiteCollectionBranding_Description;`.

7. Save the `SiteCollectionBranding` feature.

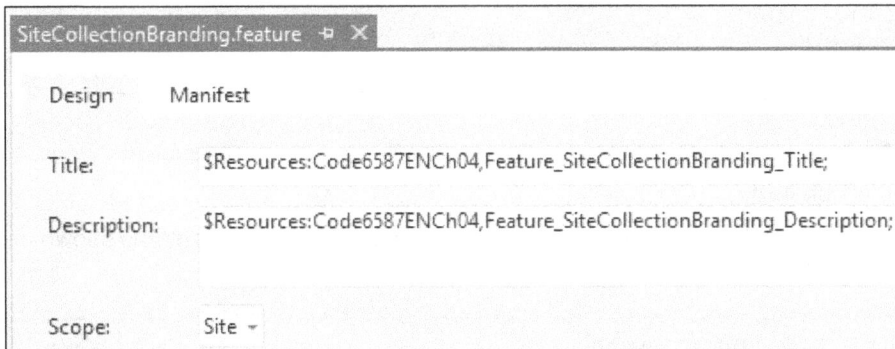

8. Right-click on the project name.

9. Click on **Add** and then select **New Item**.

10. Navigate to **Visual C# Items | Office/SharePoint** and select **Event Receiver**, as shown in the following screenshot:

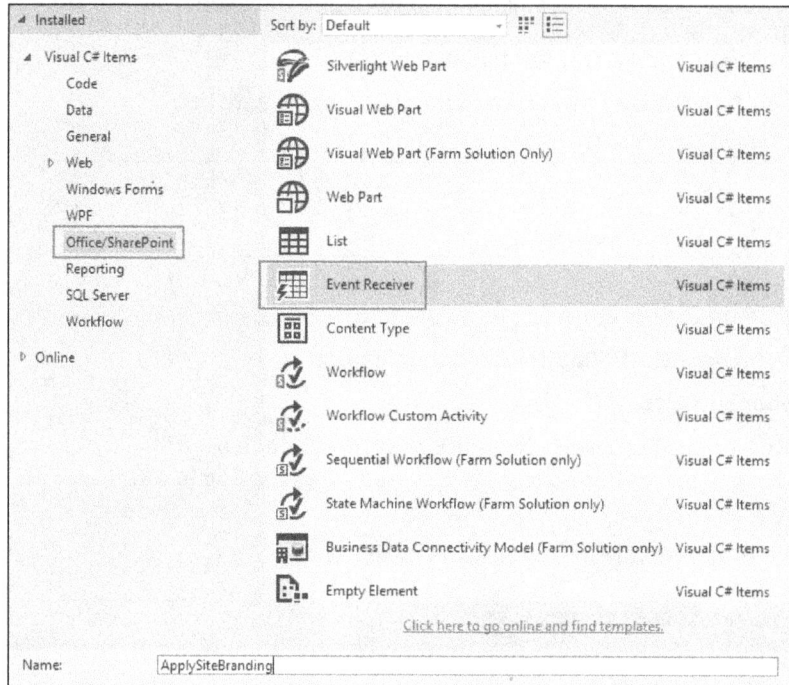

11. Give the event receiver a name (for instance, `ApplySiteBranding`).

12. Click on **Add**.

13. Select **Web Events** for **What type of event receiver do you want?** as shown in the following screenshot:

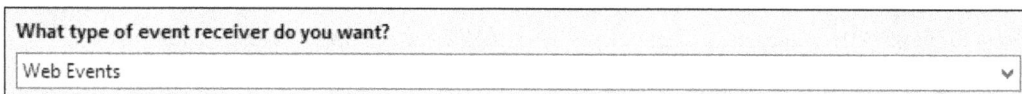

14. Select **A site was provisioned** under **Handle the following events** as shown in the following screenshot:

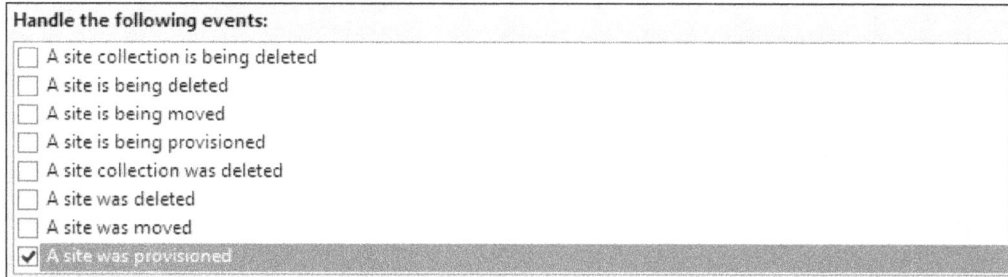

Handle the following events:

☐ A site collection is being deleted
☐ A site is being deleted
☐ A site is being moved
☐ A site is being provisioned
☐ A site collection was deleted
☐ A site was deleted
☐ A site was moved
☑ A site was provisioned

15. Click on **Finish**.

16. Open the **SiteBranding** feature.

17. Ensure that the **ApplySiteBranding** event receiver is not listed under **Items in the feature**.

18. In the **Properties** pane, make a note of the **Feature Id**. We will use this later.

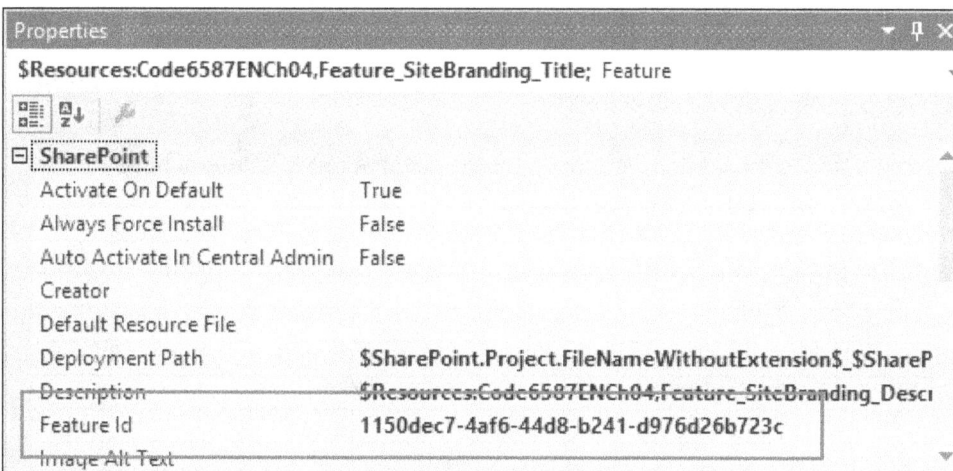

Properties	▼ 🕂 ✕
$Resources:Code6587ENCh04,Feature_SiteBranding_Title; Feature	▼

⊟ **SharePoint**

Activate On Default	True
Always Force Install	False
Auto Activate In Central Admin	False
Creator	
Default Resource File	
Deployment Path	$SharePoint.Project.FileNameWithoutExtension$_$ShareP
Description	$Resources:Code6587ENCh04,Feature_SiteBranding_Descr
Feature Id	1150dec7-4af6-44d8-b241-d976d26b723c
Image Alt Text	

19. Open the **SiteCollectionBranding** feature.

20. Ensure the **ApplySiteBranding** event receiver is listed under **Items in the feature** as shown in the following screenshot:

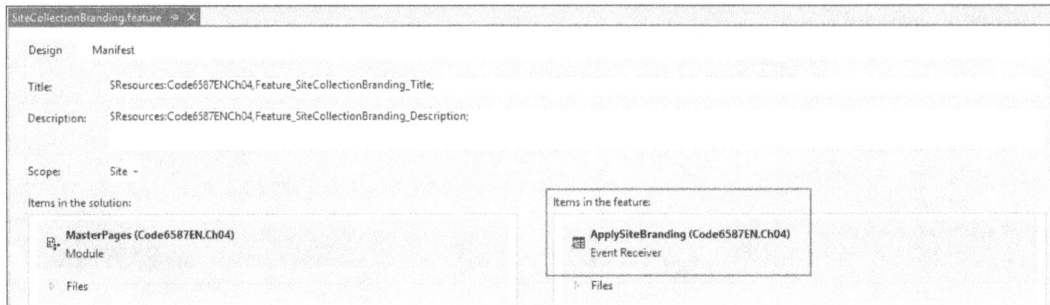

21. In the **Properties** pane, make a note of the feature ID. We will use this later.

22. In the **ApplySiteBranding** event receiver, open the `ApplySiteBranding.cs` file.

23. In the `ApplySiteBranding` class, add a static `GUID` for our **SiteBranding** feature ID. Replace the sample feature ID with the feature ID from your **SiteBranding** feature.

```
public class ApplySiteBranding : SPWebEventReceiver
{

    private static Guid BrandingFeatureId = new Guid("1150dec7-4af6-44d8-b241-d976d26b723c");
```

24. In the `WebProvisioned` method, get the site in a `using` statement as follows:

```
using (var web = properties.Web)
```

25. Ensure the site is not `null`.

```
if (web != null)
```

26. Verify the feature is in the collection of features activated on the site. If it is not activated, add the feature to the collection as follows:

```
if (web.Features[BrandingFeatureId] == null)
web.Features.Add(BrandingFeatureId);
```

27. Save the `ApplySiteBranding.cs` file.

28. Add an event receiver to the **SiteCollectionBranding** feature.

29. In the `SiteCollectionBrandingEventReceiver` class, add a static `GUID` for our **SiteBranding** feature ID. Replace the sample feature ID with the feature ID from your **SiteBranding** feature.

```
public class SiteCollectionBrandingEventReceiver :
SPFeatureReceiver
{
```

```
private static Guid BrandingFeatureId = new Guid("1150dec7-4af6-
44d8-b241-d976d26b723c");
```

30. Uncomment the `FeatureActivated` method.

31. Get the site collection in a `using` statement as follows:

```
using (var site = properties.Feature.Parent as SPSite)
```

32. Ensure the site collection is not `null`.

```
if (site != null)
```

33. Iterate through each site in the site collection.

```
foreach (SPWeb web in site.AllWebs)
```

34. Ensure the site is not `null` and that it exists.

```
if (web != null && web.Exists)
```

35. Verify the feature is in the collection of features activated on the site. If it is not activated, add the feature to the collection using the following code:

```
if (web.Features[BrandingFeatureId] == null)
web.Features.Add(BrandingFeatureId);
```

36. Save the event receiver.

How it works...

In this recipe, we first created a new feature definition for our site collection feature. We then added an event receiver that is triggered any time a new site is created in the site collection. In this event receiver, we are ensuring the site branding feature is activated on newly created sites.

Next, we added an event receiver that is triggered when our new site collection feature is activated. In this event receiver, we are iterating through each site in the site collection to ensure the site branding feature is activated on all existing sites.

The most unique identifiers for SharePoint elements created in Visual Studio, such as the **Feature Id**, will be automatically generated when the item is created.

See also

▶ The *Creating SharePoint Features* article on MSDN at http://msdn.microsoft. com/en-us/library/vstudio/ee231541(v=vs.110).aspx

▶ The *How to Create an Event Receiver* article on MSDN at http://msdn. microsoft.com/en-us/library/vstudio/ee231563.aspx

► The *SPFeatureReceiver.FeatureActivated method* topic on MSDN at `http://msdn.microsoft.com/en-us/library/microsoft.sharepoint.spfeaturereceiver.featureactivated.aspx`

► The *SPWebEventReceiver.WebProvisioned method* topic on MSDN at `http://msdn.microsoft.com/en-us/library/microsoft.sharepoint.spwebeventreceiver.webprovisioned.aspx`

Creating a timer job to ensure the site branding feature is activated

SharePoint provides a framework for tasks that can be executed at scheduled intervals called SharePoint timer jobs. These timer jobs, when configured, are executed by the SharePoint Timer Windows service. In a large site with a lot of contributors, there may be the need to enforce some rules in the environment in a more automated fashion, such as using consistent branding. In this recipe, we will create a timer job that ensures the site branding feature is activated on all sites in the site collection.

How to do it...

Follow these steps to create a timer job:

1. From the **Solution Explorer** pane, right-click on the project name.

2. Select **Add** and then select **Class**.

3. Provide a name for the class (for instance, `BrandingTimerJob`).

4. Give the class a `public` access modifier and inherit from the `SPJobDefinition` base class as follows:

    ```
    public class BrandingTimerJob : SPJobDefinition
    ```

5. In the `BrandingTimerJob` class, add a static `GUID` for our **SiteBranding** feature ID. Replace the sample feature ID with the feature ID from your **SiteBranding** feature as follows:

    ```
    private static Guid BrandingFeatureId = new Guid("1150dec7-4af6-
    44d8-b241-d976d26b723c");
    ```

6. Create the constructors for the `BrandingTimerJob` class using the following code:

    ```
    public BrandingTimerJob(SPWebApplication webApplication, string
    title) :
    base("Custom Branding Job", webApplication, null, SPJobLockType.
    ContentDatabase)
    {

    this.Title = title;
    ```

```
    }
    public BrandingTimerJob() : base() { }
```

7. Create an override for the `Execute` method as follows:

    ```
    public override void Execute(Guid targetInstanceId)
    ```

8. In the `Execute` method, attempt to get the site collection ID associated with the timer job instance using the following code:

    ```
    Guid? siteId = null;

    if (this.Properties.ContainsKey("SiteId"))
    siteId = this.Properties["SiteId"] as Guid?;
    ```

9. Get the site collection in a `using` statement as follows:

    ```
    using (var site = new SPSite(siteId.Value))
    ```

10. Ensure the site collection is not `null` as follows:

    ```
    if (site != null)
    ```

11. Iterate through each site in the site collection as follows:

    ```
    foreach (SPWeb web in site.AllWebs)
    ```

12. Ensure the site is not `null` and that it exists as follows:

    ```
    if (web != null && web.Exists)
    ```

13. Verify that the feature is in the collection of features activated on the site. If it is not activated, add the feature to the collection as follows:

    ```
    if (web.Features[BrandingFeatureId] == null)
    web.Features.Add(BrandingFeatureId);
    ```

14. Save the `BrandingTimerJob.cs` file.

15. Open the `SiteCollectionBranding.EventReceiver.cs` file.

16. Add a static string to the class for formatting the name of our timer jobs as follows:

    ```
    private static string FormatJobName = "Custom Branding Job_{0}";
    ```

17. In the `FeatureActivated` method, after the `foreach` loop iterates through each site in the site collection, create the timer job name, get the web application ID, and then get the site collection ID as follows:

    ```
    var jobName = string.Format(CultureInfo.InvariantCulture,
    FormatJobName, site.ID.ToString());

    var webAppId = site.WebApplication.Id;

    var siteId = site.ID;
    ```

18. Add a `delegate` method to be executed by the `SPSecurity.RunWithElevatedPrivleges` method as follows:

```
SPSecurity.RunWithElevatedPrivileges(delegate()
{

});
```

19. In the `delegate` method, get the web application as follows:

```
var webApplication = SPWebService.ContentService.
WebApplications[webAppId];
```

20. Using the following code, delete any timer jobs that already exist on the web application with the same name as the timer job we are about to instantiate:

```
foreach (SPJobDefinition job in webApplication.JobDefinitions.
Where(p => p.Name == jobName))
job.Delete();
```

21. Instantiate `BrandingTimerJob` and give it a daily schedule.

```
var brandingJob = new BrandingTimerJob(webApplication, jobName);

brandingJob.Properties.Add("SiteId", siteId);

brandingJob.Schedule = new SPDailySchedule() { BeginHour = 1 };

brandingJob.Update();
```

22. Uncomment the `FeatureDeactivating` method.

23. In the `FeatureDeactivating` method, get the site collection in a `using` statement as follows:

```
using (var site = properties.Feature.Parent as SPSite)
```

24. Ensure the site collection is not `null` as follows:

```
if (site != null)
```

25. Create the job name and get the web application ID as follows:

```
var jobName = string.Format(CultureInfo.InvariantCulture,
FormatJobName, site.ID.ToString());

var webAppId = site.WebApplication.Id;
```

26. Using the following code, add a `delegate` method to be executed by the `SPSecurity.RunWithElevatedPrivleges` method:

```
SPSecurity.RunWithElevatedPrivileges(delegate()
{
});
```

27. In the `delegate` method, get the web application as follows:

```
var webApplication = SPWebService.ContentService.
WebApplications[webAppId];
```

28. Delete all timer jobs on the web application that match the job name as follows:

```
foreach (SPJobDefinition job in webApplication.JobDefinitions.
Where(p => p.Name == jobName))
job.Delete();
```

29. Save the event receiver.

How it works...

A SharePoint timer job can be created for various scopes in the SharePoint farm. These scopes include the farm, a web application, a service application, and so on. In our example, we created a timer job at the web application level with the ID of the site collection. This allows for us to have multiple timer jobs in the web application for various site collections. Our timer job runs daily to ensure all sites in the site collection have the site branding feature enabled.

Using the `RunWithElevatedPrivileges` method, we can run the code as the SharePoint farm account. This essentially provides full administrator access to the SharePoint farm. As such, this technique should be used sparingly and in limited scopes. When passing variables into the delegate method, it is important to use simple types, such as strings, integers, and GUIDs. Passing complex objects, such as a site collection (`SPSite`), can result in the objects referencing the wrong SharePoint content.

See also

▶ The *SPJobDefinition class* topic on MSDN at `http://msdn.microsoft.com/en-us/library/office/microsoft.sharepoint.administration.spjobdefinition.aspx`

▶ The *Creating Timer Jobs in SharePoint 2010 That Target Specific Web Applications* article on MSDN at `http://msdn.microsoft.com/EN-US/library/hh528518(v=office.14).aspx`

Packaging and deploying the SharePoint solution

Visual Studio provides a simple one-click method to package a SharePoint project as a SharePoint solution. Once packaged, solutions can be deployed from the Visual Studio interface. In addition, packaged solutions can be deployed with PowerShell and .NET code.

How to do it...

Follow these steps to package and deploy the solution:

1. From the **Solution Explorer** pane, right-click on the project name.
2. Select **Publish** as shown in the following screenshot:

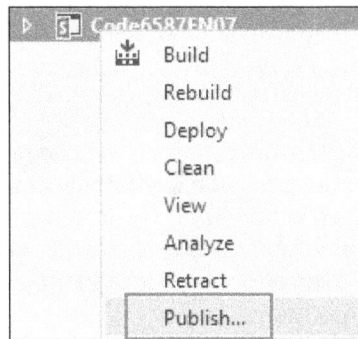

3. Provide a location to output the SharePoint solution file.
4. Click on **Publish**.

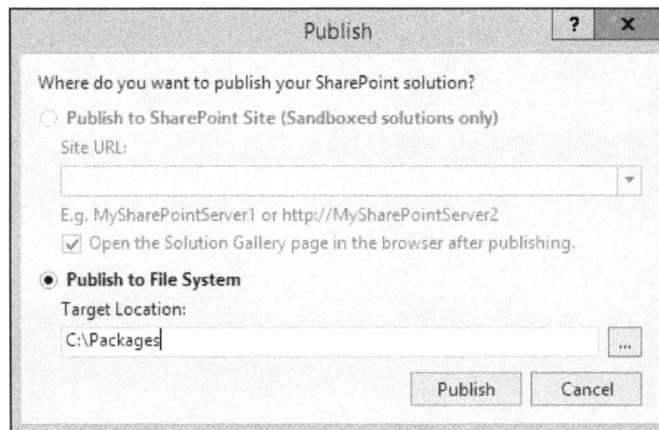

5. From the **BUILD** menu, select **Deploy Solution** as shown in the following screenshot:

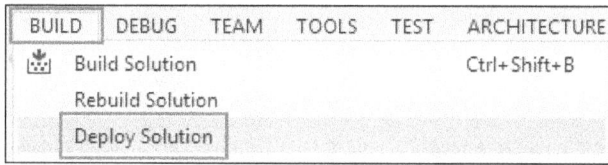

BUILD	DEBUG	TEAM	TOOLS	TEST	ARCHITECTURE
📥 Build Solution					Ctrl+Shift+B
Rebuild Solution					
Deploy Solution					

How it works...

When Visual Studio publishes (or packages) a SharePoint project, it creates a SharePoint solution file (wsp) that contains a manifest, the assemblies, and any other files that are included. The SharePoint solution is then outputted to the folder specified.

In addition, Visual Studio has the ability to deploy the solution to the local SharePoint server from the Visual Studio interface. Using this method, we will retract the solution if it already exists, and then add and deploy the solution.

There's more...

Deploying SharePoint solutions can also be accomplished with PowerShell or code using the server-side object model.

Deploying a solution using PowerShell

Follow these steps to deploy a solution using PowerShell:

1. Use the Add-SPSolution Cmdlet to add the solution to the SharePoint farm using the following code:

   ```
   Add-SPSolution -LiteralPath "C:\Packages\Code6587EN.Ch04.wsp"
   ```

2. Use the Install-SPSolution Cmdlet to deploy the solution to the SharePoint farm.

   Certain code, such as our custom timer job, requires the assembly to be in the Global Assembly Cache on the SharePoint servers so that the SharePoint Timer service can access it. To ensure our assembly gets added to the Global Assembly Cache, we will use the -GACDeployment parameter as follows:

   ```
   Install-SPSolution Code6587EN.Ch04.wsp -GACDeployment
   ```

> When deploying SharePoint solutions on a large scale, it is prudent to check if the solution already exists on the farm in order to upgrade the solution rather than installing it. In addition, if the solution contains web application resources, such as safe control entries, the `Install-SPSolution` Cmdlet will need to target web applications.
>
> The code sample included with this book for this recipe illustrates an example of identifying these parameters before performing the appropriate action.

Deploying a solution with code using the server-side object model

Follow these steps to deploy a solution with code using the server-side object model:

1. Add the following SharePoint solution to the solutions' collection on the local SharePoint farm:

   ```
   var farmSolution = SPFarm.Local.Solutions.Add("C:\\Packages\\
   Code6587EN.Ch04.wsp");
   ```

2. Deploy the SharePoint solution globally using the following command:

   ```
   farmSolution.Deploy(DateTime.Now, true, false);
   ```

See also

► The *Deploying, Publishing, and Upgrading SharePoint Solution Packages* article on MSDN at `http://msdn.microsoft.com/en-us/library/ee231559.aspx`

► The *How to Deploy and Publish a SharePoint Solution to a Local SharePoint Site* article on MSDN at `http://msdn.microsoft.com/en-us/library/ee231565.aspx`

Activating the site collection feature on all site collections with PowerShell

With our custom branding solution deployed to the SharePoint farm, we need to activate the site collection feature. The simplest method to activate the site collection feature on all site collections is using PowerShell.

How to do it...

Follow these steps to activate the feature on each site collection in the farm:

1. Assign the `SiteCollectionBranding` feature ID to a PowerShell variable, using the following command:

   `$brandingFeatureId = [GUID] "19e46226-efb9-4761-b09a-cb8711fd503a"`

2. Use the `Get-SPWebApplication` Cmdlet to get the content web applications and iterate through them as follows:

   ```
   foreach ($webApp in (Get-SPWebApplication))
   ```

3. Iterate through each site collection in the web application using the following code:

   ```
   foreach ($site in $webApp.Sites)
   ```

4. Ensure the site collection is in 2013 mode.

   ```
   if ($site.CompatibilityLevel -eq 15)
   ```

5. Verify that the `SiteCollectionBranding` feature is in the collection of activated features on the site collection. If the feature is not activated, add it to the collection as follows:

   ```
   if ($site.Features[$brandingFeatureId] -eq $null)
   {

   $site.Features.Add($brandingFeatureId)

   }
   ```

6. Use the `Dispose` method to discard the `SPSite` object.

   ```
   $site.Dispose()
   ```

How it works...

In this recipe, we retrieved all of the content web applications with the `Get-SPWebApplication` Cmdlet. For each web application we then iterated through each site collection in the `Sites` property. Lastly, we checked to ensure the site collection feature was activated on each site collection.

Adding or removing features is accomplished by adding or removing them from the collection of features exposed with the `Features` property of the web application, site collection, or site.

There's more...

Activating the site collection feature on all site collections can also be done with code using the server-side object model. Follow these steps to activate the site collection feature with code using the server-side object model:

1. Assign the `SiteCollectionBranding` feature ID to a variable as follows:

```
var featureBrandingSiteCollectionId = new Guid("19e46226-efb9-
4761-b09a-cb8711fd503a");
```

2. Iterate through each content web application.

```
foreach (SPWebApplication webApp in SPWebService.ContentService.
WebApplications)
```

3. Iterate through each site collection in the web application.

```
foreach (SPSite site in webApp.Sites)
```

4. Ensure the site collection is in 2013 mode.

```
if (site.CompatibilityLevel == 15)
```

5. Verify if the `SiteCollectionBranding` feature is in the collection of activated features on the site collection. If not, add the feature to the collection as follows:

```
if (site.Features[featureBrandingSiteCollectionId] == null)
site.Features.Add(featureBrandingSiteCollectionId);
```

See also

▶ The *Get-SPWebApplication* topic on Technet `http://technet.microsoft.com/en-us/library/ff607562.aspx`

5
Enhancing the Content Creation Process with the SharePoint Publishing Architecture

In this chapter, we will explore the publishing features of SharePoint 2013. We will cover the following recipes:

- ▶ Setting up a new publishing site
- ▶ Enabling the publishing features on an existing site
- ▶ Setting up contributor and approver access for publishing content
- ▶ Configuring the versioning settings of the Pages library
- ▶ Creating a publishing web part page
- ▶ Checking out publishing content for editing
- ▶ Checking in edited publishing content
- ▶ Publishing checked in publishing content
- ▶ Approving publishing content
- ▶ Reverting publishing content to a previous version
- ▶ Setting up a publishing site with workflow
- ▶ Creating a web part page and adding web parts with PowerShell
- ▶ Identifying all checked-out publishing pages in a site with PowerShell
- ▶ Creating an image rendition
- ▶ Inserting an image rendition into page content

Introduction

The publishing features provide the core functionality of web content management for SharePoint. At its lowest level, the publishing features are provided for a group of content authors to provide web content to a larger audience. This can include public-facing websites for customers, extranets for partners and vendors, and intranets for employees.

In a public-facing website scenario, a marketing team may collaborate on sales and product information to be viewed by customers. In an intranet scenario, a corporate communications team and a human resources team may collaborate on corporate announcements and benefits information to be viewed by employees.

Though the publishing features of SharePoint were designed with web content management in mind, they can be used for a variety of other purposes. For instance, the publishing features can be used for authoring, publishing, and approving Microsoft Word documents. A sales department might use these features when creating customer contracts that require approval from the legal department.

Setting up a new publishing site

SharePoint publishing capabilities are enabled with two SharePoint features, one at the site collection level and the other at the site level. With the site collection feature activated, the publishing site templates are made available to use when creating new sites in the site collection. These site templates automatically activate the required publishing feature at the site level. In this recipe, we will create a new publishing site in an existing site collection.

The SharePoint publishing site templates will only be available for use when the **SharePoint Server Publishing Infrastructure** site collection feature is activated.

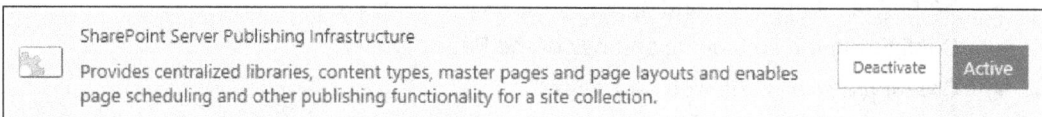

	SharePoint Server Publishing Infrastructure		
	Provides centralized libraries, content types, master pages and page layouts and enables page scheduling and other publishing functionality for a site collection.	Deactivate	Active

How to do it...

Follow these steps to set up a new publishing site:

1. Navigate to the site in your preferred web browser.
2. Select **Site contents** from the **Settings** menu.
3. Select **new subsite** from the **Subsites** section as shown in the following screenshot:

Subsites

⊕ new subsite

4. On the **New SharePoint Site** page, provide a title, description, and URL for the new site in the **Title**, **Description**, and **URL** fields.

5. Select the **Publishing Site** template from the **Publishing** tab as shown in the following screenshot:

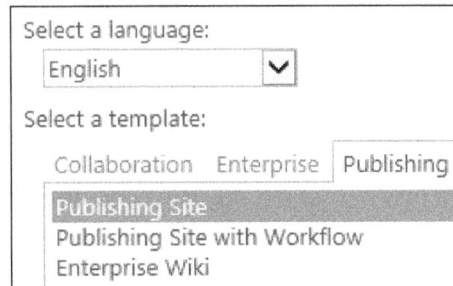

Select a language:

English ▾

Select a template:

Collaboration   Enterprise | Publishing

Publishing Site
Publishing Site with Workflow
Enterprise Wiki

6. Click on **Create**.

How it works...

Site templates in SharePoint provide instructions on how a new site is provisioned. This includes pages, features, lists, libraries, and custom provisioning handlers. The **Publishing Site** template activates the site scoped publishing feature and creates the libraries for a publishing site.

> SharePoint provides two publishing site templates: **Publishing Site** and **Publishing Site with Workflow**. A **Publishing Site with Workflow** template provides built-in workflows to schedule the publishing of content.

There's more...

SharePoint sites may also be created with PowerShell and code using the server-side object model. In PowerShell, the `New-SPWeb` Cmdlet has been provided for creating new SharePoint sites. In code, we add it to the collection of sites in the site collection object.

Setting up a new publishing site using PowerShell

To set up a new publishing site using PowerShell, use the `New-SPWeb` Cmdlet to create the site with the complete URL to the new site, the site template, a name, and a description. In addition, indicate that the site will be added to the navigation section (quick launch and top navigation) of the parent site and that the site will not inherit permissions from the parent site.

```
New-SPWeb -Url "http://sharepoint/publishing" -Template "CMSPUBLISHING#0"
-Name "Publishing Site" -Description "A publishing site. "
-AddToQuickLaunch -AddToTopNav -UniquePermissions
```

> Use the `Get-SPWebTemplate` Cmdlet to get a full list of available templates. `CMSPUBLISHING#0` is the identifier for the **Publishing Site** template.

Setting up a new publishing site with code using the server-side object model

Follow these steps to set up a new publishing site with code using the server-side object model:

1. Open the site collection in a `using` statement. For example:

   ```
   using (var site = new SPSite("http://sharepoint/"))
   ```

2. Add a new site to the site collection with the relative URL, a name, a description, a language, and the template.

   ```
   site.AllWebs.Add("publishing", "Publishing Site", "A site about
   publishing.", (uint) site.RootWeb.Locale.LCID, "CMSPUBLISHING#0",
   true, false);
   ```

> For the language, we are simply using the language of the root site in the site collection. Any language that has been installed on the SharePoint farm may be used.

See also

▶ The *New-SPWeb* topic on MSDN at `http://technet.microsoft.com/en-us/library/ff607579.aspx`

▶ The *SPSite class* topic on MSDN at `http://msdn.microsoft.com/en-us/library/microsoft.sharepoint.spsite.aspx`

▶ The *SPWebCollection.Add method* topic on MSDN at `http://msdn.microsoft.com/en-us/library/ms473439.aspx`

Enabling the publishing features on an existing site

In addition to using the SharePoint publishing site templates, publishing capabilities may be enabled on an existing site by activating the SharePoint Server Publishing feature. In this recipe, we will activate the **SharePoint Server Publishing** feature on an existing site.

How to do it...

Follow these steps to enable publishing features on an existing site:

1. Navigate to the site in your preferred web browser.
2. Select **Site settings** from the **Settings** menu.
3. Select **Manage site features** from the **Site Actions** section as shown in the following screenshot:

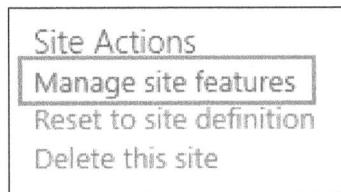

4. Activate the **SharePoint Server Publishing** feature.

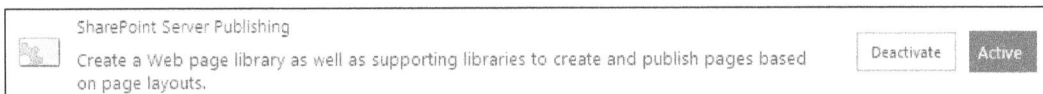

How it works...

The **SharePoint Server Publishing** feature creates the SharePoint libraries used for a publishing site. These include the **Pages** and **Images** libraries.

There's more...

SharePoint features may also be managed with PowerShell and code using the server-side object model. The feature identifier for the **SharePoint Server Publishing Infrastructure** site collection feature is `f6924d36-2fa8-4f0b-b16d-06b7250180fa` and the feature identifier for the **SharePoint Server Publishing** feature is `94c94ca6-b32f-4da9-a9e3-1f3d343d7ecb`.

Enabling the publishing features on an existing site using PowerShell

Follow these steps to enable publishing features on an existing site using PowerShell:

1. Assign the feature identifiers to variables as follows:

    ```
    $featureSiteCollection = [GUID]"f6924d36-2fa8-4f0b-b16d-
    06b7250180fa"


    $featureSite = [GUID]"94c94ca6-b32f-4da9-a9e3-1f3d343d7ecb"
    ```

2. Get the site using the `Get-SPWeb` Cmdlet as follows:

    ```
    $web = Get-SPWeb http://sharepoint/publishing
    ```

3. Ensure the site collection features collection contains the site collection feature as follows:

    ```
    if ($web.Site.Features[$featureSiteCollection] -eq $null)
    {
    $web.Site.Features.Add($featureSiteCollection)
    }
    ```

4. Ensure the site features collection contains the site feature as follows:

    ```
    if ($web.Features[$featureSite] -eq $null)
    {
    $web.Features.Add($featureSite)
    }
    ```

5. Use the following `Dispose` method to discard the `SPWeb` object:

    ```
    $web.Dispose()
    ```

Enabling the publishing features on an existing site with code using the server-side object model

Follow these steps to enable publishing features on an existing site with code using the server-side object model:

1. Assign the feature identifiers to variables as follows:

    ```
    var FeatureSiteCollection = new Guid("f6924d36-2fa8-4f0b-b16d-
    06b7250180fa");
    var FeatureSite = new Guid("94c94ca6-b32f-4da9-a9e3-
    1f3d343d7ecb");
    ```

2. Open the site collection containing the site in a `using` statement as follows:

    ```
    using (var site = new SPSite("http://sharepoint/publishing"))
    ```

3. Using the following code, ensure the site features' collection contains the site collection feature:

```
if (site.Features[FeatureSiteCollection] == null)
site.Features.Add(FeatureSiteCollection);
```

4. Open the site in a `using` statement as follows:

```
using (var web = site.OpenWeb())
```

5. Using the following code, ensure the site features collection contains the site feature:

```
if (web.Features[FeatureSite] == null)
{
web.Features.Add(FeatureSite);
}
```

See also

▸   The *SPFeatureCollection.Add method* topic on MSDN at http://msdn. microsoft.com/en-us/library/ms456927.aspx

Setting up contributor and approver access for publishing content

Using the content approval capabilities of SharePoint, we can allow for certain users to collaborate on an item and then submit it for approval before it becomes available to other users. In this recipe, we will configure content approval on the **Pages** library and set up the contributor and approver groups.

With the content approval features, we can also use SharePoint workflows to streamline the approval process. SharePoint comes with the **Publishing Approval Workflow** feature that provides a basic approval workflow. Customized workflows may also be created with SharePoint Designer and Visual Studio. For more information on workflows refer to http:// msdn.microsoft.com/en-us/library/office/jj163917.aspx.

How to do it...

Follow these steps to set up a contributor and approver access:

1. Navigate to the site in your preferred web browser.
2. Select **Site settings** from the **Settings** menu.

3. Select **Site permissions** from the **Users and Permissions** section.

> Users and Permissions
> People and groups
> Site permissions
> Site collection administrators
> Site app permissions

> [💡 If the site is inheriting permissions from the parent site, select **Stop Inheriting Permissions** from the ribbon.]

4. Select **Create Group** from the ribbon.

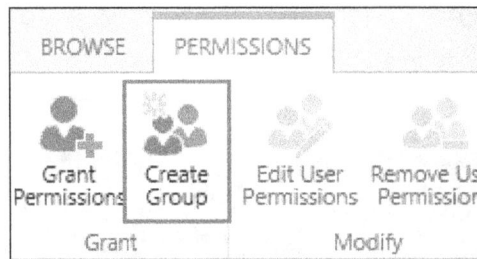

> BROWSE   PERMISSIONS
>
> Grant Permissions   Create Group   Edit User Permissions   Remove User Permission
>
> Grant   Modify

5. Name the group `Pages Contributors` and click on **Create Group**.

6. Repeat the previous step to create a group named `Pages Approvers`.

7. Select **Site contents** from the **Settings** menu.

8. Select the **Pages** library.

9. Select **Library Settings** from the **Library** tab on the ribbon.

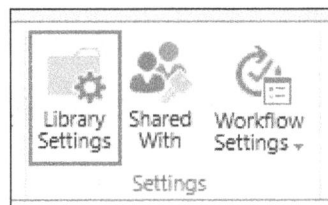

> Library Settings   Shared With   Workflow Settings
>
> Settings

10. Select **Versioning settings** from the **General Settings** section as shown in the following screenshot:

General Settings

▫ List name, description and navigation

▫ Versioning settings

▫ Advanced settings

▫ Validation settings

▫ Column default value settings

▫ Manage item scheduling

▫ Audience targeting settings

▫ Rating settings

▫ Form settings

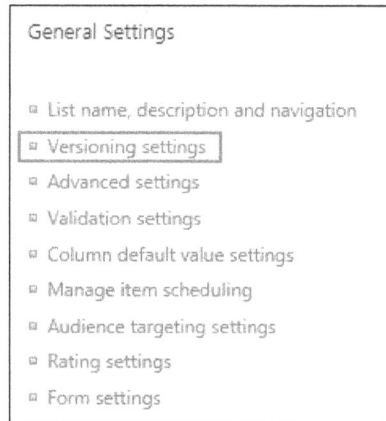

11. Set the **Require content approval for submitted items** checkbox to **Yes** as shown in the following screenshot:

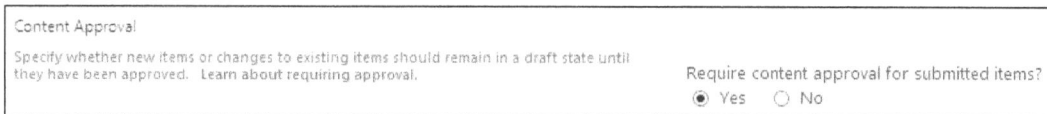

Content Approval

Specify whether new items or changes to existing items should remain in a draft state until they have been approved.   Learn about requiring approval.

Require content approval for submitted items?

◉ Yes   ○ No

12. Click on **OK**.

13. Select **Permissions for this document library** from the **Permissions and Management** section as shown in the following screenshot:

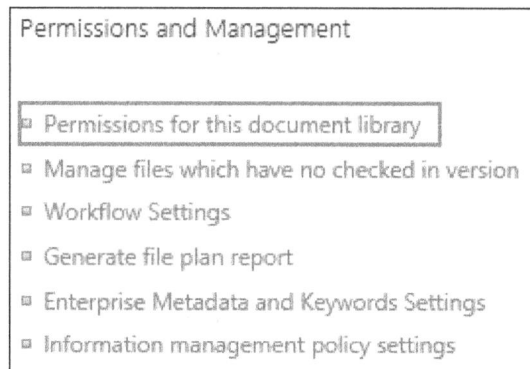

Permissions and Management

▫ Permissions for this document library

▫ Manage files which have no checked in version

▫ Workflow Settings

▫ Generate file plan report

▫ Enterprise Metadata and Keywords Settings

▫ Information management policy settings

14. Select **Stop Inheriting Permissions** from the **PERMISSIONS** tab on the ribbon as shown in the following screenshot:

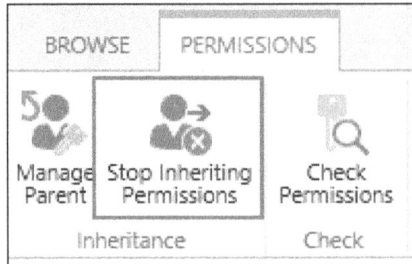

15. Select **Grant Permissions** from the **PERMISSIONS** tab on the ribbon as shown in the following screenshot:

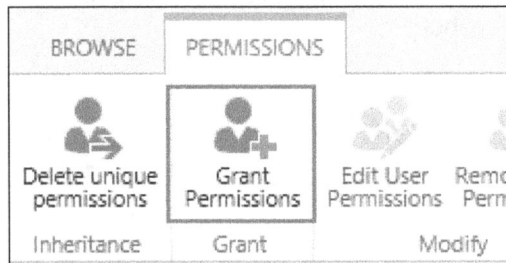

16. Enter **Pages Contributors**.

17. Select **Show Options**.

18. Select **Contribute** for the **Select a permission level** option as shown in the following screenshot:

19. Select **Share**.
20. Repeat steps 15 to 19 to provide the **Approve** permission level to the **Pages Approvers** group.

How it works...

Permissions in SharePoint are granted to a user based on the roles assigned to the user or a group the user belongs to. User and group roles, such as **Contribute**, may be assigned at the site collection, site, list, library, or individual item level. In this recipe, we provided **Approve** and **Contribute** roles to two groups at the library level.

There's more...

Managing library settings, creating SharePoint groups, and assigning SharePoint roles may also be accomplished with PowerShell or code using the server-side object model.

Setting up contributor and approver access using PowerShell

Follow these steps to set up contributor and approver access using PowerShell:

1. Assign the default username to a variable. We will use this user as the owner and first member of the SharePoint groups we are about to create.

    ```
    $defaultUserName = "domain\user"
    ```

2. Get the site using the Get-SPWeb Cmdlet as follows:

    ```
    $web = Get-SPWeb "http://sharepoint/publishing"
    ```

3. Get the **Pages** library from the site as follows:

    ```
    $pages = $web.Lists["Pages"]
    ```

4. If the **Pages** library is inheriting permissions from the site, break the inheritance. Set the parameter to false to indicate that we do not want to copy the existing permissions from the parent site.

    ```
    if ($pages.HasUniqueRoleAssignments -eq $false) { $pages.
    BreakRoleInheritance($false) }
    ```

5. Set the EnableModeration property of the **Pages** library to turn on content approval for the library.

    ```
    $pages.EnableModeration = $true
    ```

6. Update the **Pages** library using the following command:

    ```
    $pages.Update()
    ```

7. Get the default user from the site as a `Microsoft.SharePoint.SPMember` object.

```
$member = [Microsoft.SharePoint.SPMember] $web.
Users[$defaultUserName]
```

8. Get the default user from the site as a `Microsoft.SharePoint.SPUser` object
   as follows:

```
$user = [Microsoft.SharePoint.SPUser] $web.Users[$defaultUserName]
```

9. Create the **Pages Approvers** group as follows:

```
$web.SiteGroups.Add("Pages Approvers", $member, $user, "These
users can approve submissions in the Pages Library")
```

10. Create the **Pages Contributors** group as follows:

```
$web.SiteGroups.Add("Pages Contributors", $member, $user, "These
users can edit content in the Pages Library")
```

11. Get the newly created groups.

```
$approvers = $web.SiteGroups["Pages Approvers"]


$contributors = $web.SiteGroups["Pages Contributors"]
```

12. Get the **Approve** and **Contribute** roles from the site as follows:

```
$roleApprover = $web.RoleDefinitions["Approve"]


$roleContribute = $web.RoleDefinitions["Contribute"]
```

13. Assign the roles to the groups as follows:

```
$assignmentApprove = New-Object Microsoft.SharePoint.
SPRoleAssignment($approvers)


$assignmentApprove.RoleDefinitionBindings.Add($roleApprover)


$pages.RoleAssignments.Add($assignmentApprove)


$assignmentContribute = New-Object Microsoft.SharePoint.
SPRoleAssignment($contributors)


$assignmentContribute.RoleDefinitionBindings.Add($roleContribute)


$pages.RoleAssignments.Add($assignmentContribute)
```

14. Update the **Pages** library using the following command:

    ```
    $pages.Update()
    ```

15. Use the `Dispose` method to discard the `SPWeb` object as follows:

    ```
    $web.Dispose()
    ```

Setting up contributor and approver access with code using the server-side object model

Follow these steps to setup contributor and approver access with code using the server-side object model:

1. Open the site collection containing the site in a `using` statement as follows:

    ```
    using (var site = new SPSite("http://sharepoint/publishing"))
    ```

2. Open the site in a `using` statement as follows:

    ```
    using (var web = site.OpenWeb())
    ```

3. Get the **Pages** library from the site as follows:

    ```
    var pages = web.Lists["Pages"];
    ```

4. If the **Pages** library is inheriting permissions from the site, break the inheritance. Specify `false` for the parameter to indicate we do not want to copy the existing permissions from the parent site.

    ```
    if (!pages.HasUniqueRoleAssignments)
    pages.BreakRoleInheritance(false);
    ```

5. Set the `EnableModeration` property of the **Pages** library to turn on content approval as follows:

    ```
    pages.EnableModeration = true;
    ```

6. Update the **Pages** library using the following line of code:

    ```
    pages.Update();
    ```

7. Get the default user as a `Microsoft.SharePoint.SPMember` object as follows:

    ```
    var member = web.Users["USERNAME"] as SPMember;
    ```

8. Get the default user as a `Microsoft.SharePoint.SPUser` object as follows:

    ```
    var user = web.Users["USERNAME"] as SPUser;
    ```

9. Create the **Pages Approvers** group using the following code:

    ```
    web.SiteGroups.Add("Pages Approvers", member, user, "These users
    can approve submissions in the Pages Library");
    ```

10. Create the **Pages Contributors** group using the following code:

```
web.SiteGroups.Add("Pages Contributors", member, user, "These
users can edit content in the Pages Library");
```

11. Get the newly created groups as follows:

```
var approvers = web.SiteGroups["Pages Approvers"];

var contributors = web.SiteGroups["Pages Contributors"];
```

12. Get the **Approve** and **Contribute** roles from the site using the following code:

```
var roleApprover = web.RoleDefinitions["Approve"];

var roleContribute = web.RoleDefinitions["Contribute"];
```

13. Using the following code, assign the roles to the groups:

```
var assignmentApprove = new SPRoleAssignment(approvers);

assignmentApprove.RoleDefinitionBindings.Add(roleApprover);
pages.RoleAssignments.Add(assignmentApprove);

var assignmentContribute = new SPRoleAssignment(contributors);

assignmentContribute.RoleDefinitionBindings.Add(roleContribute);

pages.RoleAssignments.Add(assignmentContribute);
```

14. Update the **Pages** library using the following line of code:

```
pages.Update();
```

See also

▶ The *Getting Started with Workflows in SharePoint 2013* article on MSDN at `http://msdn.microsoft.com/en-us/library/office/jj163917.aspx`

▶ The *Workflow Development in SharePoint Designer 2013 and Visio 2013* article on MSDN at `http://msdn.microsoft.com/en-us/library/office/jj163272.aspx`

▶ The *SPRoleAssignment class* topic on MSDN at `http://msdn.microsoft.com/en-us/library/microsoft.sharepoint.sproleassignment.aspx`

▶ The *SPGroupCollection class* topic on MSDN at `http://msdn.microsoft.com/en-us/library/microsoft.sharepoint.spgroupcollection.aspx`

Configuring the versioning settings of the Pages library

The versioning features of SharePoint allow us to create published and draft versions of items in lists and libraries. We can configure how many published and draft versions to keep as well as who can see items when they are in a draft state. In this recipe, we will be configuring the versioning settings of the **Pages** library.

How to do it...

Follow these steps to configure the versioning settings of the **Pages** library:

1. Navigate to the site in your preferred web browser.
2. Select **Site contents** from the **Settings** menu.
3. Select the **Pages** library.
4. Select **Library Settings** from the **Library** tab in the ribbon.
5. Select **Versioning Settings** from the **General Settings** section.
6. Set the **Document Version History** setting to **Create major and minor (draft) versions** as shown in the following screenshot:

Document Version History

Specify whether a version is created each time you edit a file in this document library. Learn about versions.

Create a version each time you edit a file in this document library?

○ No versioning

○ Create major versions
Example: 1, 2, 3, 4

● Create major and minor (draft) versions
Example: 1.0, 1.1, 1.2, 2.0

Optionally limit the number of versions to retain:

☐ Keep the following number of major versions:

☐ Keep drafts for the following number of major versions:

7. Select both checkboxes for limiting the number of versions and set the limit to 25 for each.

8. Set the **Draft Item Security** setting to **Only users who can edit items** as shown in the following screenshot:

Draft Item Security

Drafts are minor versions or items which have not been approved. Specify which users should be able to view drafts in this document library. Learn about specifying who can view and edit drafts.

Who should see draft items in this document library?

○ Any user who can read items
◉ Only users who can edit items
○ Only users who can approve items (and the author of the item)

9. Set the **Require Check Out** setting to **Yes** as shown in the following screenshot:

Require Check Out

Specify whether users must check out documents before making changes in this document library. Learn about requiring check out.

Require documents to be checked out before they can be edited?

◉ Yes   ○ No

10. Click on **OK**.

How it works...

When versioning is enabled on a SharePoint list or library, a copy of the item is saved in the content database each time the item is edited. When the version limits are configured, the oldest version of the item will be deleted when the limit has been reached and a new version is being saved.

> By default, versioning is configured to allow an unlimited number of versions to be saved. For increased performance and limiting the amount of space used, it is recommended to set a limit to the number of versions saved.

In addition, when check out is required, users will not be able to modify the item until they check out the item.

There's more...

Managing the versioning settings of a SharePoint library may also be accomplished with PowerShell or code using the server-side object model.

Configuring the versioning settings of the Pages library using PowerShell

Follow these steps to configure the versioning settings of the **Pages** library using PowerShell:

1. Get the site using the following Get-SPWeb Cmdlet:

   ```
   $web = Get-SPWeb "http://sharepoint/publishing"
   ```

2. Get the **Pages** library from the site as follows:

   ```
   $pages = $web.Lists["Pages"]
   ```

3. Enable versioning on the library as follows:

   ```
   $pages.EnableVersioning = $true

   $pages.EnableMinorVersions = $true
   ```

4. Set the versioning limits on the library.

   ```
   $pages.MajorWithMinorVersionsLimit = 25

   $pages.MajorVersionLimit = 25
   ```

5. Set the visibility of draft items using the following code:

   ```
   $pages.DraftVersionVisibility = [Microsoft.SharePoint.
   DraftVisibilityType]::Author
   ```

6. Configure the items that require to be checked out before editing.

   ```
   $pages.ForceCheckout = $true
   ```

7. Update the **Pages** library as follows:

   ```
   $pages.Update()
   ```

8. Use the following Dispose method to discard the SPWeb object:

   ```
   $web.Dispose()
   ```

Configuring the versioning settings of the Pages library with code using the server-side object model

Follow these steps to configure the versioning settings of the **Pages** library with code using the server-side object model:

1. Open the site collection containing the site in a using statement as shown in the following line of code:

   ```
   using (var site = new SPSite("http://sharepoint/publishing"))
   ```

2. Open the site in a `using` statement as follows:

    ```
    using (var web = site.OpenWeb())
    ```

3. Get the **Pages** library from the site using the following code:

    ```
    var pages = web.Lists["Pages"];
    ```

4. Enable versioning on the library as follows:

    ```
    pages.EnableVersioning = true;

    pages.EnableMinorVersions = true;
    ```

5. Set the versioning limits on the library as follows:

    ```
    pages.MajorWithMinorVersionsLimit = 25;

    pages.MajorVersionLimit = 25;
    ```

6. Set the visibility of draft items as follows:

    ```
    pages.DraftVersionVisibility = DraftVisibilityType.Author;
    ```

7. Configure the items that require to be checked out before editing.

    ```
    pages.ForceCheckout = true;
    ```

8. Update the **Pages** library using the following line of code:

    ```
    pages.Update();
    ```

See also

▸ The *SPList properties* topic on MSDN at `http://msdn.microsoft.com/en-us/library/Microsoft.SharePoint.SPList_properties.aspx`

Creating a publishing web part page

SharePoint provides many page layouts that serve as templates when creating content pages. In this recipe, we will use the **Blank Web Part page** template to create a new content page.

How to do it...

Follow these steps to create a publishing web part page:

1. Navigate to the site in your preferred web browser.
2. Select **Site contents** from the **Settings** menu.
3. Select the **Pages** library.

4. Select **New Document** from the **FILES** tab in the ribbon as shown in the following screenshot:

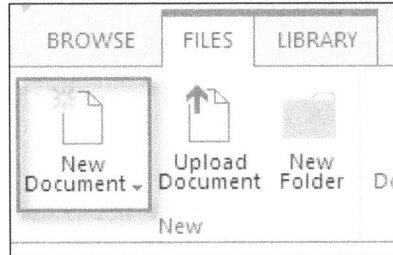

5. Provide a title, description, and URL for the new page in the **Title**, **Description**, and **URL** fields.

6. Select the **(Welcome Page) Blank Web Part page** template as shown in the following screenshot:

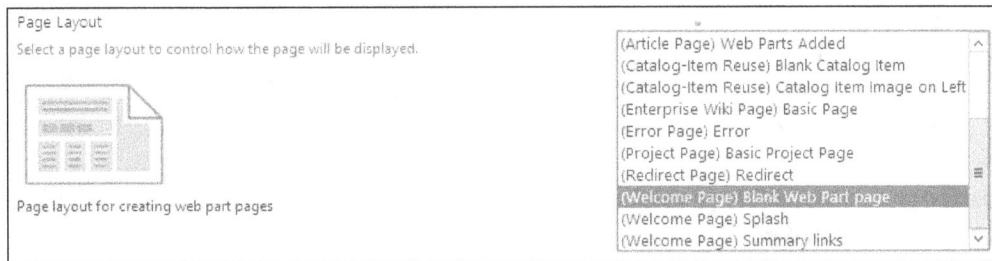

7. Click on **Create**.

How it works...

Pages in a SharePoint library are created with a page layout template. This template provides the general layout of the content within the confines of the master page.

There's more...

Publishing pages may also be created using PowerShell or code using the server-side object model.

Creating a publishing web part page using PowerShell

Follow these steps to create a publishing web part page using PowerShell:

1. Get the site using the Get-SPWeb Cmdlet as follows:

```
$web = Get-SPWeb "http://sharepoint/publishing"
```

2. Get the publishing site from the SharePoint site as follows:

```
$pubWeb = [Microsoft.SharePoint.Publishing.PublishingWeb]::GetPubl
ishingWeb($web)
```

3. Get the page layout template from the publishing site using the following command:

```
$layout = $pubWeb.GetAvailablePageLayouts() | Where-Object {
$_.Title -eq "Blank Web Part Page" }
```

4. Create a new publishing page as follows:

```
$page = $pubWeb.AddPublishingPage("PowerShellPage.aspx", $layout)
```

5. Update the publishing page object as follows:

```
$page.Update()
```

6. Set the `Title` property of the publishing page using the following commands:

```
$page.ListItem["Title"] = "PowerShell Page"


$page.ListItem.Update()
```

7. Use the `Dispose` method to discard the `SPWeb` object as follows:

```
$web.Dispose()
```

Creating a publishing web part page with code using the server-side object model

Follow these steps to create a publishing web part page with code using the server-side object model:

1. Open the site collection containing the site in a `using` statement as follows:

```
using (var site = new SPSite("http://sharepoint/publishing"))
```

2. Open the site in a `using` statement as follows:

```
using (var web = site.OpenWeb())
```

3. Get the publishing site from the SharePoint site as follows:

```
var pubWeb = PublishingWeb.GetPublishingWeb(web);
```

4. Get the page layout template from the publishing site using the following code:

```
var layout = pubWeb.GetAvailablePageLayouts().Where(p => p.Title
== "Blank Web Part Page").First();
```

5. Create a new publishing page as follows:

```
var page = pubWeb.AddPublishingPage("CodePage.aspx", layout);
```

6. Update the publishing page object as follows:

```
page.Update();
```

7. Set the `Title` property of the publishing page using the following code:

```
page.ListItem["Title"] = "Code Page";

page.ListItem.Update();
```

See also

▸ The *GetPublishingWeb method* topic on MSDN at `http://msdn.microsoft.com/en-us/library/ms497306.aspx`

▸ The *AddPublishingPage method* topic on MSDN at `http://msdn.microsoft.com/en-us/library/ee562149.aspx`

Checking out publishing content for editing

Checking out an item in SharePoint provides the user with an exclusive lock to prevent the editing of that item. This prevents multiple users from making modifications at the same time. In this recipe, we will check out the publishing page we created in the *Creating a publishing web part page* recipe.

How to do it...

Follow these steps to check out a publishing page:

1. Navigate to the SharePoint list or library that contains the item to be checked out in your preferred web browser.

> In our example, we will be using the **Pages** library and the publishing page we created in the *Creating a publishing web part page* recipe.

2. Select the item by clicking on the checkmark on the item.

3. Select **Check Out** from the **FILES** tab in the ribbon as shown in the following screenshot:

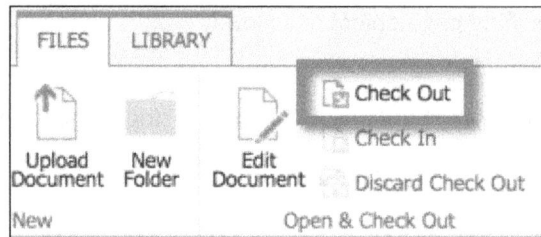

How it works...

Checking out an item in a SharePoint list or library flags it with a checked out status. This prevents other users from modifying the item. A user with a manage lists or higher role may override the check out.

There's more...

SharePoint list and library items may also be checked out with PowerShell or code using the server-side object model. There are a number of ways we could get the item to check out. In our example, we are using a CAML query to get the publishing page from the publishing site by its title. CAML is an XML-based markup language used to query SharePoint content.

Checking out publishing content using PowerShell

Follow these steps to check out a publishing content using PowerShell:

1. Get the site using the `Get-SPWeb` Cmdlet as follows:

   ```
   $web = Get-SPWeb "http://sharepoint/publishing"
   ```

2. Get the publishing site from the SharePoint site as follows:

   ```
   $pubWeb = [Microsoft.SharePoint.Publishing.PublishingWeb]::GetPubl
   ishingWeb($web)
   ```

3. Get the publishing page using the following CAML query:

   ```
   $camlQuery = "<Where><Eq><FieldRef Name='Title'></FieldRef><Value
   Type='Text'>PowerShell Page</Value></Eq></Where>"

   $page = $pubWeb.GetPublishingPages($camlQuery)
   ```

4. Check out the publishing page using the following command:

   ```
   $page.ListItem.File.CheckOut()
   ```

5. Use the `Dispose` method to discard the `SPWeb` object as follows:

```
$web.Dispose()
```

Checking out publishing content with code using the server-side object model

Follow these steps to check out a publishing content with code using the server-side object model:

1. Open the site collection containing the site in a `using` statement as follows:

```
using (var site = new SPSite("http://sharepoint/publishing"))
```

2. Open the site in a `using` statement as follows:

```
using (var web = site.OpenWeb())
```

3. Get the publishing site from the SharePoint site.

```
var pubWeb = PublishingWeb.GetPublishingWeb(web);
```

4. Get the publishing page with the following CAML query:

```
var camlQuery = "<Where><Eq><FieldRef Name='Title'></
FieldRef><Value Type='Text'>Code Page</Value></Eq></Where>";

var page = pubWeb.GetPublishingPages(camlQuery).First();
```

5. Check out the publishing page as follows:

```
page.ListItem.File.CheckOut();
```

See also

▶ The *Introduction to Collaborative Application Markup Language (CAML)* article on MSDN at `http://msdn.microsoft.com/en-us/library/office/ms426449.aspx`

▶ The *SPFile methods* topic on MSDN at `http://msdn.microsoft.com/en-us/library/microsoft.sharepoint.spfile_methods.aspx`

Checking in edited publishing content

Checking in an item in SharePoint releases the exclusive lock on the item and allows other users, who have access, to view or edit the item. In this recipe, we will check in the publishing page we created in the *Creating a publishing web part page* recipe.

How to do it...

Follow these steps to check in a publishing page:

1. Navigate to the SharePoint list or library that contains the item to check in with your preferred web browser.

2. Select the item by clicking on the checkmark on the item.

3. Select **Check In** from the **FILES** tab in the ribbon as shown in the following screenshot:

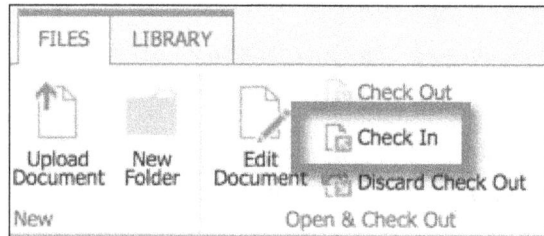

4. Provide any applicable **Check In** notes.

5. Click on **OK**.

How it works...

Checking in a SharePoint list or library item makes the modifications made by the user available to other users with the appropriate access. In addition, the item becomes available for other users with appropriate access to check out and modify the item.

There's more...

SharePoint list and library items may also be checked in with PowerShell or code using the server-side object model.

Checking in publishing content using PowerShell

Follow these steps to check in a publishing page using PowerShell:

1. Get the site using the Get-SPWeb Cmdlet as follows:

```
$web = Get-SPWeb "http://sharepoint/publishing"
```

2. Get the publishing site from the SharePoint site using the following command:

```
$pubWeb = [Microsoft.SharePoint.Publishing.PublishingWeb]::GetPubl
ishingWeb($web)
```

3. Get the publishing page using the following CAML query:

```
$camlQuery = "<Where><Eq><FieldRef Name='Title'></FieldRef><Value
Type='Text'>PowerShell Page</Value></Eq></Where>"

$page = $pubWeb.GetPublishingPages($camlQuery)
```

4. Check in the publishing page as follows:

```
$page.ListItem.File.CheckIn("My Notes")
```

5. Use the following `Dispose` method to discard the `SPWeb` object:

```
$web.Dispose()
```

Checking in publishing content with code using the server-side object model

Follow these steps to check in a publishing page with code using the server-side object model:

1. Open the site collection containing the site in a `using` statement as follows:

```
using (var site = new SPSite("http://sharepoint/publishing"))
```

2. Open the site in the following `using` statement:

```
using (var web = site.OpenWeb())
```

3. Get the publishing site from the SharePoint site.

```
var pubWeb = PublishingWeb.GetPublishingWeb(web);
```

4. Get the publishing page with the following CAML query:

```
var camlQuery = "<Where><Eq><FieldRef Name='Title'></
FieldRef><Value Type='Text'>Code Page</Value></Eq></Where>";

var page = pubWeb.GetPublishingPages(camlQuery).First();
```

5. Check in the publishing page using the following code:

```
page.ListItem.File.CheckIn("My Notes");
```

See also

▶ The *SPFile methods* topic on MSDN at `http://msdn.microsoft.com/en-us/library/microsoft.sharepoint.spfile_methods.aspx`

Publishing checked-in publishing content

Publishing an item in SharePoint makes it available to consume by users who do not have contribution rights to the item. If content approval is required, it will mark the item as **Pending Approval**. In this recipe, we will publish the publishing page we created in the *Creating a publishing web part page* recipe.

> When content approval is required, a published item will not be available to noncontributing users until it is marked as **Approved**.

How to do it...

Follow these steps to publish a publishing page:

1. Navigate to the SharePoint list or library that contains the item to be published in your preferred web browser.
2. Select the item by clicking on the checkmark on the item.
3. Select **Publish** from the **FILES** tab on the ribbon.

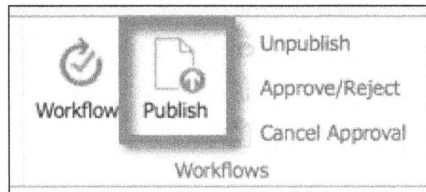

4. Provide any applicable publishing notes.
5. Click on **OK**.

How it works...

Published SharePoint list or library items are available to users with read access to the items. An item may go through multiple revisions before being published. Only the published version is made available to the users with read access. When content approval is required, only the approved and published version is made available to users with read access.

There's more...

SharePoint list and library items may also be published with PowerShell or code using the server-side object model.

Publishing a checked in publishing content using PowerShell

Follow these steps to publish a checked in publishing page using PowerShell:

1. Get the site using the `Get-SPWeb` Cmdlet as follows:

   ```
   $web = Get-SPWeb "http://sharepoint/publishing"
   ```

2. Get the publishing site from the SharePoint site.

   ```
   $pubWeb = [Microsoft.SharePoint.Publishing.PublishingWeb]::GetPubl
   ishingWeb($web)
   ```

3. Get the publishing page using the following CAML query:

   ```
   $camlQuery = "<Where><Eq><FieldRef Name='Title'></FieldRef><Value
   Type='Text'>PowerShell Page</Value></Eq></Where>"

   $page = $pubWeb.GetPublishingPages($camlQuery)
   ```

4. Publish the publishing page as follows:

   ```
   $page.ListItem.File.Publish("My Notes")
   ```

5. Use the `Dispose` method to discard the `SPWeb` object as follows:

   ```
   $web.Dispose()
   ```

Publishing a checked in publishing content with code using the server-side object model

Follow these steps to publish a checked in publishing page with code using the server-side object model:

1. Open the site collection containing the site in a `using` statement as follows:

   ```
   using (var site = new SPSite("http://sharepoint/publishing"))
   ```

2. Open the site in a `using` statement.

   ```
   using (var web = site.OpenWeb())
   ```

3. Get the publishing site from the SharePoint site as follows:

   ```
   var pubWeb = PublishingWeb.GetPublishingWeb(web);
   ```

4. Get the publishing page with the following CAML query:

   ```
   var camlQuery = "<Where><Eq><FieldRef Name='Title'></
   FieldRef><Value Type='Text'>Code Page</Value></Eq></Where>";

   var page = pubWeb.GetPublishingPages(camlQuery).First();
   ```

5. Publish the publishing page using the following code:

   ```
   page.ListItem.File.Publish("My Notes");
   ```

See also

- ► The *SPFile methods* topic on MSDN at `http://msdn.microsoft.com/en-us/ library/microsoft.sharepoint.spfile_methods.aspx`

Approving publishing content

Approving a published item in SharePoint makes it available to be viewed by users who have read access but do not have contribute access to the item. In this recipe, we will approve the publishing page we created in the *Creating a publishing web part page* recipe.

How to do it...

Follow these steps to approve a publishing page:

1. Navigate to the SharePoint list or library that contains the item to be approved in your preferred web browser.

2. Select the item by clicking on the checkmark on the item.

3. Select **Approve/Reject** from the **FILES** tab on the ribbon.

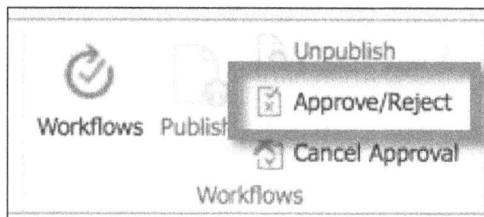

4. Select **Approved**.

5. Provide any applicable approval notes.

6. Click on **OK**.

How it works...

When content approval is required, approving a published item makes it available for the users with read access to view the item.

> In addition to approving content, content may also be rejected. Rejecting results in the version awaiting approval not being published. An item may also be unpublished.

There's more...

SharePoint list and library items may also be approved with PowerShell or code using the server-side object model.

Approving publishing content using PowerShell

Follow these steps to approve a publishing page using PowerShell:

1. Get the site using the Get-SPWeb Cmdlet as follows:

```
$web = Get-SPWeb "http://sharepoint/publishing"
```

2. Get the publishing site from the SharePoint site.

```
$pubWeb = [Microsoft.SharePoint.Publishing.PublishingWeb]::GetPubl
ishingWeb($web)
```

3. Get the publishing page using the following CAML query:

```
$camlQuery = "<Where><Eq><FieldRef Name='Title'></FieldRef><Value
Type='Text'>PowerShell Page</Value></Eq></Where>"

$page = $pubWeb.GetPublishingPages($camlQuery)
```

4. Approve the publishing page as follows:

```
$page.ListItem.File.Approve("My Notes")
```

5. Use the Dispose method to discard the SPWeb object as follows:

```
$web.Dispose()
```

Approving publishing content with code using the server-side object model

Follow these steps to approve a publishing page with code using the server-side object model:

1. Open the site collection containing the site in a using statement as follows:

```
using (var site = new SPSite("http://sharepoint/publishing"))
```

2. Open the site in the following using statement:

```
using (var web = site.OpenWeb())
```

3. Get the publishing site from the SharePoint site.

```
var pubWeb = PublishingWeb.GetPublishingWeb(web);
```

4. Get the publishing page with the following CAML query:

```
var camlQuery = "<Where><Eq><FieldRef Name='Title'></
FieldRef><Value Type='Text'>Code Page</Value></Eq></Where>";

var page = pubWeb.GetPublishingPages(camlQuery).First();
```

5. Approve the publishing page as follows:

```
page.ListItem.File.Approve("My Notes");
```

See also

▸ The *SPFile methods* topic on MSDN at `http://msdn.microsoft.com/en-us/library/microsoft.sharepoint.spfile_methods.aspx`

Reverting publishing content to a previous version

Versioned items in SharePoint allow us to revert back to a previous version when desired. In this recipe, we will revert the publishing page we created in the *Creating a publishing web part page* recipe.

How to do it...

Follow these steps to revert a publishing page:

1. Navigate to the SharePoint list or library that contains the item to be approved in your preferred web browser.

2. Select the item by clicking on the checkmark on the item.

3. Select **Check Out** from the **FILES** tab on the ribbon.

4. Select the item by clicking on the checkmark of the item.

5. Select **Version History** from the **FILES** tab on the ribbon.

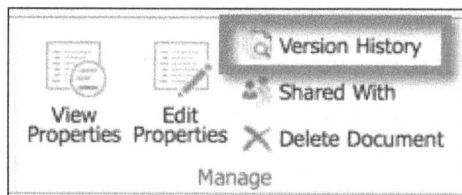

6. Select the drop-down menu from the **Modified Date** option to select the version you want to revert.

7. Select **Restore** as shown in the following screenshot:

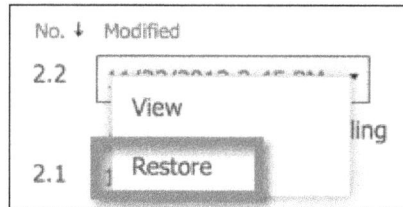

8. Click on **OK**.

9. Check in the item to complete the process using the **Check In** option.

How it works...

When a previous version of an item is restored, it copies that version and makes it the newest version. The version prior to the current one will be saved as an old version.

There's more...

SharePoint list and library items may also be reverted with PowerShell or code using the server-side object model.

Reverting publishing content using PowerShell

Follow these steps to revert a publishing page using PowerShell:

1. Get the site using the Get-SPWeb Cmdlet as follows:

```
$web = Get-SPWeb "http://sharepoint/publishing"
```

2. Get the publishing site from the SharePoint site.

```
$pubWeb = [Microsoft.SharePoint.Publishing.PublishingWeb]::GetPubl
ishingWeb($web)
```

3. Get the publishing page using the following CAML query:

```
$camlQuery = "<Where><Eq><FieldRef Name='Title'></FieldRef><Value
Type='Text'>PowerShell Page</Value></Eq></Where>"

$page = $pubWeb.GetPublishingPages($camlQuery)
```

4. Check out the publishing page as follows:

```
$page.ListItem.File.CheckOut()
```

5. Restore the item to the specified version.

```
$page.ListItem.Versions.RestoreByLabel("1.0")
```

6. Check in the publishing page as follows:

   `$page.ListItem.File.CheckIn("Reverted to 1.0")`

7. Use the `Dispose` method to discard the `SPWeb` object as follows:

   `$web.Dispose()`

Reverting publishing content with code using the server-side object model

Follow these steps to revert a publishing page with code using the server-side object model:

1. Open the site collection containing the site in a `using` statement as follows:

   `using (var site = new SPSite("http://sharepoint/publishing"))`

2. Open the site in a `using` statement.

   `using (var web = site.OpenWeb())`

3. Get the publishing site from the SharePoint site.

   `var pubWeb = PublishingWeb.GetPublishingWeb(web);`

4. Get the publishing page with the following CAML query:

   ```
   var camlQuery = "<Where><Eq><FieldRef Name='Title'></
   FieldRef><Value Type='Text'>Code Page</Value></Eq></Where>";

   var page = pubWeb.GetPublishingPages(camlQuery).First();
   ```

5. Check out the publishing page using the following line of code:

   `page.ListItem.File.CheckOut();`

6. Restore the item to the specified version.

   `page.ListItem.Versions.RestoreByLabel("1.0");`

7. Check in the publishing page using the following line of code:

   `page.ListItem.File.CheckIn("Reverted to 1.0");`

See also

▶ The *SPFile methods* topic on MSDN at `http://msdn.microsoft.com/en-us/library/microsoft.sharepoint.spfile_methods.aspx`

Setting up a publishing site with workflow

SharePoint provides a very robust workflow engine that can be incorporated into publishing sites or any other site. Built-in SharePoint workflows can be added from the web interface. Custom SharePoint workflows can be created with SharePoint Designer or Visual Studio.

In this recipe, we will create a publishing site that has a workflow for scheduling the publishing of content using a built-in site template. In addition, we will create a publishing page with a publishing schedule.

How to do it...

Follow these steps to set up a publishing site with workflow:

1. Navigate to the site in your preferred web browser.
2. Select **Site contents** from the **Settings** menu.
3. Select **new subsite** from the **Subsites** section.
4. On the **New SharePoint Site** page, provide a title, description, and URL for the new SharePoint site in the **Title**, **Description**, and **URL** fields.
5. Select the **Publishing Site with Workflow** template from the **Publishing** tab.
6. Click on **Create**.
7. In the new site, select **Site contents** from the **Settings** menu.
8. Select the **Pages** library.
9. Select **New Document** from the **FILES** tab in the ribbon and create a new publishing page.
10. Select the checkmark to select the new page in the **Pages** library.
11. Select **Edit Properties** from the **FILES** tab in the ribbon.
12. Select **Scheduling Start Date** and **Scheduling End Date** as shown in the following screenshot:

13. Click on **Save**.

How it works...

The **Publishing with Workflow** site template provides the ability to schedule publishing of content. When an item with a schedule is published and approved, it sets the approval status to **Scheduled**. Once the **Scheduling Start Date** is reached, SharePoint sets the **Approval Status** to **Approved** and becomes available to be viewed by the end users. Once the **Scheduling End Date** is reached, SharePoint sets the **Approval Status** back to **Draft** and is no longer available to be viewed by the end users.

See also

▶ The *Getting Started with Workflows in SharePoint 2013* article on MSDN at `http://msdn.microsoft.com/en-us/library/office/jj163917.aspx`

▶ The *Workflow Development in SharePoint Designer 2013 and Visio 2013* article on MSDN at `http://msdn.microsoft.com/en-us/library/office/jj163272.aspx`

▶ The *SharePoint 2013 Workflow Fundamentals* article on MSDN at `http://msdn.microsoft.com/en-us/library/jj163181.aspx`

Creating a web part page and adding web parts with PowerShell

In this recipe, we will use PowerShell to create a new publishing page and add web parts to it. This is useful in instances where a large number of these publishing pages need to be created and doing so one-by-one in the web interface would be a long and tedious process.

How to do it...

Follow these steps to create a web part page and add web parts using PowerShell:

1. Get the site with the `Get-SPWeb` Cmdlet.

   ```
   $web = Get-SPWeb "http://sharepoint/publishing"
   ```

2. Get the publishing site from the SharePoint site.

   ```
   $pubWeb = [Microsoft.SharePoint.Publishing.PublishingWeb]::GetPublishingWeb($web)
   ```

3. Get the page layout from the publishing site as follows:

   ```
   $layout = $pubWeb.GetAvailablePageLayouts() | Where-Object {
   $_.Title -eq "Blank Web Part Page" }
   ```

4. Create the publishing page.

   ```
   $page = $pubWeb.AddPublishingPage("PowerShellPageWithWebPart.
   aspx", $layout)
   ```

5. Update the publishing page object using the following command:

   ```
   $page.Update()
   ```

6. Set the `Title` property of the publishing page as follows:

   ```
   $page.ListItem["Title"] = "PowerShell Page with Web Part"


   $page.ListItem.Update()
   ```

7. Get the web part manager for the publishing page.

   ```
   $wpm = $web.GetLimitedWebPartManager($page.Url, [System.Web.
   UI.WebControls.WebParts.PersonalizationScope]::Shared)
   ```

8. Create a new content editor web part page.

   ```
   $cewp = New-Object Microsoft.SharePoint.WebPartPages.
   ContentEditorWebPart


   $cewp.Title = "PowerShell Web Part"


   $cewp.ChromeType = [System.Web.UI.WebControls.WebParts.
   PartChromeType]::TitleOnly
   ```

9. Set the `Content` property of the new web part using an `XmlDocument` object as follows:

   ```
   $xml = New-Object System.Xml.XmlDocument


   $xml.LoadXml("<Content>PowerShell Page Content</Content>")


   $cewp.Content = $xml.FirstChild
   ```

10. Add the web part to the `Header` web part zone at index `0`.

    ```
    $wpm.AddWebPart($cewp, "Header", 0)
    ```

11. Use the `Dispose` method to discard the `SPWeb` object as follows:

    ```
    $web.Dispose()
    ```

How it works...

PowerShell allows us to use .NET code to script interactions with the SharePoint object model. In this recipe, we used the publishing methods to create a new publishing page and the web part manager object to add a new web part to the page.

There's more...

Creating publishing pages and managing page web parts may also be accomplished with code using the server-side object model. Follow these steps to create a publishing page and add a web part with code using the server-side object model:

1. Get the site collection containing the site in a `using` statement as follows:

```
using (var site = new SPSite("http://sharepoint/publishing"))
```

2. Open the site in a `using` statement as follows:

```
using (var web = site.OpenWeb())
```

3. Get the publishing site from the SharePoint site.

```
var pubWeb = PublishingWeb.GetPublishingWeb(web);
```

4. Get the page layout from the publishing site.

```
var layout = pubWeb.GetAvailablePageLayouts().Where(p => p.Title
== "Blank Web Part Page").First();
```

5. Create the publishing page using the following code:

```
var page = pubWeb.AddPublishingPage("CodePageWithWebPart.aspx",
layout);
```

6. Update the publishing page object using the following code:

```
page.Update();
```

7. Set the `Title` property of the publishing page as follows:

```
page.ListItem["Title"] = "Code Page With Web Part";

page.ListItem.Update();
```

8. Get the web part manager for the publishing page.

```
var wpm = web.GetLimitedWebPartManager(page.Url,
PersonalizationScope.Shared);
```

9. Create a new content editor web part page as follows:

```
var cewp = new ContentEditorWebPart();

cewp.Title = "Code Web Part Title";

cewp.ChromeType = PartChromeType.TitleOnly;
```

10. Set the `Content` property of the web part using an `XmlDocument` object as follows:

```
var xml = new XmlDocument();

xml.LoadXml("<Content>Code Web Part Content</Content>");

cewp.Content = xml.FirstChild as XmlElement;
```

11. Add the web part to the `Header` web part zone at index 0 as follows:

```
wpm.AddWebPart(cewp, "Header", 0);
```

See also

▸ The *SPWeb.GetLimitedWebPartManager method* topic on MSDN at `http://msdn.microsoft.com/en-us/library/microsoft.sharepoint.spweb.getlimitedwebpartmanager.aspx`

Identifying all checked-out publishing pages in a site with PowerShell

Using the publishing features, SharePoint provides a great methodology for content editors to use when collaborating on items. In many cases, there is one flaw in this methodology, the users. It is very common for users to check out content and then forget to check in again. In this recipe, we will use PowerShell to identify all the publishing pages in a site that are currently checked out.

> Users with the permissions to manage the list or library, such as site administrators, have the ability to override a check out. This can be useful if the user who checked out the item is not available to check in the item.

How to do it...

Follow these steps to identify checked-out publishing pages using PowerShell:

1. Open your preferred text editor to create the `ps1` script file.

2. Get the site using the `Get-SPWeb` Cmdlet as follows:

   ```
   $web = Get-SPWeb "http://sharepoint/publishing"
   ```

3. Get the publishing site from the SharePoint site.

   ```
   $pubWeb = [Microsoft.SharePoint.Publishing.PublishingWeb]::GetPubl
   ishingWeb($web)
   ```

4. Get the publishing pages from the publishing site.

   ```
   $pages = $pubWeb.GetPublishingPages()
   ```

5. Iterate through each page in the collection of publishing pages using the following command:

   ```
   foreach ($page in $pages)
   ```

6. Check the `Level` property of the publishing page file to see if the item is checked out.

   ```
   if ($page.ListItem.File.Level -eq [Microsoft.SharePoint.
   SPFileLevel]::Checkout)
   ```

7. If the publishing page is checked out, output the details.

   ```
   Write-Host $page.Url


   Write-Host "By: " $page.ListItem.File.CheckedOutByUser.LoginName


   Write-Host "Since: " $page.ListItem.File.CheckedOutDate.ToString()


   Write-Host ""
   ```

8. Use the `Dispose` method to discard the `SPWeb` object as follows:

   ```
   $web.Dispose()
   ```

9. Save the file as a `ps1` file, for example, `getcheckedoutpages.ps1`

10. Execute the script in the PowerShell session using the following command:

   ```
   ./getcheckedoutpages.ps1
   ```

How it works...

Obtaining the SharePoint list item object associated with a publishing page provides the details necessary to identify whether a page is checked out and who has checked it out.

There's more...

Identifying checked out publishing pages may also be accomplished with code using the server-side object model. Follow these steps to identify checked-out publishing pages with code using the server-side object model:

1. Open the site collection containing the site in a `using` statement as follows:

```
using (var site = new SPSite("http://sharepoint/publishing"))
```

2. Open the site in a `using` statement as follows:

```
using (var web = site.OpenWeb())
```

3. Get the publishing site from the SharePoint site.

```
var pubWeb = PublishingWeb.GetPublishingWeb(web);
```

4. Get the publishing pages from the publishing site.

```
var pages = pubWeb.GetPublishingPages();
```

5. Iterate through each page in the collection of publishing pages using the following line of code:

```
foreach (var page in pages)
```

6. Check the `Level` property of the publishing page to see if the item is checked out.

```
if (page.ListItem.File.Level == SPFileLevel.Checkout)
```

7. If the publishing page is checked out, output the details.

```
Console.WriteLine(page.Url);

Console.WriteLine("By: " + page.ListItem.File.CheckedOutByUser.LoginName);

Console.WriteLine("Since: " + page.ListItem.File.CheckedOutDate.ToString());

Console.WriteLine("");
```

See also

▸ The *SPFile properties topic* on MSDN at `http://msdn.microsoft.com/en-us/library/microsoft.sharepoint.spfile_properties.aspx`

Creating an image rendition

Image renditions are a new feature of SharePoint 2013 that let you insert multiple sizes of the same image using the same source image. Image renditions specify the height and width to use when adding an image to a page.

Using image renditions requires BLOB cache to be enabled for the SharePoint web application. See `http://technet.microsoft.com/en-us/library/cc770229.aspx` for more information.

How to do it...

Follow these steps to create an image rendition:

1. Navigate to the site in your preferred web browser.
2. Select **Site settings** from the **Settings** menu.
3. Select **Image Renditions** from the **Look and Feel** section as shown in the following screenshot:

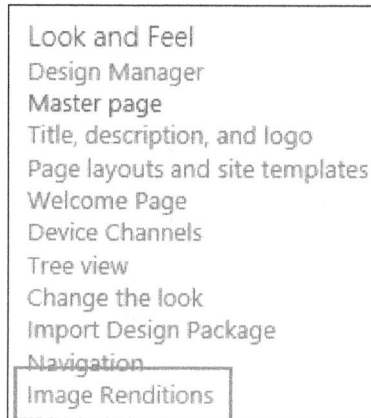

Look and Feel
Design Manager
Master page
Title, description, and logo
Page layouts and site templates
Welcome Page
Device Channels
Tree view
Change the look
Import Design Package
Navigation
Image Renditions

4. On the **Image Renditions** page, select **Add New Item**.
5. Provide a name for the image rendition in the **Name** field.
6. Provide the height and width for the image rendition in the **Height** and **Width** fields as shown in the following screenshot:

New Image Rendition

Name *	Square 50px
Width	50
Height	50

Save   Cancel

7. Click on **Save**.

How it works...

Image rendition configurations are stored as SharePoint list items. When an image rendition is applied to an image, SharePoint creates cached versions of the image in the formats dictated by the image renditions.

See also

▸ The *SharePoint 2013 Design Manager Image Renditions* article on MSDN at `http://msdn.microsoft.com/en-us/library/jj720398.aspx`

▸ The *Configure Cache Settings for a Web Application in SharePoint 2013* article on TechNet at `http://technet.microsoft.com/en-us/library/cc770229.aspx`

Inserting an image rendition into page content

Image renditions are applied to images inserted into SharePoint page content. In this recipe, we will insert an image into a page and apply an image rendition to it.

How to do it...

Follow these steps to apply an image rendition to an image in page content:

1. In your preferred web browser, navigate to the publishing page and open it for editing.
2. Place your mouse cursor in a content zone on the publishing page.

> If the publishing page does not have a content zone, a **Content Editor Web Part** may be added to a web part zone.

3. Navigate to **Picture | From SharePoint** on the **INSERT** tab in the ribbon as shown in the following screenshot:

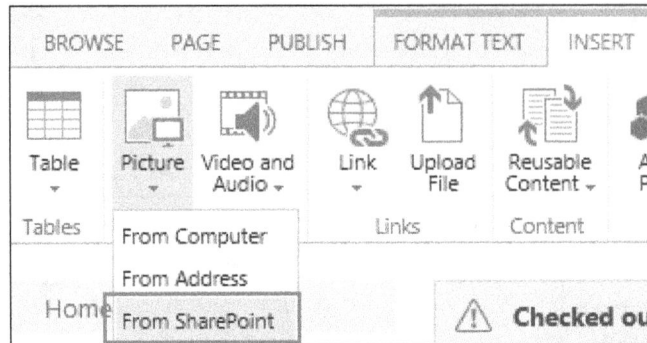

> We can also select **From Computer** to upload an image from the local filesystem to the site.

4. Select the image you want to insert.

5. Click on **Insert**.

6. Select **Pick Rendition** from the **IMAGE** tab in the ribbon.

7. Select the image rendition to be applied.

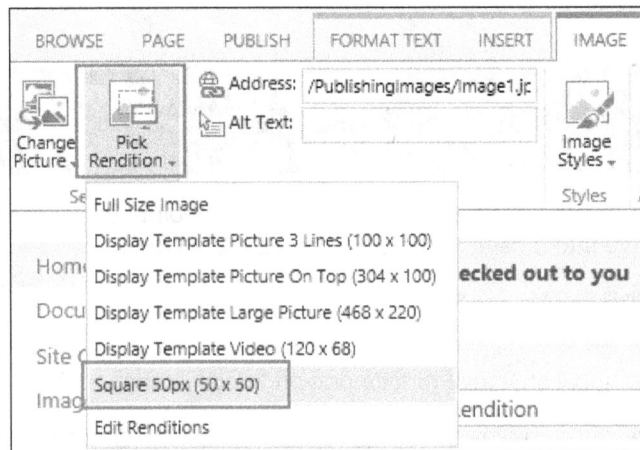

8. Save the publishing page.

> Team Site   Image Carousel   Image Rendition
>
> # Image Rendition
>
> _____
>
> IMAGE 1
>
> _____

How it works...

Applying an image rendition to an image will create a cached version of the image based on the image rendition definition. When a web browser requests the image, the cached version will be returned instead of the original image. In addition, any changes to the image rendition will automatically update the cached images.

See also

- ▶ The *SharePoint 2013 Design Manager Image Renditions* article on MSDN at `http://msdn.microsoft.com/en-us/library/jj720398.aspx`
- ▶ The *Configure Cache Settings for a web application in SharePoint 2013* article on TechNet at `http://technet.microsoft.com/en-us/library/cc770229.aspx`

6
Centralizing and Structuring Content with Cross-site Publishing and Managed Metadata

In this chapter, we will explore the cross-site publishing and managed metadata features of SharePoint 2013. We will cover the following recipes:

- ▸ Creating a new managed metadata service application
- ▸ Creating a categories term set for product catalog navigation
- ▸ Creating a product catalog authoring site collection
- ▸ Configuring the products list
- ▸ Creating a catalog document library
- ▸ Setting up a consuming site collection and connecting to the product catalog list
- ▸ Setting up a consuming site collection with separate branding

Introduction

The managed metadata features of SharePoint 2013 provide a robust set of tools for structuring taxonomy data used throughout SharePoint. Terms and term sets provided by the managed metadata services can be used for a variety of uses, including categorization of list and library items, standardized input for user profile properties, and structuring navigation. In this chapter, we will explore managed metadata from a navigation perspective.

> For more information on the other uses for the managed metadata features see http://technet.microsoft.com/en-us/library/ee424402.aspx.

New to the 2013 release of SharePoint, the cross-site publishing feature allows lists and libraries to be configured as catalog lists and catalog libraries. This allows these lists and libraries to be published and used within other site collections. Using these features, a list or library may be managed in a single location, yet provide functionality and content to a large number of other site collections.

> The cross-site publishing feature in SharePoint relies on the **search service application**. Before cross-site publishing can be implemented, the search service application must be configured and crawling the SharePoint sites. We will cover this in *Chapter 9, Configuring Search*.

Creating a new managed metadata service application

The **managed metadata service application** provides the core backend functionality for the managed metadata features in SharePoint. A SharePoint farm may contain one or more managed metadata service applications. Using multiple service applications provides the ability to isolate metadata content between web applications and also provides differing permissions.

In addition to the methods outlined in this recipe, the managed metadata service application can also be provisioned with the **Farm Configuration Wizard** in **Central Administration** when configuring the SharePoint farm for the first time.

How to do it...

Follow these steps to create a new managed metadata service application:

1. Navigate to **Central Administration** in your preferred web browser.

> If you are accessing **Central Administration** on the SharePoint server, you will need to run **SharePoint 2013 Central Administration** from the **Start** menu as an administrator.

2. In the **Application Management** section, select **Manage service applications** as shown in the following screenshot:

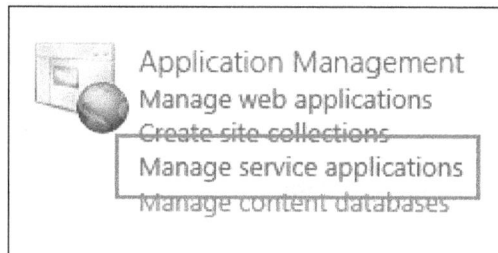

Application Management
Manage web applications
~~Create site collections~~
Manage service applications
~~Manage content databases~~

3. From the **SERVICE APPLICATIONS** tab on the ribbon, navigate to **New | Managed Metadata Service**:

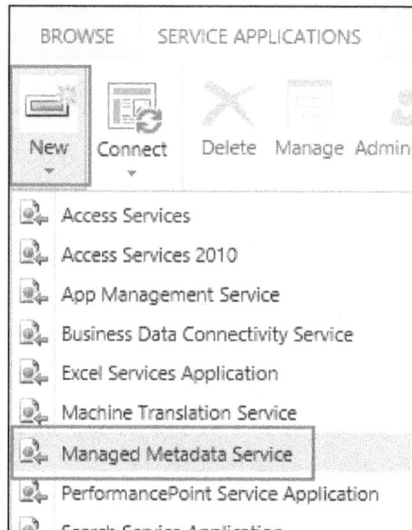

BROWSE   SERVICE APPLICATIONS

New   Connect   Delete   Manage   Admini

- Access Services
- Access Services 2010
- App Management Service
- Business Data Connectivity Service
- Excel Services Application
- Machine Translation Service
- Managed Metadata Service
- PerformancePoint Service Application
- Search Service Application

4. Provide a name, database server, and a database name.

5. Create a new or select an existing **Application Pool** for the service application to run under.

6. Click on **OK**.

7. On the **Manage service applications** page, select the row for the new service application (do not click on the link to the service application).

8. Select **Administrators** from the **SERVICE APPLICATIONS** tab on the ribbon:

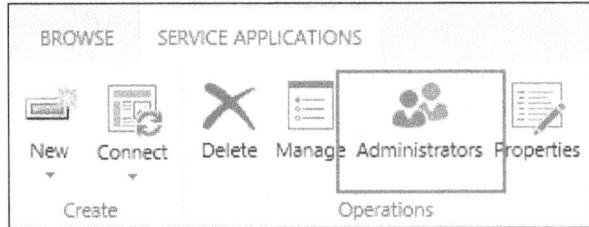

9. Enter your username and click on **Add**.

10. Mark the checkbox named **Full Control**:

11. Click on **OK**.

12. Select **System Settings** from the quick launch:

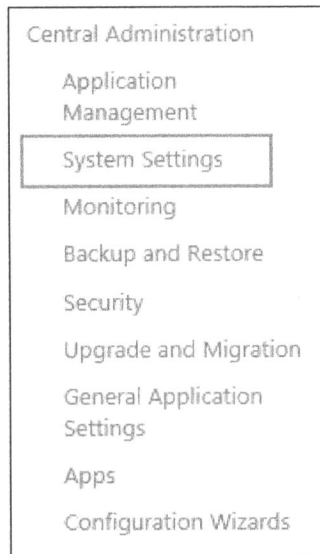

Central Administration

    Application
    Management

    System Settings

    Monitoring

    Backup and Restore

    Security

    Upgrade and Migration

    General Application
    Settings

    Apps

    Configuration Wizards

13. Select **Manage services on server** from the **Servers** section:

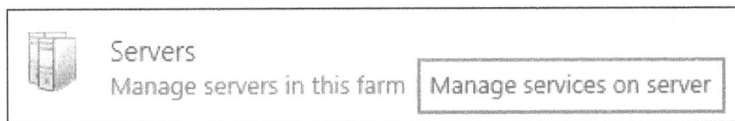

Servers
Manage servers in this farm | Manage services on server

14. Click on **Start** for the **Managed Metadata Web Service** if it is not already started. If you have more than one SharePoint server in the SharePoint farm, you can select the server in the drop-down list at the top of the page for which to manage the services.

Service	Status	Action
Excel Calculation Services	Stopped	Start
Lotus Notes Connector	Stopped	Start
Machine Translation Service	Started	Stop
Managed Metadata Web Service	Stopped	Start
Microsoft SharePoint Foundation Incoming E-Mail	Started	Stop
Microsoft SharePoint Foundation Sandboxed Code Service	Stopped	Start
Microsoft SharePoint Foundation Subscription Settings Service	Stopped	Start
Microsoft SharePoint Foundation Web Application	Started	Stop

How it works...

Service applications in SharePoint provide the backend web services and access to data storage used by many of the features throughout SharePoint. Multiple service applications of the same type may be used to isolate data between different web applications.

The managed metadata service application provides the web services and access to SQL data storage used by the managed metadata features on the frontend.

> Granting yourself full control (administrator) access to the service application provides you with full control over managing the term sets within the service application. Some functionality in the management page for the managed metadata service application will be unavailable if you do not grant full control to yourself. In addition, other users may be added who aren't necessarily farm administrators. If a user who is not a farm administrator is granted access, they will only be able to navigate to the service applications they have access to when they browse to **Central Administration**.

There's more...

Service applications may also be created with PowerShell or code using the server-side object model.

Creating a new managed metadata service application using PowerShell

Follow these steps to create a new managed metadata service application using PowerShell:

1. Use the `New-SPServiceApplicationPool` Cmdlet to create a new application pool to run our new service application and assign it to a variable. Use an existing managed account.

   ```
   $pool = New-SPServiceApplicationPool "Managed Metadata Service
   Application Pool" -Account "domain\user"
   ```

   > Alternatively, the `Get-SPServiceApplicationPool` Cmdlet may be used to retrieve an existing service application pool rather than creating a new one. In addition, to use a new service account rather than an existing one. The `New-SPManagedAccount` Cmdlet can be used to create it. The account specified must already be registered as a managed account with SharePoint before creating the application pool.

2. Use the `New-SPMetadataServiceApplication` Cmdlet to create our new service application:

```
$mms = New-SPMetadataServiceApplication -Name "Managed
Metadata Service" -ApplicationPool $pool -DatabaseName
"ManagedMetadata"
```

3. Use the `New-SPMetadataServiceApplicationProxy` Cmdlet to create the proxy to our new service application and add it to the default proxy group:

```
New-SPMetadataServiceApplicationProxy –Name "Managed Metadata
Service Proxy" -ServiceApplication $mms –DefaultProxyGroup
```

4. Start the **Managed Metadata Web Service** by getting the service instances from the SharePoint server with the `Get-SPServer` Cmdlet:

```
(Get-SPServer servername).ServiceInstances | Where-Object {
$_.TypeName -eq "Managed Metadata Web Service" } | ForEach-
Object { $_.Provision() }
```

Creating a new managed metadata service application with code using the server-side object model

Portions of the server-side object model are not publicly exposed from the SharePoint assemblies. As such, we will use .NET reflection to invoke the methods necessary to create the service application, proxy, and application pool. Follow these steps to create a new managed metadata service application with code using the server-side object model:

1. Get the `NTAccount` object for the user account the application pool will run under:

```
var account = new NTAccount("domain\\user");
```

2. Get the SharePoint managed account for the user account:

```
var processAccount =
SPProcessAccount.LookupManagedAccount((SecurityIdentifier)
account.Translate(typeof(SecurityIdentifier)));
```

3. Get the types required to instantiate a new application pool:

```
var appPoolType =
Type.GetType("Microsoft.SharePoint.Administration.
SPIisWebServiceApplicationPool, Microsoft.SharePoint,
Version=15.0.0.0, Culture=neutral,
PublicKeyToken=71e9bce111e9429c");

var appPoolOptionsType =
Type.GetType("Microsoft.SharePoint.Administration.
SPIisWebServiceApplicationPoolProvisioningOptions,
Microsoft.SharePoint, Version=15.0.0.0, Culture=neutral,
PublicKeyToken=71e9bce111e9429c");
var noneOption =
appPoolOptionsType.GetField("None").GetValue(appPoolOptionsType);
```

4. Use the `Create` and `BeginProvision` methods of the application pool type to create the new application pool:

```
var name = "Managed Metadata Service Application Pool";

var createMethod = appPoolType.GetMethod("Create",
BindingFlags.Instance | BindingFlags.NonPublic |
BindingFlags.Static, null, new Type[] { typeof(SPFarm),
typeof(string), typeof(SPProcessAccount) }, null);

var applicationPool =
(SPIisWebServiceApplicationPool)createMethod.Invoke
(null, new object[] { SPFarm.Local, name, processAccount
});

applicationPool.Update();

var beginProvision =
appPoolType.GetMethod("BeginProvision",
BindingFlags.Instance | BindingFlags.NonPublic);

beginProvision.Invoke(applicationPool, new object[]
{ noneOption });
```

5. Get the type required to instantiate the managed metadata service application:

```
var metadataAppType =
Type.GetType("Microsoft.SharePoint.Taxonomy.
MetadataWebServiceApplication,
Microsoft.SharePoint.Taxonomy, Version=15.0.0.0,
Culture=neutral, PublicKeyToken=71e9bce111e9429c");
```

6. Use the `Create` method on the service application type to create the new service application:

```
var createAppMethod = metadataAppType.GetMethod("Create",
BindingFlags.Instance | BindingFlags.NonPublic |
BindingFlags.Static, null, new Type[] { typeof(String),
typeof(String), typeof(String), typeof(String),
typeof(String), typeof(String),
typeof(SPIisWebServiceApplicationPool), typeof(String),
typeof(bool), typeof(bool), typeof(bool), typeof(int),
typeof(int), typeof(bool) }, null);

var mms = createAppMethod.Invoke(null, new object[] {
"Managed Metadata Service", "ManagedMetadataDatabase",
null, null, null, null, applicationPool, null, false,
false, false, 0, 0, false });
```

7. Get the `Uri` property for the newly created service application:

```
var mmsUri = (Uri)metadataAppType.GetProperty("Uri",
BindingFlags.Instance | BindingFlags.Public).GetValue(mms);
```

8. Get the type required to instantiate the service application proxy:

```
var metadataProxyAppType =
Type.GetType("Microsoft.SharePoint.Taxonomy.MetadataWebServ
iceApplicationProxy, Microsoft.SharePoint.Taxonomy,
Version=15.0.0.0, Culture=neutral,
PublicKeyToken=71e9bce111e9429c");
```

9. Use the `CreateProxy` method to create the service application proxy:

```
var createProxyMethod =
metadataProxyAppType.GetMethod("CreateProxy",
BindingFlags.Instance | BindingFlags.NonPublic |
BindingFlags.Static, null, new Type[] { typeof(Uri),
typeof(string), typeof(bool), typeof(bool), typeof(bool),
typeof(Uri), typeof(bool), typeof(bool), typeof(bool) },
null);

createProxyMethod.Invoke(null, new object[] { mmsUri,
"Managed Metadata Service Proxy", false, false, false,
null, false, true, false });
```

10. Start the **Managed Metadata Web Service** on the local SharePoint server:

```
((SPServiceInstance)SPServer.Local.ServiceInstances.Where
(p => p.TypeName.Equals("Managed Metadata Web Service",
StringComparison.OrdinalIgnoreCase)).First()).Provision();
```

See also

▸ The *Overview of managed metadata service applications in SharePoint Server 2013* article on TechNet at http://technet.microsoft.com/en-us/library/ee424403.aspx

▸ The *Create, update, publish, or delete a managed metadata service application* article on TechNet at http://technet.microsoft.com/en-us/library/ee530392(v=office.14).aspx

▸ The *New-SPServiceApplicationPool* topic on TechNet at http://technet.microsoft.com/en-us/library/ff607595.aspx

▸ The *New-SPMetadataServiceApplication* topic on TechNet at http://technet.microsoft.com/en-us/library/ff607557.aspx

▸ The *New-SPMetadataServiceApplicationProxy* topic on TechNet at http://technet.microsoft.com/en-us/library/ff608097.aspx

▸ The *Get-SPServer* topic on TechNet at http://technet.microsoft.com/en-us/library/ff607694.aspx

Creating a categories term set for product catalog navigation

The cross-site publishing catalog lists and libraries rely on managed metadata to organize and reference content in the lists and libraries. In this recipe, we will create a term set to use for product catalog navigation.

> Managed metadata term sets may be created and managed at both the farm (service application) and the site collection level. Term sets at the site collection level are only available for that site collection. In order for a term set to be usable with cross-site publishing between site collections, it needs to be at the farm level. In our example, we will create our term set at the farm level.

How to do it...

Follow these steps to create a categories term set:

1. Navigate to **Central Administration** in your preferred web browser.

2. Select **Manage service applications** from the **Application Management** section.

3. Select the link to the managed metadata service application, **Managed Metadata** for instance:

Machine Translation		Machine Translation Service Proxy	Started
Managed Metadata		Managed Metadata Service	Started
Managed Metadata		Managed Metadata Service Connection	Started
Search Administration Web Service for Search		Search Administration Web Service	

4. Right-click on the **Managed Metadata Service** in the tree view and then select **New Group**:

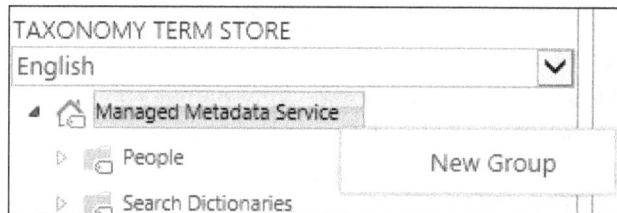

```
TAXONOMY TERM STORE
English                                    ∨
  ▲  🏠 Managed Metadata Service
     ▷  People                    New Group
     ▷  Search Dictionaries
```

5. Enter Product Categories as the group name.

6. Right-click on the drop-down menu of the **Product Categories** group and select **New Term Set**, as shown in the following screenshot:

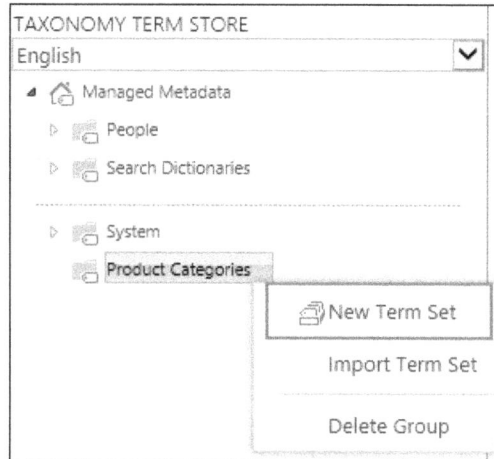

```
TAXONOMY TERM STORE
English                                                     ✔
  ⊿  🏠  Managed Metadata
      ▷  📇  People
      ▷  📇  Search Dictionaries

      ▷  📇  System
          📇  Product Categories
                              🗐 New Term Set

                              Import Term Set

                              Delete Group
```

7. Enter `Products` as the term set name.

8. Select the **Products** term set.

9. In the right-hand side pane, click on the **INTENDED USE** tab.

10. Check the **Use this Term Set for Site Navigation** checkbox. This option is required to make this term set available for use in the quick launch or header navigation of a site.

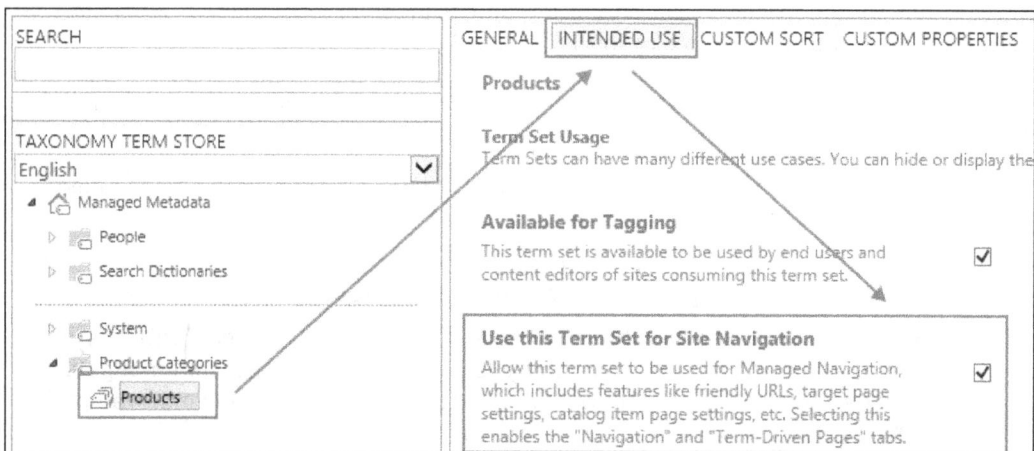

```
SEARCH                              GENERAL │ INTENDED USE │ CUSTOM SORT   CUSTOM PROPERTIES

                                    Products ↗

TAXONOMY TERM STORE                 Term Set Usage
English                     ✔       Term Sets can have many different use cases. You can hide or display the
  ⊿  🏠  Managed Metadata
      ▷  📇  People                  Available for Tagging
      ▷  📇  Search Dictionaries     This term set is available to be used by end users and          ☑
                                    content editors of sites consuming this term set.
      ▷  📇  System
      ⊿  📇  Product Categories      Use this Term Set for Site Navigation
          🗐  Products                Allow this term set to be used for Managed Navigation,          ☑
                                    which includes features like friendly URLs, target page
                                    settings, catalog item page settings, etc. Selecting this
                                    enables the "Navigation" and "Term-Driven Pages" tabs.
```

11. Click on **Save**.

12. Right-click on the drop-down menu of the **Products** term set and select **Create Term**.

13. Enter `Widgets` as the term name.

14. Right-click on the drop-down menu of the **Widgets** term and select **Create Term**.

15. Enter `Red` as the term name.

16. Press the *Enter* key to save the term and create a new one.

17. Create two more terms under the **Widgets** term, `Green` and `Blue`:

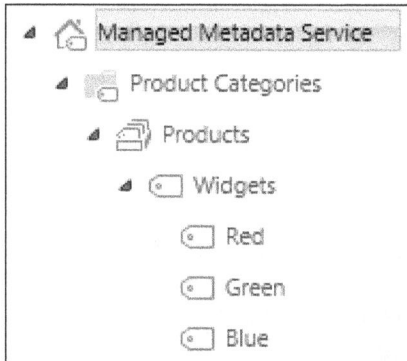

How it works...

Term sets in SharePoint provide a method for creating hierarchical structures to tag content with. In this recipe, we created a **Products** term set with a **Widgets** term that contains three subterms. We will use these to categorize our products in our product catalog later in the *Configuring the products list* recipe of this chapter.

Managed metadata taxonomy in a managed metadata service application is structured in SharePoint as follows:

- ▶ **Term store**: A term store is the root storage unit for taxonomy data per language. Term stores can only contain groups.

- ▶ **Group**: The groups are containers for term sets within term stores. Groups can only contain term sets. The group in our example was **Product Categories**.

- ▶ **Term set**: The term sets are the containers for terms within groups. Term sets can only contain terms and are usually the level of the taxonomy structure that gets attached to list columns, site navigation, and so on. The term set in our example was **Products**.

- ▶ **Term**: A term is a taxonomy item used for tagging content and many more. Terms can contain other terms in the taxonomy structure. The terms in our example included **Widgets**, **Red**, **Green**, and **Blue**.

There's more...

Managed metadata groups, term sets, and terms may also be created with PowerShell or code using the server-side object model.

Creating a categories term set for product catalog navigation using PowerShell

Follow these steps to create a categories term set using PowerShell:

1. Get the site collection with the `Get-SPSite` Cmdlet:

   ```
   $site = Get-SPSite http://sharepoint/sitecollection
   ```

2. Open a new taxonomy session with the `Get-SPTaxonomySession` Cmdlet:

   ```
   $session = Get-SPTaxonomySession –Site $site
   ```

3. Get the first term store from the taxonomy session. A term store may also be retrieved by its name; however, for simplicity we are just getting the first one:

   ```
   $termStore = $session.TermStores[0]
   ```

4. Create a new group in the term store named `PowerShell Product Categories`:

   ```
   $group = $termStore.CreateGroup("PowerShell Product
   Categories")
   ```

5. Create a new term set in the group named `Products`:

   ```
   $termSet = $group.CreateTermSet("Products")
   ```

6. Create a new term named `Widgets` in the group:

   ```
   $widgets = $termSet.CreateTerm("Widgets", 1033)
   ```

> When creating new term sets or terms in PowerShell or in code, the **locale identifier** (**LCID**) specifying the language of the item is required. We are using `1033` for U.S. English. A full list of Microsoft assigned LCIDs can be found on MSDN at `http://msdn.microsoft.com/en-us/library/microsoft.sharepoint.splocale.lcid.aspx`.

7. Create three new terms in the **Widgets** term named `Red`, `Green`, and `Blue`:

   ```
   $widgets.CreateTerm("Red", 1033)

   $widgets.CreateTerm("Green", 1033)

   $widgets.CreateTerm("Blue", 1033)
   ```

8. Commit the changes to the term store:

```
$termStore.CommitAll()
```

9. Use the `Dispose` method to discard the `SPSite` object:

```
$site.Dispose()
```

Creating a categories term set for product catalog navigation with code using the server-side object model

Follow these steps to create a categories term set with code using the server-side object model:

1. Get the site collection in a `using` statement:

```
using (var site = new
SPSite("http://sharepoint/publishing"))
```

2. Create a new taxonomy session from the site collection:

```
var session = new TaxonomySession(site);
```

3. Get the first term store in the session:

```
var termStore = session.TermStores[0];
```

4. Create a group named `Code Product Categories`:

```
var group = termStore.CreateGroup("Code Product
Categories");
```

5. Create a term set in the group named `Products`:

```
var termSet = group.CreateTermSet("Products");
```

6. Create a `Widgets` term in the `Products` term set:

```
var widgets = termSet.CreateTerm("Widgets", 1033);
```

7. Create `Red`, `Green`, and `Blue` terms in the `Widgets` term:

```
widgets.CreateTerm("Red", 1033);

widgets.CreateTerm("Green", 1033);

widgets.CreateTerm("Blue", 1033);
```

8. Commit the changes to the term store:

```
termStore.CommitAll();
```

See also

▶ The *Get-SPTaxonomySession* topic on TechNet at `http://technet.microsoft.com/en-us/library/ff608087.aspx`

▶ The *Microsoft.SharePoint.Taxonomy namespace* topic on MSDN at `http://msdn.microsoft.com/library/office/microsoft.sharepoint.taxonomy(v=office.15).aspx`

▶ The *SPLocale.LCID property* topic on MSDN at `http://msdn.microsoft.com/en-us/library/microsoft.sharepoint.splocale.lcid.aspx`

▶ The *Create and manage terms within term sets* article on the Microsoft Office help site at `http://office.microsoft.com/en-us/sharepoint-server-help/create-and-manage-terms-within-term-sets-HA101631581.aspx`

Creating a product catalog authoring site collection

In this recipe, we will create a product catalog site. The product catalog site collection will provide the source location for the products list we will use to create catalog connections with.

How to do it...

Follow these steps to create a product catalog authoring site collection:

1. Navigate to **Central Administration** in your preferred web browser.

2. Select **Create site collections** from the **Application Management** section:

Application Management
~~Manage web applications~~
Create site collections
~~Manage service applica~~tions
Manage content databases

3. Provide values for **Title**, **Description**, and **URL** for the new site collection:

Title and Description

Type a title and description for your new site. The title will be displayed on each page in the site.

Title:

Product Catalog

Description:

Product catalog site that contains our product list.

Web Site Address

Specify the URL name and URL path to create a new site, or choose to create a site at a specific path.

URL:

http://sharepoint /sites/ [▼] catalog

4. Select the **Product Catalog** template from the **Publishing** tab:

Select a template:

Collaboration   Enterprise   Publishing   Custom

Publishing Portal

Enterprise Wiki

Product Catalog

5. Enter your username for **Primary Site Collection Administrator**:

Primary Site Collection Administrator

Specify the administrator for this site collection. Only one user login can be provided; security groups are not supported.

User name:

John Chapman

6. Click on **OK**.

How it works...

Cross-site publishing requires a SharePoint site with publishing features as well as the cross-site publishing features enabled. The **Product Catalog** site collection template enables these features and creates the **Products** list.

See also

► The *Configure cross-site publishing in SharePoint 2013* article on TechNet at `http://technet.microsoft.com/en-us/library/jj656774.aspx`

Configuring the products list

In this recipe, we will add a managed metadata column and data to the **Products** list created as part of the product catalog site created in the previous recipe, *Creating a product catalog authoring site collection*. In addition, we will publish the **Products** list as a catalog list.

How to do it...

Follow these steps to configure the products list:

1. Navigate to the product catalog site we created in the *Creating a product catalog authoring site collection* recipe.

2. Select the **Products** list from the quick launch navigation:

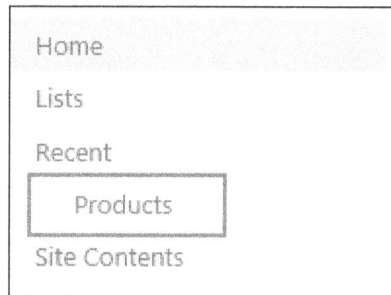

```
Home

Lists

Recent

    Products

Site Contents
```

3. From the **List** tab on the ribbon, select **List Settings**:

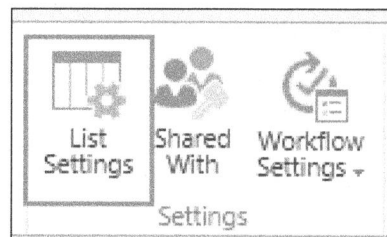

List Settings   Shared With   Workflow Settings

Settings

4. Select **Create column** from the **Columns** section:

> □ Create column
>
> □ Add from existing site columns
>
> □ Indexed columns

5. Enter `Category` as the column name.

6. Select **Managed Metadata** for the type of information:

Name and Type	
Type a name for this column, and select the type of information you want to store in the column.	Column name: `Category                                    ✕` The type of information in this column is: ○ Single line of text ○ Multiple lines of text ○ Choice (menu to choose from) ○ Number (1, 1.0, 100) ○ Currency ($, ¥, €) ○ Date and Time ○ Lookup (information already on this site) ○ Yes/No (check box) ○ Person or Group ○ Hyperlink or Picture ○ Calculated (calculation based on other columns) ○ External Data ○ Task Outcome ◉ Managed Metadata

7. Set **Require that this column contains information** to **Yes**:

Additional Column Settings	
Specify detailed options for the type of information you selected.	Description: Require that this column contains information: ◉ Yes ○ No Enforce unique values: ○ Yes ◉ No

8. Under **Term Set Settings**, navigate to and select our **Widgets** term:

Term Set Settings

Enter one or more terms, separated by semicolons, and select Find to filter the options to only include those which contain the desired values.

After finding the term set that contains the list of values to display options for this column, click on a term to select the first level of the hierarchy to show in the column. All levels below the term you select will be seen when users choose a value.

◉ Use a managed term set:
Find term sets that include the following terms.

◢ ⌂ Managed Metadata Service
　◢ ▦ Product Categories
　　◢ ▱ Products
　　　▷ ▱ **Widgets**
　▷ ▦ Search Dictionaries

9. Click on **OK**.

10. Navigate to the **Products** list.

11. Click on **New Item**.

12. Create six new list items (two for each category we created in our term set) with the following details:

Title	Item Number	Category
Widget A	001	Blue
Widget B	002	Blue
Widget C	003	Red
Widget D	004	Red
Widget E	005	Green
Widget F	006	Green

13. Select all of the list items in the **Products** list (by selecting the checkmarks to the left of each item):

Products ⓘ

⊕ new item or edit this list

All Items　Approve/reject Items　My submissions　•••　Find an item 🔍

✓	📎	🗋	Title		Item Number	Group Number	Language Tag	Rollup Image	Approval Status	Category	
✓		🗋	Widget A ✹	•••	001				Pending	Blue	
✓		🗋	Widget B ✹	•••	002				Pending	Blue	
✓		🗋	Widget C ✹	•••	003				Pending	Red	
✓		🗋	Widget D ✹	•••	004				Pending	Red	
✓		🗋	Widget E ✹	•••	005				Pending	Green	
✓		🗋	Widget F ✹	•••	006				Pending	Green	

14. Click on **Approve/Reject** from the **Items** tab on the ribbon:

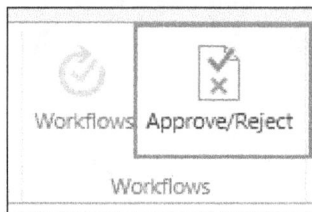

15. Select **Approved. The selected items will become visible to all users**:

Approval Status

Approve, reject, or leave the status as Pending for others with the Manage Lists permission to evaluate the selected items.

◉ Approved. The selected items will become visible to all users.

○ Rejected. The selected items will be returned to their creators and only be visible to their creators and all users who can see draft items.

○ Pending. The selected items will remain visible to their creators and all users who can see draft items.

16. Click on **OK**.

17. Select **List Settings** from the **List** tab on the ribbon.

18. Select **Catalog Settings** from the **General Settings** section:

General Settings

▫ List name, description and navigation
▫ Versioning settings
▫ Advanced settings
▫ Validation settings
▫ Rating settings
▫ Audience targeting settings
▫ Metadata navigation settings
▫ Per-location view settings
▫ Form settings
▫ Catalog Settings

19. Check the **Enable this library as a catalog** checkbox:

Catalog Sharing

Make content in this list available to other sites
and site collections through search.

☑ Enable this library as a catalog

20. Select **Enable anonymous access**:

Anonymous Access

With this option enabled, users who aren't
logged in can view, navigate, and search content
from this catalog on connected sites.

Enable anonymous access

Anonymous access off

21. Select **Make Anonymous**.

22. Add **Category** and **Item Number** to the **Selected Fields** list for **Catalog Item URL Fields**:

Catalog Item URL Fields

Select up to five fields to use as identifiers for
catalog items that may be appended to URLs for
items in this catalog on connected sites.

Available Fields

Group Number
ID
Title
Version

Add >

<
Remove

Selected Fields

Category
Item Number

23. Select **Category** as the column to categorize items for navigation:

Navigation Hierarchy

Select the managed metadata column that
contains the desired navigation hierarchy for use
on connected sites.

Select the column that categorizes items for navigation:

Category ▼

⚠ Make sure that the column's term set is global or that connected site collections have been given access to use
term set. You can verify this in the Term Store Manager.

24. Click on **OK**.

How it works...

The content provided by catalog lists and libraries is indexed and cached by the SharePoint search crawler. Once indexed, the content becomes available for consumption by other site collections. In this recipe, we have created a simple list of products categorized by a simple term set. Once consumed, the term set will provide the basis for the friendly URLs created for each item.

Making the catalog list anonymously accessible allows the catalog list to be used on sites where anonymous access is available. This is a common scenario for public-facing websites. The fields selected for **Catalog Item URL Fields** will be used when creating the friendly URLs for the list items. We will see this later on in the chapter in the *Setting up a consuming site collection and connecting to the product catalog list* recipe.

There's more...

Adding fields to lists, adding items to lists, and publishing lists as catalogs may also be accomplished with PowerShell or code using the server-side object model.

Configuring the products list using PowerShell

Follow these steps to configure the products list using PowerShell:

1. Get the site collection using the `Get-SPSite` Cmdlet:

    ```
    $site = Get-SPSite http://sharepoint/sitecollection
    ```

2. Open a new taxonomy session using the site collection with the `Get-SPTaxonomySession` Cmdlet:

    ```
    $session = Get-SPTaxonomySession -Site $site
    ```

3. Get the first term store in the taxonomy session:

    ```
    $termStore = $session.TermStores[0]
    ```

4. Get the **PowerShell Product Categories** group from the term store:

    ```
    $group = $termStore.Groups["PowerShell Product Categories"]
    ```

5. Get the **Products** term set from the group:

    ```
    $termSet = $group.TermSets["Products"]
    ```

6. Get the **Products** list from the root site of the site collection:

    ```
    $list = $site.RootWeb.Lists["Products"]
    ```

7. Create a new taxonomy (managed metadata) field named `PowerShell Category`:

    ```
    $field = [Microsoft.SharePoint.Taxonomy.TaxonomyField]
    $list.Fields.CreateNewField("TaxonomyFieldType", "PowerShell
    Category")
    ```

8. Set the anchor term ID to an empty GUID.

> When configuring a managed metadata field, a root term may be selected to limit which terms may be used in the field. This is the anchor term.

```
$field.AnchorId = [System.Guid]::Empty
```

9. Set the term store ID, group name, and term set ID on the field:

```
$field.SspId = $termStore.Id

$field.Group = "PowerShell Product Categories"

$field.TermSetId = $termSet.Id
```

10. Configure the field to only allow a single value:

```
$field.AllowMultipleValues = $false
```

11. Add the field to the collection of fields on the **Products** list:

```
$list.Fields.Add($field)
```

12. Update the **Products** list:

```
$list.Update()
```

13. Get the **Widgets** term from the term set:

```
$termWidgets = $termSet.Terms["Widgets"]
```

14. Get the **Red**, **Green**, and **Blue** terms from the **Widgets** term:

```
$termRed = $termWidgets.Terms["Red"]

$termGreen = $termWidgets.Terms["Green"]

$termBlue = $termWidgets.Terms["Blue"]
```

15. Get the **PowerShell Category** field from the **Products** list:

```
$field = [Microsoft.SharePoint.Taxonomy.TaxonomyField]
$list.Fields["PowerShell Category"]
```

16. Create a taxonomy value for the **Red**, **Green**, and **Blue** terms. Repeat this code for each term:

```
$valueRed = New-Object
Microsoft.SharePoint.Taxonomy.TaxonomyFieldValue -ArgumentList
$field

$valueRed.TermGuid = $termRed.Id.ToString()

$valueRed.Label = $termRed.Name
```

17. Add list items to the **Products** list using the **Red**, **Green**, and **Blue** taxonomy values. Repeat this code to create six items, two for each term:

```
$item001 = $list.Items.Add()

$item001["Title"] = "PowerShell Widget A"

$item001["Item Number"] = "P001"

$item001["PowerShell Category"] = $valueBlue

$item001.Update()
```

18. Update the **Products** list:

```
$list.Update()
```

19. Set the moderation status of each item to `Approved`. Repeat this code for each of the items created in step 17:

```
$item001.ModerationInformation.Status = "Approved"

$item001.Update()
```

20. Create a generic list of field names to use as the URL fields for the catalog list:

```
$urlFields = New-Object -TypeName System.Collections.Generic.
List[System.String]

$urlFields.Add("Title")

$urlFields.Add("Item Number")
```

21. Create a new `CatalogTaxonomyFieldSettings` object to configure the term set used for the navigation hierarchy of the catalog:

```
$taxFieldSetting = New-Object -TypeName
Microsoft.SharePoint.Publishing.CatalogTaxonomyFieldSettings

$field = $list.Fields["PowerShell Category"]

$taxFieldSetting.TermId = $field.AnchorId

$taxFieldSetting.TermSetId = $termSet.Id

$taxFieldSetting.TermStoreId = $termStore.Id

$taxFieldSetting.FieldId = $field.Id

$taxFieldSetting.FieldManagedPropertyName = "owstaxid" +
$field.InternalName
```

```
$taxFieldSetting.IsSelected = $true

$taxFieldSetting.FieldDisplayName = $field.StaticName
```

22. Use the `PublishCatalog` method of the `PublishingCatalogUtility` class to publish the **Products** list as a catalog list:

```
[Microsoft.SharePoint.Publishing.PublishingCatalogUtility]::
PublishCatalog($site.RootWeb, $list, $true, $urlFields,
$taxFieldSetting)
```

Configuring the products list with code using the server-side object model

Follow these steps to configure the products list with code using the server-side object model:

1. Get the site collection in a `using` statement:

    ```
    using (var site = new
    SPSite("http://sharepoint/publishing"))
    ```

2. Create a new taxonomy session from the site collection:

    ```
    var session = new TaxonomySession(site);
    ```

3. Get the **Products** term set using the following code:

    ```
    var termStore = session.TermStores[0];

    var group = termStore.Groups["Code Product Categories"];

    var termSet = group.TermSets["Products"];
    ```

4. Get the **Products** list:

    ```
    var list = site.RootWeb.Lists["Products"];
    ```

5. Add a new managed metadata field to the **Products** list using the following code snippet:

    ```
    var field = list.Fields.CreateNewField("TaxonomyFieldType", "Code
    Category") as TaxonomyField;

    field.AnchorId = Guid.Empty;

    field.SspId = termStore.Id;

    field.Group = "Code Product Categories";

    field.TermSetId = termSet.Id;

    field.AllowMultipleValues = false;

    list.Fields.Add(field);

    list.Update();
    ```

6. Get the **Red**, **Green**, and **Blue** terms from the **Widgets** term as follows:

```
var termWidgets = termSet.Terms["Widgets"];

var termRed = termWidgets.Terms["Red"];

var termGreen = termWidgets.Terms["Green"];

var termBlue = termWidgets.Terms["Blue"];
```

7. Get the managed metadata field from the list:

```
field = list.Fields["Code Category"] as TaxonomyField;
```

8. Using the following code, create taxonomy values for the **Red**, **Green**, and **Blue** terms. Repeat this code for each term.

```
var valueRed = new TaxonomyFieldValue(field);

valueRed.TermGuid = termRed.Id.ToString();

valueRed.Label = termRed.Name;
```

9. With the help of the following code, add items to the **Products** list with the term values. Repeat this code to add six items to the list, two for each term.

```
var item001 = list.Items.Add();

item001["Title"] = "Code Widget A";

item001["Item Number"] = "C001";

item001["Code Category"] = valueBlue;

item001.Update();
```

10. Update the list:

```
list.Update();
```

11. Set the moderation status of each item to `Approved`. Repeat this code for each item created in step 9.

```
item001.ModerationInformation.Status = SPModerationStatusType.
Approved;

item001.Update();
```

12. Create a generic list of field names for the URL fields of the catalog list as follows:

```
var urlFields = new List<string>();

urlFields.Add("Title");

urlFields.Add("Item Number");
```

13. Create a `CatalogTaxonomyFieldSettings` object to configure the navigation hierarchy of the catalog list using the following code snippet:

```
var taxFieldSetting = new CatalogTaxonomyFieldSettings();

field = list.Fields["Code Category"] as TaxonomyField;

taxFieldSetting.TermId = field.AnchorId;

taxFieldSetting.TermSetId = termSet.Id;

taxFieldSetting.TermStoreId = termStore.Id;

taxFieldSetting.FieldId = field.Id;

taxFieldSetting.FieldManagedPropertyName = "owstaxid" +
field.InternalName;

taxFieldSetting.IsSelected = true;

taxFieldSetting.FieldDisplayName = field.StaticName;
```

14. Publish the catalog list with the `PublishingCatalogUtility` class as follows:

```
PublishingCatalogUtility.PublishCatalog(site.RootWeb, list,
true, urlFields, new List<CatalogTaxonomyFieldSettings>()
{ taxFieldSetting });
```

See also

▶ The *Microsoft.SharePoint.Taxonomy Namespace* topic on MSDN at http://msdn.microsoft.com/en-us/library/microsoft.sharepoint.taxonomy(v=office.14).aspx

▶ The *PublishingCatalogUtility class* topic on MSDN at http://msdn.microsoft.com/en-us/library/microsoft.sharepoint.publishing.publishingcatalogutility.aspx

▶ The *Configure cross-site publishing in SharePoint Server 2013* article on TechNet at http://technet.microsoft.com/en-us/library/jj656774.aspx

Creating a catalog document library

The cross-site publishing features work ideally with list content. However, it is possible to create catalog libraries. In this recipe, we will add a new pages library to our product catalog site created in the *Creating a product catalog authoring site collection* recipe. In addition, we will publish the pages library as a catalog library.

The product catalog site template does not provide the pages library template in the list of items that can be added to the site. As such, we will create a document library and turn it into a pages library.

How to do it...

Follow these steps to create a catalog library:

1. Navigate to the product catalog site in your preferred web browser.
2. Select **Site contents** from the **Settings** menu.
3. Click on **add an app** as shown in the following screenshot:

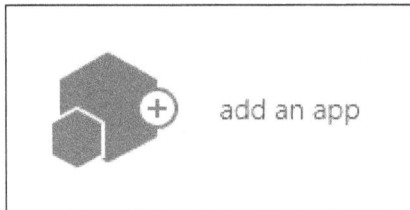

4. Select **Document Library** as shown in the following screenshot:

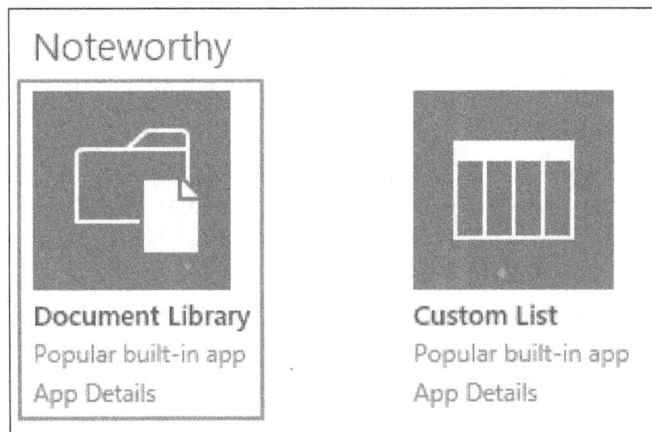

5. Provide a name for the library, Product Documents, for example, as shown in the following screenshot:

6. Click on the **Create** button.
7. Navigate to the new document library.
8. From the **Library** tab on the ribbon, select **Library Settings**.
9. Select **Advanced settings** from the **General Settings** section as shown in the following screenshot:

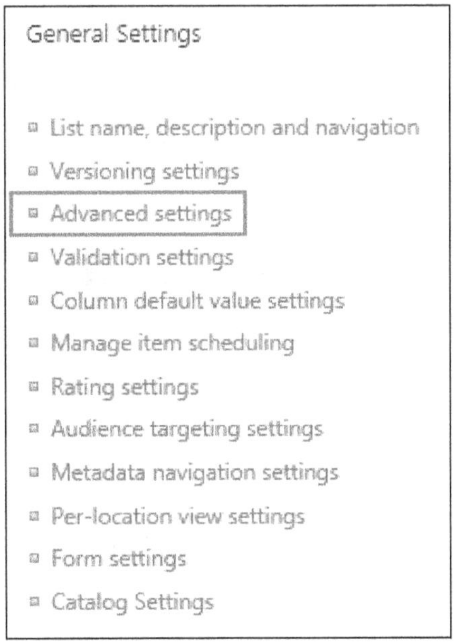

10. Set **Allow management of content types?** to **Yes**. Have a look at the following screenshot:

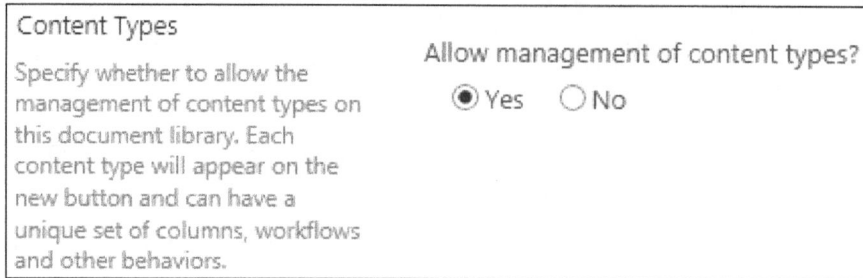

> **Content Types**
>
> Specify whether to allow the management of content types on this document library. Each content type will appear on the new button and can have a unique set of columns, workflows and other behaviors.
>
> **Allow management of content types?**
> ● Yes   ○ No

11. Click on **OK**.

12. Select **Add from existing site content types** from the **Content Types** section:

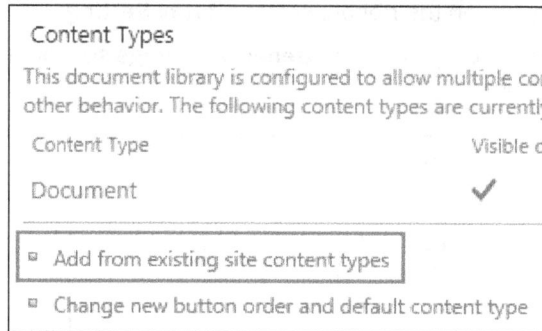

> **Content Types**
>
> This document library is configured to allow multiple con other behavior. The following content types are currently
>
> | Content Type | Visible o |
> | --- | --- |
> | Document | ✓ |
>
> ▫ Add from existing site content types
> ▫ Change new button order and default content type

13. Add the **Basic Page** content type as shown in the following screenshot:

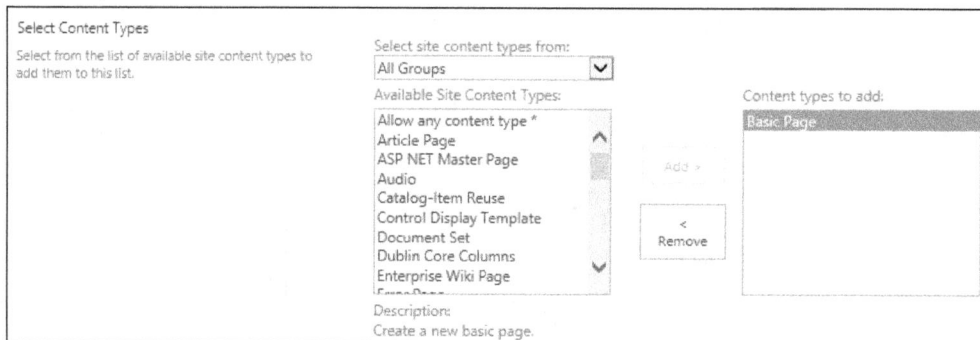

> **Select Content Types**
>
> Select from the list of available site content types to add them to this list.
>
> Select site content types from:
> All Groups ▾
>
> Available Site Content Types:
>
> Allow any content type *
> Article Page
> ASP NET Master Page
> Audio
> Catalog-Item Reuse
> Control Display Template
> Document Set
> Dublin Core Columns
> Enterprise Wiki Page
>
> Content types to add:
> Basic Page
>
> Add >
> < Remove
>
> Description:
> Create a new basic page.

14. Click on **OK**.

15. Select the **Document** content type from the **Content Types** section:

Content Types

This document library is configured to allow multiple content ty
other behavior. The following content types are currently availab

Content Type	Visible on New
Document	✓
Basic Page	✓

16. Select **Delete this content type** from the **Settings** section:

Settings

- Name and description
- Advanced settings
- Workflow settings
- Delete this content type
- Information management policy settings
- Document Information Panel settings

17. Select **Create Column** from the **Columns** section.

18. Enter category for the **Column Name**.

19. Select **Managed Metadata** for the type.

20. Set **Require that this column contains information** to **Yes**.

21. Under **Term Set Settings**, navigate to and select our **Widgets** term set.

22. Click on **OK**.

23. Navigate to the document library and select **New Document** from the **Files** tab on the ribbon.

24. Enter WidgetASpecs as the **Name** and then click on **Create**:

Site Contents › New Basic Page ⓘ

Name

Type a file name for your basic page. The file name appears in headings and links throughout the site.

Name:

WidgetASpecs   .aspx

☐ Overwrite if file already exists?

25. Edit the page and provide some text.

26. From the **PAGE** tab on the ribbon, select **Edit Properties** as shown in the following screenshot:

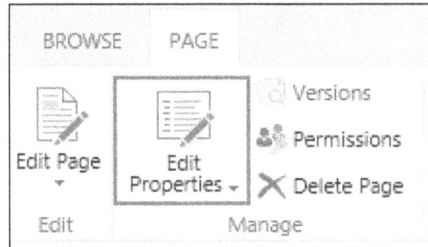

27. Select a term for the category:

28. Click on **Save**.

29. Navigate to the document library.

30. Check-in the newly created page.

31. Select **Library Settings** from the **Library** tab on the ribbon.

32. Under **General Settings**, select **Catalog Settings**.

33. Check the **Enable this library as a catalog** checkbox.

34. Click on **Enable anonymous access** and then click on **Make Anonymous**.

35. Add **Category** and **Title** to the **Selected Fields** list for **Catalog Item URL Fields**.

36. Select **Category** as the column to categorize items for navigation and click on **OK**.

How it works...

In a similar fashion to our **Products** list, the document library will be made available as a catalog library through the search services once it has been crawled. Using a catalog library may not prove as useful as a catalog list. By default, the properties of a catalog library item will be displayed in the consuming site, not the document itself. Additional customization would be required in order to retrieve the documents themselves through a catalog connection. For more information on catalog libraries, refer to `http://technet.microsoft.com/en-us/library/jj656774.aspx`.

Setting up a consuming site collection and connecting to the product catalog list

Using the cross-site publishing features provides a number of possibilities in which the content may be utilized. In this recipe, we will create a simple consuming site collection with product catalog navigation that consumes the list published from the site created in the *Creating a product catalog authoring site collection* recipe. The following is the diagram of cross-site publishing architecture:

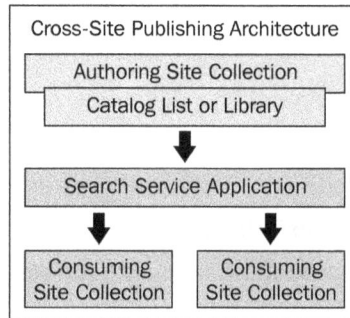

```
        Cross-Site Publishing Architecture
        ┌─────────────────────────────────┐
        │   Authoring Site Collection      │
        │   Catalog List or Library        │
        └─────────────────────────────────┘
                        │
                        ▼
        ┌─────────────────────────────────┐
        │     Search Service Application   │
        └─────────────────────────────────┘
              │                    │
              ▼                    ▼
        ┌──────────┐        ┌──────────┐
        │Consuming │        │Consuming │
        │   Site   │        │   Site   │
        │Collection│        │Collection│
        └──────────┘        └──────────┘
```

How to do it...

Follow these steps to create a consuming site collection:

1. Navigate to **Central Administration** in your preferred web browser.
2. Select **Create site collections** from the **Application Management** section.
3. Provide values for **Title**, **Description**, and **URL** for the new site collection as shown in the following screenshot:

Title and Description

Type a title and description for your new site. The title will be displayed on each page in the site.

Title:

Consumer

Description:

Publishing site that consumes the product catalog list and library.

Web Site Address

Specify the URL name and URL path to create a new site, or choose to create a site at a specific path.

URL:

http://sharepoint /sites/ ▼ consumer

4. Select the **Publishing Portal** template from the **Publishing** tab as shown in the following screenshot:

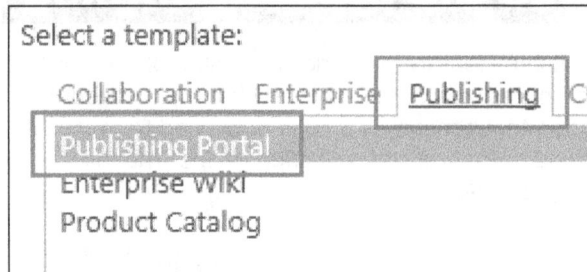

Select a template:

| Collaboration | Enterprise | **Publishing** | Cu |

Publishing Portal
Enterprise Wiki
Product Catalog

5. Enter your username for **Primary Site Collection Administrator**.

6. Click on **OK**.

7. Navigate to the consuming site collection in your preferred web browser.

8. Select **Site settings** from the **Settings** menu.

9. Select **Term store management** from the **Site Administration** section as shown in the following screenshot:

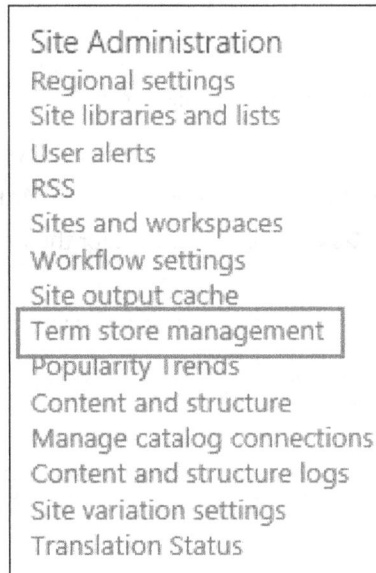

Site Administration
Regional settings
Site libraries and lists
User alerts
RSS
Sites and workspaces
Workflow settings
Site output cache
Term store management
Popularity Trends
Content and structure
Manage catalog connections
Content and structure logs
Site variation settings
Translation Status

10. Create a new group named `Navigation` and then a term set named `Site Navigation` in that group.

11. In the **INTENDED USE** tab for the **Site Navigation** term set, check the **Use this Term Set for Site Navigation** checkbox and uncheck the **Available for Tagging** checkbox, as shown in the following screenshot:

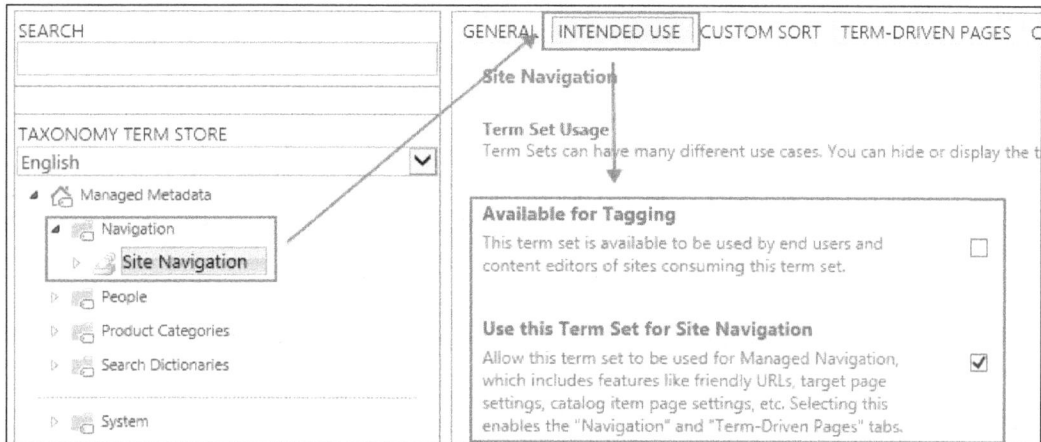

12. Click on **Save**.

> When we create our catalog connection, this newly created term set will be used to store the terms used by the site navigation. Attempting to use the product categories term set as the navigation term set will result in errors when creating the catalog connection.

13. Select **Site settings** from the **Settings** menu.

14. Select **Navigation** from the **Look and Feel** section as shown in the following screenshot:

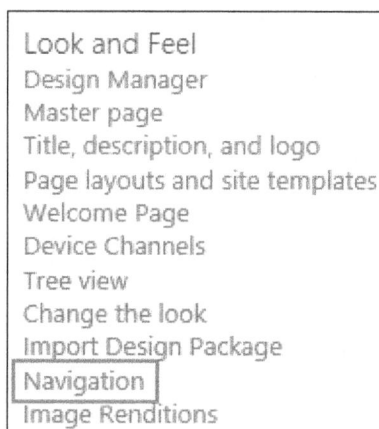

15. For both **Current Navigation** and **Global Navigation**, select **Managed Navigation** as shown in the following screenshot:

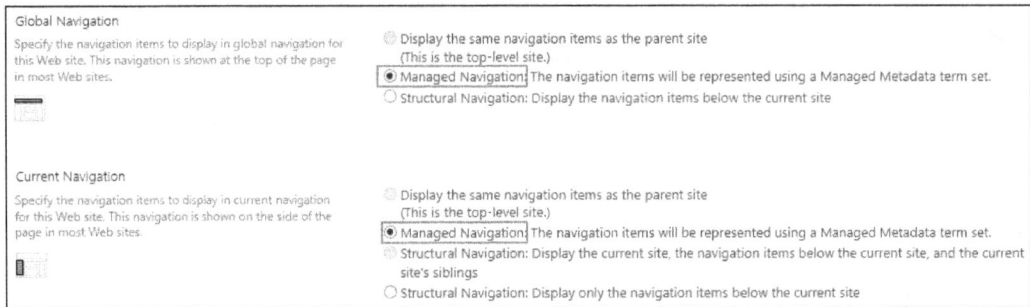

16. Select our **Site Navigation** term set from the **Managed Navigation: Term Set** section as shown in the following screenshot:

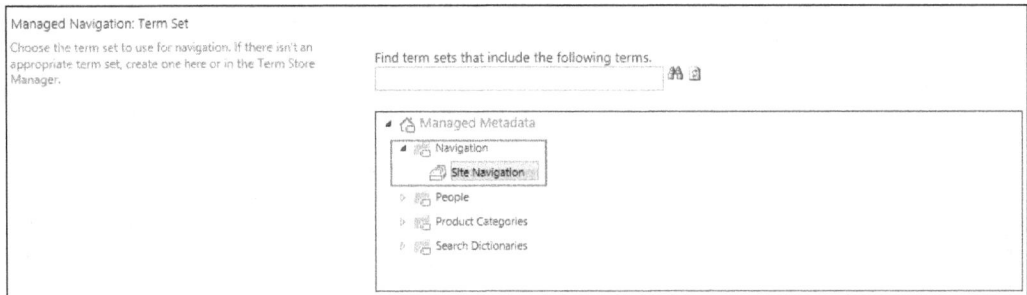

17. Click on **OK**.

18. Select **Manage catalog connections** from the **Site Administration** section:

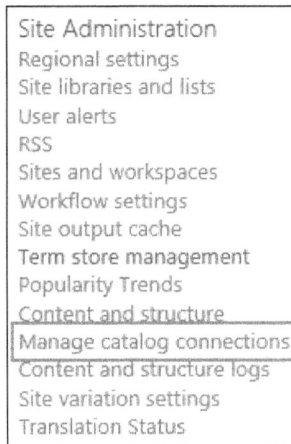

19. Click on **Connect to catalog** and then click on **Connect** for the **Products** list:

Site Settings › Manage catalog connections › Connect to catalog

⚠ **Note:** Catalogs shared in the last few minutes will not appear in this list until the next scheduled search crawl.

| | Search |

Available Catalogs:

Catalog Name	URL	
Product Catalog - Products	http://sharepoint/sites/catalog/Lists/Products	Connect

If our recently created **Products** catalog list is not available to choose from, it is most likely because the search crawler has not indexed the content yet.

20. Leave the default connection configuration options and click on **OK**.

21. Select **Site contents** from the **Settings** menu.

22. Select the **Pages** library.

23. Check-in and publish the newly created category and item pages:

Blue   Green   Product Documentation   Red   ✎ EDIT LINKS

Pages ⓘ

⊕ new item or drag files here

All Documents   ••• | Find a file   🔍 |

✓	☐	Name		Modified	Modified By	Checked Out To	Contact	Page Layout
	📑	CatalogItem-Widgets ✹	•••	3 minutes ago	☐ John Chapman	☐ John Chapman	☐ John Chapman	CatalogItem-Widgets
	📑	Category-Widgets ✹	•••	3 minutes ago	☐ John Chapman	☐ John Chapman	☐ John Chapman	Category-Widgets
	📄	default ✹	•••	39 minutes ago	☐ System Account			Blank Web Part page
	📄	PageNotFoundError ✹	•••	39 minutes ago	☐ System Account		☐ System Account	Error

24. Select one of the categories from the header or quick launch navigation to observe the newly created category page. Notice the friendly URL used when navigating to a category page, marked with a red rectangle in the following screenshot:

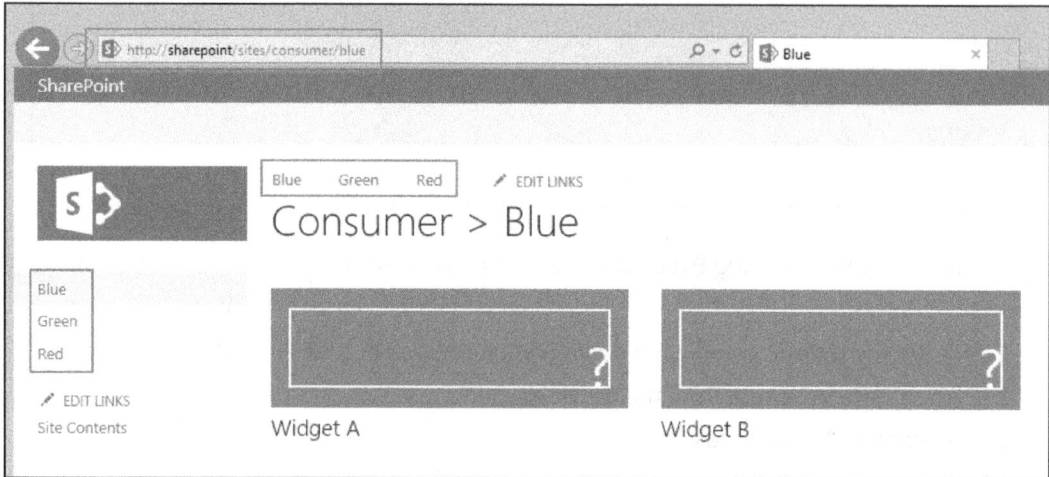

25. Select an item from the category page to observe the newly created item page. Notice the friendly URL used when navigating to the item page:

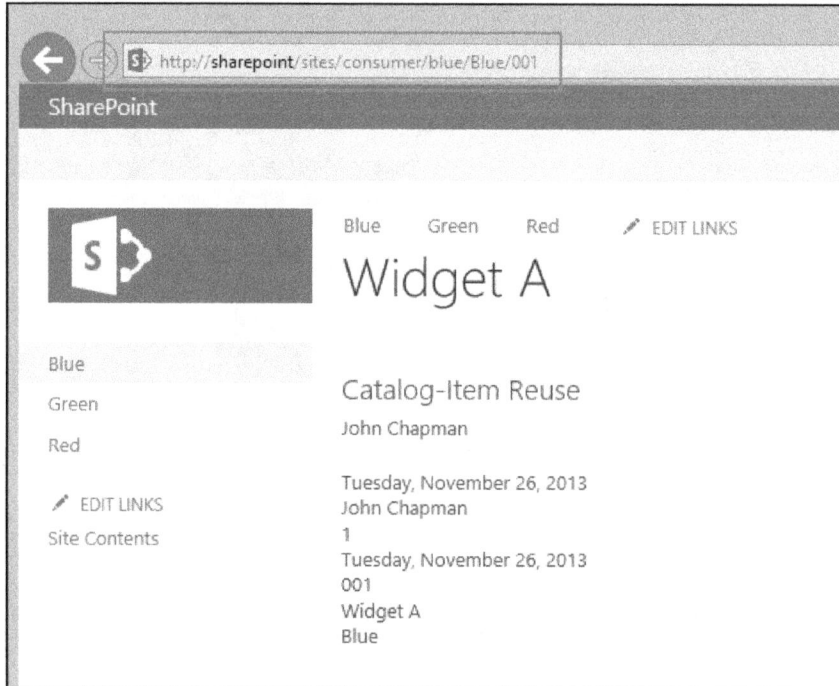

How it works...

Consuming site collections create a connection to the authoring site collection, in order to access the catalog content provided by the authoring site collection. When the SharePoint search crawler indexes the consuming site collection, it includes the catalog content as part of its content. In addition, creating the catalog connection results in category and item pages being created that are used while navigating to the categories and items.

This recipe demonstrated the basics for creating the connection to the catalog list, which resulted in pages being created to display the categories and items. These are web part pages that can be configured to display the information in whichever way it is most appropriate for the implementation.

There's more...

Creating connections to catalog lists may also be accomplished with PowerShell or code using the server-side object model.

Setting up a consuming site collection and connecting to the product catalog list using PowerShell

Follow these steps to create a consuming site collection using PowerShell:

1. Get the consuming site collection with the `Get-SPSite` Cmdlet as follows:

   ```
   $site = Get-SPSite http://sharepoint/sitecollection
   ```

2. Create a new `CatalogConnectionManager` object from the site collection using the following code:

   ```
   $catalogManager = New-Object
   Microsoft.SharePoint.Publishing.CatalogConnectionManager -
   ArgumentList $site, $true
   ```

3. Get the published catalog list using its full URL:

   ```
   $settings =
   [Microsoft.SharePoint.Publishing.PublishingCatalogUtility]::
   GetPublishingCatalog($site,
   "http://sharepoint/sites/catalog/Lists/Products")
   ```

4. Add the published catalog to the catalog connection manager as follows:

   ```
   $catalogManager.AddCatalogConnection($settings)
   ```

5. Update the connection manager as follows:

   ```
   $catalogManager.Update()
   ```

Setting up a consuming site collection and connecting to the product catalog list with code using the server-side object model

Follow these steps to create a consuming site collection with code using the server-side object model:

1. Get the site collection in a `using` statement:

    ```
    using (var site = new
    SPSite("http://sharepoint/publishing"))
    ```

2. Create a new `CatalogConnectionManager` object for the site collection.

    ```
    var manager = new CatalogConnectionManager(site, true);
    ```

3. Get the catalog list by its URL using the following code:

    ```
    var settings =
    PublishingCatalogUtility.GetPublishingCatalog(site,
    "http://sharepoint/sites/catalog/Lists/Products");
    ```

4. Add the catalog list to the connection manager and update as follows:

    ```
    manager.AddCatalogConnection(settings);
    manager.Update();
    ```

See also

▶   The *CatalogConnectionManager class* topic on MSDN at `http://msdn.microsoft.com/en-us/library/microsoft.sharepoint.publishing.catalogconnectionmanager.aspx`

▶   The *Configure cross-site publishing in SharePoint Server 2013* article on TechNet at `http://technet.microsoft.com/en-us/library/jj656774.aspx`

Setting up a consuming site collection with separate branding

Catalog lists and libraries may be consumed by multiple site collections. This is particularly useful when the same catalog data is used in sites with different branding or sites used for testing. In this recipe, we will create a second consuming site collection using a different master page to illustrate the concept.

How to do it...

Follow these steps to create a consuming site collection with separate branding:

1. Create a new site collection using the **Publishing Portal** template.

2. Navigate to the consuming site collection in your preferred web browser.

3. Select **Site settings** from the **Settings** menu.

4. Select **Master page** from the **Look and Feel** section.

5. Set the **Site Master Page** and **System Master Page** to **oslo**.

6. Click on **OK**.

7. Repeat steps 8 through 24 of the *Setting up a consuming site collection and connecting to the product catalog list* recipe to create the connection to the **Products** list.

> Create a new group in the term store for the navigation of this site. Do not reuse the **Site Navigation** group from the *Setting up a consuming site collection and connecting to the product catalog list* recipe.

8. Navigate to a category page to observe the results:

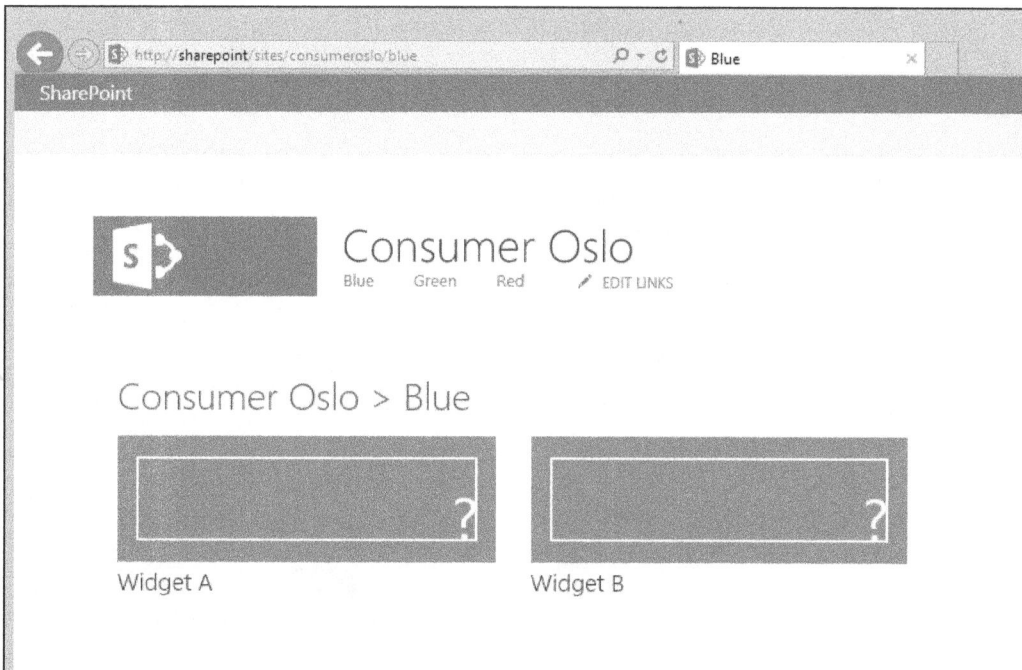

How it works...

Catalog lists and libraries may be connected to from multiple site collections. Like our first consuming site collection, the content is made available through this consuming site by the search service. This is particularly useful when multiple sites in the farm require the same information. In this recipe, we created a catalog connection from a site collection using the oslo master page.

7
Customizing the SharePoint Experience with Delegate Controls

In this chapter, we will delve into the custom-delegate control model for adding custom code to SharePoint 2013. We will cover the following recipes:

- ▶ Creating a Visual Studio solution for custom delegate controls
- ▶ Adding JavaScript and stylesheets with an AdditionalPageHead delegate control
- ▶ Customizing the suite bar branding with a SuiteBarBrandingDelegate delegate control
- ▶ Customizing the suite bar links with a SuiteLinksDelegate delegate control
- ▶ Adding Office 365-style drop-down menus to suite bar links
- ▶ Adding promoted action links with the PromotedActions delegate control
- ▶ Customizing header navigation with a TopNavigationDataSource delegate control
- ▶ Customizing quick launch navigation with a QuickLaunchDataSource delegate control
- ▶ Restoring the Navigate Up button with an AdditionalPageHead delegate control
- ▶ Adding meta tags to pages from custom library fields with an AdditionalPageHead delegate control
- ▶ Storing analytics tracking code with a site collection settings page
- ▶ Adding stored analytics tracking code to pages with an AdditionalPageHead delegate control

Introduction

Microsoft SharePoint provides a variety of ways to add custom code to enhance or customize the SharePoint experience. These include web parts, timer jobs, application pages, delegate controls, custom actions, and so on. Delegate controls provide numerous locations on each SharePoint master page where default controls may be replaced with specified custom controls. This allows for SharePoint to place different controls on the page based on the features that are activated. For instance, when publishing features are enabled, SharePoint will use the delegate controls to add the publishing controls to the page.

In addition to the delegate controls provided (and required) on each SharePoint master page, additional delegate controls can be added to custom master pages. In this chapter, however, we will stick to the ones provided by SharePoint. The commonly used delegate controls provided by SharePoint are listed in the following table:

Control ID	Purpose
AdditionalPageHead	It adds controls to the `<head>` element of the page.
SuiteBarBrandingDelegate	It adds branding text to the top-left corner in the suite bar. Displays **SharePoint** by default.
SuiteLinksDelegate	It adds the suite links to the suite bar. Displays **Newsfeed**, **SkyDrive**, and **Sites** by default.
PromotedActions	It adds additional actions to the promoted actions on the top-right corner of the page. Using this delegate control does not remove the existing promoted actions.
TopNavigationDataSource	It adds the site map provider used by the horizontal navigation at the top of the page.
QuickLaunchDataSource	It adds the site map provider used by the vertical navigation on the left-hand side of the page.
TreeViewAndDataSource	It adds the tree view control and its site map provider when enabled.
GlobalNavigation	It adds a shared navigation control that renders above all other content on the page.
SmallSearchInputBox	It adds the search box to the page.

Creating a Visual Studio solution for custom delegate controls

Delegate controls provide a mechanism for adding ASP.NET user controls. As such, to create, compile, and package custom controls, we will use a Visual Studio solution. In this recipe, we will create the Visual Studio SharePoint project that we will use for this chapter. For simplicity, we will add each subsequent recipe to this single project.

> Since the recipes in this chapter include items that will make changes to the `web.config` file of the SharePoint web application in IIS, we will be creating a farm solution.

Getting ready

In order to create a custom SharePoint solution with Visual Studio, we will need to have Visual Studio 2012 with the Office Developer Tools or Visual Studio 2013 applications installed on a computer running SharePoint Server 2013. In addition, we will need local computer administrator and SharePoint farm administrator access.

> If using PowerShell to deploy the custom SharePoint solution, SharePoint shell access to the SharePoint configuration database in SQL will also be required. Refer to `http://technet.microsoft.com/en-us/library/ff607596.aspx` for more information on adding a SharePoint shell administrator.

How to do it...

Follow these steps to create a Visual Studio solution for custom-delegate controls:

1. Open Visual Studio running as administrator.
2. From the **File** menu, select **New Project**.

3. Select the **SharePoint 2013 – Empty Project** template by navigating to **Templates |
Visual C# | Office/SharePoint | SharePoint Solutions** as shown in the
following screenshot:

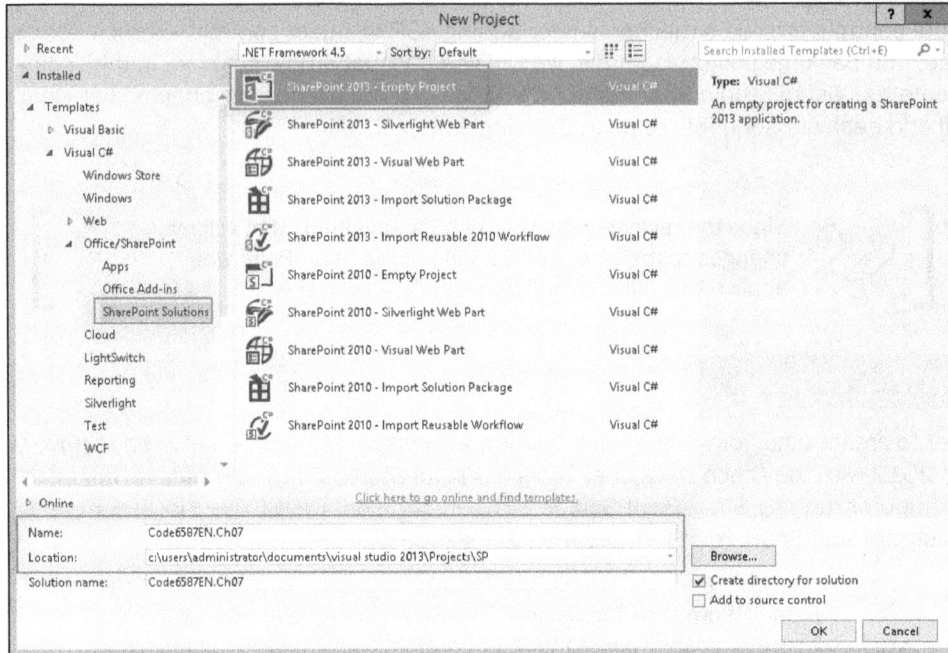

4. Provide values in the **Name** and **Location** textboxes for the project and click on **OK**.

5. Provide the URL to the local SharePoint site you will be testing with:

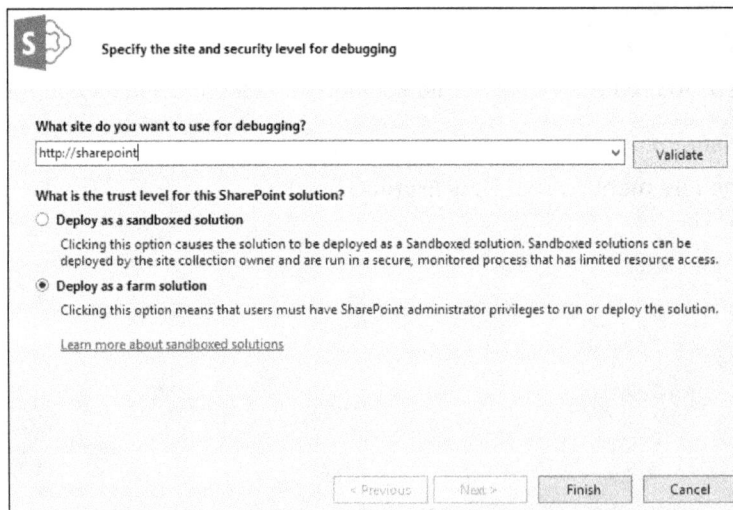

6. Select **Deploy as a farm solution** and click on **Finish**.

7. Add project references to `System.Configuration` and `Microsoft.SharePoint.Publishing`. The `Microsoft.SharePoint.Publishing` assembly can be found at `C:\Program Files\Common Files\Web Server Extensions\15\ISAPI`.

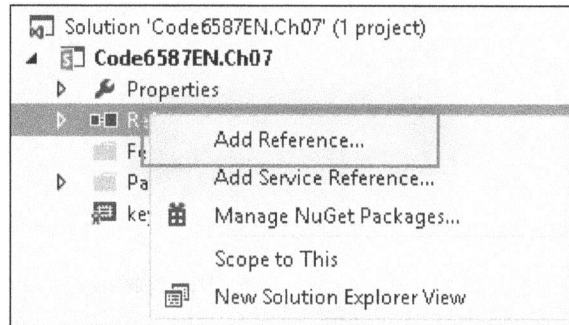

8. Right-click on the project name in the **Solution Explorer** pane.

9. Navigate to **Add | New Folder** as shown in the following screenshot:

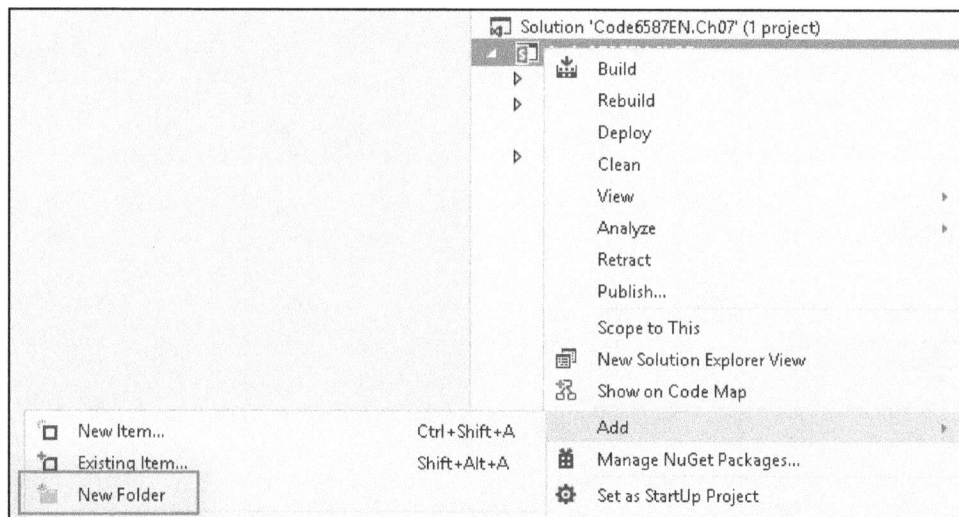

10. Create a folder named `Controls`. We will use the `Controls` folder later in the chapter to store all of our code-only user controls.

11. Right-click on the project name.

12. Navigate to **Add | SharePoint Mapped Folder...** as shown in the following screenshot:

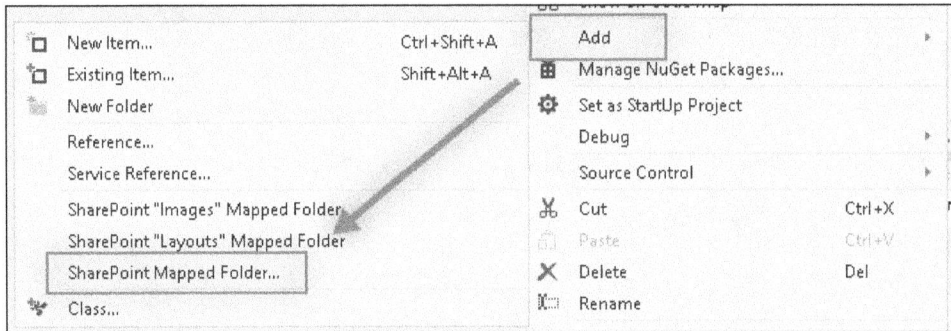

13. Select the CONTROLTEMPLATES folder under the TEMPLATE folder. We will use the CONTROLTEMPLATES mapped folder to store all of our ASCX user controls later in the chapter.

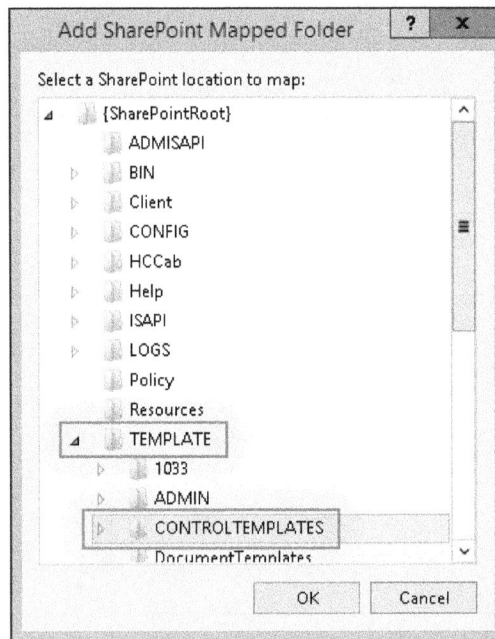

14. Click on **OK**.

15. Add a folder in the CONTROLTEMPLATES mapped folder with the same name as the project. When working with mapped folders, it is important to place items in a subfolder that is unique. This will alleviate any collisions with files of the same names included with SharePoint or provided by other custom solutions.

16. Click on the **SharePoint "Layouts" Mapped Folder** option to add the Layouts mapped folder, which we will use later in the chapter to store our application page, stylesheets, and JavaScript:

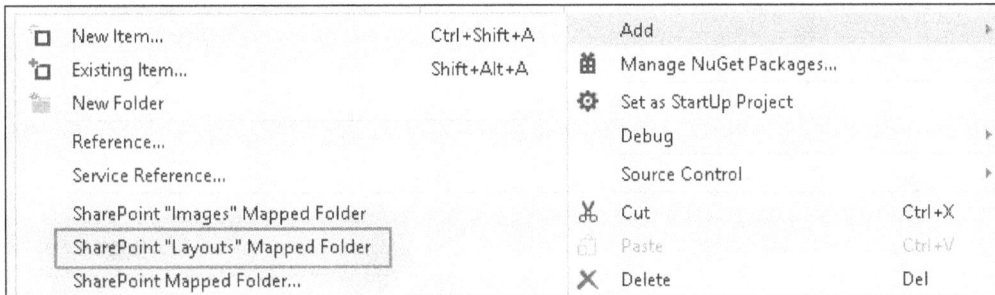

☐ New Item...	Ctrl+Shift+A	Add	▶
☐ Existing Item...	Shift+Alt+A	📦 Manage NuGet Packages...	
New Folder		⚙ Set as StartUp Project	
Reference...		Debug	▶
Service Reference...		Source Control	▶
SharePoint "Images" Mapped Folder		✂ Cut	Ctrl+X
SharePoint "Layouts" Mapped Folder		Paste	Ctrl+V
SharePoint Mapped Folder...		✕ Delete	Del

17. Click on **Save All** from the toolbar or **File** menu.

How it works...

Our Controls folder will act like a folder does in a standard .NET class library to provide organization and namespaces. The CONTROLTEMPLATES mapped folder will instruct SharePoint to deploy the ASCX files for our user controls to the appropriate place on the filesystem (C:\Program Files\Common Files\Microsoft Shared\Web Server Extensions\15\TEMPLATE\CONTROLTEMPLATES). The Layouts mapped folder will instruct SharePoint to deploy our application page, stylesheets, and JavaScript to the appropriate place on the filesystem to allow them to be accessed from the client web browsers (C:\Program Files\Common Files\Microsoft Shared\Web Server Extensions\15\TEMPLATE\LAYOUTS).

See also

▶ The *Add-SPShellAdmin* topic on TechNet at http://technet.microsoft.com/en-us/library/ff607596.aspx

▶ The *Developing SharePoint Solutions* article on MSDN at http://msdn.microsoft.com/en-us/library/vstudio/ee231517.aspx

▶ The *How To: Add and Remove Mapped Folders* article on MSDN at http://msdn.microsoft.com/en-us/library/vstudio/ee231521(v=vs.110).aspx

Adding JavaScript and stylesheets with an AdditionalPageHead delegate control

The `AdditionalPageHead` control is one of the most commonly used delegate controls by developers to add custom code to the page. Controls registered to the `AdditionalPageHead` control are added to the `<head>` element of each page and multiple controls may be added, unlike most other delegate controls that only allow one user control.

In this recipe, we will create an `ASCX` user control that will add references to a custom stylesheet and custom JavaScript. We will then register the control to be added to the `AdditionalPageHead` delegate control. Using an `AdditionalPageHead` delegate control allows us to add our custom stylesheet and custom JavaScript to every SharePoint page, regardless of which master page is being used. This is particularly useful when a custom master page is not required and when managing the master pages for sites on a large scale becomes impractical.

Getting ready

We should have already created our Visual Studio project in the *Creating a Visual Studio solution for custom delegate controls* recipe of this chapter before starting this recipe.

How to do it...

Follow these steps to create a delegate control to add JavaScript and stylesheet references to each page:

1. Open the project created in the *Creating a Visual Studio solution for custom delegate controls* recipe of this chapter in Visual Studio.

2. Right-click on the folder that was created under the `Layouts` mapped folder.

3. Navigate to **Add | New Item...** as shown in the following screenshot:

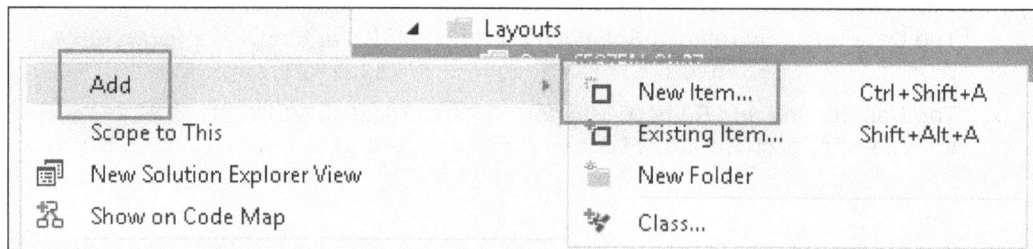

4. Select **Style Sheet** by navigating to **Visual C# Items | Web**:

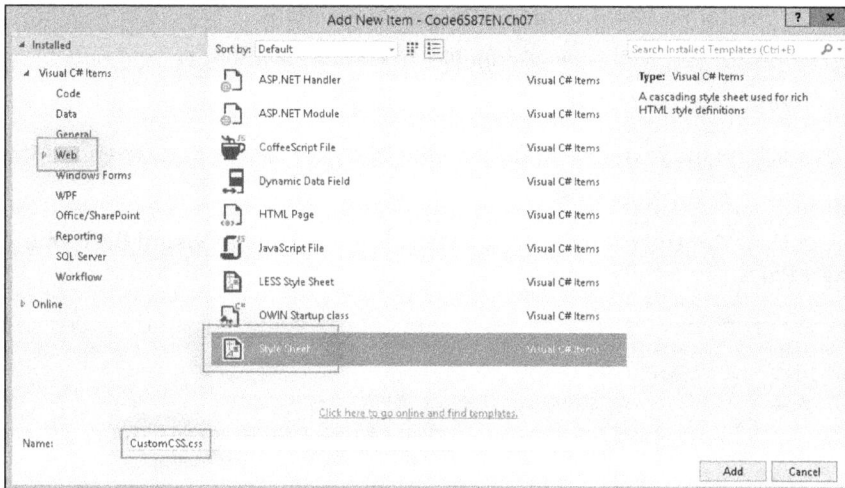

5. Provide the item a name, `CustomCSS.css`, for example.

6. Add some content to the stylesheet, at least a CSS comment:

```
/* CSS Comment */
```

> As of this writing, there is an unusual behavior between SharePoint and Google Chrome that causes the file to be repeatedly requested by the browser if the file has no content.

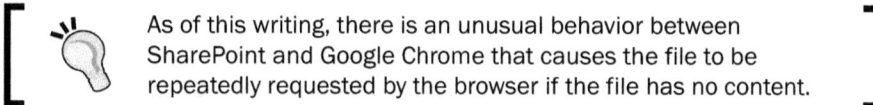

7. Right-click on the folder again and navigate to **Add | New Item**.

8. Select **JavaScript File** by navigating to **Visual C# Items | Web** as shown in the following screenshot:

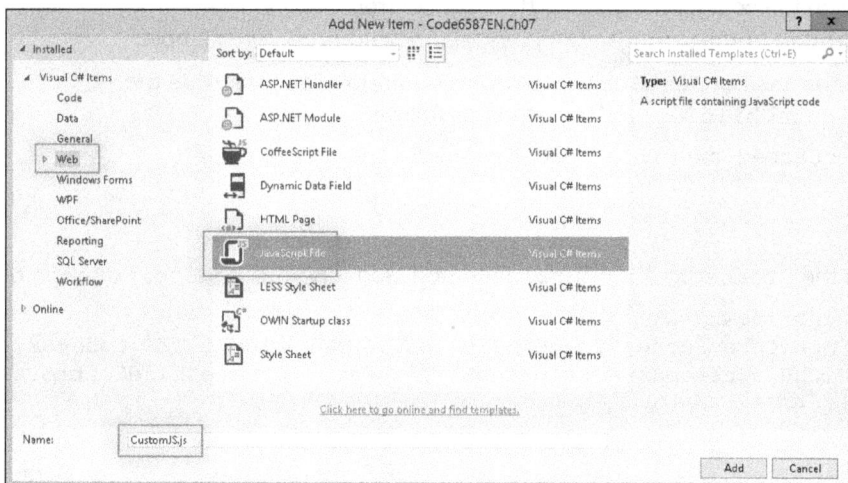

9. Provide the item a name, `CustomJS.js`, for example.

10. Add some content to the JavaScript file, at least a JavaScript comment:

    ```
    // JavaScript Comment
    ```

11. Right-click on the folder we created in the `CONTROLTEMPLATES` mapped folder.

12. Navigate to **Add | New Item**.

13. Select **User Control (Farm Solution Only)** by navigating to **Visual C# Items | Office/ SharePoint**:

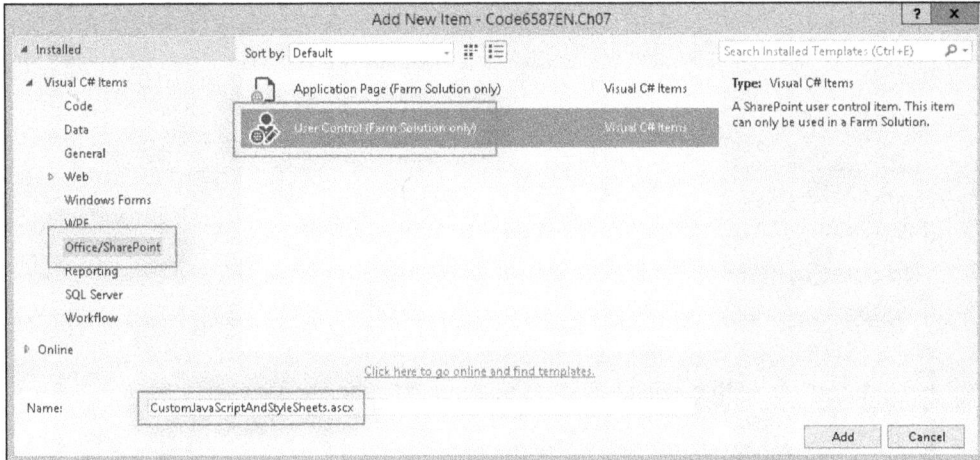

14. Provide the item a name, `CustomJavaScriptAndStyleSheets.ascx`, for example.

15. Click on **Add**.

16. Open the code-behind file for the user control, `CustomJavaScriptAndStyleSheets.ascx.cs`, for example.

17. In the `CustomJavaScriptAndStyleSheets` class, override the `CreateChildControls` method as follows:

    ```
    protected override void CreateChildControls()
    {
    }
    ```

18. In the `CreateChildControls` method, add a new `SPMonitoredScope` object:

    ```
    using (new
    SPMonitoredScope("Code6587EN.Ch07.CONTROLTEMPLATES.Code6587
    EN.Ch07.CustomJavaScriptAndStyleSheets::CreateChildControls
    "))
    {
    }
    ```

19. Get the URL to our custom JavaScript file with the relative URL of the current site:

```
var url =
SPContext.Current.Web.ServerRelativeUrl.TrimEnd('/') +
"/_layouts/15/Code6587EN.Ch07/CustomJS.js";
```

20. Register the JavaScript file with the `ClientScriptManager` object of the current page:

```
this.Page.ClientScript.RegisterClientScriptInclude("CustomJ
S", url);
```

21. Open the `ASCX` user control, `CustomJavaScriptAndStyleSheets.ascx` for example.

22. Add a reference to our custom CSS file using a SharePoint `CssRegistration` control:

```
<SharePoint:CssRegistration ID="customCssRegistration"
Name="<%
$SPUrl:~Site/_layouts/15/Code6587EN.Ch07/CustomCSS.css %>"
runat="server"></SharePoint:CssRegistration>
```

> Stylesheet references may also be added using C# code in the code-behind file. We are adding it in the `ASCX` file to demonstrate the use of the `ASCX` user controls.

23. Right-click on the project name in the **Solution Explorer** pane.

24. Navigate to **Add | New Item**.

25. Select **Empty Element** by navigating to **Visual C# Items | Office/SharePoint** as shown in the following screenshot:

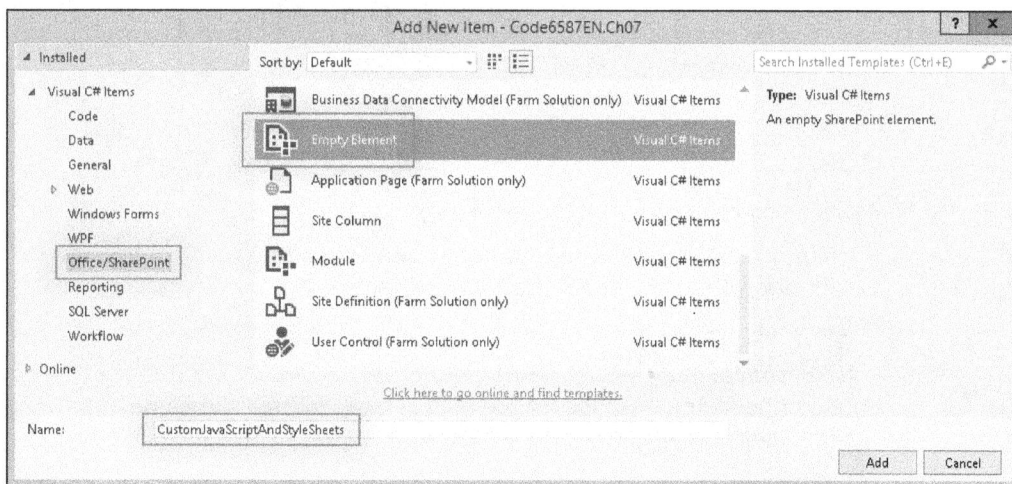

26. Provide the item a name, `CustomJavaScriptAndStyleSheets`, for example.

27. Click on **Add**.

28. In the `Elements.xml` file of the new element, register our custom control with the `AdditionalPageHead` control using the following code:

```xml
<?xml version="1.0" encoding="utf-8"?>
<Elements xmlns="http://schemas.microsoft.com/sharepoint/">
  <Control Id="AdditionalPageHead" Sequence="10"
  ControlSrc="~/_controltemplates/15/Code6587EN.Ch07/
  CustomJavaScriptAndStyleSheets.ascx">
  </Control>
</Elements>
```

In similar fashion to the `Layouts` mapped folder, items in a SharePoint 2013 solution within the `CONTROLTEMPLATES` mapped folder will be located under `/_CONTROLTEMPLATES/15/`.

29. Select the new element (not the `Elements.xml` file within it) in the **Solution Explorer** pane.

30. In the **Properties** pane, click on the ellipsis for the **Safe Control Entries** option as shown in the following screenshot:

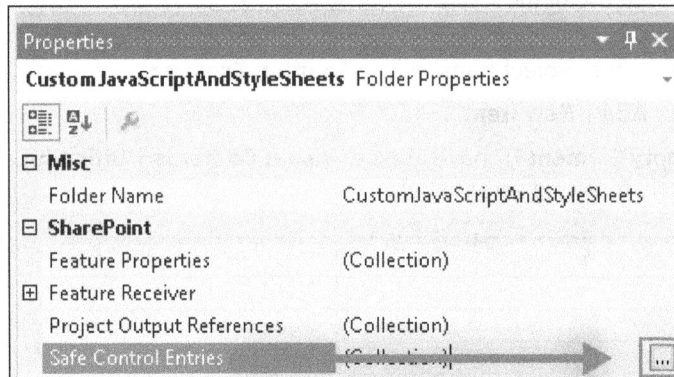

31. Add a new safe control entry with the following details:

   ❑ **(Name)**: `CustomJavaScriptAndStyleSheets` (the name of the user control we created without the `.ascx` extension)

   ❑ **Assembly**: `$SharePoint.Project.AssemblyFullName$`

   ❑ **Namespace**: `Code6587EN.Ch07.CONTROLTEMPLATES.Code6587EN.Ch07` (the full namespace for the user control, without the name of the class itself)

   ❑ **Safe**: `True`

- ❑ **Safe Against Script**: True
- ❑ **Type Name**: CustomJavaScriptAndStyleSheets (the name of the class for the user control)

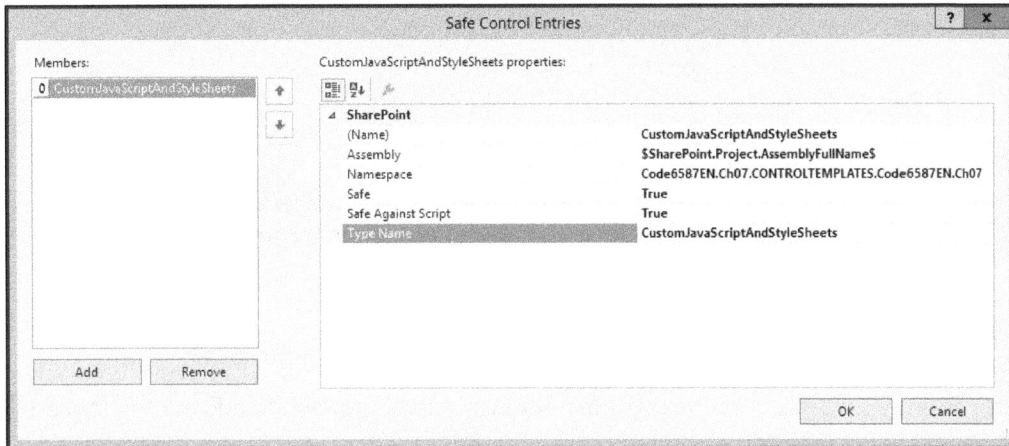

32. Click on **OK**.

33. When the **Empty Element** item was added, it also added a new feature in the Features folder. Rename the feature to the project name. Each of the elements we add in the recipes for this chapter will automatically be added to this feature:

34. Open the feature and provide it an appropriate name, Code6587EN.Ch07 Delegate Controls, for example as shown in the following screenshot:

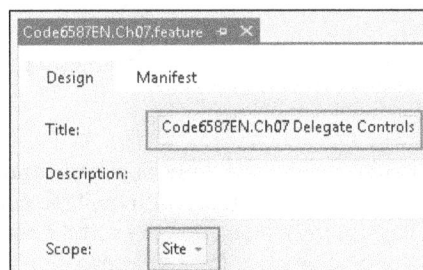

35. Set the scope to **Site**.

36. Click on **Start** from the toolbar to package the solution, deploy it to the local SharePoint server, activate the feature, and attach the debugger to the IIS process:

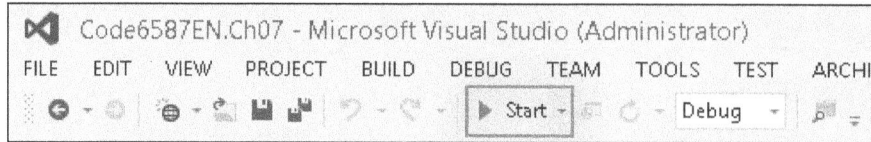

```
Code6587EN.Ch07 - Microsoft Visual Studio (Administrator)
FILE   EDIT   VIEW   PROJECT   BUILD   DEBUG   TEAM   TOOLS   TEST   ARCHI

   ⟳ ▾  ⟳ ▾  ⊜ ▾  ⌂  ⊟ ⊟   ⟲ ▾ ⟳ ▾   ▶ Start ▾   ⌐ ⟳ ▾   Debug   ▾   ⌂ ▾
```

37. Once the SharePoint site is loaded in the web browser (after clicking on **Start**), view the source of the page to observe the references to our custom stylesheet and JavaScript files.

How it works...

The `Elements.xml` file of our **Empty Element** instructs SharePoint to add our referenced user control to the delegate control with the `Id` of `AdditionalPageHead`. The sequence provides SharePoint the order in which to add controls referencing the same `Id` to the page. For delegate controls that accept just one control, only the registered control with the lowest sequence will be added.

An `SPMonitoredScope` object allows developers to designate portions of code to be monitored for usage statistics in the **Unified Logging Service** (**ULS**) logging and the developer dashboard. Using them is not a requirement; however, they do make it easier to identify bottlenecks and other potential issues in custom code. As a matter of best practice, I find it is valuable to use `SPMonitoredScopes` whenever a block of code affects what is rendered on a page. They do not provide a whole lot of value for backend code that doesn't affect the user interface. The name provided for the scope is a bit arbitrary. You can use whatever you want. However, I find it helpful to use a standard pattern. The pattern used in the examples for this book is `Namespace.ClassName::Method`. This pattern provides the information required to know exactly where the code is in our project.

Adding our safe control entry to **Safe Control Entries** of the **Empty Element** item will add the safe control entry to the SharePoint web application's `web.config` configuration file. Without this registration, SharePoint will throw an exception indicating the control is not safe when attempting to load it.

Once loaded, our user control will add references to our custom stylesheet and JavaScript files to the page.

> Using the `ClientScriptManager` object to register our custom JavaScript allows it to be registered with multiple controls, but only added to the page once. It also adds the script references in one group, which is a best practice for web applications in general.

See also

▸ The *Using SPMonitoredScope* article on MSDN at `http://msdn.microsoft.com/en-us/library/ff512758(v=office.14).aspx`

▸ The *Delegate Controls* article on MSDN at `http://msdn.microsoft.com/en-us/library/sharepoint/ms478826.aspx`

▸ The *Control Element (Delegate Control)* topic on MSDN at `http://msdn.microsoft.com/en-us/library/sharepoint/ms469179.aspx`

▸ The *ClientScriptManager.RegisterClientScriptInclude Method* topic on MSDN at `http://msdn.microsoft.com/en-us/library/system.web.ui.clientscriptmanager.registerclientscriptinclude.aspx`

▸ The *CssRegistration class* topic on MSDN at `http://msdn.microsoft.com/en-us/library/microsoft.sharepoint.webcontrols.cssregistration.aspx`

Customizing the suite bar branding with a SuiteBarBrandingDelegate delegate control

The out-of-the-box master pages included with SharePoint 2013 provide a delegate control to place branding text in the top-left corner of the page. For standard SharePoint instances, the text **SharePoint** is displayed. For SharePoint on Office 365, **Office 365** is displayed instead.

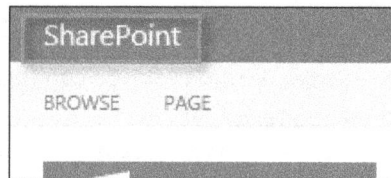

In this recipe, we will simply replace the control with a custom control that displays our own text. The text could also be replaced by editing the master page or by modifying the `SuiteBarBrandingElementHtml` property on the SharePoint web application. Using the custom control provides us the ability to add additional functionality if desired. For instance, the control could be used to add additional links, a menu, or other interactive content.

Getting ready

We should have already created our Visual Studio project in the *Creating a Visual Studio solution for custom delegate controls* recipe of this chapter before starting this recipe.

How to do it...

Follow these steps to replace the suite bar branding text using a delegate control:

1. Open the project created in the *Creating a Visual Studio solution for custom delegate controls* recipe of this chapter in Visual Studio.

2. Right-click on the subfolder we previously created in the CONTROLTEMPLATES mapped folder.

3. Navigate to **Add | New Item**.

4. Select **User Control** by navigating to **Visual C# Items | Office/SharePoint**.

5. Provide the item a name, CustomSuiteBarBranding.ascx for example and then click on **Add**.

6. Open the newly created ASCX file if it is not already open.

7. In the body of the user control, add our custom branding text as follows:

```
<div class="ms-core-brandingText">
Custom SharePoint Branding Text</div>
```

8. Right-click on the project name in the **Solution Explorer** pane.

9. Navigate to **Add | New Item**.

10. Select **Empty Element** by navigating to **Visual C# Items | Office/SharePoint**.

11. Provide the new item a name, CustomSuiteBarBranding for example.

12. Click on **Add**.

13. In the newly created Elements.xml file from the new element, register our custom control with the SuiteBarBrandingDelegate control as follows:

```
<?xml version="1.0" encoding="utf-8"?>
<Elements xmlns="http://schemas.microsoft.com/sharepoint/">
  <Control Id="SuiteBarBrandingDelegate"
  Sequence="10"
  ControlSrc="~/_controltemplates/15/Code6587EN.Ch07/
  CustomSuiteBarBranding.ascx">
  </Control>
</Elements>
```

14. Add a new safe control entry to the new element with the following details:

   ❑ **(Name)**: CustomSuiteBarBranding (the name of the user control we created without the .ascx extension)

   ❑ **Assembly**: $SharePoint.Project.AssemblyFullName$

   ❑ **Namespace**: Code6587EN.Ch07.CONTROLTEMPLATES.Code6587EN. Ch07 (the full namespace for the user control, without the name of the class itself)

- ❑ **Safe**: True

- ❑ **Safe Against Script**: True

- ❑ **Type Name**: CustomSuiteBarBranding (the name of the class for the user control)

15. Open the feature created previously. Ensure that the new element is included in the feature:

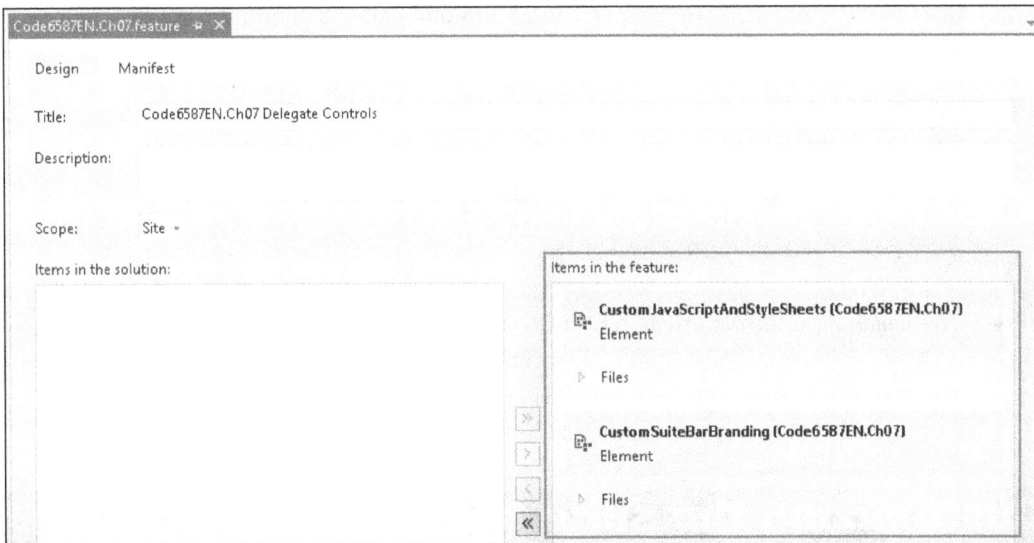

16. Click on **Start** from the toolbar to deploy the solution and attach the debugger.

17. Once the SharePoint site is loaded in the web browser (after clicking on **Start**), observe the new branding text as shown in the following screenshot:

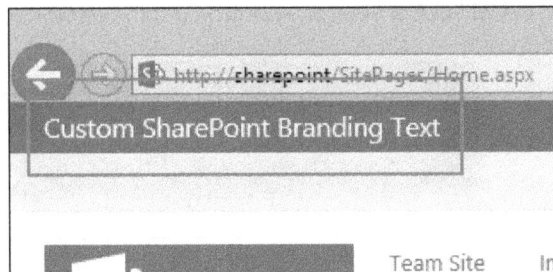

How it works...

The out-of-the-box control used by the `SuiteBarBrandingDelegate` delegate control displays the HTML snippet stored in the `SuiteBarBrandingElementHtml` property of the current SharePoint web application. In this recipe, we replaced the default control with our own delegate control that adds our text to the page.

We are using the same CSS class that the out-of-the-box text uses to allow the content to display with the standard style. Relying on the SharePoint classes allows the content to inherit the styles provided by the current SharePoint theme.

See also

► The *SPWebApplication.SuiteBarBrandingElementHtml property* topic on MSDN at `http://msdn.microsoft.com/en-us/library/microsoft.sharepoint.administration.spwebapplication.suitebarbrandingelementhtml.aspx`

► The *Delegate Controls* article on MSDN at `http://msdn.microsoft.com/en-us/library/sharepoint/ms478826.aspx`

► The *Control Element (Delegate Control)* topic on MSDN at `http://msdn.microsoft.com/en-us/library/sharepoint/ms469179.aspx`

Customizing the suite bar links with a SuiteLinksDelegate delegate control

In addition to the branding text, out-of-the-box SharePoint master pages include a delegate control to display a series of links in the suite bar. These links include **Newsfeed**, **SkyDrive**, and **Sites** by default. Since SharePoint provides no configuration options to add or modify the links in the suite bar, we will use a delegate control in this recipe and in the next recipe to customize the links displayed.

Getting ready

We should have already created our Visual Studio project in the *Creating a Visual Studio solution for custom delegate controls* recipe of this chapter before starting this recipe.

How to do it...

Follow these steps to customize the suite bar links with a delegate control:

1. Open the project created in the *Creating a Visual Studio solution for custom delegate controls* recipe of this chapter in Visual Studio.

2. Right-click on the `Controls` folder we created previously.

3. Navigate to **Add | Class**.

4. Provide a name for the item, `CustomSuiteBarLinks.cs` for example.

5. Click on **Add**.

6. Set the access modifier for the `CustomSuiteBarLinks` class to `public`, set the class to inherit from the `UserControl` base class, and implement the `IDesignTimeHtmlProvider` interface:

   ```
   public class CustomSuiteBarLinks  : UserControl,
   IDesignTimeHtmlProvider
   ```

7. Override the `CreateChildControls` method and in a monitored scope instruct the script manager to load the applicable SharePoint JavaScript files using the following code:

   ```
   protected override void CreateChildControls()
   {
     using (new SPMonitoredScope("Code6587EN.Ch07.Controls.
     CustomSuiteBarLinks::CreateChildControls"))
     {
       ScriptLink.RegisterScriptAfterUI(this, this.Page,
       "sp.js", false);
       ScriptLink.RegisterScriptAfterUI(this, this.Page,
       "SP.UI.MySiteNavigation.js", false);
       ScriptLink.RegisterScriptAfterUI(this, this.Page,
       "suitelinks.js", false);
       ScriptLink.RegisterScriptAfterUI(this, this.Page,
       "MyLinks.js", false);
     }
   }
   ```

8. Implement the `GetDesignTimeHtml` method from the `IDesignTimeHtmlProvider` interface and in a monitored scope return the HTML output from the `Render` method using `HtmlTextWriter` as follows:

   ```
   public string GetDesignTimeHtml()
   {
     using (new SPMonitoredScope("Code6587EN.Ch07.Controls.
     CustomSuiteBarLinks::GetDesignTimeHtml"))
     {
   ```

```
        StringWriter writer = new
        StringWriter(CultureInfo.CurrentCulture);
        HtmlTextWriter writer2 = new HtmlTextWriter(writer);
        this.Render(writer2);
        writer2.Close();
        return writer.ToString();
    }
}
```

9. Add a private method named `RenderSuiteLink` that we will use to render the HTML for each individual suite bar link and add a monitored scope using the following code:

```
private static void RenderSuiteLink(HtmlTextWriter writer,
string url, string name, string linkId, bool isActiveLink)
{
    using (new SPMonitoredScope("Code6587EN.Ch07.Controls.
    CustomSuiteBarLinks::GetDesignTimeHtml"))
    {
    }
}
```

When rendering each suite bar link, we will use `HtmlTextWriter` instantiated in the `GetDesignTimeHtml` method to append the HTML code for the link.

10. In the monitored scope of our `RenderSuiteLink` method, add an HTML list item element with `ms-core-SuiteLink` as its CSS class:

```
writer.AddAttribute(HtmlTextWriterAttribute.Class,
"ms-core-suiteLink");
writer.RenderBeginTag(HtmlTextWriterTag.Li);
```

When we use an `HtmlTextWriter` to construct HTML, we use the `AddAttribute` method to add HTML attributes to an HTML element prior to rendering its beginning tag.

11. Add an HTML link element with `ms-core-suiteLink-a` as the CSS class, the provided URL as the `HREF` attribute, and the provided link ID for the `ID` attribute:

```
writer.AddAttribute(HtmlTextWriterAttribute.Class, "ms-
core-suiteLink-a");
writer.AddAttribute(HtmlTextWriterAttribute.Href, url);
writer.AddAttribute(HtmlTextWriterAttribute.Id, linkId);
writer.RenderBeginTag(HtmlTextWriterTag.A);
```

12. Add an HTML `SPAN` element that will contain the text to display in the suite link bar:

```
writer.RenderBeginTag(HtmlTextWriterTag.Span);
```

13. Add the text to display in the SPAN element:

```
writer.Write(name);
```

14. If the link is the active link, add a SPAN element with the carat image that SharePoint uses to indicate an active link:

```
if (isActiveLink)
{
  writer.AddAttribute(HtmlTextWriterAttribute.Id,
  "Suite_ActiveLinkIndicator_Clip");
  writer.AddAttribute(HtmlTextWriterAttribute.Class,
  "ms-suitenav-caratBox");
  writer.RenderBeginTag(HtmlTextWriterTag.Span);
  writer.AddAttribute(HtmlTextWriterAttribute.Id,
  "Suite_ActiveLinkIndicator");
  writer.AddAttribute(HtmlTextWriterAttribute.Class,
  "ms-suitenav-caratIcon");
  writer.AddAttribute(HtmlTextWriterAttribute.Src,
  SPUtility.GetThemedImageUrl(SPUrlUtility.CombineUrl
  (SPUtility.ContextImagesRoot, "spcommon.png"),
  "spcommon"));
  writer.RenderBeginTag(HtmlTextWriterTag.Img);
  writer.RenderEndTag();
  writer.RenderEndTag();
}
```

15. Using the following code add the end tags for the SPAN, link, and list item elements:

```
writer.RenderEndTag();
writer.RenderEndTag();
writer.RenderEndTag();
```

16. Override the Render method and add a monitored scope as follows:

```
protected override void Render(HtmlTextWriter writer)
{
  using (new SPMonitoredScope("Code6587EN.Ch07.
  Controls.CustomSuiteBarLinks::GetDesignTimeHtml"))
  {
  }
}
```

17. In the monitored scope, add the HTML DIV element to contain our suite bar links with Suite_NavBar as the ID attribute:

```
writer.AddAttribute(HtmlTextWriterAttribute.Id,
"Suite_NavBar");
writer.RenderBeginTag(HtmlTextWriterTag.Div);
```

18. Add the unordered list element to contain the list items created in the
    `RenderSuiteLink` method with `ms-core-SuiteLinkList` as the CSS class and
    `Suite_TopMenu` as the `ID` attribute using the following code:

    ```
    writer.AddAttribute(HtmlTextWriterAttribute.Id,
    "Suite_TopMenu");
    writer.AddAttribute(HtmlTextWriterAttribute.Class,
    "ms-core-suiteLinkList");
    writer.RenderBeginTag(HtmlTextWriterTag.Ul);
    ```

19. Add two or more suite links with the `RenderSuiteLink` method:

    ```
    RenderSuiteLink(writer, "/", "Home", "suiteLinkHome",
    true);
    RenderSuiteLink(writer, "http://www.bing.com", "Bing",
    "suiteLinkBing", false);
    ```

    In our example, we are simply setting the **Home** link as the active link. It would be
    prudent to add your own method for determining which link is active by the current
    page URL or by some other appropriate method.

20. Add the end tags for the unordered list and `DIV` elements as follows:

    ```
    writer.RenderEndTag();
    writer.RenderEndTag();
    ```

21. Add a new **Empty Element** item to the project to register our custom suite link's bar
    control.

22. In the `Elements.xml` file of our new element, register our custom suite bar links
    control with the `SuiteLinksDelegate` delegate control using the following code:

    ```
    <?xml version="1.0" encoding="utf-8"?>
    <Elements xmlns="http://schemas.microsoft.com/sharepoint/">
      <Control Id="SuiteLinksDelegate"
    Sequence="1"
      ControlClass="Code6587EN.Ch07.Controls.
      CustomSuiteBarLinks"
      ControlAssembly="$SharePoint.Project.AssemblyFullName$">
      </Control>
    </Elements>
    ```

23. Add a new safe control entry to the new element with the following details:

    ❑ **(Name):** `CustomSuiteBarLinks` (the name of the class for our
      custom control)

    ❑ **Assembly:** `$SharePoint.Project.AssemblyFullName$`

    ❑ **Namespace:** `Code6587EN.Ch07.Controls` (the full namespace for the
      class, without the name of the class itself)

    ❑ **Safe:** `True`

❑ **Safe Against Script**: True

❑ **Type Name**: CustomSuiteBarLinks (the name of the class)

24. Open the feature created previously. Ensure that the new element is included in the feature.

25. Click on **Start** from the toolbar to deploy the solution and attach the debugger.

26. Once the SharePoint site is loaded in the web browser (after clicking on **Start**), observe the new suite bar links as shown in the following screenshot:

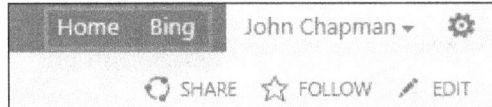

How it works...

Our custom suite bar links control implements the SharePoint IDesignTimeHtmlProvider interface. When our control is rendered, SharePoint calls the GetDesignTimeHtml method that we implemented to get the HTML markup to add to the page. Our code composes the HTML markup to render our custom suite links bar using the same styles and structure as the out-of-the-box suite links bar control. This ensures that our custom suite links work well with SharePoint themes and other customized styles.

In this recipe, we are using an HtmlTextWriter to compose the HTML content of the suite bar links control. This HTML content is output to a string using a StringWriter object. There are a variety of ways HTML code may be composed and added to the page. The out-of-the-box control for the suite links uses the HtmlTextWriter methodology. In your own suite links control, you could use any applicable method you like for composing HTML. For instance, you could add the HTML markup to an ASCX control rather than creating it programmatically.

See also

▶ The *IDesignTimeHtmlProvider interface* topic on MSDN at http://msdn. microsoft.com/en-us/library/microsoft.sharepoint.webcontrols. idesigntimehtmlprovider.aspx

▶ The *IDesignTimeHtmlProvider.GetDesignTimeHtml method* topic on MSDN at http://msdn.microsoft.com/en-us/library/microsoft.sharepoint. webcontrols.idesigntimehtmlprovider.getdesigntimehtml.aspx

▶ The *HtmlTextWriter Class* topic on MSDN at http://msdn.microsoft.com/en-us/library/system.web.ui.htmltextwriter.aspx

Adding Office 365-style drop-down menus to suite bar links

SharePoint on Office 365 includes additional links related to Office 365 services in the suite bar, including a drop-down menu of links. Standard installations of SharePoint include the CSS styles and basic JavaScript required to handle these Office 365 drop-down menus. They do not, however, include a way to utilize the styles and JavaScript. The following screenshot illustrates how the drop-down menu looks on Office 365:

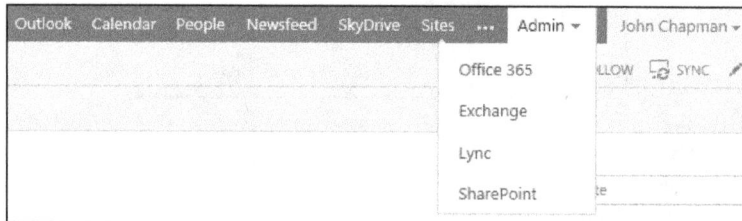

In this recipe, we will add a drop-down menu using the provided CSS styles and a bit of custom JavaScript of our own using the delegate control we created in the previous recipe. The JavaScript code provided out-of-the-box is designed to only work with Office 365. We will use a modified version of the methods from the out-of-the-box JavaScript to work with our custom drop-down menu.

Getting ready

For this recipe, we should already have the delegate control created in the *Customizing the suite bar links with a SuiteLinksDelegate delegate control* recipe.

How to do it...

Follow these steps to add a drop-down menu to our suite links delegate control:

1. Open the project created in the *Creating a Visual Studio solution for custom delegate controls* recipe of this chapter in Visual Studio.

2. Add a new JavaScript file to the subfolder we created in the `Layouts` mapped folder.

3. In our new JavaScript file, add a function to hide the suite bar menu by setting its CSS style and removing the active CSS class from its parent container as follows:

```
function CustomSuiteBarMenu_Hide (menuDivID, popupOwnerID) {
  var menuDiv = document.getElementById(menuDivID);
  if (menuDiv)
  {
```

```
    menuDiv.style.display = "none";
    menuDiv.style.top = "-10000px";
    var popupOwner = document.getElementById(popupOwnerID);
    RemoveCssClassFromElement(popupOwner,
    "ms-core-suiteLink-active");
  }
}
```

4. Add a function to get the location of the element provided using the following code:

```
function CustomSuiteBarMenu_GetRectangle (elem) {
  var rWin = elem.getBoundingClientRect();
  var xOff = Boolean(window.pageXOffset) ?
  window.pageXOffset : document.documentElement.scrollLeft;
  var yOff = Boolean(window.pageYOffset) ?
  window.pageYOffset : document.documentElement.scrollTop;
  var rDoc = {};
  rDoc.left = rWin.left + xOff;
  rDoc.right = rWin.right + xOff;
  rDoc.top = rWin.top + yOff;
  rDoc.bottom = rWin.bottom + yOff;
  return rDoc;
}
```

5. Add a function to show the suite bar menu as follows:

```
function CustomSuiteBarMenu_ShowMenu(popupOwnerID,
menuDivID, navBarID)
```

6. In our new function to show the suite bar menu, determine if the current page is displaying text left-to-right or right-to-left:

```
var IsRtl = window.document.documentElement.
getAttribute("dir") == "rtl";
```

7. Get the menu element, the suite link element containing the menu, and the suite links bar element:

```
var menuDiv = document.getElementById(menuDivID);
var popupOwner = document.getElementById(popupOwnerID);
var navBar = document.getElementById(navBarID);
```

8. Call our function to hide the menu that will ensure we are not applying the styles to display the menu multiple times:

```
CustomSuiteBarMenu_Hide(menuDivID, popupOwnerID);
```

9. Add the `ms-core-suiteLink-active` CSS class to the suite link element containing the suite bar menu as follows:

```
AddCssClassToElement(popupOwner,
"ms-core-suiteLink-active");
```

10. Get the location of the suite link element containing the menu:

```
var currentMenuOwnerBoundingRect =
CustomSuiteBarMenu_GetRectangle(popupOwner);
```

11. Get the location of the suite links bar:

```
var navBarBoundingRect =
CustomSuiteBarMenu_GetRectangle(navBar);
```

12. Using the following code set the `display` style of the suite bar menu to `inline-block`:

```
menuDiv.style.display = "inline-block";
```

13. Set the location of the suite bar menu based on the location of the suite link containing the menu, the location of the suite links bar, and the direction of the text on the page, with the help of the following code snippet:

```
var menuLeft;
var menuWidth = menuDiv.offsetWidth;
if (IsRtl) {
  menuLeft = currentMenuOwnerBoundingRect.
  right - menuWidth;
}
else {
  menuLeft = currentMenuOwnerBoundingRect.left;
}
var winWidth = document.documentElement.clientWidth;
var winLeft =
Boolean(window.pageXOffset) ? window.pageXOffset :
document.documentElement.scrollLeft;
var winRight = winLeft + winWidth;
if (menuLeft < winLeft) {
  menuLeft = winLeft;
}
else if (menuLeft + menuWidth > winRight) {
  menuLeft = winRight - menuWidth;
}
menuDiv.style.left =
String(Math.max(winLeft, menuLeft)) + "px";
menuDiv.style.top =
String(navBarBoundingRect.bottom) + "px";
```

14. In our monitored scope within the `CreateChildControls` method of our `CustomSuiteBarLinks` class, instruct the script manager to add a reference to our custom JavaScript file to the page as follows:

```
this.Page.ClientScript.RegisterClientScriptInclude
("CustomSuiteBarLinks
", SPContext.Current.Web.ServerRelativeUrl.TrimEnd('/') + "/_
layouts/15/Code6587EN.Ch07/CustomSuiteBarLinks.js");
```

15. In our `CustomSuiteBarLinks` class, add a new method to render our suite bar menu with a monitored scope using the following code:

```
private static void RenderSuiteLinkMenu(HtmlTextWriter writer,
string name, string menuId, List<Tuple<string, string, string>>
subItems)
{
  using (new
  SPMonitoredScope("Code6587EN.Ch07.Controls.
  CustomSuiteBarLinks::GetDesignTimeHtml"))
  {
  }
}
```

To contain the list of links that we will render in the menu, we are using a list of tuples. Tuples are a simple way to instantiate anonymous objects. You could also use a collection of custom class objects or whatever other method of passing a collection of links that suit your needs.

16. Add the HTML list item element to contain the suite bar menu with `ms-core-suiteLink` for the CSS class:

```
writer.AddAttribute(HtmlTextWriterAttribute.Class,
"ms-core-suiteLink");
writer.RenderBeginTag(HtmlTextWriterTag.Li);
```

17. Using the following code add the HTML link element to contain the suite bar menu and add the JavaScript handlers to show or hide the suite bar menu:

```
writer.AddAttribute(HtmlTextWriterAttribute.Class,
"ms-core-suiteLink-a");
writer.AddAttribute(HtmlTextWriterAttribute.Href, "#");
writer.AddAttribute(HtmlTextWriterAttribute.Id,
"Suite_MainLink_" + menuId);
writer.AddAttribute("onfocus",
"CustomSuiteBarMenu_ShowMenu('Suite_MainLink_" + menuId +
"', 'Suite_PopupMenu_" + menuId + "', 'Suite_NavBar');");
writer.AddAttribute("onclick",
"CustomSuiteBarMenu_ShowMenu('Suite_MainLink_" + menuId +
"', 'Suite_PopupMenu_" + menuId + "', 'Suite_NavBar');");
```

```
writer.AddAttribute("onblur",
"CustomSuiteBarMenu_Hide('Suite_PopupMenu_" + menuId + "',
'Suite_MainLink_" + menuId + "');");
writer.RenderBeginTag(HtmlTextWriterTag.A);
```

18. Add the HTML SPAN element to contain the display text for the menu and add the JavaScript handler to hide the suite bar menu as follows:

```
writer.AddAttribute("onblur",
"CustomSuiteBarMenu_Hide('Suite_PopupMenu_" + menuId + "',
'Suite_MainLink_" + menuId + "');");
writer.RenderBeginTag(HtmlTextWriterTag.Span);
```

19. Add the display text for the suite bar menu name:

```
writer.Write(name);
```

20. Add the HTML SPAN element and image to display the drop-down menu icon with the use of the following code:

```
writer.AddAttribute(HtmlTextWriterAttribute.Class,
"ms-suitenav-downarrowBox");
writer.AddAttribute("onblur",
"CustomSuiteBarMenu_Hide('Suite_PopupMenu_" + menuId + "',
'Suite_MainLink_" + menuId + "');");
writer.RenderBeginTag(HtmlTextWriterTag.Span);
writer.AddAttribute(HtmlTextWriterAttribute.Class,
"ms-suitenav-downarrowIcon");
writer.AddAttribute(HtmlTextWriterAttribute.Src,
SPUtility.GetThemedImageUrl(SPUrlUtility.CombineUrl
(SPUtility.ContextImagesRoot, "spcommon.png"),
"spcommon"));
writer.RenderBeginTag(HtmlTextWriterTag.Img);
```

21. Add the end tags for the image, image SPAN, display text SPAN, and link elements:

```
writer.RenderEndTag();
writer.RenderEndTag();
writer.RenderEndTag();
writer.RenderEndTag();
```

22. Add the HTML DIV element to contain the suite bar menu items with ms-core-menu-box ms-core-suitemenu for the CSS class using the following code:

```
writer.AddAttribute(HtmlTextWriterAttribute.Class,
"ms-core-menu-box ms-core-suitemenu");
writer.AddAttribute(HtmlTextWriterAttribute.Id,
"Suite_PopupMenu_" + menuId);
writer.RenderBeginTag(HtmlTextWriterTag.Div);
```

23. Add the HTML unordered list element to contain the list of menu items with `ms-core-menu-list` as the CSS class as follows:

```
writer.AddAttribute(HtmlTextWriterAttribute.Class,
"ms-core-menu-list");
writer.RenderBeginTag(HtmlTextWriterTag.Ul);
```

24. For each link in our collection of links, add the HTML elements to render the menu item using the following code listing:

```
foreach (var subItem in subItems)
{
  writer.AddAttribute(HtmlTextWriterAttribute.Class,
  "ms-core-menu-item");
  writer.RenderBeginTag(HtmlTextWriterTag.Li);
  writer.AddAttribute(HtmlTextWriterAttribute.Class,
  "ms-core-menu-link");
  writer.AddAttribute(HtmlTextWriterAttribute.Href,
  subItem.Item3);
  writer.AddAttribute(HtmlTextWriterAttribute.Id,
  "Suite_SubLink_" + subItem.Item2);
  writer.RenderBeginTag(HtmlTextWriterTag.A);
  writer.AddAttribute(HtmlTextWriterAttribute.Class,
  "ms-core-menu-label");
  writer.RenderBeginTag(HtmlTextWriterTag.Div);
  writer.AddAttribute(HtmlTextWriterAttribute.Class,
  "ms-core-menu-title");
  writer.RenderBeginTag(HtmlTextWriterTag.Span);
  writer.Write(subItem.Item1);
  writer.RenderEndTag();
  writer.RenderEndTag();
  writer.RenderEndTag();
  writer.RenderEndTag();
}
```

25. Add the end tags for the unordered list, suite bar menu container `DIV`, and the list item element containing the menu.

26. Click on **Start** from the toolbar to deploy the solution and attach the debugger.

27. Once the SharePoint site is loaded in the web browser (after clicking on **Start**), observe the new suite bar links drop-down menu. The following screenshot shows how it will look:

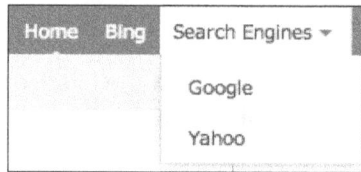

How it works...

The JavaScript and CSS styles provided by SharePoint out-of-the-box include the functionality to render a drop-down menu in the suite links bar for Office 365. In this recipe, we added a modified copy of the applicable JavaScript to allow us to render our own drop-down menu using the same styles. We could use other JavaScript-based method for displaying a custom drop-down menu. However, for this recipe, we used the Office 365 methodology to keep the example simple.

See also

▶   The *Tuple Class* topic on MSDN at `http://msdn.microsoft.com/en-us/library/system.tuple.aspx`

Adding promoted action links with the PromotedActions delegate control

The out-of-the-box master pages included with SharePoint contain a series of promoted actions on the top-right corner of the page. These JavaScript-based actions are displayed as links and include functions such as **FOLLOW** and **SHARE** as shown in the following screenshot. The `PromotedActions` delegate control allows us to add additional actions, but does not replace the existing actions.

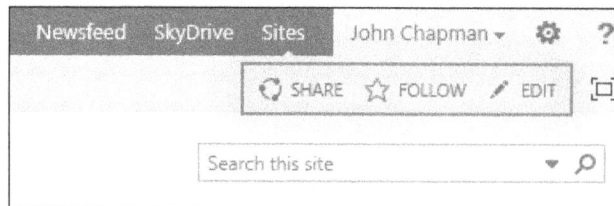

In this recipe, we will add a custom promoted action that fires a JavaScript alert. Promoted actions could be used for a variety of purposes related to the page or site the user is currently viewing. For instance, a promoted action could be created to post a link to the page on social network sites.

Getting ready

We should have already created our Visual Studio project in the *Creating a Visual Studio solution for custom delegate controls* recipe of this chapter before starting this recipe.

How to do it...

Follow these steps to add a promoted action with a delegate control:

1. Open the project created in the *Creating a Visual Studio solution for custom delegate controls* recipe of this chapter in Visual Studio.

2. Add a new class to our `Controls` folder.

3. Set the access modifier of the class to `public`, inherit from the `UserControl` base class, and implement the `IDesignTimeHtmlProvider` interface:

```
public class CustomPromotedAction : UserControl,
IDesignTimeHtmlProvider
```

4. Implement the `GetDesignTimeHtml` method and return the HTML provided by the `Render` method in a monitored scope using the following code:

```
public string GetDesignTimeHtml()
{
  using (new SPMonitoredScope("Code6587EN.Ch07.Controls.
  CustomPromotedAction::GetDesignTimeHtml"))
  {
    StringWriter writer = new StringWriter
    (CultureInfo.CurrentCulture);
    HtmlTextWriter writer2 = new HtmlTextWriter(writer);
    this.Render(writer2);
    writer2.Close();
    return writer.ToString();
  }
}
```

5. Override the `Render` method and add a monitored scope as follows:

```
protected override void Render(HtmlTextWriter writer)
{
```

```
       using (new SPMonitoredScope("Code6587EN.Ch07.
       Controls.CustomPromotedAction::Render"))
       {
       }
    }
}
```

6. Get the URL to the common SharePoint image sprite for the currently applied theme:

```
var iconUrl = SPUtility.GetThemedImageUrl
("/_layouts/15/images/spcommon.png", "spcommon");
```

We will use this image to display an icon for our promoted action. You can use a different image and modify the CSS accordingly for positioning.

7. Add a `STYLE` element to provide the CSS styles that we will use to render our custom action as follows:

```
writer.AddAttribute(HtmlTextWriterAttribute.Type,
"text/css");
writer.RenderBeginTag(HtmlTextWriterTag.Style);
writer.Write("#customPromotedActionIcon { height:16px;
width:16px; position:relative; display:inline-block;
overflow:hidden; background-image: url('" + iconUrl + "');
background-position: -218px -48px; }");
writer.RenderEndTag();
```

8. Add the HTML link element to display our custom promoted action with its JavaScript handler to fire when clicked:

```
writer.AddAttribute(HtmlTextWriterAttribute.Id,
"customPromotedAction");
writer.AddAttribute(HtmlTextWriterAttribute.Class,
"ms-promotedActionButton");
writer.AddAttribute(HtmlTextWriterAttribute.Href, "#");
writer.AddAttribute("onclick",
"alert('You clicked the promoted action.');");
writer.RenderBeginTag(HtmlTextWriterTag.A);
```

9. Add the HTML `SPAN` element to display our custom promoted action image:

```
writer.AddAttribute(HtmlTextWriterAttribute.Class,
"s4-clust ms-promotedActionButton-icon");
writer.AddAttribute(HtmlTextWriterAttribute.Id,
"customPromotedActionIcon");
writer.RenderBeginTag(HtmlTextWriterTag.Span);
writer.Write(" ");
writer.RenderEndTag();
```

10. Add the HTML SPAN element to contain the display text for our custom promoted action:

```
writer.AddAttribute(HtmlTextWriterAttribute.Class,
"ms-promotedActionButton-text");
writer.RenderBeginTag(HtmlTextWriterTag.Span);
writer.Write("Custom Action");
writer.RenderEndTag();
```

11. Add the end tag for our HTML link element:

```
writer.RenderEndTag();
```

12. Add a new **Empty Element** item to our project.

13. In the Elements.xml file of our new element, register our custom promoted action control with the PromotedActions delegate control:

```
<?xml version="1.0" encoding="utf-8"?>
<Elements xmlns="http://schemas.microsoft.com/sharepoint/">
  <Control Id="PromotedActions" Sequence="90"
  ControlClass="Code6587EN.Ch07.Controls.
  CustomPromotedAction" ControlAssembly=
  "$SharePoint.Project.AssemblyFullName$">
  </Control>
</Elements>
```

14. Add a new safe control entry to the new element with the following details:

   - **(Name)**: CustomPromotedAction (the name of the class for our custom control)
   - **Assembly**: $SharePoint.Project.AssemblyFullName$
   - **Namespace**: Code6587EN.Ch07.Controls (the full namespace for the class, without the name of the class itself)
   - **Safe**: True
   - **Safe Against Script**: True
   - **Type Name**: CustomPromotedAction (the name of the class)

15. Open the feature created previously. Ensure that the new element is included in the feature.

16. Click on **Start** from the toolbar to deploy the solution and attach the debugger.

17. Once the SharePoint site is loaded in the web browser (after clicking on **Start**), observe the promoted action. The following screenshot shows how it will look:

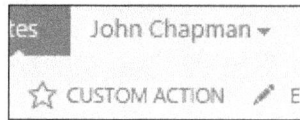

How it works...

Promoted actions in SharePoint provide a series of JavaScript-based actions for end users. The default actions include **FOLLOW** and **SHARE**. Adding a custom promoted action adds actions rather than replacing the existing ones. The promoted action in our recipe simply fires the JavaScript `alert` function to display a message to the user.

See also

▶ The *SPUtility.GetThemedImageUrl method* topic on MSDN at `http://msdn.microsoft.com/en-us/library/microsoft.sharepoint.utilities.sputility.getthemedimageurl.aspx`

Customizing header navigation with a TopNavigationDataSource delegate control

SharePoint provides two primary navigation structures by default: the quick launch displayed vertically on the left-hand side of the page and the top navigation displayed horizontally at the top of the page. The items displayed in these navigation structures may be customized in a variety of methods, including manually per site, using managed metadata, and using custom site map providers. The following screenshot shows the horizontal navigation provided by SharePoint at the top of the page:

In this recipe, we will create a custom site map provider and register it with the `TopNavigationDataSource` delegate control. There are a variety of techniques to create custom site map providers from code. The site map providers used by SharePoint are derived from the `SiteMapProvider` class provided by the .NET framework in the `System.Web` assembly. For the purpose of this recipe, we will create a very simple class derived from the `PortalSiteMapProvider` class.

Getting ready

We should have already created our Visual Studio project in the *Creating a Visual Studio solution for custom delegate controls* recipe of this chapter before starting this recipe.

How to do it...

Follow these steps to customize the top navigation with a delegate control:

1. Open the project created in the *Creating a Visual Studio solution for custom delegate controls* recipe of this chapter in Visual Studio.

2. Add a new class to our `Controls` folder.

3. Set the access modifier for our new class to `public` and inherit from the `PortalSiteMapProvider` base class:

```
public class CustomSiteMapProvider : PortalSiteMapProvider
```

4. Add a field to the class containing the list of links to return from the custom site map provider using the following code:

```
private Dictionary<string, string> links = new Dictionary<string,
string>() {
    { "Bing", "http://www.bing.com" },
    { "Google", "http://www.google.com" },
    { "Yahoo", "http://www.yahoo.com" }
};
```

If you were always using a constant list of links, this would be sufficient. However, if you had a dynamic source for the link data, you could replace this with your own method for getting links.

5. Add a `bool` field to the class to determine whether or not we should include the SharePoint configured navigation data in the list of links we will return. In our method to return the collection of links, we will use this to indicate whether or not we should include the SharePoint-provided links, along with our own links. You could remove this or make it configurable depending upon your circumstances.

```
private bool renderSharePointLinks = false;
```

6. Override the `GetChildNodes` method and add a monitored scope as follows:

```
public override SiteMapNodeCollection GetChildNodes(SiteMapNode
node)
{
    using (new SPMonitoredScope("Code6587EN.Ch07.Controls.
    CustomSiteMapProvider::GetChildNodes"))
```

```
        {
        }
}
```

The `GetChildNodes` method will be called by SharePoint when looking for the links to render for each navigation node. We will return our links when the node provided is for the current SharePoint site.

7. In our monitored scope, instantiate a new `SiteMapNodeCollection` object:

    ```
    var nodes = new SiteMapNodeCollection();
    ```

8. Cast the provided node as `PortalSiteMapNode`:

    ```
    PortalSiteMapNode portalNode = node as PortalSiteMapNode;
    ```

9. Ensure the casted node is not null:

    ```
    if (portalNode != null)
    ```

10. Ensure the node is for the current SharePoint site with the help of the following code:

    ```
    if (portalNode.Type == NodeTypes.Area && portalNode.WebId
    == SPContext.Current.Site.RootWeb.ID)
    ```

11. For each link in our collection of links, add a new node to the nodes collection:

    ```
    foreach (var link in links)
    nodes.Add(new SiteMapNode(this, link.Key, link.Value,
    link.Key));
    ```

12. If we are adding the SharePoint configured links, add the nodes from the `GetChildNodes` method of the `PortalSiteMapProvider` base class:

    ```
    if (renderSharePointLinks)
    nodes.AddRange(base.GetChildNodes(portalNode));
    ```

13. Return our collection of nodes:

    ```
    return nodes;
    ```

14. Add a new **Empty Element** item to our project.

15. In the `Elements.xml` file of our new element, register the `SiteMapDataSource` class from the `System.Web` assembly with the `TopNavigationDataSource` delegate control. Add our custom site map provider as the value for the `SiteMapProvider` property of the control using the following code snippet:

    ```
    <?xml version="1.0" encoding="utf-8"?>
    <Elements xmlns="http://schemas.microsoft.com/sharepoint/">
      <Control Sequence="1" Id="TopNavigationDataSource"
      ControlClass=
      "System.Web.UI.WebControls.SiteMapDataSource"
    ```

```
ControlAssembly="System.Web, Version=2.0.0.0,
Culture=neutral, PublicKeyToken=b03f5f7f11d50a3a">
  <Property Name="ID">topSiteMap</Property>
  <Property Name="SiteMapProvider">
CustomSiteMapProvider</Property>
  <Property Name="EnableViewState">false</Property>
  <Property Name="ShowStartingNode">true</Property>
</Control>
</Elements>
```

16. Open the feature created previously, **Code6587EN.Ch07** for instance. Ensure that the new element is included in the feature.

17. Right-click on the feature in the **Solution Explorer** pane and select **Add Event Receiver** as shown in the following screenshot:

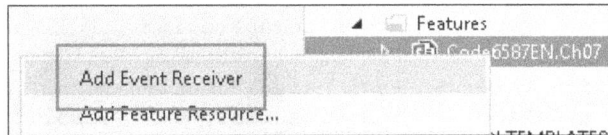

18. Uncomment the `FeatureActivated` and `FeatureDeactivating` event receiver override methods.

19. In our `FeatureActivated` override method, add a scope to run with elevated privileges:

```
SPSecurity.RunWithElevatedPrivileges(() =>
{
});
```

> Executing our code with elevated privileges runs the code as the farm account rather than as the current user. This helps to prevent access denied errors if the current user does not have direct access to perform the current action. It is only recommended to use this methodology when performing actions that affect a SharePoint web application or the farm itself. Allowing code to run with full control over the farm can open potential security risks if we are allowing users who do not have farm administrator access to make farm-level changes.
>
> If elevated permissions only to the current site or site collection are required, open the site collection with the user token of the system account instead. See http://msdn.microsoft.com/en-us/library/office/microsoft.sharepoint.spusertoken.systemaccount.aspx for more information on retrieving the system account user token.

20. In our elevated scope, get the current content web service:

```
SPWebService service = SPWebService.ContentService;
```

21. With the help of the following code, create a new `web.config` modification record to add our custom site map provider to the configured site map providers:

```
SPWebConfigModification myModification = new
SPWebConfigModification();
myModification.Path =
"configuration/system.web/siteMap/providers";
myModification.Name = "add[@name='CustomSiteMapProvider']";
myModification.Sequence = 0;
myModification.Owner = "Code6587ENCustomSiteMapProvider";
myModification.Type =
SPWebConfigModification.SPWebConfigModificationType.
EnsureChildNode;
var typeName = typeof(CustomSiteMapProvider).FullName + ",
" + typeof(CustomSiteMapProvider).Assembly.FullName;
myModification.Value = "<add name=\"CustomSiteMapProvider\"
type=\"" + typeName + "\" NavigationType=\"Global\" />";
```

22. Add our new modification to the collection of modifications:

```
service.WebConfigModifications.Add(myModification);
```

23. Update the content web service and apply the `web.config` modifications:

```
service.Update();
service.ApplyWebConfigModifications();
```

24. In our `FeatureDeactivating` override method, add a scope to run with elevated privileges:

```
SPSecurity.RunWithElevatedPrivileges((() =>
{
});
```

25. In our elevated scope, get the content web service:

```
SPWebService service = SPWebService.ContentService;
```

26. Get the collection of `web.config` modifications from the content web service:

```
Collection<SPWebConfigModification> modsCollection =
service.WebConfigModifications;
```

27. Iterate through each configuration. If you have added the modification, remove it using the following code:

```
int modsCount1 = modsCollection.Count;
for (int i = modsCount1 - 1; i > -1; i--)
```

```
{
  if (modsCollection[i].Owner.Equals
  ("Code6587ENCustomSiteMapProvider"))
  {
    modsCollection.Remove(modsCollection[i]);
  }
}
```

28. Update the content web service and apply the `web.config` modifications:

    ```
    service.Update();
    service.ApplyWebConfigModifications();
    ```

29. Click on **Start** from the toolbar to deploy the solution and attach the debugger.

30. Once the SharePoint site is loaded in the web browser (after clicking on **Start**), observe the links displayed in the top navigation.

How it works...

A `SiteMapProvider` class provides the data for the top navigation control in SharePoint. In our recipe, we created a custom `SiteMapProvider` class based on the `PortalSiteMapProvider` base class. Rather than replacing the `TopNavigationDataSource` delegate control with a custom control, we registered the default `SiteMapProvider` control and configured it to use our custom site map provider. In addition, we registered our custom site map provider in the `web.config` file of the SharePoint web application programmatically.

See also

▸ The *SiteMapProvider Class* topic on MSDN at `http://msdn.microsoft.com/en-us/library/system.web.sitemapprovider.aspx`

▸ The *PortalSiteMapProvider class* topic on MSDN at `http://msdn.microsoft.com/en-us/library/sharepoint/microsoft.sharepoint.publishing.navigation.portalsitemapprovider.aspx`

▸ The *How To: Add and Remove Web.Config Settings Programmatically* article on MSDN at `http://msdn.microsoft.com/en-us/library/bb861909(v=office.14).aspx`

▸ The *SPWebConfigurationModification class* topic on MSDN at `http://msdn.microsoft.com/en-us/library/microsoft.sharepoint.administration.SPWebConfigModification.aspx`

▸ The *SPSecurity.RunWithElevatedPriviliges method* topic on MSDN at `http://msdn.microsoft.com/en-us/library/microsoft.sharepoint.spsecurity.runwithelevatedprivileges.aspx`

> ▶ The *SPSite constructor (String, SPUserToken)* topic on MSDN at `http://msdn.microsoft.com/en-us/library/ms469253.aspx`

> ▶ The *SPUserToken.SystemAccount property* topic on MSDN at `http://msdn.microsoft.com/en-us/library/microsoft.sharepoint.spusertoken.systemaccount.aspx`

Customizing quick launch navigation with a QuickLaunchDataSource delegate control

In this recipe, we will register the custom site map provider, which we created in the previous recipe, *Customizing header navigation with a TopNavigationDataSource delegate control*, with the `QuickLaunchDataSource` delegate control. Since we have already created our custom site map provider and registered it in the `web.config` modifications, we will simply configure the `QuickLaunchDataSource` delegate control to use this site map provider. The `QuickLaunchDataSource` delegate control provides the data for the navigation illustrated in the following screenshot:

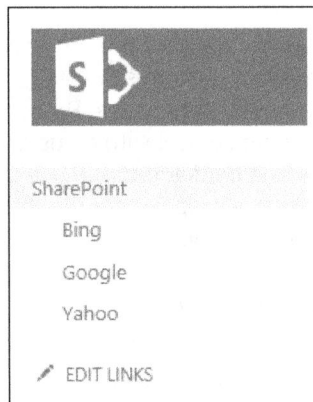

Getting ready

For this recipe, we should already have the custom site map provider created from the *Customizing header navigation with a TopNavigationDataSource delegate control* recipe.

How to do it...

Follow these steps to register our custom site map provider with the quick launch navigation:

1. Open the project created in the *Creating a Visual Studio solution for custom delegate controls* recipe of this chapter in Visual Studio.

2. In the `Elements.xml` file from the **Empty Element** item created in the previous recipe, add another control registration for the `QuickLaunchDataSource` delegate control using the following code:

```xml
<?xml version="1.0" encoding="utf-8"?>
<Elements xmlns="http://schemas.microsoft.com/sharepoint/">
  <Control Sequence="1" Id="TopNavigationDataSource"
  ControlClass="System.Web.UI.WebControls.
  SiteMapDataSource" ControlAssembly="System.Web,
  Version=2.0.0.0, Culture=neutral,
  PublicKeyToken=b03f5f7f11d50a3a">
    <Property Name="ID">topSiteMap</Property>
    <Property Name="SiteMapProvider">
    CustomSiteMapProvider</Property>
    <Property Name="EnableViewState">false</Property>
    <Property Name="ShowStartingNode">true</Property>
  </Control>

  <Control Sequence="1" Id="QuickLaunchDataSource"
  ControlClass="System.Web.UI.WebControls.
  SiteMapDataSource" ControlAssembly="System.Web,
  Version=2.0.0.0, Culture=neutral,
  PublicKeyToken=b03f5f7f11d50a3a">
    <Property Name="ID">QuickLaunchSiteMap</Property>
    <Property Name="SiteMapProvider">
    CustomSiteMapProvider</Property>
    <Property Name="EnableViewState">false</Property>
    <Property Name="ShowStartingNode">true</Property>
  </Control>
</Elements>
```

3. Click on **Start** from the toolbar to deploy the solution and attach the debugger.

4. Once the SharePoint site is loaded in the web browser (after clicking on **Start**), observe the links displayed in the quick launch.

How it works...

Site map providers registered in the `web.config` modifications of an ASP.NET web application, including SharePoint, can be utilized by any navigation control in the web application. This enables us to use the same provider for both the top navigation and quick launch navigation controls. In this recipe, we registered the custom site map provider, created in the previous *Customizing header navigation with a TopNavigationDataSource delegate control* recipe, as the data source for the `QuickLaunchDataSource` control. This resulted in the data from our custom provider being used when rendering the links for the quick launch navigation.

Restoring the Navigate Up button with an AdditionalPageHead delegate control

The out-of-the-box master pages from SharePoint 2010 included a breadcrumb control that would allow a user to easily navigate up the current site hierarchy. The out-of-the-box master pages in SharePoint 2013 have hidden this control. We previously accomplished this in a master page in *Chapter 3, Branding SharePoint with Custom Master Pages and Page Layouts*. In this recipe, however, we will accomplish this with an `AdditionalPageHead` delegate control. This allows us to restore the button regardless of which master page is being used. The following screenshot illustrates the restored breadcrumb control:

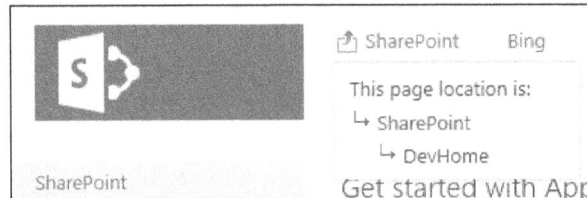

Getting ready

We should have already created our Visual Studio project with the help of the *Creating a Visual Studio solution for custom delegate controls* recipe of this chapter before starting this recipe.

How to do it...

Follow these steps to restore the navigate up button with a delegate control:

1. Open the project created in the *Creating a Visual Studio solution for custom delegate controls* recipe of this chapter in Visual Studio.

2. Add a new class to our `Controls` folder.

3. Set the access modifier of our new class to `public` and inherit from the `UserControl` base class:

   ```
   public class RestoreBreadcrumb : UserControl
   ```

4. Override the `CreateChildControls` method and add a monitored scope as follows:

   ```
   protected override void CreateChildControls()
   {
     using (new
     SPMonitoredScope("Code6587EN.Ch07.Controls.
   ```

```
RestoreBreadcrumb::CreateChildControls"))
  {
  }
}
```

5. Get the master page from the current page:

```
var masterPage = this.Page.Master;
```

6. Get the `AjaxDelta` control that contains the breadcrumb control:

```
var delta =
masterPage.FindControl("DeltaBreadcrumbDropdown") as
AjaxDelta;
```

7. Ensure the `AjaxDelta` control is not null:

```
if (delta != null)
```

8. Get the breadcrumb control from the `AjaxDelta` control:

```
var breadcrumb =
delta.FindControl("GlobalBreadCrumbNavPopout") as
PopoutMenu;
```

9. Ensure the `breadcrumb` control is not null:

```
if (breadcrumb != null)
```

10. Set the `breadcrumb` control to be visible, set the `ThemeKey` property, and set the `IconUrl` property using the following code:

```
breadcrumb.Visible = true;
breadcrumb.ThemeKey = "spcommon";
breadcrumb.IconUrl = "/_layouts/15/images/spcommon.png";
```

11. Add a `STYLE` element to set the display style of the `breadcrumb` container to `inline-block`.

12. Add a new **Empty Element** item.

13. In the `Elements.xml` file of the new element, register our control with the `AdditionalPageHead` delegate control using the following code:

```
<?xml version="1.0" encoding="utf-8"?>
<Elements xmlns="http://schemas.microsoft.com/sharepoint/">
  <Control Id="AdditionalPageHead" Sequence="11"
  ControlClass="Code6587EN.Ch07.Controls.RestoreBreadcrumb"
  ControlAssembly="$SharePoint.Project.AssemblyFullName$">
  </Control>
</Elements>
```

14. Add a new safe control entry to the new element with the following details:

- ❑ **(Name):** `RestoreBreadcrumb` (the name of the class for our custom control)
- ❑ **Assembly:** `$SharePoint.Project.AssemblyFullName$`
- ❑ **Namespace:** `Code6587EN.Ch07.Controls` (the full namespace for the class, without the name of the class itself)
- ❑ **Safe:** `True`
- ❑ **Safe Against Script:** `True`
- ❑ **Type Name:** `RestoreBreadcrumb` (the name of the class)

15. Open the feature created previously. Ensure that the new element is included in the feature.
16. Click on **Start** from the toolbar to deploy the solution and attach the debugger.
17. Once the SharePoint site is loaded in the web browser (after clicking on **Start**), observe the restored `breadcrumb` control.

How it works...

The out-of-the-box master pages included with SharePoint 2013 already include the required controls on the page to render the breadcrumb control. However, they are hidden. In our `AdditionalPageHead` delegate control, we are locating the control, instructing it to display, and configuring the icon to be correctly inherited from the currently applied SharePoint theme.

See also

▶ The *PopoutMenu class* topic on MSDN at `http://msdn.microsoft.com/en-us/library/office/microsoft.sharepoint.webcontrols.popoutmenu.aspx`

Adding meta tags to pages from custom library fields with an AdditionalPageHead delegate control

One of the common search engine optimization techniques used is adding the `META` tags to the `HEAD` element of a page to include additional information about the page. These `META` tags can include author information, keywords, a description, copyright information, and so on. For sites where this information is the same for every page, we can simply add the `META` tags to the master page. However, for sites that require different information for each page, we can use an `AdditionalPageHead` control to dynamically add the `META` tags.

In this recipe, we will add the `META` tags to the `HEAD` element of pages that have specific list item fields.

Getting ready

We should have already created our Visual Studio project in the *Creating a Visual Studio solution for custom delegate controls* recipe of this chapter before starting this recipe. In addition, on the **Pages** library we are testing this recipe with, we should have added two custom columns: **Meta Keywords** and **Meta Description**. For one or more of the pages in the library, we should have set the value for these fields on the properties of the pages.

How to do it...

Follow these steps to add the META tags with a delegate control:

1. Open the project created in the *Creating a Visual Studio solution for custom delegate controls* recipe of this chapter in Visual Studio.

2. Add a new class to our `Controls` folder.

3. Set the access modifier of our new class to `public` and inherit from the `UserControl` base class:

   ```
   public class CustomMetaTags : UserControl
   ```

4. Set constant values for the names of the fields to look for and the formats of the `<meta>` elements as follows:

   ```
   private const string FieldNameKeywords = "Meta Keywords";
   private const string FieldNameDescription =
   "Meta Description";
   private const string FormatMetaTagKeywords =
   "<meta name=\"keywords\" content=\"{0}\" />";
   private const string FormatMetaTagDescription =
   "<meta name=\"description\" content=\"{0}\" />";
   ```

5. Override the `CreateChildControls` method and add a monitored scope:

   ```
   protected override void CreateChildControls()
   {
     using (new SPMonitoredScope("Code6587EN.Ch07.Controls.
     CustomMetaTags::CreateChildControls"))
     {
     }
   }
   ```

6. Ensure the current SharePoint context is not null, it has a file, and that the file has a list item:

   ```
   if (SPContext.Current != null
   && SPContext.Current.File !=
   null
   && SPContext.Current.File.Item != null)
   ```

7. Get the list item associated with the current file as follows:

```
var item = SPContext.Current.File.Item;
```

8. Ensure the list has the **Meta Keywords** column and that the current item has a value assigned:

```
if (item.Fields.ContainsField(FieldNameKeywords) &&
item[FieldNameKeywords] != null
&&
!string.IsNullOrEmpty(item[FieldNameKeywords].ToString()))
```

9. Add a `<meta>` element to the page using the format for the keywords tag and the value of the list item field:

```
this.Controls.Add(new LiteralControl
(string.Format(CultureInfo.InvariantCulture,
FormatMetaTagKeywords,
item[FieldNameKeywords].ToString())));
```

10. Ensure the list has a **Meta Description** column and that the current item has a value assigned:

```
if (item.Fields.ContainsField(FieldNameDescription)
&&
item[FieldNameDescription] != null
&&
!string.IsNullOrEmpty(item[FieldNameDescription].ToString()
))
```

11. Add a `<meta>` element to the page using the format for the description tag and the value of the list item field:

```
this.Controls.Add(new LiteralControl
(string.Format(CultureInfo.InvariantCulture,
FormatMetaTagDescription,
item[FieldNameDescription].ToString())));
```

12. Add a new **Empty Element** item to the project.

13. In the `Elements.xml` file of the new element, register our custom control with the `AdditionalPageHead` delegate control using the following code:

```
<?xml version="1.0" encoding="utf-8"?>
<Elements xmlns="http://schemas.microsoft.com/sharepoint/">
  <Control Id="AdditionalPageHead" Sequence="12"
  ControlClass="Code6587EN.Ch07.Controls.CustomMetaTags"
  ControlAssembly="$SharePoint.Project.
  AssemblyFullName$"></Control>
</Elements>
```

14. Add a new safe control entry to the new element with the following details:

    ❑ **(Name)**: `CustomMetaTags` (the name of the class for our custom control)

    ❑ **Assembly**: `$SharePoint.Project.AssemblyFullName$`

    ❑ **Namespace**: `Code6587EN.Ch07.Controls` (the full namespace for the class, without the name of the class itself)

    ❑ **Safe**: `True`

    ❑ **Safe Against Script**: `True`

    ❑ **Type Name**: `CustomMetaTags` (the name of the class)

15. Open the feature created previously. Ensure that the new element is included in the feature.

16. Click on **Start** from the toolbar to deploy the solution and attach the debugger.

17. Once the SharePoint site is loaded in the web browser (after clicking on **Start**), navigate to a page with either the **Meta Keywords** field or the **Meta Description** field populated. View the source of the page to observe the addition of the `<meta>` elements.

How it works...

In this recipe, if the current SharePoint content has a file associated with it, such as a web page, our control is looking at the list item for the file. If the list item has a **Meta Keywords** field or a **Meta Description** field, we are adding `<meta>` tags to the page with the content of the fields.

See also

▸ The *HTML <meta> Tag* article on W3 Schools at `http://www.w3schools.com/tags/tag_meta.asp`

Storing analytics tracking code with a site collection settings page

Though SharePoint includes some analytic features, many still prefer to use third-party web analytics providers such as Google Analytics. These analytics providers use a snippet of JavaScript code that is added to each page in most cases.

In this recipe, we will create a settings page to allow site collection administrators to store the JavaScript code on a per site collection basis.

Getting ready

We should have already created our Visual Studio project in the *Creating a Visual Studio solution for custom delegate controls* recipe of this chapter before starting this recipe.

How to do it...

Follow these steps to create a settings page for our tracking code:

1. Open the project created in the *Creating a Visual Studio solution for custom-delegate controls* recipe of this chapter in Visual Studio.

2. Add a new **Application Page** item to the subfolder we created in the Layouts mapped folder as shown in the following screenshot:

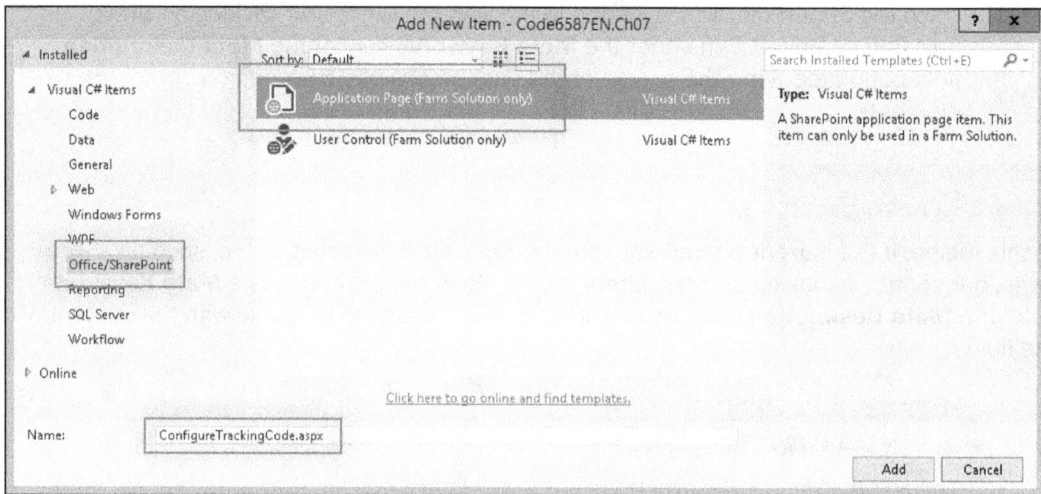

3. In the ASPX page, register the settings page user controls as follows:

```
<%@ Register TagPrefix="wssuc" TagName="InputFormSection"
src="/_controltemplates/InputFormSection.ascx" %>
<%@ Register TagPrefix="wssuc" TagName="InputFormControl"
src="/_controltemplates/InputFormControl.ascx" %>
<%@ Register TagPrefix="wssuc" TagName="ButtonSection"
src="~/_controltemplates/ButtonSection.ascx" %>
```

4. In the title content placeholders, add the title for our settings page as follows:

```
<asp:Content ID="PageTitle"
ContentPlaceHolderID="PlaceHolderPageTitle" runat="server">
Configure Analytics Tracking Code
</asp:Content>
```

```
<asp:Content ID="PageTitleInTitleArea"
ContentPlaceHolderID="PlaceHolderPageTitleInTitleArea"
runat="server" >
Configure Analytics Tracking Code
</asp:Content>
```

5. In the main content placeholder, add a `<table>` element to contain our settings page sections:

```
<asp:Content ID="Main"
ContentPlaceHolderID="PlaceHolderMain" runat="server">
  <table width="100%">
    <tr>
      <td>
      </td>
    </tr>
  </table>
</asp:Content>
```

The settings page user controls were designed to be placed inside a `<table>` element.

6. In our `<table>` element, add an `InputFormSection` control with a `TextBox` control to input our analytics tracking code as follows:

```
<wssuc:InputFormSection Title="Analytics Tracking Code"
id="trackingCodeSection" runat="server" Description="The
script block entered here will be rendered on each page in
this SharePoint site.">
<template_inputformcontrols>
  <wssuc:InputFormControl LabelText="Analytics Tracking
  Code Script Block" runat="server"
  LabelAssociatedControlId="txtScriptBlock">
  <Template_control>
    <asp:TextBox runat="server" Width="100%"
    ID="txtScriptBlock" TextMode="MultiLine"
    Height="300px" />
  </Template_control>
  </wssuc:InputFormControl>
</template_inputformcontrols>
</wssuc:InputFormSection>
```

7. Add a `ButtonSection` control with a `Button` control to submit our analytics tracking code:

```
<wssuc:ButtonSection runat="server">
<Template_Buttons>
```

```
<asp:Button UseSubmitBehavior="false" runat="server"
class="ms-ButtonHeightWidth" OnClick="BtnSubmit_Click"
Text="OK" id="BtnSaveChanges"
accesskey="<%$Resources:wss,okbutton_accesskey%>"/>
</Template_Buttons>
</wssuc:ButtonSection>
```

8. In the code-behind file of our application page, add a constant string for the name of the property we will save our analytics code within:

```
private const string PropertyName = "CustomAnalyticsCode";
```

9. In a monitored scope within the `Page_Load` method, set the `TextBox` content to the existing value of the analytics property:

```
protected void Page_Load(object sender, EventArgs e)
{
  using (new SPMonitoredScope
  ("Code6587EN.Ch07.Layouts.Code6587EN.Ch07.
  ConfigureTrackingCode::Page_Load"))
  {
    if (!IsPostBack)
      if
      (SPContext.Current.Site.RootWeb.AllProperties.
      ContainsKey(PropertyName))
        txtScriptBlock.Text =
        SPContext.Current.Site.RootWeb.
        AllProperties[PropertyName].ToString();
  }
}
```

10. Add the `BtnSubmit_Click` method with a monitored scope to execute when the **Submit** button is clicked:

```
protected void BtnSubmit_Click(object sender, EventArgs e)
{
  using (new
  SPMonitoredScope("Code6587EN.Ch07.Layouts.
  Code6587EN.Ch07.ConfigureTrackingCode::BtnSubmit_Click"))
  {
  }
}
```

11. If the root site of the site collection already contains the analytics property, set its value as follows:

```
if
(SPContext.Current.Site.RootWeb.AllProperties.ContainsKey
(PropertyName))
```

```
SPContext.Current.Site.RootWeb.
AllProperties[PropertyName] = txtScriptBlock.Text;
```

12. If the root site of the site collection does not already contain the analytics property, add it and set its value as follows:

```
else
    SPContext.Current.Site.RootWeb.AllProperties.
    Add(PropertyName, txtScriptBlock.Text);
```

13. Update the root site of the site collection and redirect to the **Site settings** page:

```
SPContext.Current.Site.RootWeb.Update();
SPUtility.Redirect(SPContext.Current.Web.ServerRelativeUrl.
TrimEnd('/') + "/_layouts/15/Settings.aspx",
SPRedirectFlags.Default, HttpContext.Current);
```

14. Add an **Empty Element** item to the project.

15. In the `Elements.xml` file of the new element, register our custom action with the URL to our application page:

```
<?xml version="1.0" encoding="utf-8"?>
<Elements xmlns="http://schemas.microsoft.com/sharepoint/">
<CustomAction Id="AnalyticsCode"
GroupId="SiteCollectionAdmin"
Location="Microsoft.SharePoint.SiteSettings"
Sequence="1000" Title="Configure Analytics Code">
<UrlAction
Url="~sitecollection/_layouts/15/Code6587EN.Ch07/
ConfigureTrackingCode.aspx"/>
</CustomAction>
</Elements>
```

16. Open the feature created previously. Ensure that the new element is included in the feature.

17. Click on **Start** from the toolbar to deploy the solution and attach the debugger.

18. Once the SharePoint site is loaded in the web browser (after clicking on **Start**), navigate to the **Site settings** page, and select the **Configure Analytics Code** link under **Site Collection Administration**, as shown in the following screenshot:

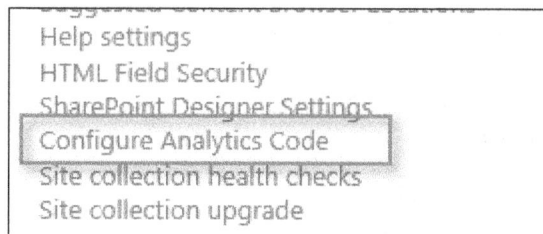

19. Add your analytics tracking code including the `<script>` tags and submit by clicking on **OK**:

Configure Analytics Tracking Code

Analytics Tracking Code

The script block entered here will be rendered on each page in this SharePoint site.

Analytics Tracking Code Script Block

```
<script type="text/javascript">

var _gaq = _gaq || [];
_gaq.push(['_setAccount', 'UA-XXXXXXXX-1']);
_gaq.push(['_trackPageview']);

(function() {
  var ga = document.createElement('script'); ga.type
= 'text/javascript'; ga.async = true;
  ga.src = ('https:' ==
document.location.protocol ? 'https://ssl' : 'http://www')
+ '.google-analytics.com/ga.js';
  var s = document.getElementsByTagName('script')[0];
s.parentNode.insertBefore(ga, s);
  })();

</script>
```

OK   Cancel

How it works...

In this recipe, we have created a basic settings page that allows us to store our analytics tracking code as a property of the root site in the current site collection. This page uses the settings page user controls used by the majority of SharePoint settings pages. In addition, we used a custom action registration to add our settings page to the list of links on the **Site settings** page in the **Site Collection Administration** section.

See also

▶ The *Custom Action* topic on MSDN at `http://msdn.microsoft.com/en-us/library/ms458635(v=office.14).aspx`

▶ The *SPWeb.AllProperties property* topic on MSDN at `http://msdn.microsoft.com/en-us/library/microsoft.sharepoint.spweb.allproperties.aspx`

Adding stored analytics tracking code to pages with an AdditionalPageHead delegate control

With the analytics tracking code being stored from the previous recipe, we will use an `AdditionalPageHead` delegate control to insert the snippet of analytics tracking code on each page.

Getting ready

For this recipe, we should already have the settings page created in the *Storing analytics tracking code with a site collection settings page* recipe.

How to do it...

Follow these steps to add the stored analytics tracking code with a delegate control:

1. Open the project created in the *Creating a Visual Studio solution for custom delegate controls* recipe of this chapter in Visual Studio.

2. Add a new class to our `Controls` folder.

3. Set the access modifier of our new class to `public` and inherit from the `UserControl` base class:

   ```
   public class CustomAnalyticsCode : UserControl
   ```

4. Add a constant string with the name of the property we are storing the analytics code with as follows:

   ```
   private const string PropertyName = "CustomAnalyticsCode";
   ```

5. Override the `CreateChildControls` method and add a monitored scope using the following code:

   ```
   protected override void CreateChildControls()
   {
     using (new SPMonitoredScope("Code6587EN.Ch07.Controls.
     CustomAnalyticsCode::CreateChildControls"))
     {
     }
   }
   ```

6. If the root site of the site collection contains the analytics property and it has a value, add it to the controls collection of the current page form:

```
if (SPContext.Current.Site.RootWeb.AllProperties.
ContainsKey(PropertyName)
&& !string.IsNullOrEmpty(SPContext.Current.Site.RootWeb.
AllProperties[PropertyName].ToString()))
   this.Page.Form.Controls.Add(new LiteralControl
   (SPContext.Current.Site.RootWeb.
   AllProperties[PropertyName].ToString()));
```

7. In the `Elements.xml` file of the **Empty Element** item we created in the previous recipe, add the registration for our custom control with the `AdditionalPageHead` delegate control:

```
<Control Id="AdditionalPageHead" Sequence="13"
ControlClass="Code6587EN.Ch07.Controls.CustomAnalyticsCode"
ControlAssembly="$SharePoint.Project.AssemblyFullName$">
</Control>
```

8. Click on **Start** from the toolbar to deploy the solution and attach the debugger.

9. Once the SharePoint site is loaded in the web browser (after clicking on **Start**), view the source of the page to observe the added analytics code.

How it works...

In this recipe, we are retrieving the analytics code we stored as a property of the root site in the current site collection from the previous recipe. We are then adding the script to the collection of controls on the current page form in our `AdditionalPageHead` control using a `LiteralControl`. A `LiteralControl` renders the provided content directly on the page.

See also

▶ The *SPWeb.AllProperties property* topic on MSDN at `http://msdn.microsoft.com/en-us/library/microsoft.sharepoint.spweb.allproperties.aspx`

8
Enhancing User Input with InfoPath Forms

In this chapter, we will explore the abilities of Microsoft InfoPath to customize the end user's input experience in SharePoint. We will cover the following recipes:

- Customizing the SharePoint list entry form templates with InfoPath
- Creating InfoPath forms that are submitted to the SharePoint form libraries
- Creating a SharePoint list to provide a drop-down menu data to InfoPath
- Adding a drop-down menu to InfoPath using SharePoint list data
- Paginating InfoPath forms with views
- Validating data in InfoPath forms
- Calculating field values in InfoPath based on the values of other fields
- Adding custom .NET code to an InfoPath form
- Preparing InfoPath forms for approval by SharePoint administrators
- Approving submitted InfoPath forms in SharePoint
- Creating libraries using approved InfoPath forms in SharePoint
- Creating a survey InfoPath form that gets locked after submission and populates the SharePoint fields

Introduction

In the collection of tools available to enhance and customize the SharePoint experience, Microsoft InfoPath is often overlooked. Microsoft InfoPath is a powerful tool to create interactive form templates. These form templates can be used in the InfoPath Filler application that is available on the users' desktops or can be used in SharePoint as web-based forms.

Microsoft InfoPath is designed like the rest of the Microsoft Office applications and can be easily used by power users and developers alike. It comes as a part of the Professional Plus edition of Microsoft Office 2013.

Using InfoPath in web content management applications allows us to provide a robust user input experience without involving custom code. This is particularly useful for content authors who need to create forms but do not have development experience. An entire cookbook could be dedicated to InfoPath. In this chapter, however, we will only cover the basics of how to use InfoPath to customize the way users input information in SharePoint.

For most InfoPath forms, the InfoPath Designer application is all that is required. However, in order to add custom .NET code to an InfoPath form, the Microsoft Visual Studio Tools for Applications are required in addition to Microsoft Visual Studio. They can be obtained from `http://www.microsoft.com/en-us/download/details.aspx?id=38807`.

> Do not install Microsoft InfoPath on the same computer as Microsoft SharePoint Server. The assemblies included with the InfoPath client applications often conflict with the assemblies included with SharePoint. You may receive exceptions in SharePoint, in both the web interface and the logs, if the InfoPath client applications are installed on the SharePoint server.

Customizing the SharePoint list entry form templates with InfoPath

With SharePoint Server 2010, Microsoft added the ability to use Microsoft InfoPath form templates to replace the default entry form pages illustrated in the following screenshot. The default entry form pages use a basic layout and offer only a few validation and calculation options.

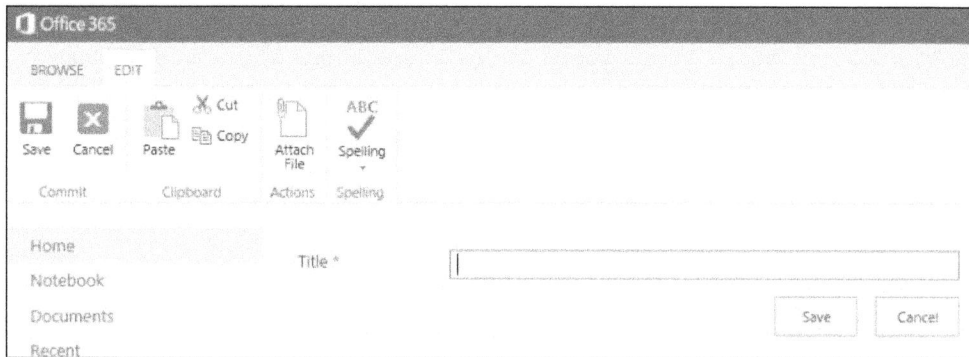

Though entry forms may also be customized in SharePoint Designer and Visual Studio, using InfoPath is a much simpler approach, particularly for power users who do not have development experience. In this recipe, we will create a SharePoint list and customize the entry form template with InfoPath.

How to do it...

Follow these steps to customize the input form for SharePoint:

1. Navigate to the SharePoint site using Internet Explorer.

> Launching InfoPath Designer to customize list forms is only available with Internet Explorer. It is not available from other web browsers such as Google Chrome or Mozilla Firefox.

2. Select **Site contents** from the **Settings** menu.
3. Click on **Add an app**.
4. Click on **Custom List**.
5. Provide a name for the list in the **Name** field and click on **Create**.
6. On the **Site contents** page, select the newly created list.
7. Select **Customize Form** from the **LIST** tab in the ribbon as shown in the following screenshot:.

Internet Explorer may ask for your permission to open the form template in InfoPath.

8. Add some text to the form template.

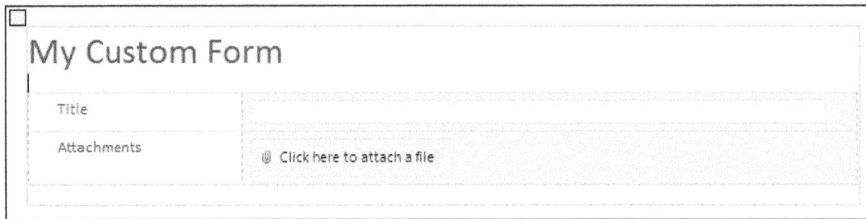

9. Select **Quick Publish** from the **Info** menu as shown in the following screenshot:

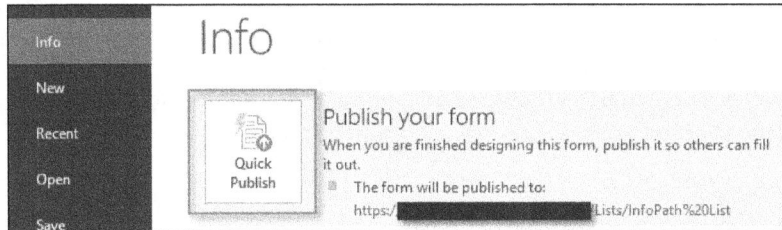

10. Once the form has been published, select **Open the SharePoint list in the browser** and click on **OK**, as shown in the following screenshot:

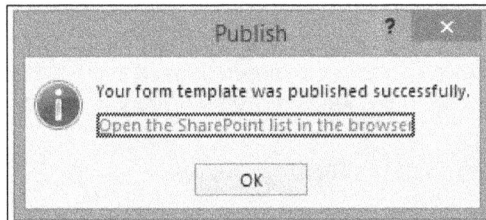

11. From the **ITEMS** tab in the ribbon, select **New Item** to observe the results of the newly customized InfoPath form template:

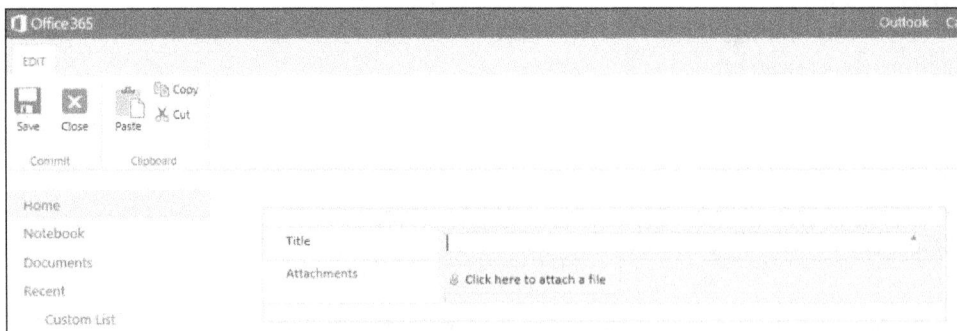

How it works...

By default, SharePoint lists use automatically generated forms within web part pages to create, view, and edit list item data. These web part pages can be customized with tools such as Microsoft SharePoint Designer or Microsoft Visual Studio. They may also be replaced with an InfoPath form template. When selecting **Customize Form** on the ribbon, SharePoint automatically creates the InfoPath form template based on the list columns, configures the list to use the InfoPath form template in place of the web part pages, and opens the form template in InfoPath Designer for editing.

The **Quick Publish** option is only available for a form template that has already been published. When customizing a list entry form template, SharePoint has already published it. We will cover the initial publishing of a new form template later in the *Creating InfoPath forms that are submitted to the SharePoint form libraries* recipe of this chapter.

Using InfoPath form templates in SharePoint requires a state service application to be configured. If this has not been configured, you may receive the following error message:

```
The form cannot be rendered. This may be due to a
misconfiguration of the Microsoft SharePoint Server
State Service. For more information, contact your
server administrator.
```

A new state service application can be configured with the `New-SPStateServiceApplication` Cmdlet in PowerShell.

See also

▸ The *New-SPStateServiceApplication* topic on TechNet at `http://technet.microsoft.com/en-us/library/ff608084.aspx`

▸ The *Customize a SharePoint List Form* article on Microsoft Office at `http://office.microsoft.com/en-us/infopath-help/customize-a-sharepoint-list-form-HA101821257.aspx`

Creating InfoPath forms that are submitted to the SharePoint form libraries

Customizing list item entry form templates is one of the two common types of InfoPath form templates. The second common type is a self-contained form that is submitted to a SharePoint form library as a document. These types of forms are particularly useful in place of paper documents. For instance, this type of form could be used for creating web-based tests or quizzes. In this recipe, we will create a simple InfoPath form template and publish it to a library.

How to do it...

Follow these steps to create a form template that submits to a SharePoint form:

1. Open Microsoft InfoPath Designer 2013.

2. From the **New** section of the **File** menu, select **SharePoint Form Library** as shown in the following screenshot:

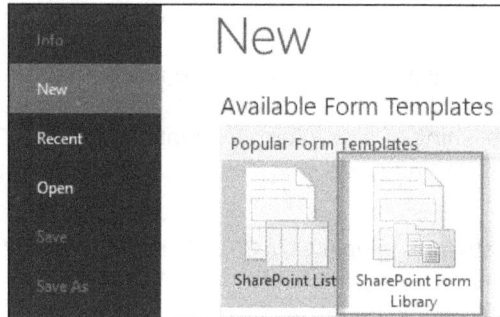

3. Click on **Design Form**.

4. In the newly created form template, populate the title and two headings, as shown in the following screenshot:

Newly created form templates include a default table layout. You can modify the provided layout or replace it with a different one. New table layouts may be added from the **INSERT** tab in the ribbon. Modifying table layouts in InfoPath is nearly identical to using tables in Microsoft Word. In addition, predefined page layouts can be accessed from the **PAGE DESIGN** tab in the ribbon.

5. In the first column with the **Add label** watermark, click inside the table cell to place your mouse cursor and enter a label for the first field, such as `Customer Name`.

6. In the corresponding column with the **Add control** watermark, click inside the table cell to place your mouse cursor.

7. From the **HOME** tab in the ribbon, select **Text Box** in the **Controls** section as shown in the following screenshot:

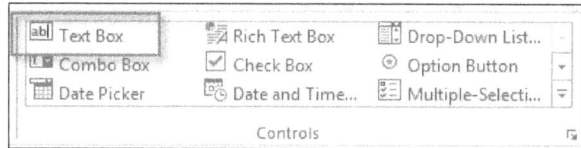

8. With the newly created field selected, in the ribbon, navigate to **CONTROL TOOLS | PROPERTIES**.

9. Provide a more meaningful name for the control, `customerName`, for instance:

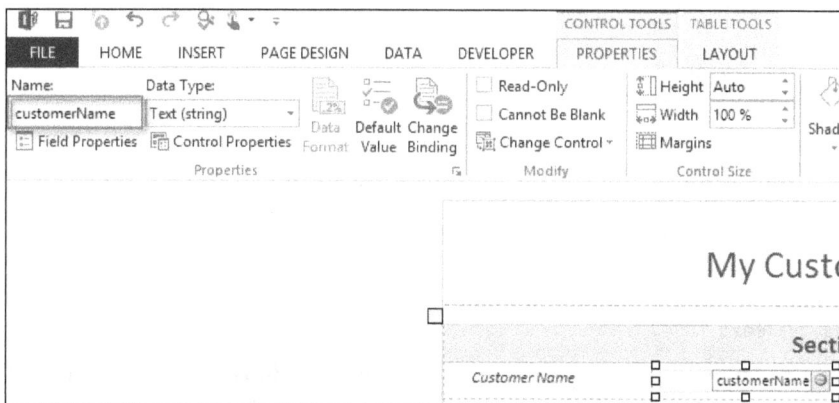

10. Repeat steps 5 through 9 to add a label and control for each place provided. Add textboxes, checkboxes, and person/group pickers for the control types.

11. Click on **Save** from the **File** menu to save the form template to your local computer.

> When working with form templates created in InfoPath Designer, keeping a saved copy will make it easier to edit and publish updated versions in the future. They can also be saved as documents in a SharePoint document library to allow collaboration and versioning on the form templates.

12. From the **Publish** section of the **File** menu, select **SharePoint Server** as shown in the following screenshot:

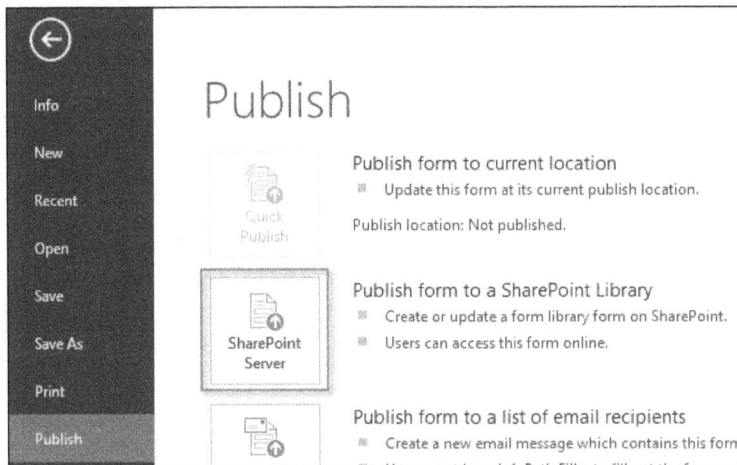

13. Provide the complete URL to the SharePoint site we are publishing the form to and click on **Next**.

14. Ensure **Enable this form to be filled out by using a browser** is selected and select **Form Library** for **What do you want to create or modify**.

15. Click on **Next**.

16. Select **Create a new form library** and click on **Next**. Publishing a form template may also be used to update an existing document library.

17. In the **Name** and **Description** fields, provide a name and description for the form library and click on **Next**.

18. For the fields that will be available as columns in SharePoint, click on **Add**.

19. Select the first field we created, verify that the column name matches the name of the field, and click on **OK** as shown in the following screenshot:

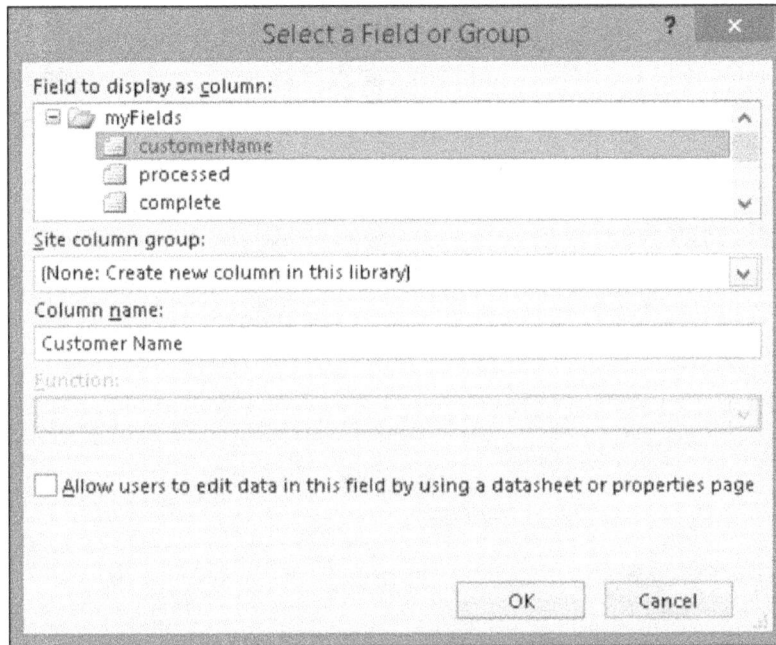

20. Repeat steps 19 and 20 for each of the fields we added to the form template. For each of the fields made available as columns, data entered in those fields will be populated as column data on the document in the form library when submitted. The **People/Group Picker** fields create groups of fields with the **Display Name**, **Account Id**, and **Account Type** attributes of the user or group selected. When adding a **People/Group Picker** field as a column, you will need to select one of those values.

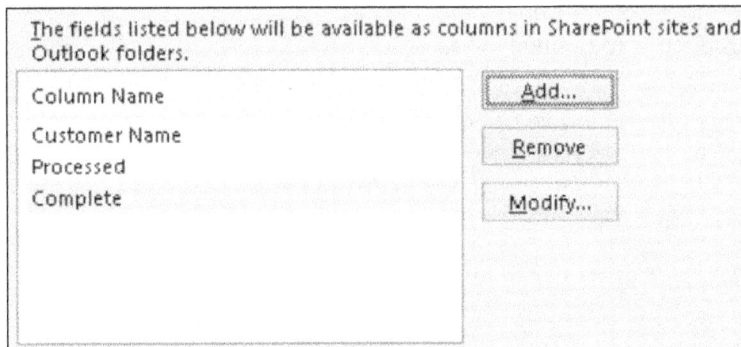

21. Click on **Next** and then on **Publish**.

22. Select **Open this Form in the Browser**.

23. Fill out the form and click on **Save**.

> The default save action requires the user to provide a filename. In the *Creating a survey InfoPath form that gets locked after submission and populates the SharePoint fields* recipe of this chapter, we will cover using submit buttons to automatically generate the filename that does not require the user to specify it.

24. Navigate to the form library to view the newly created document and its properties.

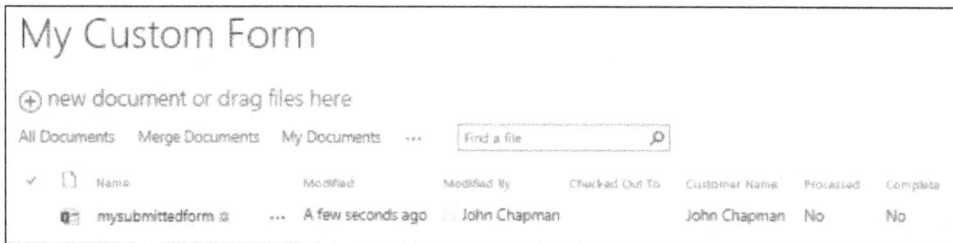

	Name	Modified	Modified By	Checked Out To	Customer Name	Processed	Complete
	mysubmittedform	A few seconds ago	John Chapman		John Chapman	No	No

My Custom Form

⊕ new document or drag files here

All Documents   Merge Documents   My Documents   ···   Find a file

How it works...

Publishing an InfoPath form template that submits to a SharePoint form library creates a new content type in the SharePoint site with the form template as the document template for the content type. A content type is a reusable set of columns and other settings for a category of list items or documents. The form library is then configured to use this newly created content type. When a user saves a completed form, it is added to the form library as an XML document.

See also

▸ The *Introduction to Content Types* article on MSDN at http://msdn.microsoft.com/en-us/library/office/ms472236(v=office.14).aspx

▸ The *Publish a form* article on Microsoft Office at http://office.microsoft.com/en-us/infopath-help/publish-a-form-HA101783381.aspx

Creating a SharePoint list to provide a drop-down menu data to InfoPath

InfoPath can use data from SharePoint and other sources, such as web services, to populate choices in data-driven controls such as drop-down menus. In this recipe, we will create a simple SharePoint list to provide data to InfoPath for the next recipe, adding a drop-down menu to InfoPath using SharePoint list data.

How to do it...

Follow these steps to create our SharePoint list:

1. Navigate to the SharePoint site in your preferred web browser.
2. From the **Settings** menu, select **Site contents**.
3. Select **Add an app** and then click on **Custom List**.
4. Provide a name such as `Categories` for the custom list in the **Name** field.
5. Select the newly created list on the **Site contents** page.
6. Add new items to the list such as `Customer Request`, `Internal Request`, and `Automated Request`.

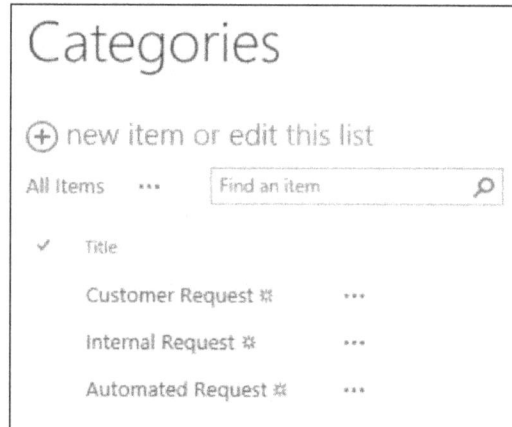

How it works...

InfoPath form templates have the ability to communicate with SharePoint to retrieve list data. Like SharePoint Designer, InfoPath communicates with SharePoint using web services. This allows form templates to be published and connections to lists from remote computers.

Adding a drop-down menu to InfoPath using SharePoint list data

In this recipe, we will add a drop-down menu that uses data provided by the custom list we created previously in the *Creating a SharePoint list to provide drop-down menu data to InfoPath* recipe.

Getting ready

For this recipe, we should have a SharePoint list created to retrieve data from.

How to do it...

Follow these steps to create a drop-down menu that uses SharePoint list data:

1. Create a new form template or open an existing one in Microsoft InfoPath Designer 2013.

2. Select **From SharePoint List** from the **DATA** tab present in the ribbon as shown in the following screenshot:

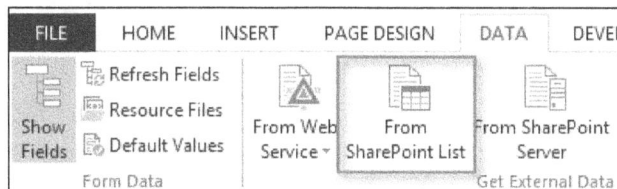

3. Provide the URL to the SharePoint site that contains the list and click on **Next**.

4. Select the list and click on **Next**.

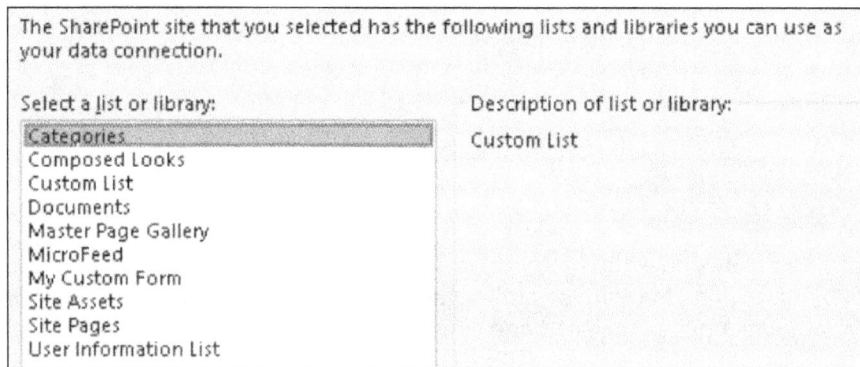

5. Select the field you want to display in the drop-down menu. In the case of our **Categories** list, select **Title** as shown in the following screenshot:

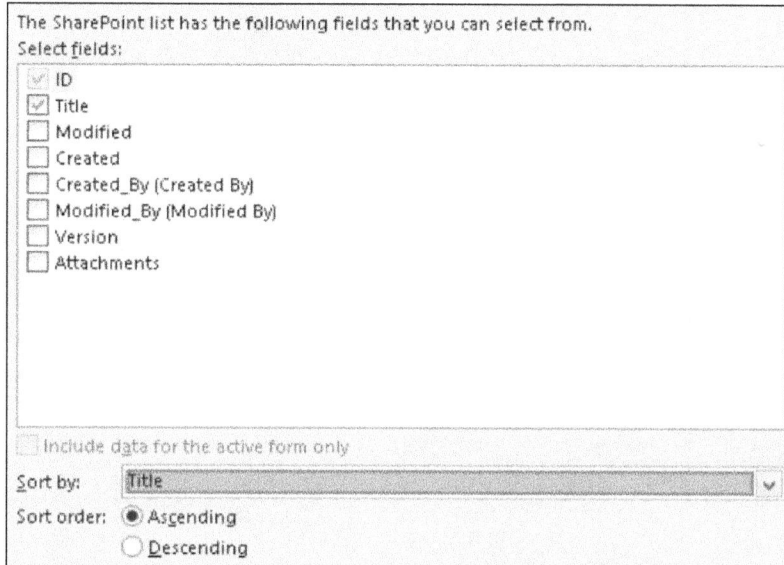

The SharePoint list has the following fields that you can select from.
Select fields:

- [✓] ID
- [✓] Title
- [ ] Modified
- [ ] Created
- [ ] Created_By (Created By)
- [ ] Modified_By (Modified By)
- [ ] Version
- [ ] Attachments

[ ] Include data for the active form only

Sort by: Title

Sort order: (●) Ascending
            ( ) Descending

6. In the **Sort By** field, select **Title** to sort the fields according to their title.

7. Click on **Next**, then again on **Next**, and then click on **Finish**.

8. Add a **Combo Box** control to the form template and provide the control an appropriate name, such as `category`.

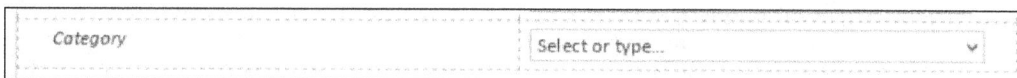

Category   Select or type...   ∨

9. Select the control.

10. Navigate to **CONTROL TOOLS | PROPERTIES** and select **Edit Choices** as shown in the following screenshot:

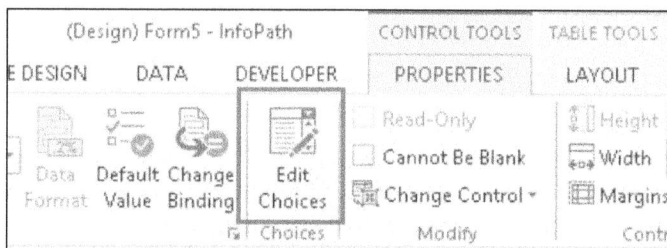

(Design) Form5 - InfoPath   CONTROL TOOLS   TABLE TOOLS

DESIGN   DATA   DEVELOPER   PROPERTIES   LAYOUT

Data   Default   Change   Edit   Read-Only   Height
Format   Value   Binding   Choices   Cannot Be Blank   Width
                              Change Control ▾   Margins
                    Choices   Modify   Contr

11. Select **Get choices from an external data source** as shown in the following screenshot:

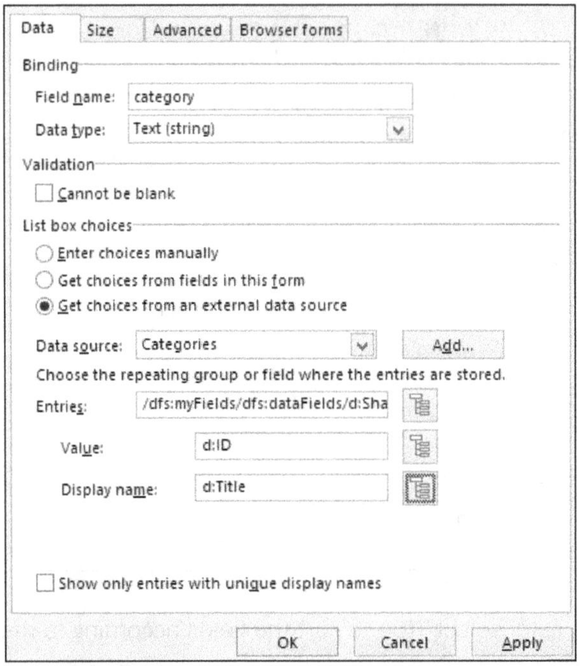

12. Set **Categories** for **Data source**, **ID** for **Value**, and **Title** for the **Display** name and then click on **OK**.

13. From the **HOME** tab, select **Preview** to observe the newly created drop-down menu. When testing your InfoPath form, you can use the **Preview** function. This allows you to test your form without publishing it to SharePoint. Observe the drop-down list for the **Category** field as shown in the following screenshot:

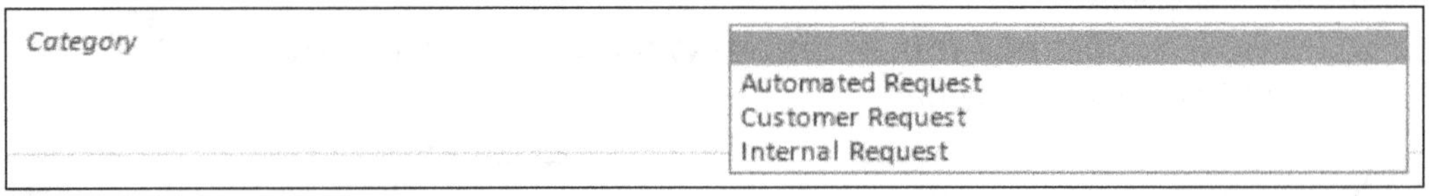

How it works...

When creating a connection to SharePoint list data, InfoPath uses the SharePoint web services to connect to, and retrieve information about, the SharePoint list. SharePoint uses this connection information to retrieve the list data when rendering the form in the web browser. List data can be retrieved when the form is opened or can be retrieved when triggered by a user action.

▸ The *SharePoint List Data Connections in InfoPath* article on MSDN at `http://blogs.msdn.com/b/infopath/archive/2010/05/06/sharepoint-list-data-connections-in-infopath-2010.aspx`

Paginating InfoPath forms with views

Forms with a lot of input fields and information can be cumbersome to the user if everything is displayed all at once. With InfoPath, we can organize content into separate views. In this recipe, we will create a form with two views and buttons to toggle between.

How to do it...

Follow these steps to create pages in a form using views:

1. Create a new form template or open an existing one in Microsoft InfoPath Designer 2013.

2. Select **New View** from the **PAGE DESIGN** tab in the ribbon as shown in the following screenshot:

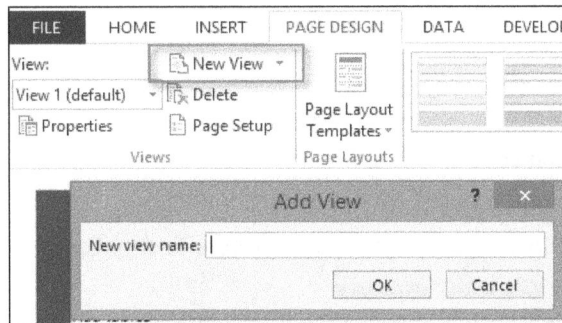

3. Provide the view (or page) with a name and select **OK**. To toggle between views when designing a form template, select the view from the drop-down list on the **PAGE DESIGN** tab in the ribbon:

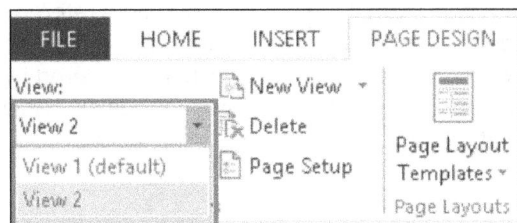

4. Add a **Button** control to each view.

5. Select the **Button** control in the first view.

6. Navigate to **CONTROL TOOLS | PROPERTIES** and provide the **Button** control with an appropriate label, such as `Next`.

7. Navigate to **CONTROL TOOLS | PROPERTIES** and select **Rules** in the **Button** section as shown in the following screenshot:

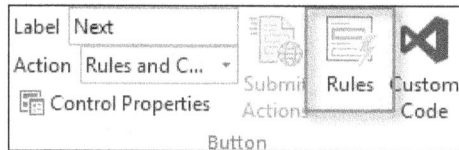

8. In the **Rules** pane (on the right-hand side of the window), select **Action** from the **New** menu.

9. Provide the **Action** with a name, such as `Switch to View 2`.

10. Under **Run these actions**, select **Switch views** from the **Add** menu as shown in the following screenshot:

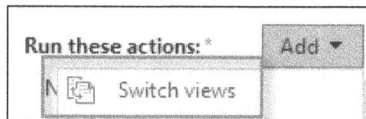

11. Select the second view and click on **OK**.

12. Select the **Button** control created on the second view.

13. Provide an appropriate label for it, such as `Previous`.

14. Repeat steps 7 to 11 to provide an **Action Rule** to change the view back to the first view.

15. Using the **Preview** button, preview the form template to observe the results of clicking on each button.

How it works...

A view in InfoPath acts like a page with its own layout and field references. Each view may have a unique layout independent of other views. In this recipe, we added a secondary view in addition to a button on each view. We then used actions triggered by button clicks to switch between our views. Actions allow us to perform various operations in the form, such as switching views or manipulating data.

InfoPath views can be used for a variety of purposes beyond paging. Examples include using a read-only view to display the data entered after a form has been submitted, using views to display the form in different languages, and hiding or showing areas of the form based on the previous input.

See also

▸ The *Add, delete, and switch views (pages) in a form* article on Microsoft Office at `http://office.microsoft.com/en-us/infopath-help/add-delete-and-switch-views-pages-in-a-form-HA101732801.aspx`

Validating data in InfoPath forms

When it comes to forms, it is usually important to ensure that the correct type of information is collected in each form field. In InfoPath, fields can be configured to be required or to only allow certain types of information, such as numbers. In addition, we can use validation rules to ensure the data entered meets the specified requirements, such as being a number greater than the number entered into the previous field.

In this recipe, we will create a required field that only allows whole numbers between 10 and 20.

How to do it...

Follow these steps to create a required field with a validation rule:

1. Create a new form template or open an existing one in Microsoft InfoPath Designer 2013.

2. Add a **Text Box** control to the form.

3. Navigate to **CONTROL TOOLS | PROPERTIES** and with the **Text Box** control selected, change **Data Type** to **Whole Number (Integer)** as shown in the following screenshot:

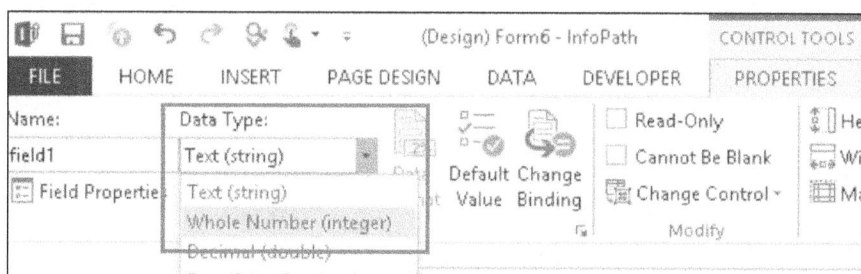

4. Select **Field Properties** from the **Properties** section of the ribbon.

5. Select the **Cannot be blank** option as shown in the following screenshot:

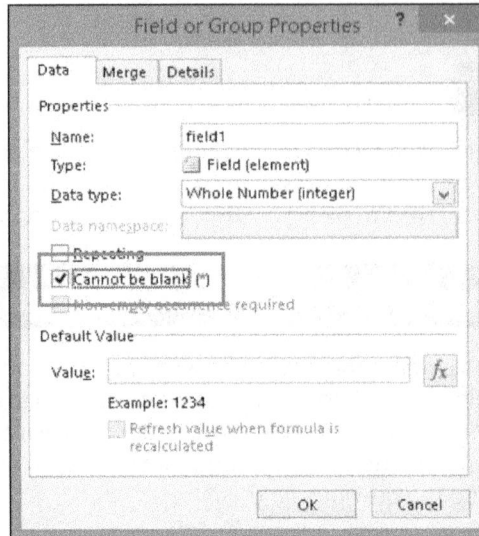

6. Click on **OK**.

7. If the **Rules** pane is not currently displayed, select **Manage Rules** from the ribbon to display it.

8. Select **Validation** from the **New** menu in the **Rules** pane.

9. Provide a name for the rule, such as Between 10 and 20.

10. Under **Condition**, select the **None** link.

11. Set the conditions to check if the value of the textbox is less than 10 or greater than 20 as shown in the following screenshot:

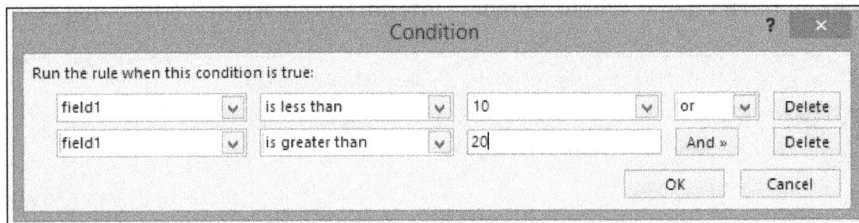

12. Click on **OK**.

13. Enter a **ScreenTip** to be displayed to the user, such as Value Must be Between 10 and 20.

14. Using the **Preview** option, preview the form template to observe the behavior of the field when entering non-numeric values, numbers greater than 20 or less than 10, and numbers between 10 and 20.

How it works...

When data in a field does not meet the requirements specified, we can prevent the form from being submitted. This allows the user to correct the information before submitting it again. These requirements are enforced using validation rules in the InfoPath engine. The **Cannot be blank** option makes the field required. The **Condition** for a validation rule may be quite complex. Custom formulas can be used, the conditions can vary depending upon the values of other fields, and so on. In this recipe, we simply ensured that our field is not empty and that it has a value between 10 and 20.

See also

▶   The *Add rules for validation* article on Microsoft Office at `http://office.microsoft.com/en-us/infopath-help/add-rules-for-validation-HA101783369.aspx`

Calculating field values in InfoPath based on the values of other fields

With InfoPath, we can perform calculations automatically when users input information. For instance, in an expense report form, we can automatically calculate the sum of the items as each one is entered. In addition, we can calculate information with non-numeric information. For instance, we can create a quiz that automatically calculates the score when the user submits the form.

In this recipe, we will create a field that automatically calculates the sum of two other fields.

How to do it...

Follow these steps to create a field that automatically calculates the sum of two other fields:

1.   Create a new form template or open an existing one in Microsoft InfoPath Designer 2013.

2. Add three Text Box controls to the form template as shown in the following screenshot:

SIMPLE CALCULATOR
Value 1
Value 2
Sum

3. In the **Data Type** field, set the data type for each **Text Box** control to **Whole Number (Integer)**.

4. Select the third **Text Box** control.

5. Select **Control Properties** from the **Properties** section by navigating to **CONTROL TEMPLATES | PROPERTIES**.

6. Select the **Display** tab.

7. Select **Read-only** and click on **OK**, as shown in the following screenshot:

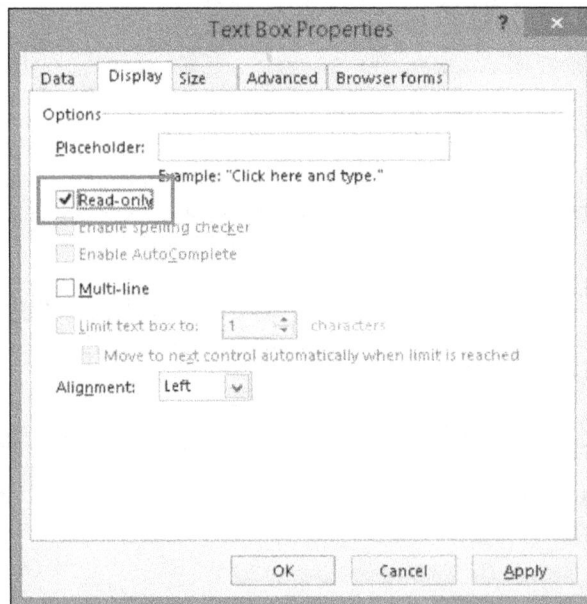

8. Select the first **Text Box** field.

9. Add a new action rule with an appropriate name, such as `Calculate Sum`.

10. Under **Run these actions**, select **Set a field's value** from the **Add** menu as shown in the following screenshot:

11. Select the third **Text Box** field for the field to set the value for.
12. Select the function button for the **Value** field.
13. In the **Formula** field, select **Insert Field or Group**.
14. Select the first **Text Box** control and click on **OK**.
15. Add a plus symbol to the formula.
16. Insert the second **Text Box** field. The formula should look something similar to the one seen in the following screenshot:

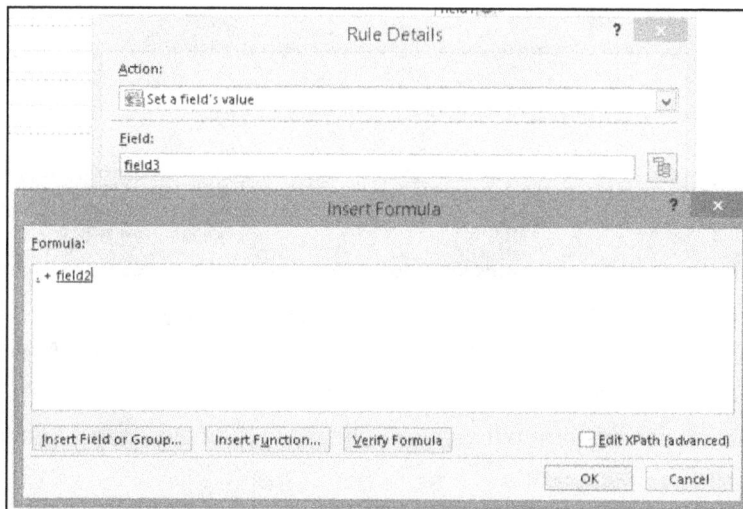

17. Click on **OK** to save the formula.

18. Click on **OK** again to save the rule details.

19. Select the second **Text Box** and repeat steps 9 to 18 to create the same **Action Rule** for the second **Text Box**.

20. Using the **Preview** feature, preview the form template to observe the value of the third **Text Box** when entering numbers into the other fields.

SIMPLE CALCULATOR
Value 1
10
Value 2
5
Sum
15

How it works...

When a user performs an action in a form, such as entering information or clicking a button, a series of actions can be performed automatically. These are called **action rules**. The InfoPath engine executes action rules automatically when the action that triggers them occurs. In addition, setting a control to be read-only prevents the user from entering information directly into the control. In this recipe, we created a simple action rule that sets the value of a field by calculating the sum of the values in the first two fields in the form.

See also

▶ The *Add rules for performing other actions* article on Microsoft Office at `http://office.microsoft.com/en-us/infopath-help/add-rules-for-performing-other-actions-HA101783373.aspx`

Adding custom .NET code to an InfoPath form

The Microsoft Visual Studio Tools for Applications allows code-based customization of documents in Microsoft Office. This has replaced the older **Visual Basic for Applications** (**VBA**) methodology for using custom code in Microsoft Office.

In this recipe, we will add custom code that sets the value of a field when a button is clicked.

How to do it...

Follow these steps to add custom .NET code to an InfoPath form:

1. Create a new form template or open an existing one in Microsoft InfoPath Designer 2013.

2. Add a **Text Box** control to the form template and give it an appropriate name, such as `currentDate`.

3. Add a **Button** control to the form template and give it an appropriate label, such as `Get Date`.

4. Save the form template.

5. With the **Button** control selected, click on **Custom Code** by navigating to **CONTROL TOOLS | PROPERTIES** in the **Properties** section. Selecting **Custom Code** will automatically start Visual Studio and create the project for the InfoPath form template. It will then create the method to be executed when the button is clicked and add the appropriate event handler. In addition, it will add a comment to the method to indicate where to add your custom code.

6. In the newly created method, where it says `// Write your code here`, get the `XPathNavigator` object from the XML data source representing the form template.

   ```
   var navigator = this.MainDataSource.CreateNavigator();
   ```

7. Get the XML node representing the **Text Box** control using its XML path.

   ```
   var node = navigator. SelectSingleNode("//my:currentDate", this.
   NamespaceManager);
   ```

8. Set the value of the node to the current date using the following line of code:

   ```
   node.SetValue(DateTime.Now.ToString());
   ```

9. Build the Visual Studio solution by right-clicking on the project name in the **Solution Explorer** and selecting **Build**.

10. Return to the InfoPath form template in the InfoPath Designer.

11. Preview the form template to observe the action taken when clicking the button.

How it works...

InfoPath form templates are XML based. When interacting with form content from our custom code, we are using an XML `XPathNavigator` object to find the field by its XML path. Once located, we are setting the value of the field by setting the value of its XML node within the XML of the form document.

See also

▸ The *Getting Started Developing Form Templates with Code* article on MSDN at `http://msdn.microsoft.com/en-us/library/office/aa944896.aspx`

Preparing InfoPath forms for approval by SharePoint administrators

A farm administrator must approve InfoPath form templates that contain custom .NET code before they can be used in SharePoint. Form templates are prepared for approval in the InfoPath Designer and then sent to the farm administrator for approval.

In this recipe, we will prepare the form we created in the previous recipe *Adding custom .NET code to an InfoPath form* for approval.

Getting ready

For this recipe, we will need the InfoPath form created in the previous recipe *Adding custom .NET code to an InfoPath form*.

How to do it...

Follow these steps to prepare our InfoPath form for approval:

1. With our form template containing .NET code open, select **SharePoint Server** from the **Publish** section of the **File** menu.

2. Provide the URL to the site collection we will publish the form to in the end and click on **Next**.

> The URL provided here should be a URL from the farm we are publishing to. It does not necessarily have to be the site collection URL.

3. Select **Administrator-approved form template (advanced)** and click on **Next**, as shown in the following screenshot:

☑ Enable this form to be filled out by using a browser

What do you want to create or modify?

○ Form Library

Publish this form template as a template in a form library. A form library stores forms based on this form template. Users can open and fill out forms in the library. You can specify which fields in the template appear as columns in the library.

○ Site Content Type (advanced)

A site content type allows this form template to be used in multiple libraries and sites. You can specify which fields in the template appear as columns in the library.

◉ Administrator-approved form template (advanced)

Prepare this form template for an administrator approval.

4. Specify a location to save the prepared form and click on **Next**. Since we will be uploading the form, we can save it to our local hard drive. When providing the form to a farm administrator, we could save the form to a SharePoint library, a network file share, and so on.

5. Provide any applicable SharePoint columns for the form template to populate and click on **Next**.

6. Click on **Publish**.

How it works...

InfoPath form templates with custom .NET code must run with full trust in SharePoint. In order for a template to be approved, it must be uploaded by a farm administrator in **Central Administration**. Publishing an administrator-approved form template prepares the form template to be uploaded. Alternatively, InfoPath forms may be included as part of a custom SharePoint solution in Visual Studio.

See also

▸ The *Publish a form* article on Microsoft Office at `http://office.microsoft.com/en-us/infopath-help/publish-a-form-HA101783381.aspx`

▸ The *Manage administrator-approved form templates* article on TechNet at `http://technet.microsoft.com/en-us/library/cc262921.aspx`

Approving submitted InfoPath forms in SharePoint

In order to approve an InfoPath form template, an administrator must upload the form template in **Central Administration**. In this recipe, we will upload the form template prepared in the previous recipe, *Preparing InfoPath forms for approval by SharePoint administrators,* as an administrator-approved form template.

Getting ready

For this recipe, we will need the InfoPath form created in the *Adding custom .NET code to an InfoPath form* and *Preparing InfoPath forms for approval by SharePoint administrators* recipes.

How to do it...

Follow these steps to approve our InfoPath form template:

1. Navigate to **Central Administration** in your preferred web browser.

2. Select **General Application Settings**.

3. Select **Upload form template** under **InfoPath Forms Services** as shown in the following screenshot:

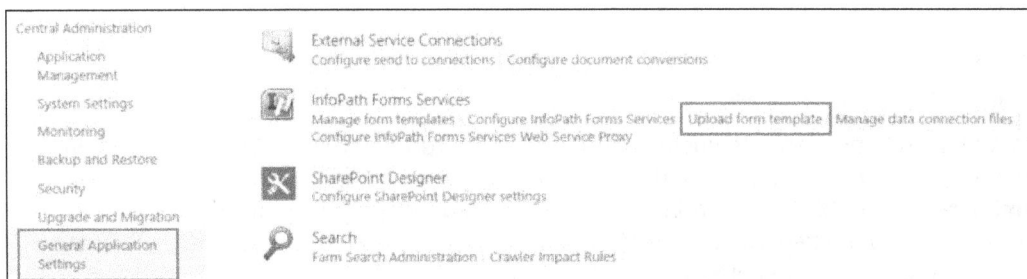

4. Select the file we prepared in the *Preparing InfoPath forms for approval by SharePoint administrators* recipe.

5. Select **Verify** to ensure there are no issues with the form template.

6. Select **Upload**. Once the status on the **Manage Form Templates** page shows **Ready**, we can continue to the *Creating libraries using approved InfoPath forms in SharePoint* recipe.

How it works...

Uploading an administrator-approved InfoPath form template creates a site-collection-scoped feature for the form template. Activating the site collection feature adds the form template to the **Form Templates** library within the root site of the site collection and adds a new content type for the form template.

See also

▶   The *Manage administrator-approved form templates* article on TechNet at `http://technet.microsoft.com/en-us/library/cc262921.aspx`

Creating libraries using approved InfoPath forms in SharePoint

In this recipe, we will activate the site collection feature for our form template and add our form template content type to a form library.

Getting ready

For this recipe, we will need the administrator-approved form uploaded in the previous recipe, *Approving submitted InfoPath forms in SharePoint*.

How to do it...

Follow these steps to add our form template to a form:

1. Navigate to the SharePoint site collection in your preferred web browser.
2. Select **Site settings** from the **Settings** menu.
3. Select **Site Collection Features** from the **Site Collection Administration** section.
4. Activate the feature for our form template. The name of the feature will match the name of the form.
5. Navigate to a form library in the site collection. You can create a new one or use an existing one.
6. Select **Library Settings** from the **Library** tab in the ribbon.
7. Select **Advanced Settings** from the **General Settings** section.
8. Set **Allow Management of Content Types** to **Yes**.
9. Click on **OK**.

10. Select **Add from Existing Site Content Types** from the **Content Types** section.

11. Add our form template and click on **OK**. Our form template will be listed in the **Microsoft InfoPath** group.

12. Navigate back to the document library.

13. From the **Files** tab in the ribbon, select the drop-down menu for **New Document**.

14. Select our form template to observe the results.

How it works...

Activating the site collection feature for the form template adds our form template to the root site of the site collection. In addition, a content type for the form template is created. With the content type, we are able to add our form template to any library in the site collection.

Creating a survey InfoPath form that gets locked after submission and populates the SharePoint fields

In this recipe, we will create a simple survey form template that switches to a read-only view of the form data when it is opened again.

How to do it...

Follow these steps to create a survey form template:

1. Create a new **SharePoint Form Library** form template in InfoPath Designer.

2. Add a few labels and controls for the survey input.

3. Select the whole table, including the labels and fields.

4. Copy the selection to the clipboard.

5. Add a new view to the form template named Submitted.

6. Paste the selection to the new view.

7. For each control in the Submitted view, set the field to be **Read-Only** in the **Display** tab of the **Control Properties** tab.

8. For each control in the Submitted view that are not **Text Box** controls, select **Change Control** by navigating to **CONTROL TOOLS | PROPERTIES** and select **Text Box**.

Survey

Questions

Are you happy with your experience?		When did you shop?	
Will you shop here again?		Comments?	
How many items did you buy?			

9. Return to the first view in the form template and add a **Button** control with Submit as the label.

10. Publish the form to a SharePoint form library. Before we can create our Submit action, we need the document library to be already created. We will publish the form again, once we set up the Submit action.

11. From the **DATA** tab in the ribbon, select **To SharePoint Library** in the **Submit Form** section.

12. Enter the URL to the document library we created when publishing the form in step 11.

13. Provide a formula for the name of the submitted documents, for example, concat(now(), " - ", userName()). Formulas in InfoPath work very similar to formulas in Microsoft Excel and SharePoint- calculated columns.

14. Click on **Next** and then on **Finish**.

15. In the **Fields** pane, select **Add** from the drop-down menu for **myFields** as shown in the following screenshot:

16. Enter Completed for the **Name** and select **True/False (Boolean)** for the **Data Type**. We will use this field to indicate that the form is complete when we open the form to view it.

17. Click on **OK**.

18. Select **Form Load** from the **Rules** section of the **DATA** tab. The **Form Load** rules run when the form template first loads, before the user can interact with the form.

19. Add a new **Action Rule**.

20. For **Condition**, check whether the value of the **Completed** field we created is TRUE.

21. Under **Run These Actions**, add an action to switch the view to the Submitted view.

22. Select the **Submit** button in the first view and add an **Action Rule**.

23. Under **Run These Actions**, add an action to set the value of the **Completed** field to true (lowercase).

24. Under **Run These Actions**, add a **Submit Data** action. Leave the options set to the defaults and click on **OK**.

25. Under **Run These Actions**, add an action to **Close the Form**.

26. From the **Info** section of the **File** menu, select **Form Options**.

27. In the **Web Browser** category, uncheck the **Show InfoPath Commands in Ribbon or Toolbar** option. The options in this category control what options are displayed in the ribbon when displaying the form template in SharePoint. We are choosing not to display the ribbon at all.

28. Click on **OK**.

29. From the **Info** section of the **File** menu, select **Quick Publish**. The **Quick Publish** feature will republish the form template with the same configuration used during the previous publish.

30. Navigate to the form library in SharePoint and select **New Document** from the **Files** tab in the ribbon. Fill out the form and submit.

31. Navigate to the form library to observe the newly created document and open the newly created document to observe the read-only version of the submitted form.

How it works...

When a control is added to a form template, a corresponding field is created automatically. The field may be attached to additional controls allowing multiple places to display or interact with the same field content. In this recipe, we created a second view containing read-only versions of the controls we added to the first view. Doing so allowed us to create a locked, or read-only, view of the form data.

In this recipe, we also created a button for the user to submit the form. This allowed us to take control over the submit process to automatically provide a document name without having the user to provide it.

9
Configuring Search

In this chapter, we will cover configuring the search features of SharePoint 2013. We will cover the following recipes:

- ▸ Provisioning a search service application
- ▸ Configuring a search content source
- ▸ Creating a search center site
- ▸ Connecting a site collection to a search center
- ▸ Creating a search scope
- ▸ Using a search query rule to promote an item in search results
- ▸ Configuring search engine optimization settings

Introduction

Search is often one of the key components of a successful web content management system. Without the ability to search, users may have difficulty locating the content they are looking for. Since the very first iteration of SharePoint, SharePoint Portal Server 2001, search has been an integral part of the SharePoint experience. For SharePoint Server 2010, Microsoft made available FAST Search for SharePoint as a separate product that would integrate with the SharePoint 2010 farm. The combination of SharePoint 2010 and FAST Search provided all of the functionality of a search appliance, rivaling and even surpassing some abilities of a Google search appliance, such as indexing line-of-business data.

With SharePoint 2013, Microsoft has incorporated most of the FAST Search product features into the SharePoint Server 2013 product. This provides, out of the box, one of the most powerful search appliances available in the market today. SharePoint search can be configured to index SharePoint content, web content, file shares, Microsoft Exchange public folders, and line-of-business data.

Using the SharePoint search capabilities out of the box works well for smaller sites. However, for larger content-heavy sites, configuring the search behavior can greatly enhance the experience for the end user. In this chapter, we will cover the basic configuration of the search capabilities of SharePoint 2013.

Provisioning a search service application

The search service application handles the core functionality of search in SharePoint. In this recipe, we will provision a new search service application.

> You can create multiple search service applications for a farm. This can be useful to segment indexed content for different web applications. For instance, the search service application used by a public-facing web application may be configured to index the content of the public-facing sites only, whereas a separate search service application used by an internal-facing web application may be configured to index all of the content on the farm.

How to do it...

Follow these steps to provision a search service application:

1. Navigate to **Central Administration** in your preferred web browser.

2. Click on **Manage service applications** from the **Application Management** section as shown in the following screenshot:

Application Management
Manage web applications
Create site collections
Manage service applications
Manage content databases

3. Click on **Search Service Application** in the **New** menu from the **SERVICE APPLICATIONS** tab in the ribbon as shown in the following screenshot:

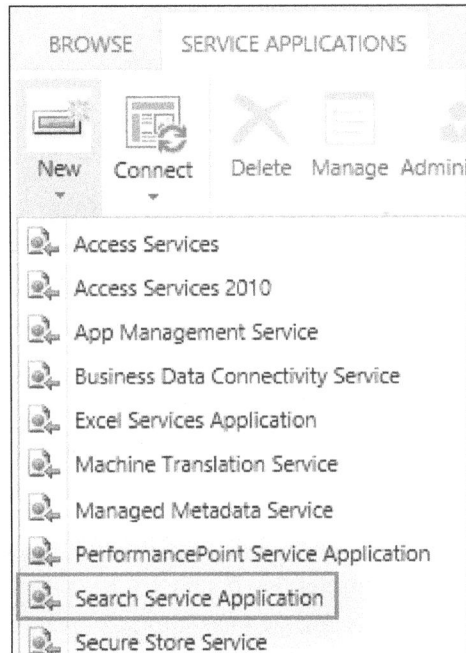

4. Provide a name, such as `Search Service Application`, in the **Name** field for the service application.

5. Select a managed account to use for the **Search Service Account**. The **Search Service Account** is used when indexing content. Any content that requires authentication should provide read access to this account.

6. Provide a name and select a managed account for the **Application Pool for Search Admin Web Service**. The managed account selected does not have to be the same account used for the **Search Service Account**.

Application Pool for Search Admin Web Service	○ Use existing application pool
Choose the Application Pool to use for this Service Application. This defines the account and credentials that will be used by this web service.	Managed Metadata Service Application Pool ▾
	◉ Create new application pool
	Application pool name
	Search Admin Web Service
You can choose an existing application pool or create a new one.	Select a security account for this application pool
	○ Predefined
	Network Service ▾
	◉ Configurable
	WESTEROS\sp_services ▾
	Register new managed account

7. Provide a name and select a managed account for the **Application Pool for Search Query and Site Settings Web Service** options.

8. Click on **OK**. The operation will take a few minutes to complete.

How it works...

The search service application handles all of the core functionality of the SharePoint search. This includes indexing content, accessing the search databases, processing search queries, and so on. When a user searches in a SharePoint site, the query is processed by the search service application that is associated with the SharePoint web application in which the site is contained.

Service applications in SharePoint use application pools in **Internet Information Services** (**IIS**) to run their web services. The search service application uses two application pools, one for the administrative components and the other for the query and site-level components.

There's more...

Search service applications may also be provisioned with PowerShell.

Provisioning a search service application using PowerShell

Follow these steps to provision a search service application using PowerShell:

1. Create a new application pool for the search service and assign it to a variable using the `New-SPServiceApplicationPool` Cmdlet as follows:

   ```
   $appPool = New-SPServiceApplicationPool -Name "Search Service
   Application Pool" -Account domain\searchuser
   ```

   [
   To use an existing application pool, the `Get-SPServiceApplicationPool` Cmdlet may be used instead.
   ]

2. Create a new search service application using the `New-SPEnterpriseSearchServiceApplication` Cmdlet and assign it to a variable as follows:

   ```
   $ssa = New-SPEnterpriseSearchServiceApplication -Name "Search
   Service Application" -ApplicationPool $appPool
   ```

3. Create a new proxy for the search service application using the `New-SPEnterpriseSearchServiceApplicationProxy` Cmdlet as follows:

   ```
   New-SPEnterpriseSearchServiceApplicationProxy -Name "Search
   Service Application Proxy" -SearchApplication $ssa
   ```

See also

- The *Create and configure a Search service application in SharePoint Server 2013* article on TechNet at `http://technet.microsoft.com/en-us/library/gg502597.aspx`

- The *New-SPServiceApplicationPool* topic on TechNet at `http://technet.microsoft.com/en-us/library/ff607595.aspx`

- The *Get-SPServiceApplicationPool* topic on TechNet at `http://technet.microsoft.com/en-us/library/ff607544.aspx`

- The *New-SPEnterpriseSearchServiceApplication* topic on TechNet at `http://technet.microsoft.com/en-us/library/ff607751.aspx`

- The *New-SPEnterpriseSearchServiceApplicationProxy* topic on TechNet at `http://technet.microsoft.com/en-us/library/ff607722.aspx`

Configuring a search content source

Once a search service application is configured, it needs data for indexing. In this recipe, we will add a new content source for our search service application.

Getting ready

For this recipe, we should have a search service application created in the *Provisioning a search service application* recipe.

How to do it...

Follow these steps to add a new content source to our search service application:

1. Navigate to **Central Administration** in your preferred web browser.
2. Click on **Manage service applications** from the **Application Management** section.
3. Click on the **Search Service Application** link we created in the previous recipe.

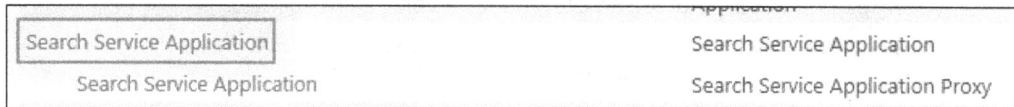

Search Service Application	Search Service Application
Search Service Application	Search Service Application Proxy

4. In the quick launch, click on **Content Sources** from the **Crawling** section as shown in the following screenshot:

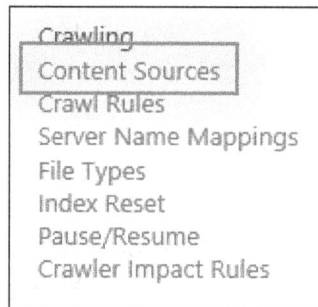

Crawling
Content Sources
Crawl Rules
Server Name Mappings
File Types
Index Reset
Pause/Resume
Crawler Impact Rules

5. Click on **New Content Source**.
6. Provide a name, such as `Local SharePoint Sites`, for the content source in the **Name** field.
7. Select **SharePoint Sites** for the **Content Source Type** as shown in the following screenshot:

Name	Name: *
Type a name to describe this content source.	Local SharePoint Sites
Content Source Type	Select the type of content to be crawled:
Select what type of content will be crawled.	
Note: This cannot be changed after this content source is created because other settings depend on it.	⦿ SharePoint Sites
	◯ Web Sites
	◯ File Shares
	◯ Exchange Public Folders
	◯ Line of Business Data
	◯ Custom Repository

8. Add the URL to the root SharePoint site to index to the **Start Addresses** section, `http://sharepoint/` for instance. Multiple SharePoint sites may be indexed as a single content source. To add more SharePoint sites, add them on a new line in the **Start Addresses** field.

Start Addresses	Type start addresses below (one per line): *
Type the URLs from which the search system should start crawling.	http://sharepoint
This includes all SharePoint Server sites and Microsoft SharePoint Foundation sites.	
	Example: http://intranetsite

9. Select **Crawl Everything Under the Hostname for Each Start Address** in the **Crawl Settings**.

> The content source can be configured to index only the site collection that matches the URL provided or to index everything under that URL. For instance, when enabled, `http://sharepoint/site` will be indexed when `http://sharepoint/` is added to the **Start Addresses** field.

10. Select **Enable Continuous Crawl** in the **Crawl Schedules**.

> **Continuous Crawl** is a new feature of SharePoint 2013 that crawls content as it is modified or added to the sites. This can be resource intensive on large SharePoint sites. Alternatively, crawls can be scheduled for specific times.

11. Click on **OK**.

How it works...

Search crawls in SharePoint are conducted on a per content source basis. Content sources define what is being crawled and how often. They can include SharePoint sites, websites, file shares, Microsoft Exchange public folders, line-of-business data from business data connectivity services connections, and custom repositories. Each content source defined can use multiple content sources of the same content type. For instance, a content source could include multiple, different websites. A content source, however, could not include both a website and a line-of-business data connection.

There's more...

Content sources can also be created and configured with PowerShell.

Configuring a search content source using PowerShell

Follow these steps to configure a content source using PowerShell:

1. Assign our search service application to a variable using the `Get-SPEnterpriseSearchServiceApplication` Cmdlet:

   ```
   $ssa = Get-SPEnterpriseSearchServiceApplication "Search Service
   Application"
   ```

2. Create a new content source with the `New-SPEnterpriseSearchCrawlContentSource` Cmdlet and assign it to a variable:

   ```
   $cs = New-SPEnterpriseSearchCrawlContentSource -Name
   "SharePoint Sites" -SearchApplication $ssa -Type SharePoint
   -SharePointCrawlBehavior CrawlVirtualServers -StartAddresses
   "http://sharepoint/"
   ```

   The `SharePointCrawlBehavior` parameter is the equivalent of the **Crawl Settings** section in the web interface. `CrawlVirtualServers` instructs the indexer to index all content under the URL provided and `CrawlSites` instructs the indexer to only index the site collection at the URL provided.

3. Enable **Continuous Crawl** and then update the content source using the following commands:

   ```
   $cs.EnableContinuousCrawls = $true
   ```

   ```
   $cs.Update()
   ```

▸ The *Add, Edit, or Delete a content source in SharePoint 2013* article on TechNet at
   `http://technet.microsoft.com/en-us/library/jj219808.aspx`

▸ The *Get-SPEnterpriseSearchServiceApplication* topic on TechNet at `http://technet.microsoft.com/en-us/library/ff608050.aspx`

▸ The *New-SPEnterpriseSearchCrawlContentSource* topic on TechNet at `http://technet.microsoft.com/en-us/library/ff607867.aspx`

Creating a search center site

Search queries can be conducted in a variety of different ways. The two common methods are searching within a SharePoint site and searching in a search center site. Searching within a SharePoint site typically uses the default search results page located in the `/_layouts/` folder. These search queries are limited to only return results from the current SharePoint site.

Searching in a search center site uses web parts on customizable web part pages to submit and display the results of search queries. The results can include all of the content indexed by the search service application, regardless of where the content is located. In this recipe, we will create a new SharePoint site with a search center template. A search center site may be created as the root site of a new site collection from **Central Administration** or as a subsite of an existing site collection. In this recipe, we are adding the search center as a subsite to an existing site collection.

How to do it...

Follow these steps to create a new search center site:

1. In your preferred web browser, navigate to the site collection to which we added our search site.

2. Click on **Site contents** from the **Settings** menu.

3. Click on **new subsite** from the **Subsites** section as shown in the following screenshot:

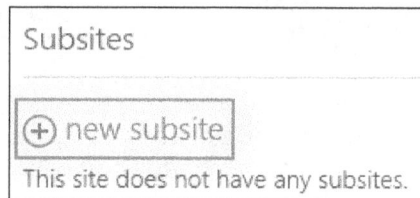

4. Provide a title, description, and URL for the new site in the **Title**, **Description**, and **URL** fields.

5. Under **Template Selection**, select **Enterprise Search Center** from the **Enterprise** tab as shown in the following screenshot:

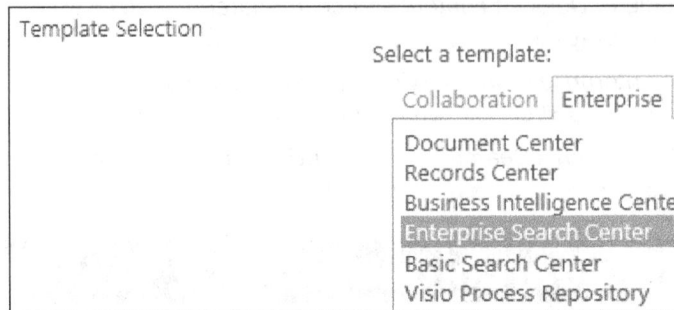

```
Template Selection
                                    Select a template:

                            Collaboration │ Enterprise

                            Document Center
                            Records Center
                            Business Intelligence Center
                            Enterprise Search Center
                            Basic Search Center
                            Visio Process Repository
```

6. Click on **Create**.

How it works...

The search center site templates create sites with the intended purpose of searching. These templates include the required components, such as the search web parts for searching and displaying results. These templates use a minimalistic master page that is conducive to display search results in a user-friendly manner. In addition, unlike the search result page used when searching individual sites, the web part pages used in the search center sites can be easily customized.

There's more...

SharePoint sites may also be created with PowerShell or with code using the server-side object model. We covered this previously in the *Setting up a new publishing site* recipe in *Chapter 5, Enhancing the Content Creation Process with the SharePoint Publishing Architecture*; however, the site template to use when creating an **Enterprise Search Center** site is SRCHCEN#0.

Connecting a site collection to a search center

In order for SharePoint site collections to forward search queries to a search center, the connection to the search center must be configured. In this recipe, we will configure our site collection to forward search queries to the search center we created in the *Creating a search center site* recipe.

How to do it...

Follow these steps to connect a site collection to a search center:

1. In your preferred web browser, navigate to the site collection to which we are connecting the search center.

2. Click on **Site settings** from the **Settings** menu.

3. Select **Search Settings** under **Site Collection Administration** as shown in the following screenshot:

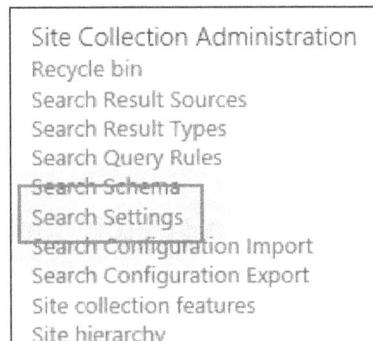

Site Collection Administration
Recycle bin
Search Result Sources
Search Result Types
Search Query Rules
Search Schema
Search Settings
Search Configuration Import
Search Configuration Export
Site collection features
Site hierarchy

4. Enter the URL to the **Pages** library in the search center. For instance, if the search center is at `http://sharepoint/sites/search`, enter `http://sharepoint/sites/search/pages` for the URL as shown in the following screenshot:

Enter a Search Center URL

When you've specified a search center, the search system displays a message to all users offering them the ability to try their search again from that Search Center.

Search Center URL:

`/sites/search/pages`

Example: /SearchCenter/Pages or http://server/sites/SearchCenter/Pages

> If the search center is on the same web application host as the site collection, a relative URL may be used instead. For instance, `/sites/search/pages` may be used instead of `http://sharepoint/sites/search/pages`.

5. Click on **OK**.

How it works...

Site collections not configured to forward search queries to a search center are limited to only searching within the current site. These searches use the basic search results page found in the /_layouts/ folder of each site. When search queries are forwarded to a search center, the results include all indexed content the user has access to.

> The URL to the search center is stored as a property on the root site of the site collection.

There's more...

The search center URL configured for a site collection may also be configured with PowerShell or code using the server-side object model.

Connecting a site collection to a search center using PowerShell

Follow these steps to connect a site collection to a search center using PowerShell:

1. Assign the site collection to a variable with the Get-SPSite Cmdlet:

   ```
   $site = Get-SPSite http://sharepoint
   ```

2. Set the SRCH_ENH_FTR_URL_SITE property of the root site to the URL of the **Pages** library in the search center:

   ```
   $site.RootWeb.AllProperties["SRCH_ENH_FTR_URL_SITE"] = "/sites/
   search/pages"
   ```

3. Update the root site of the site collection:

   ```
   $site.RootWeb.Update()
   ```

Connecting a site collection to a search center with code using the server-side object model

Follow these steps to connect a site collection to a search center with code using the server-side object model:

1. Open the site collection in a `using` statement:

   ```
   using (var site = new SPSite("http://sharepoint"))
   ```

2. Set the `SRCH_ENH_FTR_URL_SITE` property of the root site to the URL of the **Pages** library in the search center:

   ```
   site.RootWeb.AllProperties["SRCH_ENH_FTR_URL_SITE"] = "/sites/
   search/pages";
   ```

3. Update the root site of the site collection:

   ```
   site.RootWeb.Update();
   ```

Creating a search scope

SharePoint 2007 and 2010 included the option to add scopes to a drop-down list next to search boxes in the sites. This would allow site administrators to create narrowed down search results for specific uses. For instance, a scope could be created to only return items from a specific library.

With SharePoint 2013, Microsoft has removed the concept of search scopes. Instead, we will need to create a new search results page with a limited search query. In this recipe, we will add a new search results page to our search center to return only images.

How to do it...

Follow these steps to create a new search results page for images:

1. Navigate to our search center in your preferred web browser.
2. Click on **Site contents** from the **Settings** menu.
3. Select the **Pages** library.

4. From the **FILES** tab in the ribbon, click on **Welcome Page** from the **New Document** drop-down menu as shown in the following screenshot:

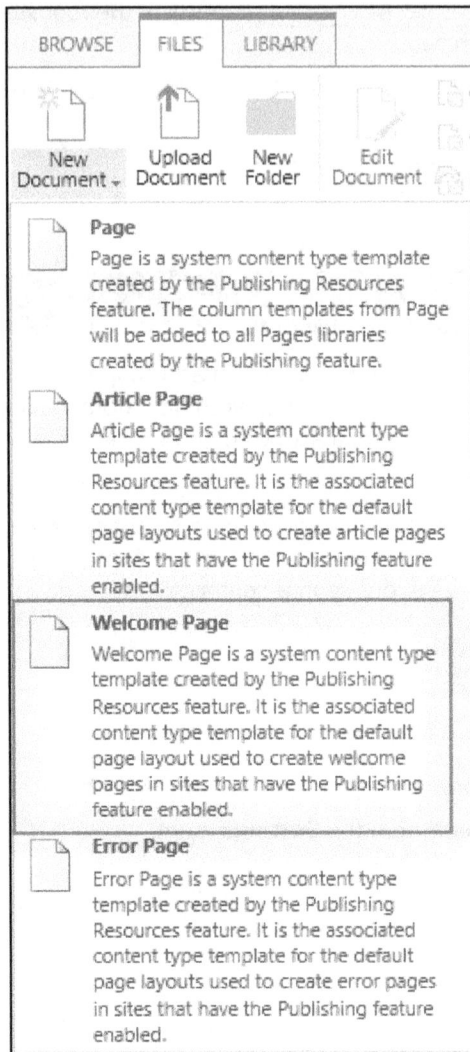

5. Provide a title and URL for the page, for instance, Images in the **Title** and **URL** fields.

6. Select **(Welcome Page) Search results** for the **Page Layout** feature in the following screenshot:

Page Title and Description

Enter a URL name, title, and description for this page.

Title:

Images

Description:

URL Name:

Pages/ Images .aspx

Page Layout

Select a page layout to control how the page will be displayed.

(Welcome Page) Search results

This page layout contains a tab control, and search Web Parts. It has Web Part zones arranged in a right column, header, footer, 2 columns and 2 rows.

7. Click on **Create**.

8. Click on the **Images** page in the **Pages** library to navigate to it.

9. Click on **Edit** page from the **Settings** menu.

10. Click on **Edit Web Part** from the drop-down menu on the **Search Results** web part as shown in the following screenshot:

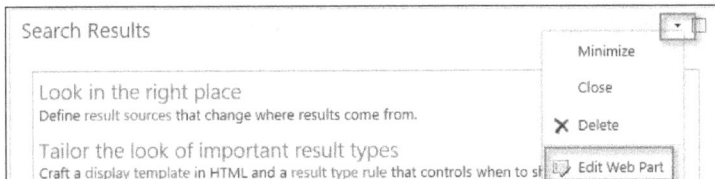

Search Results

Minimize

Close

Look in the right place
Define result sources that change where results come from.

✕ Delete

Tailor the look of important result types
Craft a display template in HTML and a result type rule that controls when to sh

🗐 Edit Web Part

11. Click on **Change query** in the web part edit pane as shown in the following screenshot:

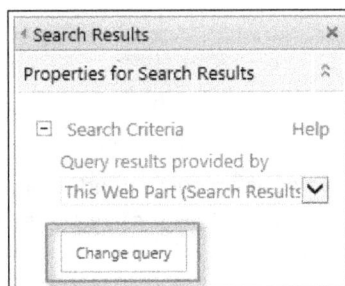

◁ Search Results ✕

Properties for Search Results ☆

⊟ Search Criteria Help

Query results provided by

This Web Part (Search Results ✔

Change query

12. Set the **Property Filter** to **ContentType Contains Image** as shown in the following screenshot:

Keyword filter	Property filter
Query from the search box ⌄	ContentType ⌄
Add keyword filter	Contains ⌄ Image ⌄
	Add property filter

Query text

{searchboxquery}
ContentType:0x0101009148F5A04DDD49CBA7127AADA5FB792B00AADE34325A8B49CDA8BB4DB5
3328F214*

13. Click on the **Add property** filter.

14. Click on **OK**.

15. In the web part edit pane, click on **OK**.

16. Click on **Publish** from the **PUBLISH** tab in the ribbon. Click on **Continue** to publish the page.

17. Click on **Site settings** from the **Settings** menu.

18. Click on **Search Settings** from the **Search** section as shown in the following screenshot:

Search
Result Sources
Result Types
Query Rules
Schema
Search Settings
Searchable columns
Search and offline availability
Configuration Import
Configuration Export

19. In the **Configure Search Navigation** section, add a link to the newly created page. For instance, Images with /sites/search/pages/Images.aspx as the URL as shown in the following screenshot:

Configure Search Navigation

Search Navigation allows users to move quickly between search experiences listed in the Navigation. Navigation is displayed in the Quick Launch control on search pages, and can also be shown as a drop-down menu from the search box.

   ⚐ Move Up   Move Down   🏛 Edit...   ✕ Delete   🏛 Add Link...

🏛 Everything
🏛 People
🏛 Conversations
🏛 Videos
🏛 Images

Selected Item

Title: Images
URL: /sites/search/pages/Images.aspx
Description:
Type: 🏛 Link

20. Click on **OK**.

21. Navigate to the search center home page.

22. Enter a keyword to search for and press the *Enter* key.

23. Click on the newly added **Images** navigation option to observe the filtered results.

Search...   🔍

Everything   People   Conversations   Videos   Images

How it works...

The search results web parts on search results pages use search-specific queries to determine which results to show for a particular search. For instance, the **Conversations** search results page uses a search query that returns only the **Newsfeed** items. In this recipe, we created a new search results page that queried only for the **Image** items by their content type.

See also

▶ The *Configure search web parts in SharePoint Server 2013* article on TechNet at `http://technet.microsoft.com/en-us/library/jj679900.aspx`

Using a search query rule to promote an item in search results

Search indexers use complex algorithms to determine the order in which items should return in a search query. The factors include the number of times an item is linked to by other pages or items, the frequency of a keyword in the item, and the author of the item. As a result, it is not uncommon for items that are very important, but only use a particular keyword once or twice, to not appear at the top of the search results. For instance, a human resources site may have a number of blog posts and announcements related to retirement accounts. In addition, the site may have a document simply named *Retirement Account Enrollment*. When searching for information about retirement accounts, users may see results for the announcements and blog posts ahead of the enrollment document.

When the most important item, the enrollment document, doesn't return at the top of the search results, users may never find the item. To alleviate this, we can manually instruct SharePoint to display certain results first using query rules. This allows the site administrators of the human resources site to ensure users can easily find the enrollment document.

How to do it...

Follow these steps to create a search query rule:

1. Navigate to our search center in your preferred web browser.
2. Select **Site settings** from the **Settings** menu.
3. Select **Query Rules** from the **Search** section as shown in the following screenshot:

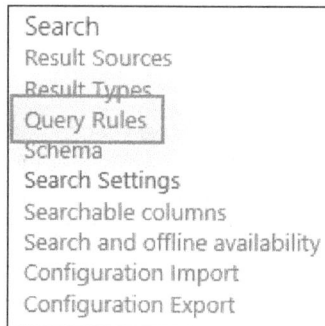

Search
Result Sources
Result Types
Query Rules
Schema
Search Settings
Searchable columns
Search and offline availability
Configuration Import
Configuration Export

4. Select the **Documents (System)** results source from the drop-down menu as shown in the following screenshot:

For what context do you want to configure rules?

Select a Result Source...
Conversations (System)
Documents (System)
Items matching a content type (System)
Items matching a tag (System)
Items related to current user (System)
Items with same keyword as this item (System)
Local People Results (System)
Local Reports And Data Results (System)
Local SharePoint Results (System)
Local Video Results (System)
Pages (System)
Pictures (System)
Popular (System)
Recently changed items (System)
Recommended Items (System)
Wiki (System)
All Sources

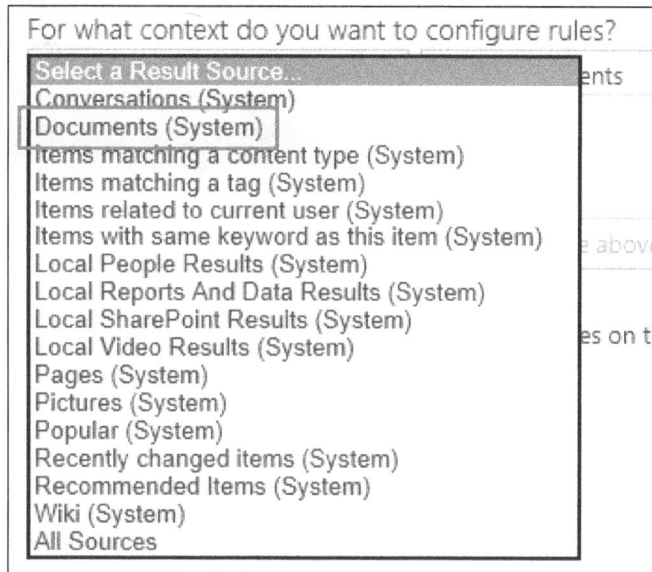

5. Select **New Query Rule** as shown in the following screenshot:

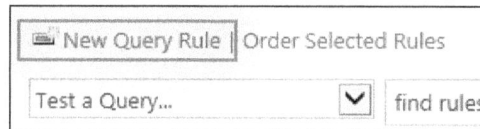

New Query Rule | Order Selected Rules

Test a Query...   ✔ find rules

6. Provide a name for the query rule.

7. In the **Query Conditions** section, select **Query Matches Keyword Exactly** and enter the keywords to match the query. The keywords are separated with semicolons.

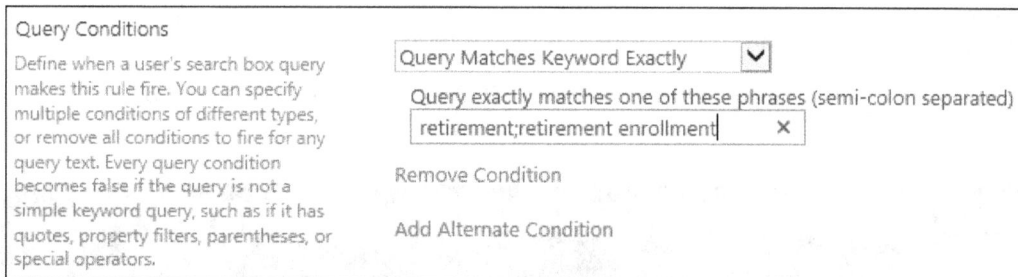

Query Conditions

Define when a user's search box query makes this rule fire. You can specify multiple conditions of different types, or remove all conditions to fire for any query text. Every query condition becomes false if the query is not a simple keyword query, such as if it has quotes, property filters, parentheses, or special operators.

Query Matches Keyword Exactly   ✔

Query exactly matches one of these phrases (semi-colon separated)

retirement;retirement enrollment   ✕

Remove Condition

Add Alternate Condition

8. Under **Actions**, click on **Add Promoted Result**.

9. Enter a title, URL, and description for the promoted result in the **Title**, **URL**, and **Description** fields. This information will be displayed in the search results.

Add Promoted Result ✕

Title

Retirement Enrollment Form

URL

http://sharepoint/sites/hr/documents/retirementenrollment.pdf

☐ Render the URL as a banner instead of as a hyperlink

Description

Use the retirement enrollment form to sign up for your retirement accounts.

---

10. Click on **Save** to add the promoted result.
11. Click on **Save** to save the query rule.

How it works...

Search query rules are used as a factor in the complex algorithms used by the SharePoint search service. Using query rules allows the site administrator to modify the positioning or importance of certain content that might otherwise be considered as less important by the search algorithm.

See also

▶ The *Manage query rules in SharePoint 2013* article on TechNet at http://technet.microsoft.com/en-us/library/jj871676.aspx

Configuring search engine optimization settings

SharePoint 2013 provides a few basic but important features for optimizing sites for external search engines, such as Bing. These features include generating site maps and adding META tags to each page. In this recipe, we will enable and configure the site map and the META tag options.

In order for site maps to be accessible by external search engines, anonymous access to the site should be configured. This is covered in *Chapter 12, Configuring Anonymous Access*.

How to do it...

Follow these steps to configure the search engine optimization settings:

1. In your preferred web browser, navigate to the site collection for which we are configuring search engine optimization settings.

2. Click on **Site settings** from the **Settings** menu.

3. Select **Site collection features** from the **Site Collection Administration** section as shown in the following screenshot:

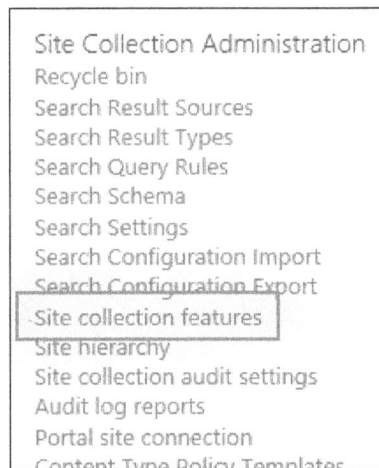

Site Collection Administration
Recycle bin
Search Result Sources
Search Result Types
Search Query Rules
Search Schema
Search Settings
Search Configuration Import
Search Configuration Export
Site collection features
Site hierarchy
Site collection audit settings
Audit log reports
Portal site connection
Content Type Policy Templates

4. Activate the **Search Engine Sitemap** feature.

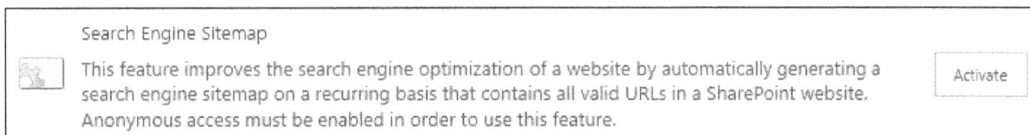

Search Engine Sitemap

This feature improves the search engine optimization of a website by automatically generating a search engine sitemap on a recurring basis that contains all valid URLs in a SharePoint website. Anonymous access must be enabled in order to use this feature.

[Activate]

5. Select **Site settings** from the **Settings** menu.

6. Select **Search engine optimization settings** from the **Site Collection Administration** section as shown in the following screenshot:

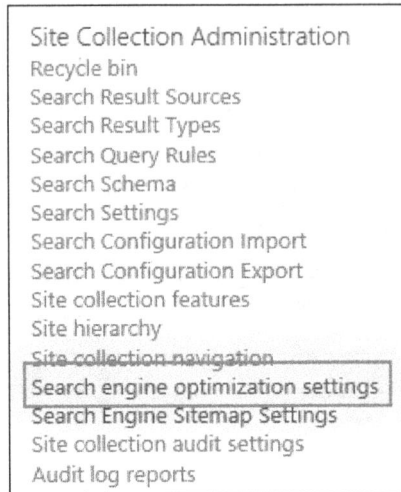

Site Collection Administration
Recycle bin
Search Result Sources
Search Result Types
Search Query Rules
Search Schema
Search Settings
Search Configuration Import
Search Configuration Export
Site collection features
Site hierarchy
Site collection navigation
Search engine optimization settings
Search Engine Sitemap Settings
Site collection audit settings
Audit log reports

7. Select **Include these meta tags in pages**.

8. Add a META tag as follows:

```
<meta name="author" content="John Chapman" />
```

Verify ownership of this site with search engines

Some Internet search engines offer Webmaster Tools that aggregate search-related statistics about websites. To access these statistics, you'll need verify to the search engine that you own this website. Here's how:

1. Visit a search engine's Webmaster Tools website and sign up.
2. Copy the <meta> tag provided by the search engine and paste the tag on this page.
3. Select "Include these meta tags in pages."
4. Ask the search engine to verify your ownership of this website.

○ Do not include these meta tags in pages
◉ Include these meta tags in pages

```
<meta name="author" content="John Chapman" />
```

9. Click on **OK**.

How it works...

Site maps are simple XML files, usually stored at the root of a website, which provide a list of the pages the website includes. This makes it simpler for search engines to locate all of the pages on the site that may or may not have direct links to them from elsewhere on the site. When enabled, SharePoint will generate these XML files automatically based on the content of the site. In addition, exclusions can be configured that will also generate a `robots.txt` file. The `robots.txt` file, also usually stored at the root of a website, instructs search engines as to which content should be excluded from being indexed.

Adding META tags to pages in a site provides additional information about the page or site when being crawled by a search engine. This allows for additional information to be included about the page that is not part of the content of the page, such as the author. The META tags are stored in the `seocustommetatagpropertyname` property of the root site of the site collection.

There's more...

Activating the **Search Engine Sitemap** feature and configuring the META tags can both be accomplished with PowerShell and code using the server-side object model. We have activated site collection features previously in the *Enabling the publishing features on an existing site* recipe in *Chapter 5, Enhancing the Content Creation Process with the SharePoint Publishing Architecture*. We have also previously updated site properties in the *Connecting a site collection to a search center* recipe in this chapter. The property name for the META tags is `seocustommetatagpropertyname` and the feature ID for the search engine sitemap feature is `77fc9e13-e99a-4bd3-9438-a3f69670ed97`.

See also

 ▸ The *Enabling the publishing features on an existing site* recipe in *Chapter 5, Enhancing the Content Creation Process with the SharePoint Publishing Architecture*

 ▸ The *HTML <meta> tag* topic on W3 Schools at `http://www.w3schools.com/tags/tag_meta.asp`

 ▸ The *Site map* article on Wikipedia at `http://en.wikipedia.org/wiki/Site_map`

10
Creating Multilingual Sites with SharePoint Variations

In this chapter, we will explore the translation and multilingual site features of SharePoint 2013. We will cover the following recipes:

- ▶ Installing SharePoint language packs
- ▶ Configuring SharePoint with installed language packs
- ▶ Provisioning a machine translation service application
- ▶ Configuring machine translation timer jobs
- ▶ Configuring site collection variation settings
- ▶ Creating the primary language variation label
- ▶ Creating the secondary language variation labels
- ▶ Checking the status of the variation hierarchy
- ▶ Creating, publishing, and updating targets with a new publishing page
- ▶ Creating translation packages for human translation
- ▶ Uploading translation packages
- ▶ Translating content with the machine translation service

Introduction

Microsoft SharePoint provides one of the most comprehensive sets of tools for creating multilingual sites. In conjunction with the publishing features, the multilingual features provide an end-to-end solution for creating, publishing, and translating web content. Introduced in SharePoint Server 2013, the machine translation service uses the **Microsoft Translator** service, formerly the Bing Translation service, to provide automated machine translations of content. The Microsoft Translator service is one of the web services offered through the Microsoft Windows Azure Marketplace. Refer to `https://datamarket.azure.com/dataset/bing/microsofttranslator` for more details about the Microsoft Translator service.

In this chapter, we will configure the machine translation service and create a multilingual site using SharePoint variations. We will create site variations for multiple languages.

Installing SharePoint language packs

Language packs for SharePoint allow administrators to configure sites of different languages without separate SharePoint installations. Installing language packs adds the resources necessary to support languages other than the language of the SharePoint installation. This includes resource strings, XML files for site definitions and features, and so on. The following table contains the 44 language packs currently available for SharePoint Server 2013:

Language	ID
Arabic	1025
Basque	1069
Bulgarian	1026
Catalan	1027
Chinese (Simplified)	2052
Chinese (Traditional)	1028
Croatian	1050
Czech	1029
Danish	1030
Dutch	1043
English	1033
Estonian	1061
Finnish	1035
French	1036
Galician	1110
German	1031

Language	ID
Greek	1032
Hebrew	1037
Hindi	1081
Hungarian	1038
Indonesian	1057
Italian	1040
Japanese	1041
Kazakh	1087
Korean	1042
Latvian	1062
Lithuanian	1063
Malay (Malaysia)	1086
Norwegian (Bokmål)	1044
Polish	1045
Portuguese (Brazil)	1046
Portuguese (Portugal)	2070
Romanian	1048
Russian	1049
Serbian (Cyrillic)	3098
Serbian (Latin)	2074
Slovak	1051
Slovenian	1060
Spanish	3082
Swedish	1053
Thai	1054
Turkish	1055
Ukrainian	1058
Vietnamese	1066

When downloading and installing language packs, there is a separate download for each service pack in addition to the language pack. Installing a language pack requires the language pack in addition to any service packs, to match the service pack level of SharePoint. For example, if SP1 is installed on SharePoint, both the language pack and SP1 for the language pack will need to be installed.

In this recipe, we will download and install the SharePoint 2013 language pack for the French language. We will use the French language later on in the *Creating the secondary language variation labels* recipe. You can use whichever available language you desire, simply replace the language used in the *Creating the secondary language variation labels* recipe with the one of your choosing.

How to do it...

Follow these steps to install the French language pack for SharePoint:

1. Navigate to the **Language Packs for SharePoint 2013** download page (`http://www.microsoft.com/en-us/download/details.aspx?id=37140`). If one or more service packs are installed on SharePoint, we will need to repeat this process to obtain the language pack for each service pack installed.

2. Select the language name for the language pack that you want to download, **French** for example.

3. Click on the **Download** button and save the file on the local filesystem. When selecting a different language, the page will redirect to the download page in that language. Pay attention to the styling of the download button so that you know which button to click on the page in that language. For instance, if you select Spanish, the download page itself will display in Spanish. Alternatively, if you have an MSDN subscription, you can download the language packs from MSDN.

4. Run the downloaded executable to install the language pack. Language packs must be installed on every SharePoint server in the SharePoint farm. The install application for each language pack will display in the language of the language pack as illustrated for the French language pack in the following screenshot:

Language Pack for SharePoint and Project Server 2013 - French/Français

Lire les termes du contrat de licence logiciel Microsoft

Vous devez accepter les termes de ce contrat pour continuer. Si vous ne voulez pas accepter les termes du contrat de licence logiciel Microsoft, fermez cette fenêtre pour annuler l'installation.

REMARQUE : votre utilisation du présent logiciel est régie par les termes du contrat de licence au titre duquel vous avez acquis ledit logiciel. Par exemple, si vous êtes :
• un client de licence en volume, l'utilisation de ce logiciel est régie par votre contrat de licence en volume;
• un client MSDN, l'utilisation de ce logiciel est régie par le contrat MSDN. Vous n'êtes pas autorisé à utiliser ce logiciel si vous n'avez pas acquis une licence valide du logiciel auprès de Microsoft ou de l'un de ses distributeurs agréés.

EULAID:O15_RTM_SERVERLP.1_RTM_FR

✔ J'accepte les termes de ce contrat.   Continuer

How it works...

Language packs include the resources, XML files, and images required to support the language in all display elements of SharePoint. Installing the language pack adds the files to the local filesystem, but does not configure SharePoint to use them. We will configure SharePoint to recognize the installed language packs in the next recipe, *Configuring SharePoint with installed language packs*.

See also

▸ The *Language packs in SharePoint 2013* article on TechNet at `http://technet.microsoft.com/en-us/library/ff463597.aspx`

▸ The *Language packs for SharePoint 2013* download page on Microsoft at `http://www.microsoft.com/en-us/download/details.aspx?id=37140`

Configuring SharePoint with installed language packs

Installing service packs, cumulative updates, and language packs for SharePoint each require running the **SharePoint Products Configuration Wizard** to configure SharePoint to use the newly installed software. In this recipe, we will run the wizard to complete the installation of our language packs.

How to do it...

Follow these steps to run the SharePoint Products Configuration Wizard:

1. Select the **SharePoint 2013 Products Configuration Wizard** from the **Microsoft SharePoint 2013 Products** folder in the **Start** menu.

2. Complete the wizard with the default options to configure the language pack on the local SharePoint server. The **SharePoint Products Configuration Wizard** must be run on each SharePoint server, one at a time. Since the wizard makes changes to the SharePoint configuration database, running the wizard on multiple servers at the same time is not supported.

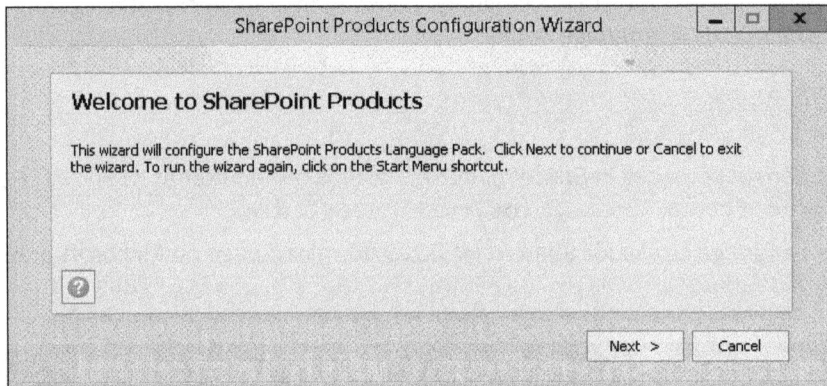

SharePoint Products Configuration Wizard	—	□	X

Welcome to SharePoint Products

This wizard will configure the SharePoint Products Language Pack. Click Next to continue or Cancel to exit the wizard. To run the wizard again, click on the Start Menu shortcut.

[Next >] [Cancel]

How it works...

When language packs are installed on a SharePoint farm, they are not available to SharePoint until the **SharePoint Products Configuration Wizard** has been run. The **SharePoint Products Configuration Wizard** registers the language pack with the SharePoint farm and makes it available for use.

See also

▶   The *Install or uninstall language packs for SharePoint 2013* article on TechNet at `http://technet.microsoft.com/en-us/library/cc262108.aspx`

Provisioning a machine translation service application

The machine translation service application is a new feature of SharePoint Server 2013 that provides an API for SharePoint and developers to translate content with the Microsoft Translator service at no additional cost. Using the Microsoft Translator service in custom code without the SharePoint 2013 machine translation service would incur additional costs after a certain number of characters are translated.

[![note icon] The machine translation service requires access to the Microsoft Translator service via the Internet from the SharePoint server.]

In this recipe, we will provision a new machine translation service application.

How to do it...

Follow these steps to provision a machine translation service application:

1. Navigate to **Central Administration** in your preferred web browser.

2. Select **Manage service applications** from the **Application Management** section as shown in the following screenshot:

3. Click on **Machine Translation Service** under the **New** menu from the **SERVICE APPLICATIONS** tab on the ribbon:

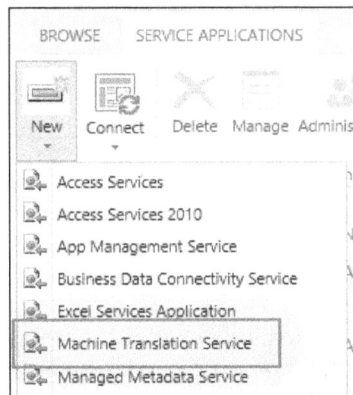

4. Provide a name and choose an application pool for the service application:

Name

The name for the new
service application.

Name

Machine Translation Service

Application Pool

Choose the Application Pool
to use for this Service
Application. This defines the
account and credentials that
will be used by this web
service.

You can choose an existing
application pool or create a
new one.

○ Use existing application pool

Managed Metadata Service Application Pool   ∨

⦿ Create new application pool
Application pool name

Machine Translation Service

Select a security account for this application pool

○ Predefined

Network Service ∨

⦿ Configurable

WESTEROS\sp_services ∨
Register new managed account

5. Check the **Add this service application's proxy to the farm's default proxy list** checkbox under **Add to Default Proxy List**. Adding a service application to the default proxy group will make it available to all web applications using the default proxy group.

Add to Default Proxy List

Specify if this service
application's proxy should
be added to the default
proxy list.

☑ Add this service application's proxy to the farm's default
proxy list.

6. Click on **OK**.

How it works...

The machine translation service application provides the web service endpoints for the translation API used by SharePoint. It creates a service application, instantiates the endpoints in **Internet Information Services** (**IIS**), and makes the API available to SharePoint and custom code deployed to SharePoint.

There's more...

Machine translation service applications may also be provisioned with PowerShell. Follow these steps to provision a machine translation service application using PowerShell:

1. Create a new application pool with the `New-SPServiceApplicationPool` Cmdlet, or get an existing application pool with the `Get-SPServiceApplicationPool` Cmdlet, and assign it to a variable:

   ```
   $appPool = Get-SPServiceApplicationPool "SharePoint Web
   Services Default"
   ```

2. Create a new machine translation service application using the `New-SPTranslationServiceApplication` Cmdlet and assign it to a variable:

   ```
   $mts = New-SPTranslationServiceApplication -Name
   "Machine Translation Service" -ApplicationPool $appPool
   ```

3. Create a proxy for the new machine translation service application and assign it to the default proxy group with the `New-SPTranslationServiceApplicationProxy` Cmdlet:

   ```
   New-SPTranslationServiceApplicationProxy -Name
   "Machine Translation Service Proxy" -ServiceApplication $mts -
   DefaultProxyGroup
   ```

See also

► The *Turn on automated translation of documents in SharePoint Server 2013* article on TechNet at `http://technet.microsoft.com/en-us/library/jj553772(v=office.15).aspx`

► The *New-SPServiceApplicationPool* topic on TechNet at `http://technet.microsoft.com/en-us/library/ff607595.aspx`

► The *Get-SPServiceApplicationPool* topic on TechNet at `http://technet.microsoft.com/en-us/library/ff607544.aspx`

► The *New-SPTranslationServiceApplicationProxy* topic on TechNet at `http://technet.microsoft.com/en-us/library/jj219763.aspx`

► The *New-SPTranslationServiceApplication* topic on TechNet at `http://technet.microsoft.com/en-us/library/jj219712.aspx`

Configuring machine translation timer jobs

The machine translation service receives translation jobs from SharePoint content and other sources that get translated in batches. The frequency of translating these batches as well as other configuration options, such as connecting through a web proxy, may be configured for the machine translation service.

There are many configuration options for the machine translation service. In this recipe, we will only focus on the interval at which the queued translation jobs are processed.

How to do it...

Follow these steps to configure the machine translation timer jobs:

1. Navigate to **Central Administration** in your preferred web browser.

2. Select **Manage service applications** from the **Application Management** section.

3. Select the link to the newly created machine translation service:

	Application Proxy	
Machine Translation	Machine Translation Service	Started
Machine Translation	Machine Translation Service Proxy	Started

4. In the **Translation Throughput** section, set the **Frequency with which to start translations (minutes)** to 15:

Translation Throughput	Frequency with which to start translations (minutes):
Specify the frequency with which groups of translations are started, and the number of translations within each group. Setting these values too high or too low can affect performance.	15

5. Click on **OK** to save the change.

How it works...

The machine translation service uses a SharePoint timer job to process queued translation requests. The default interval at which this job runs is 15 minutes. This can be configured to run more or less frequently. The machine translation service can use a considerable amount of resources on the server. These settings allow us to adjust the translation service based on the needs of the implementation.

There's more...

The machine translation service configuration options may also be set using PowerShell. Follow these steps to configure the machine translation timer job using PowerShell:

1. Use the `Get-SPServiceApplication` Cmdlet to obtain the unique identifier for the machine translation service application on the local farm:

    Get-SPServiceApplication

    You will see a screen similar to the one shown in the following screenshot after issuing the preceding command:

```
                          SharePoint 2013 Management Shell                    _ □ x
PS C:\Users\Administrator> Get-SPServiceApplication

DisplayName            TypeName              Id
-----------            --------              --
Secure Store           Secure Store Serv...  4e889567-58f1-402a-b4b3-a8c2056f6fb8
Managed Metadata       Managed Metadata ...  d4ff2e7b-e983-4147-985e-6079e74f3a4d
App Management         App Management Se...  857d2c4d-cd16-4d62-a77d-136b25ad40b6
Security Token Se...   Security Token Se...  1e1e4ad9-1bdc-4d8f-a3fb-169785f5c54f
Machine Translation    Machine Translati...  bc6a1336-3e12-49e0-bb4b-4d159b7670c8
Application Disco...   Application Disco...  ecdded3b-8736-41d5-9922-d6460e4fa135
WSS_UsageApplication   Usage and Health ...  4299c4d8-286b-4ffc-91fc-76e79e155846
Search Administra...   Search Administra...  58ebf23f-4d3d-421a-9c53-318757bc867c
Search Administra...   Search Administra...  13196f9b-df01-446e-a10d-98e1a2b4b987
User Profile           User Profile Serv...  2d8cd6b1-3334-4137-a913-081a860dfbae
Business Data Con...   Business Data Con...  ea8cd8c6-a569-4e64-8897-f66ea063a581
Work Management        Work Management S...  2417ae92-d45c-4a53-b719-a0633857c3e2
Search                 Search Service Ap...  870c9823-4109-479e-8f45-2c9cdb1765e8
Search Service Ap...   Search Service Ap...  e9387b70-65ed-485c-846c-01beaa539270


PS C:\Users\Administrator> _
```

2. Use the `Set-SPTranslationServiceApplication` Cmdlet to set the timer job frequency, replace `Identity` with the unique identity from the previous step:

    Set-SPTranslationServiceApplication –Identity bc6a1336-3e12-49e0-bb4b-4d159b7670c8 –TimerJobFrequency 15

See also

▸ The *Turn on automated translation of documents in SharePoint Server 2013* article on TechNet at `http://technet.microsoft.com/en-us/library/jj553772(v=office.15).aspx`

▸ The *Get-SPServiceApplication* topic on TechNet at `http://technet.microsoft.com/en-us/library/ff607714.aspx`

▸ The *Set-SPTranslationServiceApplication* topic on TechNet at `http://technet.microsoft.com/en-us/library/jj219583.aspx`

Configuring site collection variation settings

Variations in SharePoint allow site administrators to create multiple versions of the same site in various languages. This provides a simple yet powerful tool for creating multilingual websites. In a site collection with variations, a source variation site (or label) is configured as the primary location for content to be authored. For each variation (or language), a target site (or label) is created that receives its content from the source site.

In this recipe, we will cover the basic settings for site collection variations that we will use when we create our source and target labels in the *Creating the primary language variation label* and *Creating the secondary language variation labels* recipes.

> The site containing the variations must be a publishing site. The root site of the site collection does not need to be a publishing site, just the site that will contain the variations. Trying to configure variations in a site that is not a publishing site will generate error messages.

How to do it...

Follow these steps to configure the site collection variation settings:

1. Navigate to the site collection that will contain the source and target variations in your preferred web browser.

2. Click on **Site settings** from the **Settings** menu.

3. Select **Variations Settings** from the **Site Collection Administration** section as shown in the following screenshot:

Site Collection Administration
Recycle bin
Search Result Sources
Search Result Types
Search Query Rules
Search Schema
Search Settings
Search Configuration Import
Search Configuration Export
Site collection features
Site hierarchy
Search engine optimization settings
Search Engine Sitemap Settings
Site collection navigation
Site collection audit settings
Audit log reports
Portal site connection
Content Type Policy Templates
Storage Metrics
Site collection app permissions
Site Policies
Content type publishing
Popularity and Search Reports
Variations Settings
Variation labels
Variation logs
Translatable columns
Suggested Content Browser Locations

4. Under **Site, List, and Page Creation Behavior**, select **Create Everywhere**.
   Alternatively, **Create Selectively** may be selected in case you want to choose if a new
   piece of content should be published manually rather than automatically publishing
   all new content to the target sites:

Site, List, and Page Creation Behavior

Choose how the Variations feature behaves when a new
site, list, or page is created in the source label.

You can define how target labels handle updates to
existing content when creating each target label.

◉ Create Everywhere

Best for organizations where the majority of content applies to all target sites.

When I publish a new page, that content will be copied to all target language sites as a draft version.

○ Create Selectively

Best for organizations where significant portions of content apply to some but not all target sites.

When I create new content, I can choose which language sites (if any) that content should be synced to.

5. Under **Recreate Deleted Target Page**, select **Recreate a new target page when the source page is republished**. If a page is deleted in one of the target sites, this option will recreate the page if the source site publishes it again.

Recreate Deleted Target Page

Choose whether a new target page should be recreated when the source page is republished if the previous target page has been deleted.

⦿ Recreate a new target page when the source page is republished.

○ Do not recreate a new target page when the source page is republished.

6. Under **Update Target Page Web Parts**, select **Update Web Part changes to target pages when variation source page update is propagated**. If the web parts on a target page have been personalized, this will revert them to the state of the web parts in the source page.

Update Target Page Web Parts

Choose whether Web Part changes from source page should be updated to existing target pages. Note that Web Parts personalization will be lost when update is made.

⦿ Update Web Part changes to target pages when variation source page update is propagated.

○ Do not update Web Part changes to target pages when variation source page update is propagated.

7. Click on **OK**.

How it works...

The site collection variation settings control how the variations of the site collection should behave when content is created or updated. These settings allow us to choose whether or not content should automatically be published to target sites, whether or not pages in target sites that have been deleted should be recreated if the page is published again, and whether or not web parts customized in the target sites should be overwritten when a page is published again.

Determining which options to select depends upon the implementation. If very little is customized directly on the target sites, the default options to automatically publish new content, recreate deleted pages, and overwrite web part customizations are ideal. However, if customizations are made to pages in the target sites, configuring the options to not publish content automatically, not recreate deleted pages, and not overwrite web part customizations may be appropriate.

See also

▸ The *Variations overview in SharePoint 2013* article on TechNet at `http://technet.microsoft.com/en-us/library/ff628966.aspx`

▸ The *Create a multi-language website* article on the Microsoft Office help website at `http://office.microsoft.com/en-us/sharepoint-server-help/create-a-multi-language-website-HA102886546.aspx`

Creating the primary language variation label

In SharePoint 2013, a variation is a version of a site in a different language than the original. A variation label defines each site variation. The first variation label created defines the source site for the target sites to receive the published content from. In this recipe, we will create the primary language variation label.

How to do it...

Follow these steps to create the primary language variation label:

1. Navigate to the site collection that will contain the source and target variations in your preferred web browser.

2. Click on **Site settings** from the **Settings** menu.

3. Click on **Variation labels** from the **Site Collection Administration** section as shown in the following screenshot:

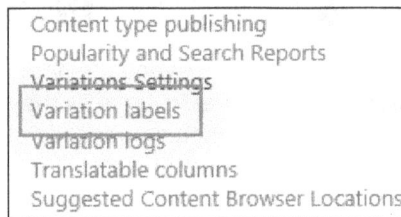

Content type publishing
Popularity and Search Reports
Variations Settings
Variation labels
Variation logs
Translatable columns
Suggested Content Browser Locations

4. Select **New Label** and set the language and locale of the source site:

Language

Select a language pack from the list. This will set the default user interface language for this variation label. More than one variation label can reference the same language pack.

Site Template Language:

English

Locale

Select the locale that content in this label represents. The source label should contain content generally applicable to all target labels.

Locale:

English (United States)

5. Set the location where the source and target sites will be contained. For instance, entering / will contain the sites in the root of the current site collection.

6. Click on **OK**.

How it works...

The primary variation label defines the source language and the source site variations for the site collection. Subsequent variation labels will rollup to receive their content from the content published in the primary variation label based on the settings configured in the *Configuring site collection variation settings* recipe. The sites created for each label will be added to the site specified in the **Location** field for the **Variations Home** option.

See also

- ▸ The *Variations overview in SharePoint 2013* article on TechNet at `http://technet.microsoft.com/en-us/library/ff628966.aspx`
- ▸ The *Create a multi-language website* article on the Microsoft Office help website at `http://office.microsoft.com/en-us/sharepoint-server-help/create-a-multi-language-website-HA102886546.aspx`

Creating the secondary language variation labels

With our primary variation label created in the *Creating the primary language variation label* recipe, we will create a secondary variation label to serve as the target site for the content published in our primary variation label site. When creating variation labels, the label name is used in the URL for the sites. For instance, a label name of `fr-fr` results in the site URL of `/fr-fr/`. In this recipe, we will be using the French language for our target label. If you chose to install the language pack for a different language, use that language instead.

How to do it...

Follow these steps to create a secondary language variation label:

1. Navigate to the site collection that will contain the source and target variations in your preferred web browser.
2. Click on **Site settings** from the **Settings** menu.
3. Select **Variation labels** from the **Site Collection Administration** section.
4. Click on **New Label**.
5. Select a language and locale for the new variation label as shown in the following screenshot:

Language

Select a language pack from the list. This will set the default
user interface language for this variation label. More than one
variation label can reference the same language pack.

Site Template Language:

French ⌄

Locale

Select the locale for this variation. This value will be used to
redirect customers to your site based on their browser
language setting. This value cannot be changed once it has
been set.

Locale:

French (France) ⌄

6. Click on **Continue**.

7. Select **Publishing Sites, Lists with Variations, and All Pages** under the
    Hierarchy Creation:

Hierarchy Creation

This label's structure will be built based on the source
hierarchy during Hierarchy Creation. Select the portion of the
source hierarchy you would like copied.

◉ Publishing Sites, Lists with Variations, and All Pages
○ Publishing Sites Only
○ Root Site Only

8. Click on **Continue**.

9. Select **Allow human translation on this target label** and **Allow Machine Translation
    on this target label**:

Create Translation Package

Enabling human translation on this target will allow users to
export content to an XLIFF file. Users may then send the file to
a translator for professional translation.

○ Disable human translation on this target label
◉ Allow human translation on this target label
Translator Language
French (France) ⌄

Machine Translation

Enabling machine translation on this target will allow users to
send content online to Microsoft for translation. We may use
content users send us to improve the quality of translations.
Learn more.

○ Disable Machine Translation on this target label
◉ Allow Machine Translation on this target label
Machine Translation Language
French ⌄

10. Click on **Continue**.

11. Select **Automatically update target variation pages**.

12. Click on **Continue**.

13. Review the details of the new variation label and click on **Finish**.

How it works...

Creating the secondary variation label adds a new target site in the site collection. When content is published in the primary variation label site, it will be published to the target site based on the settings configured in the *Configuring site collection variation settings* recipe. Once content has been published to a target variation label site, it can then be translated into that language using human or machine translation.

When a variation label is created, a job to create the variation hierarchy will be automatically queued. A timer job will process the queue the next time it runs, which is once per hour by default. We will check the status of our variation hierarchy in the next recipe, *Checking the status of the variation hierarchy*.

See also

▶ The *Variations overview in SharePoint 2013* article on TechNet at `http://technet.microsoft.com/en-us/library/ff628966.aspx`

▶ The *Create a multi-language website* article on the Microsoft Office help website at `http://office.microsoft.com/en-us/sharepoint-server-help/create-a-multi-language-website-HA102886546.aspx`

Checking the status of the variation hierarchy

Once variation labels have been created, a job to create the variation hierarchy is queued. The variation hierarchy defines the flow of content from the source variation labels to the target variation labels. In our example, our content simply flows from the source label to both the target labels. In more complex scenarios, the content could flow through multiple levels of target labels. For this recipe, we will check the status of the hierarchy for the variation labels we created in the *Creating the secondary language variation labels* recipe.

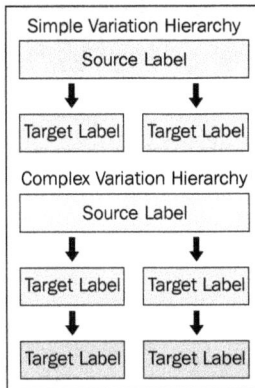

Simple Variation Hierarchy / Source Label / Target Label / Target Label
Complex Variation Hierarchy / Source Label / Target Label / Target Label / Target Label / Target Label

How to do it...

Follow these steps to check the status of the variation hierarchy:

1. Navigate to the site collection that contains the source and target variations in your preferred web browser.

2. Click on **Site settings** from the **Settings** menu.

3. Click on **Variation labels** from the **Site Collection Administration** section.

4. The status of the hierarchy is displayed under **Hierarchy Is Created** as illustrated in the following screenshot. In addition, more detailed logging information is available by clicking on the **Variation Logs** link.

Label	Display Name	Language	Locale	Human Translation	Machine Translation	Is Source	Description	Hierarchy Is Created
en-us	English (United States)	English (United States)	English (United States)	Disabled	Disabled	Yes		Yes
fr-fr	French (France)	French (France)	French (France)	French (France)	French	No		Yes

How it works...

The hierarchy of variation labels determines how and what content is published from the source site to the target sites. Content will not be published to a target variation label site until the hierarchy is created.

See also

▶ The *Variations overview in SharePoint 2013* article on TechNet at `http://technet.microsoft.com/en-us/library/ff628966.aspx`

▶ The *Create a multi-language website* article on the Microsoft Office help website at `http://office.microsoft.com/en-us/sharepoint-server-help/create-a-multi-language-website-HA102886546.aspx`

Creating, publishing, and updating targets with a new publishing page

With our variation labels and variation hierarchy created, we will now create a new publishing page in the source site and publish it to the target site.

How to do it...

Follow these steps to create a new page and publish it to the target variation label site:

1. Navigate to the site collection that contains the source and target variations in your preferred web browser.
2. Click on **Site settings** from the **Settings** menu.
3. Select **Variation labels** from the **Site Collection Administration** section.
4. Click on the display name for the source variation label, such as **English (United States)**, to navigate to the source site as shown in the following screenshot:

New Label | Create Hierarchies | Variations Settings | Variation Logs

Label	Display Name	Language	Locale
en-us	English (United States)	English (United States)	English (Unit States)
fr-fr	French (France)	French (France)	French (Fran

5. Click on **Site contents** from the **Settings** menu and select the **Pages** library.
6. Select **New Document** from the **FILES** tab on the ribbon.
7. Provide the page a name and URL and click on **Create**.
8. Edit the page and add some content.

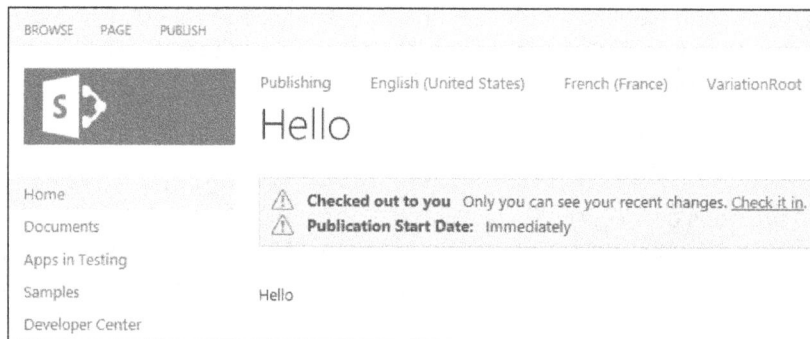

BROWSE   PAGE   PUBLISH

Publishing   English (United States)   French (France)   VariationRoot

Hello

Home

Documents

Apps in Testing

Samples

Developer Center

⚠ **Checked out to you** Only you can see your recent changes. Check it in.

⚠ **Publication Start Date:** Immediately

Hello

9. Select **Publish** from the **PUBLISH** ribbon tab and click on **Continue**.

10. Navigate to the site collection that contains the source and target variations in your preferred web browser.

11. From the **Settings** menu, select **Site settings**.

12. Select **Variation labels** from the **Site Collection Administration** section.

13. Select the display name for the target variation label to navigate to the target site as shown in the following screenshot:

New Label | Create Hierarchies | Variations Settings | Variation Logs			
Label	Display Name	Language	Locale
en-us	English (United States)	English (United States)	English (Uni States)
fr-fr	French (France)	French (France)	French (Fran

14. Click on **Site contents** from the **Settings** menu. These options will be displayed in the language of the target label site. In our French site, **Site contents** will be displayed as **Contenu du site**.

15. Select the **Pages** library.

16. Observe the page published from the source site. If the page is not yet there, the timer job to publish the source site content has not yet completed. This job runs every fifteen minutes by default. Once it is done, the page will appear similar to the following screenshot:

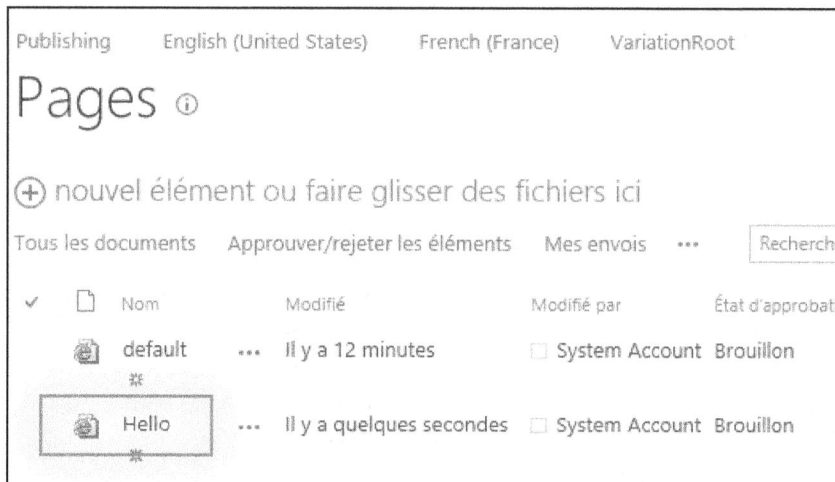

Publishing   English (United States)   French (France)   VariationRoot

Pages ⓘ

⊕ nouvel élément ou faire glisser des fichiers ici

Tous les documents	Approuver/rejeter les éléments	Mes envois •••	Recherche

		Nom	Modifié	Modifié par	État d'approbati
	🗐	default •••	Il y a 12 minutes	☐ System Account	Brouillon
	🗐	Hello •••	Il y a quelques secondes	☐ System Account	Brouillon

How it works...

When configured, changes to content in the source site will automatically be published to the target site. Automatic publishing of content happens in timer jobs that run every fifteen minutes by default. Once published to the target site, content can then be human or machine translated.

The three timer jobs to publish content to target sites are instantiated per web application. These timer jobs include **Variations Propagate List Items Job Definition**, **Variations Propagate Page Job Definition**, and **Variations Propagate Page Job Definition**. The frequency of these timer jobs can be configured individually per job, per web application.

See also

▶ The *Variations overview in SharePoint 2013* article on TechNet at `http://technet.microsoft.com/en-us/library/ff628966.aspx`

▶ The *Create a multi-language website* article on the Microsoft Office help website at `http://office.microsoft.com/en-us/sharepoint-server-help/create-a-multi-language-website-HA102886546.aspx`

Creating translation packages for human translation

Content published from a source site will retain the original text in the target site until it has been translated. In this recipe, we will create a translation package for human translation.

The target site will display elements in the language of the variation label. The instructions in this recipe refer to the items in English; however, they will be actually displayed in the language of the variation label.

How to do it...

Follow these steps to create a translation package:

1. Navigate to the newly published page from the *Creating, publishing, and updating targets with a new publishing page* recipe in the target site.

2. Click on **Create Translation Package** from the **VARIATIONS** tab on the ribbon. In our French target site, these will display as **VARIANTES** and **Créer un package de traduction** as shown in the following screenshot:

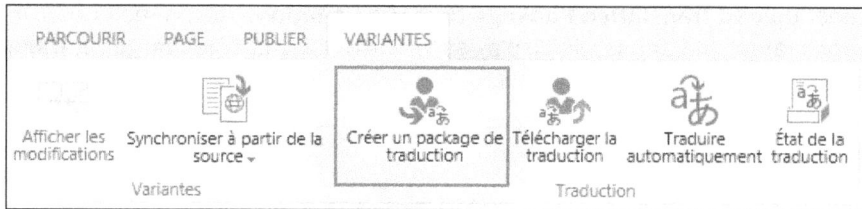

3. Click on **OK**.

How it works...

When requested, a job will be added to the translation queue to create a translation package for download. This translation package contains the items to be translated in the standard **XML Localisation Interchange File Format** (**XLIFF**) format. In most circumstances, this package is provided to an external company to perform the translation. Once the job to create the package is complete, you will be e-mailed with a link to download the package.

See also

▶ The *XLIFF* article on Wikipedia at `http://en.wikipedia.org/wiki/XLIFF`

▶ The *Variations overview in SharePoint 2013* article on TechNet at `http://technet.microsoft.com/en-us/library/ff628966.aspx`

▶ The *Create a multi-language website* article on the Microsoft Office help website at `http://office.microsoft.com/en-us/sharepoint-server-help/create-a-multi-language-website-HA102886546.aspx`

Uploading translation packages

In this recipe, we will upload the translation package we created in the *Creating translation packages for human translation* recipe.

Since we have not actually done any translation in the package, it will process the file without actually saving any translation. You can modify the translation package to add your own translation for demonstration purposes.

How to do it...

Follow these steps to upload a translation package:

1. Navigate to the newly published page from the *Creating, publishing, and updating targets with a new publishing page* recipe in the target site.

2. Select **Upload Translation Package** from the **Variations** tab on the ribbon. In our French target site, these will display as **VARIANTES** and **Télécharger la traduction** as shown in the following screenshot:

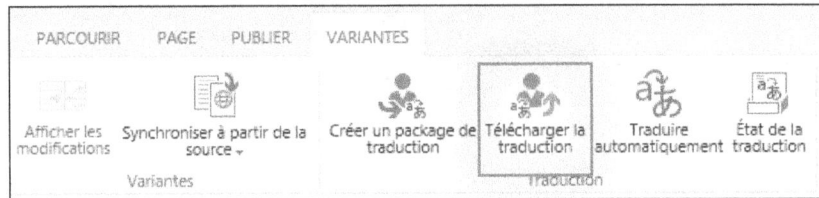

3. Select the translation package on the local filesystem.

4. Provide a name for the translator. This is just for record keeping.

5. Click on **OK**.

How it works...

Uploading a translation package creates a new queued job to process the package. Once processed, the items translated will be updated in the site.

See also

▶ The *Variations overview in SharePoint 2013* article on TechNet at `http://technet.microsoft.com/en-us/library/ff628966.aspx`

▶ The *Create a multi-language website* article on the Microsoft Office help website at `http://office.microsoft.com/en-us/sharepoint-server-help/create-a-multi-language-website-HA102886546.aspx`

Translating content with the machine translation service

In this recipe, we will translate our publishing page from the *Creating, publishing, and updating targets with a new publishing page* recipe in the target site using the machine translation service.

How to do it...

1. Navigate to the newly published page from the *Creating, publishing, and updating targets with a new publishing page* recipe in the target site.

2. Select **Machine Translation** from the **Variations** tab on the ribbon. In our French target site, these will display as **VARIANTES** and **Traduire automatiquement** as shown in the following screenshot:

3. Click on **OK**. A new translation job will be added to the machine translation job queue.

4. Once the translation job has been completed, navigate to the publishing page in the target site to observe the results. It will look similar to the following screenshot:

How it works...

When requested, a new translation job will be queued for the page content. The machine translation service will process the translation job using the Microsoft Translator API and update the page content accordingly.

See also

▶ The *Variations overview in SharePoint 2013* article on TechNet at `http://technet.microsoft.com/en-us/library/ff628966.aspx`

▶ The *Create a multi-language website* article on the Microsoft Office help website at `http://office.microsoft.com/en-us/sharepoint-server-help/create-a-multi-language-website-HA102886546.aspx`

11
Configuring Content Deployment

In this chapter, we will look at the content deployment features of SharePoint 2013. We will cover the following recipes:

- ▶ Configuring the source site collection for content deployment
- ▶ Configuring the farm content deployment settings
- ▶ Creating the content deployment path
- ▶ Creating the content deployment job
- ▶ Performing content deployment

Introduction

With public facing or large intranet sites it is common for organizations to stage content before it is made available to the end users. This allows for collaboration and testing of content before it is made available in the production sites. For instance, an e-commerce site might perform weeks of testing site changes before making those changes available to public users.

Introduced in Microsoft Office SharePoint Server 2007, the content deployment features allow authoring content in one site collection and then deploying the content of the site collection to another. The target site collection can be on the same SharePoint farm or an entirely different SharePoint farm. SharePoint also allows chains of content deployment. For instance, the content could be authored in a site collection that is deployed to a staging environment. Once the content has been tested and approved, it is then deployed from the staging environment to the production environment.

In this chapter, we will set up a source site collection, a target site collection, and the content deployment connection. In addition, we will schedule the content deployment operation to occur on a scheduled interval.

Configuring the source site collection for content deployment

Content deployment in SharePoint 2013 is handled at the site collection level. New to SharePoint 2013, we must first activate the **Content Deployment Source Feature**. This new feature provides a report containing a list of features currently activated that are not supported by content deployment. In addition, this feature makes the site collection available in the list of site collections to use as the source when creating our content deployment connection in the *Creating the content deployment path* recipe.

Getting ready

For this recipe, we should have a source site collection and a target site collection created. They should both be created with the same site template, such as the **Publishing Site** template.

> The source and target site collections must be in separate content databases. They can be in the same web application as long as they are in separate content databases.

How to do it...

Follow these steps to configure the source site collection for content deployment:

1. Navigate to the source site collection in your preferred web browser.
2. Click on **Site settings** from the **Settings** menu.
3. Click on **Site Collection Features** from the **Site Collection Administration** section.
4. Activate the **Content Deployment Source Feature**.
5. Click on **Site settings** from the **Settings** menu.
6. Click on **Content Deployment Source Status** from the **Site Collection Administration** section. The **Content Deployment Source Status** page displays a list of features and other content that would result in a failed content deployment operation as shown in the following screenshot:

Site Settings › Content Deployment Source Status ⓘ

This page lists all the errors that will prevent successful Content Deployment from this Site Collection.

Site	Error	How to fix it
Deployment Source	Ratings: This Site Collection feature is not supported	This feature is hidden. It must be deactivated using powershell
Deployment Source	SignaturesWorkflowSPD1033: This Site Collection feature is not supported	This feature is hidden. It must be deactivated using powershell
Deployment Source	RollupPages: This Site feature is not supported	This feature is hidden. It must be deactivated using powershell

7. Deactivate any features and delete any content listed on the **Content Deployment Source Status** page. For any features listed as hidden, they can be deactivated using PowerShell. For instance, the **Ratings** feature can be deactivated by removing the feature identifier that matches the feature from the collection of features activated on the site collection:

```
$site = Get-SPSite http://sharepoint/sitecollection

$site.Features | Where-Object { $_.Definition.DisplayName -
eq "Ratings" } | ForEach-Object { $site.Features.Remove($_.
DefinitionId) }
```

8. Once each item has been addressed, the **Content Deployment Source Status** page will indicate that the site collection is ready for content deployment as shown in the following screenshot:

Site Settings › Content Deployment Source Status ⓘ

There are no errors and this Site Collection is ready for Content Deployment.

How it works...

SharePoint 2013 uses the **Content Deployment Source Feature** to identify which site collections to make available when configuring a content deployment path. A content deployment path defines the source and the target for deploying content. In addition, this feature makes available the **Content Deployment Source Status** page that displays features from the source site collection known not to be compatible with content deployment.

The **Content Deployment Source Status** page will only list incompatible features that are included with SharePoint. If you have third-party or custom solutions, you should test them in a nonproduction environment to ensure they work with content deployment operations.

There's more...

Activating a site collection feature may also be accomplished with PowerShell or code using the server-site object model. When doing so the feature identifier for the **Content Deployment Source Feature** is cd1a49b0-c067-4fdd-adfe-69e6f5022c1a.

Configuring the source site collection for content deployment using PowerShell

Follow these steps to activate the site collection feature using PowerShell:

1. Get the source site collection with the `Get-SPSite` Cmdlet as follows:

    ```
    $site = Get-SPSite http://sharepoint/sitecollection
    ```

2. Ensure the feature is not already activated on the site collection. If the following command returns a value, it is already activated:

    ```
    $site.Features[[GUID] "cd1a49b0-c067-4fdd-adfe-69e6f5022c1a"]
    ```

3. Activate the feature by adding the feature identifier to the features collection on the site collection as follows:

    ```
    $site.Features.Add([GUID] "cd1a49b0-c067-4fdd-adfe-69e6f5022c1a")
    ```

Configuring the source site collection for content deployment with code using the server-side object model

Follow these steps to activate the site collection feature with code using the server-side object model:

1. Get the source site collection in a `using` statement as follows:

    ```
    using (var site = new SPSite("http://sharepoint/sitecollection"))
    ```

2. Ensure the feature is not already activated on the site collection. If the following command returns a value, it is already activated:

    ```
    if (site.Features[new Guid("cd1a49b0-c067-4fdd-adfe-
    69e6f5022c1a")] == null)
    ```

3. Activate the feature by adding the feature identifier to the features collection on the site collection as follows:

    ```
    site.Features.Add(new Guid("cd1a49b0-c067-4fdd-adfe-
    69e6f5022c1a"));
    ```

Configuring the farm content deployment settings

Before we can configure a content deployment connection, we need to enable incoming content deployment jobs on the SharePoint farm to which we are deploying our content. Even if we are deploying to the same SharePoint farm the content is being deployed from, we still need to enable the incoming jobs. In this recipe, we will enable incoming content deployment jobs for our SharePoint farm.

How to do it...

Follow these steps to configure incoming content deployment jobs:

1. Navigate to **Central Administration** on the target SharePoint farm in your preferred web browser.

2. Click on **General Application Settings** as shown in the following screenshot:

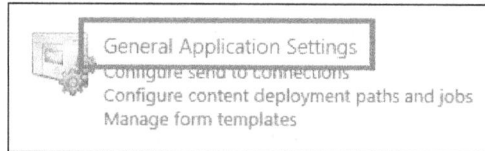

General Application Settings
Configure send to connections
Configure content deployment paths and jobs
Manage form templates

3. Click on **Configure content deployment** from the **Content Deployment** section as shown in the following screenshot:

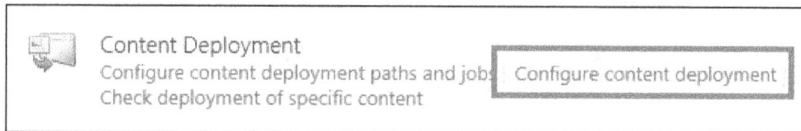

Content Deployment
Configure content deployment paths and jobs   Configure content deployment
Check deployment of specific content

4. Select **Accept incoming content deployment jobs** as shown in the following screenshot:

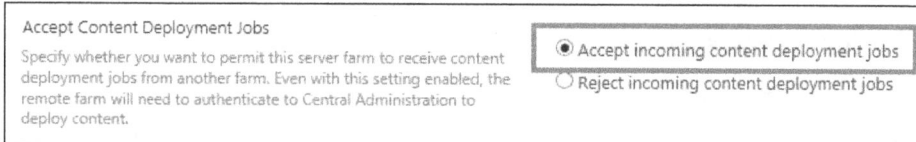

Accept Content Deployment Jobs

Specify whether you want to permit this server farm to receive content deployment jobs from another farm. Even with this setting enabled, the remote farm will need to authenticate to Central Administration to deploy content.

⦿ Accept incoming content deployment jobs
◯ Reject incoming content deployment jobs

5. If SSL is not configured for the **Central Administration** web application (it is not configured by default) set the **Connection Security** setting to **Do not require encryption** as shown in the following screenshot:

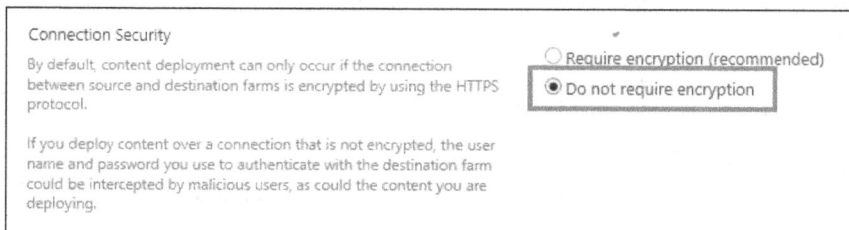

Connection Security

By default, content deployment can only occur if the connection between source and destination farms is encrypted by using the HTTPS protocol.

If you deploy content over a connection that is not encrypted, the user name and password you use to authenticate with the destination farm could be intercepted by malicious users, as could the content you are deploying.

◯ Require encryption (recommended)
⦿ Do not require encryption

6. Click on **OK**.

How it works...

The target SharePoint farm will only allow content deployment connections if it has been configured to do so. In addition, requiring encryption will only allow connections using the **Central Administration** URL over SSL.

There's more...

The farm content deployment configuration options may also be set with PowerShell or code using the server-side object model.

Configuring the farm content deployment settings using PowerShell

Follow these steps to configure the farm content deployment settings using PowerShell:

1. Get the content deployment configuration instance for the local SharePoint farm as follows:

   ```
   $cd = [Microsoft.SharePoint.Publishing.Administration.ContentDeplo
   ymentConfiguration]::GetInstance()
   ```

2. Set the `AcceptIncomingJobs` property to `true` and `RequiresSecureConnection` property to `false` as follows:

   ```
   $cd.AcceptIncomingJobs = $true

   $cd.RequiresSecureConnection = $false
   ```

3. Update the configuration instance using the following command:

   ```
   $cd.Update()
   ```

Configuring the farm content deployment settings with code using the server-side object model

Follow these steps to configure the farm content deployment settings with code using the server-side object model:

1. Get the content deployment configuration instance for the local SharePoint farm as follows:

   ```
   var cd = Microsoft.SharePoint.Publishing.Administration.
   ContentDeploymentConfiguration.GetInstance();
   ```

2. Set the `AcceptIncomingJobs` property to `true` and `RequiresSecureConnection` property to `false` as follows:

   ```
   cd.AcceptIncomingJobs = true;
   cd.RequiresSecureConnection = false;
   ```

3. Update the configuration instance using the following line of code:

```
cd.Update();
```

See also

▶ The *ContentDeployementConfiguration* class topic on MSDN at `http://msdn.microsoft.com/en-us/library/Microsoft.SharePoint.Publishing.Administration.ContentDeploymentConfiguration(v=office.14).aspx`

Creating the content deployment path

Content deployment connections are managed in two parts: a path and a job. The content deployment path defines where the content is coming from and where it is going. The content deployment job defines when and how often the content should be deployed. In this recipe, we will create the content deployment path. We will create the content deployment job in the *Creating the content deployment job* recipe.

How to do it...

Follow these steps to create a content deployment path:

1. Navigate to **Central Administration** on the source SharePoint farm in your preferred web browser.
2. Click on **General Application Settings**.
3. Click on **Configure content deployment paths and jobs** from the **Content Deployment** section as shown in the following screenshot:

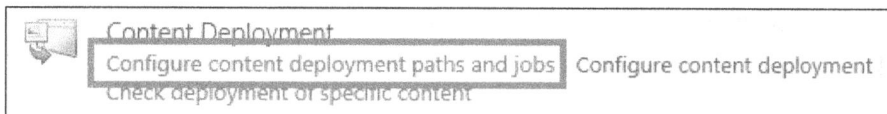

4. Click on **New Path**.

5. Provide a name and description for the new path as shown in the following screenshot:

Name and Description

Specify the name and description of the content deployment path.

Type the name of this path:

Staging Deployment Path

Type the description of the content deployment path:

Deploy /sites/source to /sites/target.

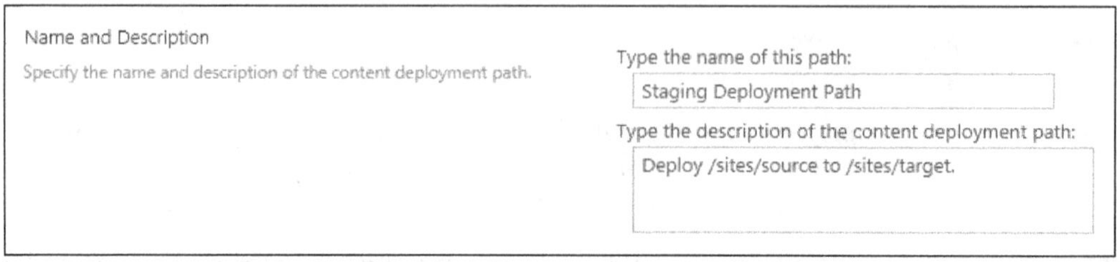

6. Select the values for **Source web application** and **Source site collection** as shown in the following screenshot:

Source Web Application and Site Collection

Specify the web application and site collection on the source server. The specified site collection must have the "Content Deployment Source" feature activated.

Source web application:

SharePoint - 80

Source site collection:

sites/source

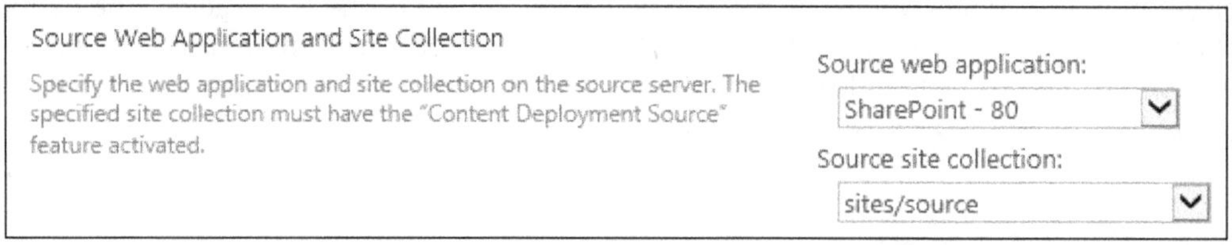

7. Enter the Central Administration URL for the target SharePoint farm in the **Type the URL of the destination Central Administration Server** textbox:

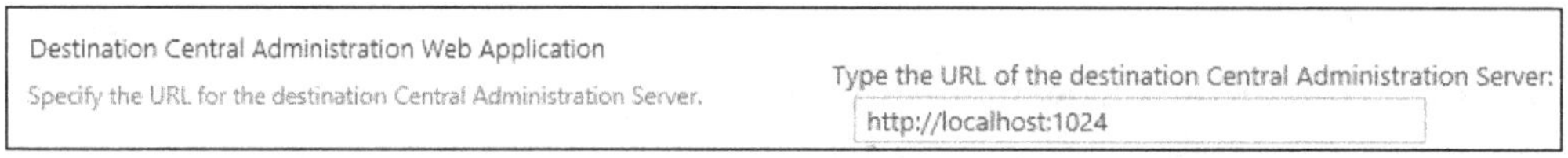

Destination Central Administration Web Application

Specify the URL for the destination Central Administration Server.

Type the URL of the destination Central Administration Server:

http://localhost:1024

8. Enter the credentials to use when connecting to the target SharePoint farm.

9. Click on **Connect**.

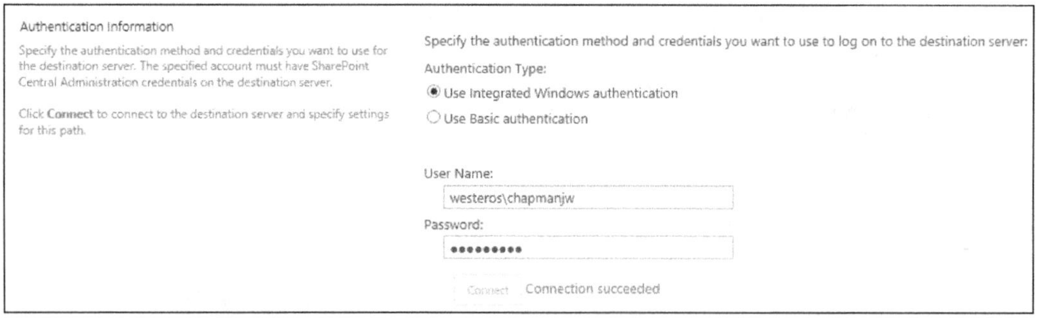

Authentication Information

Specify the authentication method and credentials you want to use for the destination server. The specified account must have SharePoint Central Administration credentials on the destination server.

Click **Connect** to connect to the destination server and specify settings for this path.

Specify the authentication method and credentials you want to use to log on to the destination server:

Authentication Type:

◉ Use Integrated Windows authentication

○ Use Basic authentication

User Name:

westeros\chapmanjw

Password:

●●●●●●●●

Connect   Connection succeeded

10. Select the **Destination web application** and **Destination Site Collection** as shown in the following screenshot:

Destination web application and site collection

Specify the URL for the destination web application and site collection.

Destination web application:

| SharePoint - 80 | ∨ |

Destination Site Collection:

| sites/target | ∨ |

11. Click on **OK**. Observe the newly created content deployment path.

	New Path | New Job					
Type	Name	Next Run	Last Run	Status	Created By
	Staging Deployment Path				
	Quick Deploy job for path 'Staging Deployment Path'	None Scheduled	Not Yet Run		System Account

How it works...

The content deployment path defines where the content is coming from and where it is going. The target SharePoint farm is communicated with through the **Central Administration** site.

> If you receive an access denied error when attempting to create the content deployment path, try accessing Central Administration from a different computer and retry the operation. There is a bug in the initial release of SharePoint Server 2013 that occasionally throws an access denied error when trying to verify the status of the source site collection when accessing Central Administration from the server hosting Central Administration.

There's more...

Content deployment paths may also be created with PowerShell or code using the server-side object model.

Creating the content deployment path using PowerShell

Follow these steps to create the content deployment path using PowerShell:

1. Get the source site collection using the `Get-SPSite` Cmdlet as follows:

```
$source = Get-SPSite http://sharepoint/source
```

2. Get the credentials to use for the connection. Simply using the `Get-Credential` Cmdlet will prompt you to enter the user credentials.

```
$credentials = Get-Credential
```

3. Create the content deployment path with the `New-SPContentDeploymentPath` Cmdlet.

```
New-SPContentDeploymentPath -Name "Test Deployment" -
SourceSPWebApplication $source.WebApplication -SourceSPSite
$source -DestinationCentralAdministrationURL "http://
sharepointcentraladmin" -DestinationSPWebApplication
"http://sharepointdestination" -DestinationSPSite "http://
sharepointdestination/site" -PathAccount $credentials
```

Creating the content deployment path with code using the server-side object model

Follow these steps to create the content deployment path with code using the server-side object model:

1. Create a new `ContentDeploymentPath` object as follows:

```
var path = Microsoft.SharePoint.Publishing.Administration.
ContentDeploymentPath.GetAllPaths().Add();
```

2. Set the properties for the content deployment path as follows:

```
path.Name = "Deployment Path";
path.IncludeSecurity = Microsoft.SharePoint.Deployment.
SPIncludeSecurity.All;
path.EnableEventReceivers = true;
path.EnableCompression = true;
path.IsPathEnabled = true;
path.AuthenticationType = "NTLM";
path.UserId = "domain\\username";
path.Password = "password";
path.SourceServerUri = new Uri("http://sharepoint");
path.SourceSiteCollection = "/source";
path.DestinationAdminServerUri = new Uri("http://
destinationcentraladmin");
path.DestinationServerUri = new Uri("http://
sharepointdestination");
path.DestinationSiteCollection = "/target";
```

3. Update the content deployment path.

```
path.Update();
```

See also

▶ The *Get-Credential* topic on TechNet at `http://technet.microsoft.com/en-us/library/hh849815.aspx`

▶ The *New-SPContentDeploymentPath* topic on TechNet at `http://technet.microsoft.com/en-us/library/ff607765.aspx`

Creating the content deployment job

In this recipe, we will create the second portion of the content deployment connection, the content deployment job. We will use the content deployment path created in the *Creating the content deployment path* recipe.

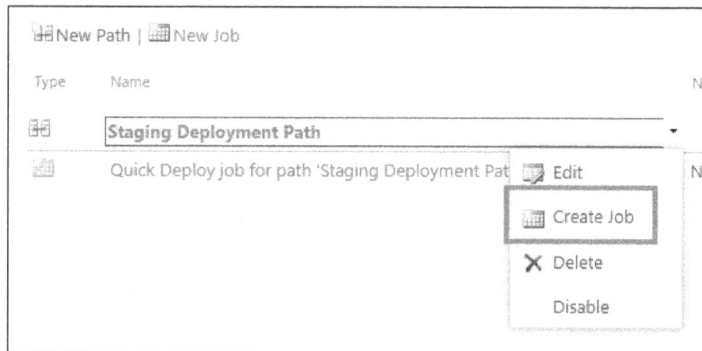

How to do it...

Follow these steps to create the content deployment job:

1. Navigate to **Central Administration** in your preferred web browser.

2. Click on **General Application Settings**.

3. Click on **Configure content deployment paths and jobs** from the **Content Deployment** section.

4. Select **Create Job** from the drop-down menu for the content deployment path created in the *Creating the content deployment path* recipe:

	New Path | New Job	
Type	Name	Ne
	Staging Deployment Path ▾	
	Quick Deploy job for path 'Staging Deployment Pat'	No

Edit
Create Job
✕ Delete
Disable

5. Provide a name and description for the content deployment job in the **Name** and **Description** fields as shown in the following screenshot:

Name and Description	
Specify a unique name and description for this content deployment job.	**Name:** Staging Deployment Job
	Description: Job to deploy /sites/source to /sites/target

6. Select the content deployment path we created in the *Creating the content deployment path* recipe if it is not already selected.

Path

Select the path this job is associated with.

Select a content deployment path:

Staging Deployment Path ▼

7. Select **Run this job on the following schedule** for **Frequency**. The default schedule is once per day. You can configure the schedule to suit your needs.

Frequency

Specify how often you want to run this content deployment job. Show me more information.

☑ Run this job on the following schedule:

○ One time only
   Date:
   12/24/2013   🗓 1 PM ▼ 51 ▼

○ Every
   15 minutes ▼

○ Once an hour
   At minute: 00

◉ Once a day
   At time:
   3 AM ▼ 00 ▼

○ Once a week
   Day: Monday ▼

   At time:
   3 AM ▼ 00 ▼

○ Once a month
   Day: 1 ▼

   At time:
   3 AM ▼ 00 ▼

8. Click on **OK**.

How it works...

The content deployment job defines when and how the content defined in a content deployment path should be deployed. For content deployment jobs with a repeating schedule, a SharePoint timer job will execute the job at the specific interval.

There's more...

A content deployment job may also be created with PowerShell or code using the server-side object model.

Creating the content deployment job using PowerShell

Follow these steps to create the content deployment job using PowerShell:

1. Get the content deployment path with the `Get-SPContentDeploymentPath` Cmdlet as follows:

```
$path = Get-SPContentDeploymentPath "Staging Deployment Path"
```

2. Create a new `SPDailySchedule` object as follows:

```
$schedule = New-Object Microsoft.SharePoint.SPDailySchedule
$schedule.BeginHour = 3
```

> Any `SPSchedule` object may be used for the job schedule. This includes `SPDailySchedule`, `SPHourlySchedule`, and `SPMinuteSchedule`.

3. Create the content deployment job using the `New-SPContentDeploymentJob` Cmdlet as follows:

```
New-SPContentDeploymentJob -Name "Staging Deployment Job" -
SPContentDeploymentPath $path -Schedule $schedule -ScheduleEnabled
$true
```

Creating the content deployment job with code using the server-side object model

Follow these steps to create the content deployment job with code using the server-side object model:

1. Get the content deployment path as follows:

```
var path = Microsoft.SharePoint.Publishing.Administration.
ContentDeploymentPath.GetInstance("Staging Deployment Path");
```

2. Create a new content deployment job as follows:

```
var job = Microsoft.SharePoint.Publishing.Administration.
ContentDeploymentJob.GetAllJobs().Add();
```

3. Set the properties of the content deployment job as follows:

```
job.Name = "Staging Deployment Job";
job.IsEnabled = true;
job.Path = path;
```

4. Update the content deployment job using the following line of code:

   ```
   job.Update();
   ```

5. Create an `SPDailySchedule` object as follows:

   ```
   var schedule = new SPDailySchedule();
   schedule.BeginHour = 3;
   ```

6. Assign the schedule to the `TimerJobDefintion` object of the content deployment job as follows:

   ```
   job.TimerJobDefinition.Schedule = schedule;
   ```

7. Update the content deployment job using the following line of code:

   ```
   job.Update();
   ```

See also

▸ The *ContentDeploymentPath* class topic on MSDN at `http://msdn. microsoft.com/en-us/library/Microsoft.SharePoint.Publishing. Administration.ContentDeploymentPath(v=office.14).aspx`

▸ The *ContentDeploymentJob* class topic on MSDN at `http://msdn. microsoft.com/en-us/library/microsoft.sharepoint.publishing. administration.contentdeploymentjob(v=office.14).aspx`

▸ The *New-SPContentDeploymentJob* topic on TechNet at `http://technet. microsoft.com/en-us/library/ff607805.aspx`

▸ The *Get-SPContentDeploymentPath* topic on TechNet at `http://technet. microsoft.com/en-us/library/ff607782.aspx`

Performing the content deployment

Content deployment jobs can be configured to run on a specific schedule or to only run when instructed to manually. In either case, we can manually start the content deployment job. In this recipe, we will manually start the deployment job created in the *Creating the content deployment job* recipe.

How to do it...

Follow these steps to start the content deployment job:

1. Navigate to **Central Administration** in your preferred web browser.

2. Click on **General Application Settings**.

3. Click on **Configure content deployment paths and jobs** from the **Content Deployment** section.

4. Select **Run Now** from the drop-down menu for the content deployment job as shown in the following screenshot:

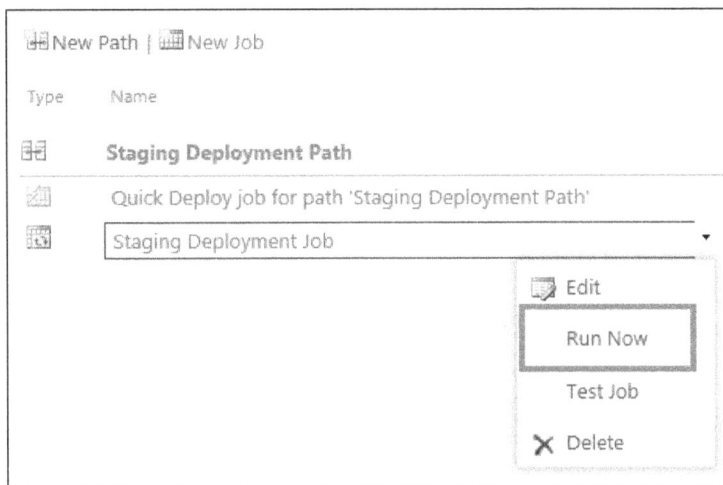

How it works...

Manually starting the content deployment job instructs the SharePoint timer job associated with the content deployment job to execute at the current date and time. Once the timer job runs, it will start the deployment job.

There's more...

Starting a content deployment job may also be accomplished with PowerShell or code using the server-side object model.

Performing content deployment using PowerShell

Follow these steps to start the content deployment job using PowerShell:

1. Get the name of the content deployment job using the `Get-SPContentDeploymentJob` Cmdlet as follows:

```
Get-SPContentDeploymentJob
```

2. Start the content deployment job using the `Start-SPContentDeploymentJob` Cmdlet:

```
Start-SPContentDeploymentJob "Staging Deployment Job"
```

Performing content deployment with code using the server-side object model

Follow these steps to start the content deployment job with code using the server-side object model:

1. Get the content deployment job as follows:

    ```
    var job = Microsoft.SharePoint.Publishing.Administration.
    ContentDeploymentJob.GetInstance("Job Name");
    ```

2. Start the content deployment job using the following line of code:

    ```
    job.Run();
    ```

See also

▶ The *ContentDeploymentJob class* topic on MSDN at `http://msdn.`
    `microsoft.com/en-us/library/microsoft.sharepoint.publishing.`
    `administration.contentdeploymentjob(v=office.14).aspx`

▶ The *Get-SPContentDeploymentJob* topic on TechNet at `http://technet.`
    `microsoft.com/en-us/library/ff607681.aspx`

▶ The *Start-SPContentDeploymentJob* topic on TechNet at `http://technet.`
    `microsoft.com/en-us/library/ff608077.aspx`

12
Configuring Anonymous Access

In this chapter, we will cover configuring a SharePoint 2013 site with anonymous access. We will cover the following recipes:

- ► Configuring anonymous access for web applications
- ► Configuring anonymous access for site content
- ► Limiting access to application pages
- ► Identifying anonymously accessible content with PowerShell
- ► Verifying anonymous access to content with PowerShell

Introduction

Hosting public-facing websites on SharePoint usually requires anonymous access to the SharePoint content. Anonymous access allows users to view content on a site without logging in. SharePoint 2013 provides the necessary functionality to configure anonymous access to SharePoint web applications and content. In addition, it provides a few security mechanisms to prevent anonymous users from accessing pages and other content they aren't supposed to. In this chapter, we will cover the basics of configuring anonymous access for a web application and a site collection.

Configuring anonymous access for web applications

Allowing anonymous access to SharePoint content is configured in two parts, at the web application level and at the content level. In this recipe, we will enable anonymous access to our SharePoint web application.

How to do it...

Follow these steps to configure anonymous access at the web application level:

1. Navigate to **Central Administration** in your preferred web browser.

2. Click on **Manage web applications** in the **Application Management** section as shown in the following screenshot:

3. Select the web application that we are enabling anonymous access for.

4. Click on **Authentication Providers** in the **WEB APPLICATIONS** tab on the ribbon as shown in the following screenshot:

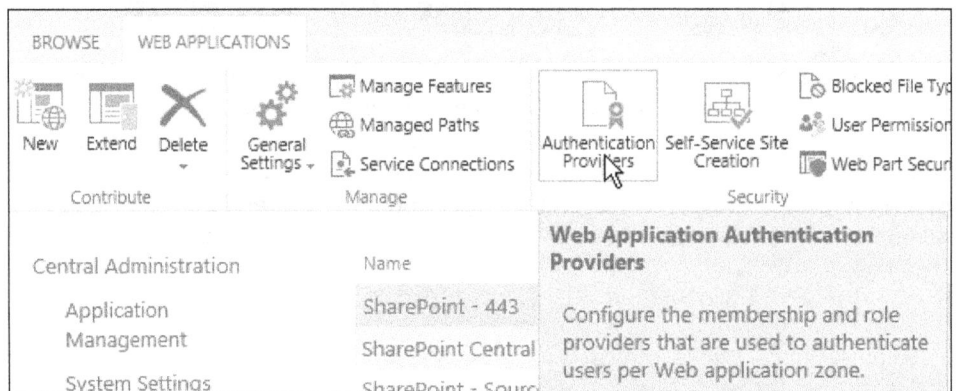

5. Click on the **Default** zone.

Authentication Providers   ✕

Zone	Membership Provider Name
Default	Claims Based Authentication

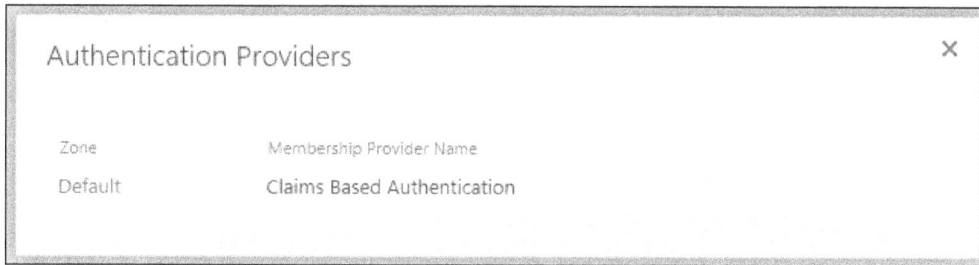

6. Select **Enable anonymous access** as shown in the following screenshot:

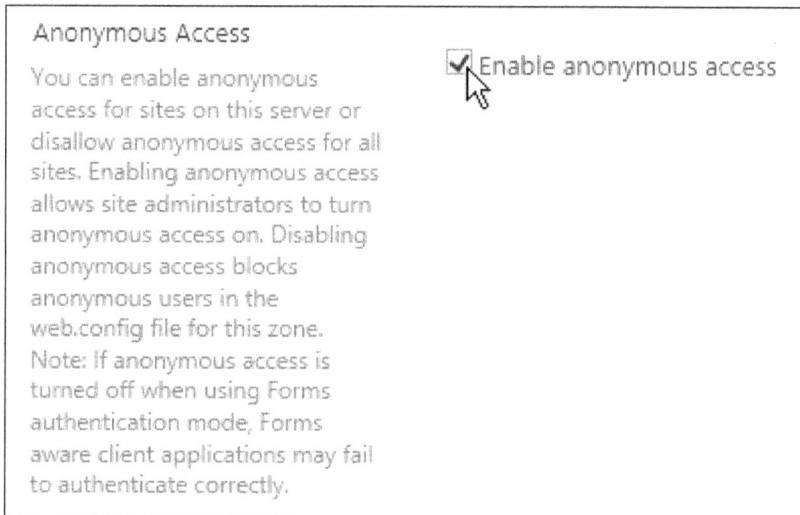

Anonymous Access

You can enable anonymous
access for sites on this server or
disallow anonymous access for all
sites. Enabling anonymous access
allows site administrators to turn
anonymous access on. Disabling
anonymous access blocks
anonymous users in the
web.config file for this zone.
Note: If anonymous access is
turned off when using Forms
authentication mode, Forms
aware client applications may fail
to authenticate correctly.

☑ Enable anonymous access

7. Click on **Save**.

How it works...

Authentication for SharePoint is handled at the web application level. A SharePoint web
application represents a site in **Internet Information Services (IIS)**. Authentication
configuration for the SharePoint web application configures the IIS site accordingly to allow
anonymous, unauthenticated users to access the web application.

There's more...

Configuring anonymous access at the SharePoint web application level can also be
accomplished with PowerShell or code using the server-side object model.

Configuring anonymous access for web applications using PowerShell

Follow these steps to configure anonymous access for a web application using PowerShell:

1. Get the SharePoint web application with the following `Get-SPWebApplication` Cmdlet:

   ```
   $webApp = Get-SPWebApplication http://sharepoint
   ```

2. Set the `AllowAnonymous` property for the IIS settings of the `Default` zone to `true`:

   ```
   $webApp.IisSettings[[Microsoft.SharePoint.Administration.
   SPUrlZone]::Default].AllowAnonymous = $true
   ```

3. Update the web application using the following command:

   ```
   $webApp.Update()
   ```

Configuring anonymous access for web applications with code using the server-side object model

Follow these steps to configure anonymous access for a web application with code using the server-side object model:

1. Get the SharePoint web application by its URL:

   ```
   var webApp = SPWebApplication.Lookup(new Uri("http://
   sharepoint"));
   ```

2. Set the `AllowAnonymous` property for the IIS settings of the `Default` zone to `true`:

   ```
   webApp.IisSettings[SPUrlZone.Default].AllowAnonymous = true;
   ```

3. Update the web application using the following line of code:

   ```
   webApp.Update();
   ```

See also

► The *Get-SPWebApplication* topic on TechNet at `http://technet.microsoft.com/en-us/library/ff607562.aspx`

Configuring anonymous access for site content

With anonymous access configured for the SharePoint web application in the *Configuring anonymous access for web applications* recipe, anonymous users are now able to access the SharePoint web application. Without granting anonymous users access to the content itself, SharePoint will display the generic **Access Denied** error page when trying to access the content. In this recipe, we will configure anonymous access for the site content.

How to do it...

Follow these steps to configure anonymous access to the site content:

1. Navigate to the site collection we are enabling anonymous access for in your preferred web browser.
2. Click on **Site settings** from the **Settings** menu.
3. Click on **Site permissions** from the **Users and Permissions** section as shown in the following screenshot:

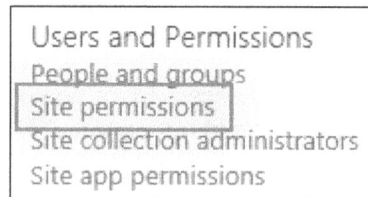

4. Click on **Anonymous Access** from the **PERMISSIONS** tab in the ribbon as shown in the following screenshot:

5. Select **Entire Web site**. Selecting **Lists and libraries** allows you to specify which content to allow anonymous access to on a more granular level.

> **Anonymous Access**
>
> Specify what parts of your Web site (if any) anonymous users can access. If you select Entire Web site, anonymous users will be able to view all pages in your Web site and view all lists and items which inherit permissions from the Web site. If you select Lists and libraries, anonymous users will be able to view and change items only for those lists and libraries that have enabled permissions for anonymous users.
>
> Anonymous users can access:
> - ● Entire Web site
> - ○ Lists and libraries
> - ○ Nothing

6. Click on **OK**.

How it works...

Content in SharePoint is only made available to users who have the appropriate access to the content. Configuring anonymous access at the site level provides anonymous users with appropriate access to the content. Without access to the content, anonymous users would receive the generic SharePoint **Access Denied** error page.

There's more...

Configuring anonymous access at the site level may also be accomplished with PowerShell or code using the server-side object model.

Configuring anonymous access for site content using PowerShell

Follow these steps to configure anonymous access to site content using PowerShell:

1. Get the SharePoint site using the `Get-SPWeb` Cmdlet:

```
$web = Get-SPWeb http://sharepoint
```

2. Set the `AnonymousState` property to `On` as follows:

```
$web.AnonymousState = [Microsoft.SharePoint.SPWeb.
WebAnonymousState]::On
```

> For the `AnonymousState` property `Disabled` is equivalent to **Nothing**, `Enabled` is equivalent to **Lists and libraries**, and `On` is equivalent to **Entire Web site**.

3. Update the SharePoint site using the following command:

```
$web.Update()
```

Configuring anonymous access for site content with code using the server-side object model

Follow these steps to configure anonymous access to site content with code using the server-side object model:

1. Get the SharePoint site collection containing the site in a `using` statement as follows:

```
using (var site = new SPSite("http://sharepoint"))
```

2. Open the SharePoint site in a `using` statement as follows:

```
using (var web = site.OpenWeb())
```

3. Set the `AnonymousState` property to `On` as follows:

```
web.AnonymousState = SPWeb.WebAnonymousState.On;
```

4. Update the SharePoint site using the following line of code:

```
web.Update();
```

See also

▶ The *SPWeb.WebAnonymousState enumeration* topic on MSDN at `http://msdn.microsoft.com/en-us/library/office/microsoft.sharepoint.spweb.webanonymousstate.aspx`

▶ The *Get-SPWeb* topic on TechNet at `http://technet.microsoft.com/en-us/library/ff607807.aspx`

Limiting access to application pages

In previous versions of SharePoint, enabling anonymous access allowed users to access application pages such as the **Site contents** page. Preventing access to the application pages (`/_layouts`) previously required some manual configuration. In SharePoint 2013, access to application pages can be restricted using the new **Limited-access user permission lockdown mode** feature. In this recipe, we will activate this feature on our site collection.

How to do it...

Follow these steps to enable the site collection feature to limit access to application pages:

1. Navigate to the site collection in your preferred web browser.
2. Select **Site settings** from the **Settings** menu.
3. Select **Site collection features** from the **Site Collection Administration** section.
4. Activate the **Limited-access user permission lockdown mode** feature.

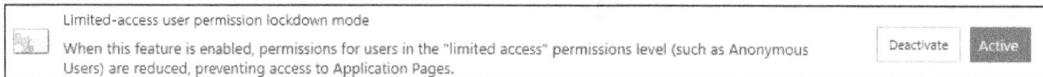

Limited-access user permission lockdown mode

When this feature is enabled, permissions for users in the "limited access" permissions level (such as Anonymous Users) are reduced, preventing access to Application Pages.   Deactivate   Active

How it works...

With the **Limited-access user permission lockdown mode** feature enabled anonymous users will no longer be able to access pages within the `/_layouts` folder. This prevents these users from accessing pages such as the **Site contents** page and reduces the surface area for anonymous users to identify or exploit content in the site.

Using the **Site contents** page is one way hackers attempt to identify content on SharePoint sites in an attempt to exploit the site. Using this feature helps to eliminate that option for anonymous users.

There's more...

The **Limited-access user permission lockdown mode** site collection feature may also be activated with PowerShell or code using the server-side object model. We have covered how to activate site collection features in the *Enabling the publishing features on an existing site* recipe of *Chapter 5, Enhancing the Content Creation Process with the SharePoint Publishing Architecture*. The feature identifier to use when activating the feature is `7c637b23-06c4-472d-9a9a-7c175762c5c4`.

Identifying anonymously accessible content with PowerShell

Granular permissions, such as permissions on individual documents or list items, in SharePoint can be difficult to manage and identify. We can identify permissions given to content in PowerShell. In this recipe, we will check the anonymous status of a SharePoint site, which content in the site provides permissions to anonymous users, and which content does not.

How to do it...

Follow these steps to identify anonymous access to content using PowerShell:

1. Get the SharePoint site with the `Get-SPWeb` Cmdlet:

   ```
   $web = Get-SPSite http://sharepoint
   ```

2. Output the anonymous access configuration for the site from the `AnonymousState` property as follows:

   ```
   $web.AnonymousState
   ```

3. Output the lists in the site that provide permissions to anonymous users by filtering the site lists on the `AnonymousPermMask64` property. The `AnonymousPermMask64` property contains the permissions granted to anonymous users. The `EmptyMask` value indicates that no permissions have been granted.

   ```
   $web.Lists | Where-Object { $_.AnonymousPermMask64 -ne "EmptyMask" } | Format-Table -Property Title
   ```

4. Output the lists in the site that do not provide permissions to anonymous users by filtering the site lists on the `AnonymousPermMask64` property as follows:

   ```
   $web.Lists | Where-Object { $_.AnonymousPermMask64 -eq "EmptyMask" } | Format-Table -Property Title
   ```

How it works...

Permissions are assigned to content in SharePoint using permission masks. A permission mask is an enumeration of specific permission-level items, such as viewing versions. When no permissions are assigned an empty permissions mask will be returned. The permission mask for anonymous users on a SharePoint list is accessed with the `AnonymousPermMask64` property.

The `AnonymousPermMask` property has been deprecated from previous versions of SharePoint.

There's more...

Identifying the SharePoint sites that are configured for anonymous access and the permissions assigned to the SharePoint lists may also be accomplished with code using the server-side object model.

Follow these steps to identify anonymously accessible content with code using the server-side object model:

1. Get the SharePoint site collection containing the site in a `using` statement as follows:

   ```
   using (var site = new SPSite("http://sharepoint"))
   ```

2. Open the SharePoint site in a `using` statement as follows:

   ```
   using (var web = site.OpenWeb())
   ```

3. Output the anonymous configuration for the site.

   ```
   Console.WriteLine(web.AnonymousState);
   ```

4. Output the lists in the site that provide permissions to anonymous users by filtering the site lists on the `AnonymousPermMask64` property as follows:

   ```
   foreach (SPList list in web.Lists)
   if (list.AnonymousPermMask64 != SPBasePermissions.EmptyMask)
   Console.WriteLine(list.Title);
   ```

5. Output the lists in the site that do not provide permissions to anonymous users by filtering the site lists on the `AnonymousPermMask64` property as follows:

   ```
   foreach (SPList list in web.Lists)
   if (list.AnonymousPermMask64 == SPBasePermissions.EmptyMask)
   Console.WriteLine(list.Title);
   ```

See also

▸ The *SPList.AnonymousPermMask64 property* topic on MSDN at `http://msdn.microsoft.com/en-us/library/microsoft.sharepoint.splist.anonymouspermmask64.aspx`

▸ The *SPBasePermissions enumeration* topic on MSDN at `http://msdn.microsoft.com/en-us/library/microsoft.sharepoint.spbasepermissions.aspx`

Verifying anonymous access to content with PowerShell

In this recipe, we will use PowerShell to ensure that anonymous users can access the home page of our SharePoint site but cannot access the **Site contents** page.

How to do it...

Follow these steps to verify the anonymous access to content with PowerShell:

1. Create a new `WebClient` object. We are using the `WebClient` object to make simple, unauthenticated web requests against our SharePoint site.

   ```
   $client = New-Object System.Net.WebClient
   ```

2. Use the `DownloadString` method to make a request for the home page of our site as follows:

   ```
   $client.DownloadString("http://sharepoint")
   ```

   If we receive the HTML content for our page, our request was successful. However, if we receive an exception with a 401 or 403 HTTP response, anonymous access is most likely not available for that page.

3. Use the `DownloadString` method to make a request for the **Site contents** page on our site:

   ```
   $client.DownloadString("http://sharepoint/_layouts/viewlsts.aspx")
   ```

   If the page is correctly blocked for anonymous users, an exception should be thrown with a 401 or 403 HTTP response. If we receive the HTML content for the page, it indicates that the page request was successful and our page is not being blocked for anonymous users.

How it works...

Using the `DownloadString` method of the `WebClient` object, we are making simple HTTP requests in the same manner that a web browser would request the content. When the request is successful, it returns the content of the page as a plain text `string` object. When the request fails, an exception is thrown with the HTTP response code returned by the web server.

There's more...

Using the `WebClient` object to make HTTP requests against our SharePoint site may also be accomplished with code using the server-side object model. Follow these steps to verify anonymous access to content with code using the server-side object model:

1. Create a new `WebClient` object as follows:

   ```
   var client = new WebClient();
   ```

2. Use the `DownloadString` method to make a request for the home page of our site.

    ```
    var homePageContent = client.DownloadString("http://sharepoint");
    ```

    If we receive the HTML content for our page, our request was successful. However, if we receive an exception with a 401 or 403 HTTP response, anonymous access is most likely not available for that page.

3. Use the following `DownloadString` method to make a request for the **Site contents** page on our site:

    ```
    var viewAllContent = client.DownloadString("http://sharepoint/_
    layouts/viewlsts.aspx");
    ```

    If the page is correctly blocked for anonymous users, an exception should be thrown with a 401 or 403 HTTP response. If we receive the HTML content for the page, it indicates that the page request was successful and our page is not being blocked for anonymous users.

See also

▸   The *WebClient class* topic on MSDN at `http://msdn.microsoft.com/en-us/library/system.net.webclient(v=vs.100).aspx`

Index

Symbols

A

C

[PACKT] PUBLISHING enterprise

professional expertise distilled

Thank you for buying
SharePoint 2013 WCM Advanced Cookbook

About Packt Publishing

Packt, pronounced 'packed', published its first book *"Mastering phpMyAdmin for Effective MySQL Management"* in April 2004 and subsequently continued to specialize in publishing highly focused books on specific technologies and solutions.

Our books and publications share the experiences of your fellow IT professionals in adapting and customizing today's systems, applications, and frameworks. Our solution-based books give you the knowledge and power to customize the software and technologies you're using to get the job done. Packt books are more specific and less general than the IT books you have seen in the past. Our unique business model allows us to bring you more focused information, giving you more of what you need to know, and less of what you don't.

Packt is a modern, yet unique publishing company, which focuses on producing quality, cutting-edge books for communities of developers, administrators, and newbies alike. For more information, please visit our website: www.PacktPub.com.

About Packt Enterprise

In 2010, Packt launched two new brands, Packt Enterprise and Packt Open Source, in order to continue its focus on specialization. This book is part of the Packt Enterprise brand, home to books published on enterprise software – software created by major vendors, including (but not limited to) IBM, Microsoft and Oracle, often for use in other corporations. Its titles will offer information relevant to a range of users of this software, including administrators, developers, architects, and end users.

Writing for Packt

We welcome all inquiries from people who are interested in authoring. Book proposals should be sent to author@packtpub.com. If your book idea is still at an early stage and you would like to discuss it first before writing a formal book proposal, contact us; one of our commissioning editors will get in touch with you.

We're not just looking for published authors; if you have strong technical skills but no writing experience, our experienced editors can help you develop a writing career, or simply get some additional reward for your expertise.

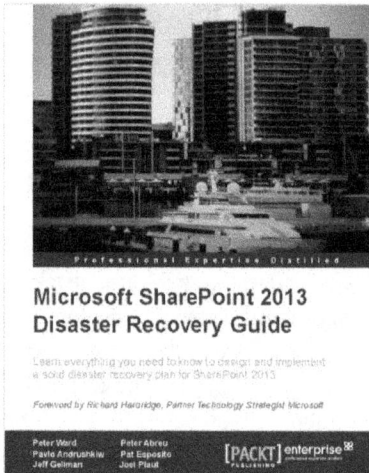

Microsoft SharePoint 2013 Disaster Recovery Guide

ISBN: 978-1-84968-510-8   Paperback: 278 pages

Learn everything you need to know to design and implement a solid disaster recovery plan for SharePoint 2013

1. Design, implement, test, and execute solid disaster recovery plans for your SharePoint environment with this essential guide

2. Learn out-of-the-box backup and restore procedures

3. Implement a solid disaster recovery strategy for custom development environments

4. A quick hands-on guide to get familiar with procedures to secure your data

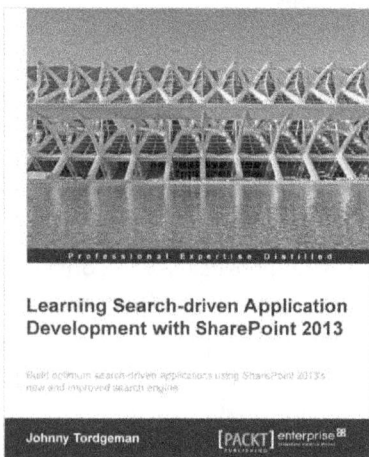

Microsoft SharePoint 2013 Disaster Recovery Guide

Learn everything you need to know to design and implement a solid disaster recovery plan for SharePoint 2013

Foreword by Richard Harbridge, Partner Technology Strategist Microsoft

Peter Ward   Peter Abreu
Pavlo Andrushkiw   Pat Esposito
Jeff Gellman   Joel Plaut

[PACKT] enterprise 🞧

Learning Search-driven Application Development with SharePoint 2013

ISBN: 978-1-78217-100-3   Paperback: 106 pages

Build optimum search-driven applications using SharePoint 2013's new and improved search engine

1. Create search-driven applications using the new SharePoint 2013 enterprise search engine

2. Learn how to respond intelligently to user's search queries using Query Rules

3. Filled with helpful tips, diagrams, and practical examples to make your organization's search experience smarter

Learning Search-driven Application Development with SharePoint 2013

Build optimum search-driven applications using SharePoint 2013's new and improved search engine

Johnny Tordgeman   [PACKT] enterprise 🞧

Please check **www.PacktPub.com** for information on our titles

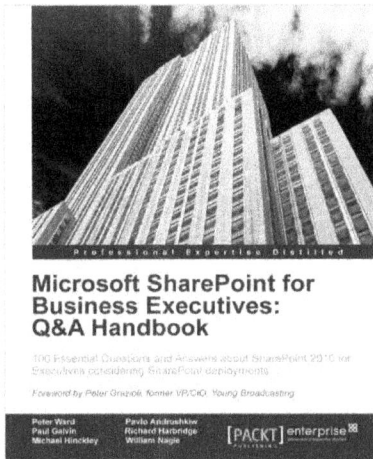

Microsoft SharePoint for Business Executives: Q&A Handbook

ISBN: 978-1-84968-610-5   Paperback: 236 pages

100 Essential Questions and Answers about SharePoint 2010 for Executives considering SharePoint deployments

1. Forget lengthy technical SharePoint guides more suited for hands-on technical staff; get equipped with the knowledge of SharePoint's business potential before deployment

2. Get to grips with SharePoint governance, the Cloud, staffing, development, and much more from a business perspective in this book and e-book

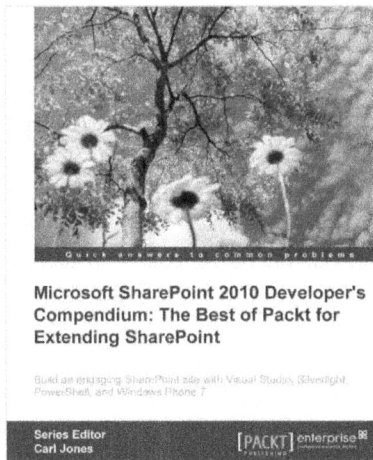

Microsoft SharePoint for Business Executives: Q&A Handbook

100 Essential Questions and Answers about SharePoint 2010 for Executives considering SharePoint deployments

Foreword by Peter Grapiok, former VP/CIO, Young Broadcasting

Peter Ward   Pavlo Andrushkiw
Paul Galvin   Richard Harbridge
Michael Hinckley   William Nagle   [PACKT] enterprise 88

Microsoft SharePoint 2010 Developer's Compendium: The Best of Packt for Extending SharePoint

ISBN: 978-1-84968-680-8   Paperback: 392 pages

Build an engaging SharePoint site with Visual Studio, Silverlight, PowerShell, and Windows Phone 7

1. Get to grips with extending SharePoint with a range of different tools in this comprehensive guide which draws on the value of five separate Packt SharePoint titles

2. Learn about developing and extending SharePoint through both step-by-step tutorial and cookbook chapters in this book and e-book

Microsoft SharePoint 2010 Developer's Compendium: The Best of Packt for Extending SharePoint

Build an engaging SharePoint site with Visual Studio, Silverlight, PowerShell, and Windows Phone 7

Series Editor
Carl Jones   [PACKT] enterprise 88

Please check **www.PacktPub.com** for information on our titles

www.ingramcontent.com/pod-product-compliance
Lightning Source LLC
Chambersburg PA
CBHW080138220326
41598CB00032B/5101